Encyclopedia of
LOVE & SEX

**A comprehensive guide to the
physiology of sex, the art of loving, and the
psychology of love**

CRESCENT BOOKS
New York

Printed and bound in Spain.

This 1988 edition is published by Crescent Books.

This volume is not to be sold outside the
United States of America, Canada and the
Philippines.

This edition first printed 1972.

Library of Congress Cataloging in Publication Data
Main entry under title:
Encyclopedia of love & sex.
   Reprint. Originally published: London: Cavendish,
1972.
   1. Sexual intercourse. 2. Hygiene, Sexual. 3. Sex.
(Psychology) 4. Love. I. Title: Encyclopedia of love
and sex.
HQ31.E74 1982   613.9′5   81-22132
ISBN 0-517-10550-0   AACR2

FOREWORD

The chapters of this book deal frankly, simply, and in
vivid pictorial terms with some of the basic problems of sex and
sexual relationships.

The sexual physiology of men
and women is clearly illustrated.

Basic questions are posed and
answered. Here is a wealth of
fascinating information aimed at throwing a

light on those areas of doubt
and difficulty that are often the product
of fear and of ignorance.

This book, therefore, aims at contributing to the sensible
discussion of sexual matters and of the whole infinitely
complicated and varied relationship between men and women
in simple yet lucid and authoritative terms.

The subjects are divided into three main sections—
the physiology of sex, the art of loving, and, finally, the
psychology of love.

CONTENTS

1

THE PHYSIOLOGY OF SEX

The chemistry of love

In a darkened room, two people make love. They are sharing perhaps the most personal, as well as the most beautiful, of all human experiences.

But in this case there is a difference. The couple are not in their own bedroom, but in a laboratory. During intercourse, their pulses, blood pressures, and other important measurements have been recorded by machines linked to their bodies and noted down by experienced researchers.

Many people, quite understandably, recoil from this coolly clinical attitude to the investigation of sexual function. Certainly, the average person's mind takes a little while to adjust to the idea of couples volunteering to make love with scientific instruments attached to them, or in front of observers—even though those observers may be doctors and scientists who are trying to obtain information of value to the furthering of human happiness.

Yet this research is one of the most important pieces of scientific work ever carried out. Under the direction of Dr. William H. Masters and psychologist Virginia E. Johnson, a team of scientists at the Reproductive Biology Research Foundation in St. Louis, Missouri, have been able to find out more about the physiology of sexual intercourse than all their predecessors in this field put together.

Thanks to Masters and Johnson, doctors at last actually know something about the bodily changes that take place during intercourse—the 'chemistry of love'.

Until 1966 (when Masters and Johnson published an account of their research in their remarkable book *Human Sexual Response*), medical men literally knew next to nothing about this aspect of human physiology. As a result, medical books and marriage manuals contained much that was misleading and, sometimes, wrong.

Even today, a great deal is unknown about the mechanisms of intercourse—but because of the work done by the St. Louis team (and, of course, the hundreds of husbands and wives who helped them), far more is understood than ever before. The value of this knowledge in combating widespread sexual problems and anxieties that affect human beings is immense.

What physical alterations do take place in a husband and wife during intercourse? There are certain changes common in both partners.

To begin with, as the couple's interest in love-making is aroused, their pulse rates increase and their blood pressures rise. At the same time, the pupils of the eyes widen slightly—which tends to increase a woman's beauty. In medieval times, and sometimes even in this century, girls put the plant-extract belladonna—which means 'beautiful woman'—into their eyes to try to reproduce this appearance.

As intercourse begins, these changes become more marked. The emotional excitement of both partners becomes greater and greater. The highest pitch of ecstasy is reached at the moment called 'orgasm' or 'climax', and from that instant, both bodily and mental excitement seem to fall away with great suddenness.

Generations of writers have accurately compared this phenomenon to an emotional ascent of a steep mountain peak, followed by a rapid and immediate descent. Recent scientific research has confirmed this view, in a slightly modified form.

A clear understanding of how the human body behaves during intercourse emerges when the reactions of the man and woman are considered separately.

A man's first reaction when thoughts of intercourse enter his head is, of course, erection. This process is started off by a series of nerve impulses that flow from the brain and spinal cord, down the nerves that lead to the genital organs. In response, the sponge-like tissues of the interior of the penis become filled drum-tight with blood, causing the organ to stiffen and rise upwards.

This phenomenon, whereby human tissues become turgid with blood, is called 'vasocongestion' and it occurs in both the male and female sex organs during sexual excitement.

The man's heart rate and blood pressure then increase. These are effects of adrenalin—the hormone poured out in reaction to *any* form of excitement by the adrenal glands which are situated above the kidneys. It is this same hormone that makes his pupils dilate, his nostrils flare slightly, his skin perspire, and his breathing become

faster and heavier. His skin is likely to become flushed, and his muscles tensed.

Now, as he passes through what physiologists call the 'excitement phase', corresponding to the first steep ascent of the mountain, changes are taking place in the man's sex organs of which he is probably unaware. The scrotum (the pouch containing the testicles) becomes tenser and thicker. At the same time, the testicles themselves are drawn markedly upwards, so that they are tight against the body.

If intercourse proceeds satisfactorily, the initial increase in excitement levels out. Keeping the metaphor of the ascent of the mountain, physiologists call this levelling out the 'plateau phase'. This phase is important, for it gives the man time to take control of his own reactions, and to ensure that intercourse is prolonged for as long as he and his partner desire. The man's plateau phase may go on for a very long time indeed, particularly when both man and woman are happy and relaxed in love-making. On the other hand, one of the most common of all sexual problems occurs when the man's plateau phase is short, even practically non-existent, so that he reaches his climax too soon to satisfy his partner.

During this plateau phase, there is additional vasocongestion of the penis, so that its smooth 'cap' (the glans) increases even further in size—it appears to be almost bursting—and may become a deeper, purplish colour. No

significant changes take place in the scrotum, but the testicles usually increase in size to a variable degree.

Now comes the orgasm—the 'final assault' on the mountain peak. The intensity of the sexual climax has always been far beyond the descriptive powers of mankind. Great surges of nerve impulses flow back and forth between the man's brain and his sex organs and all the muscles along the passages that carry seminal fluid contract violently.

At this moment, the man knows that ejaculation of sperm is imminent and feels that there is nothing whatever he can do to stop it. The part of the urethra (or urinary passage) nearest to the prostate gland is forcibly distended by seminal fluid to several times the normal diameter. This not only produces an immensely pleasant sensation, but provokes a tremendous contraction of the urethra that drives the fluid up the penis to emerge at its tip. So powerful is this thrust that, if the penis was not in the vagina, the drops of fluid would spurt anything up to six inches.

A series of contractions follows at a rate slightly faster than one a second, each producing a smaller volume of semen than before, and depositing a pool of living sperms within the body of the woman. Eventually, the contractions die away, as the man goes into the 'resolution phase' of intercourse.

In many ways, the changes that a woman experiences in intercourse parallel those

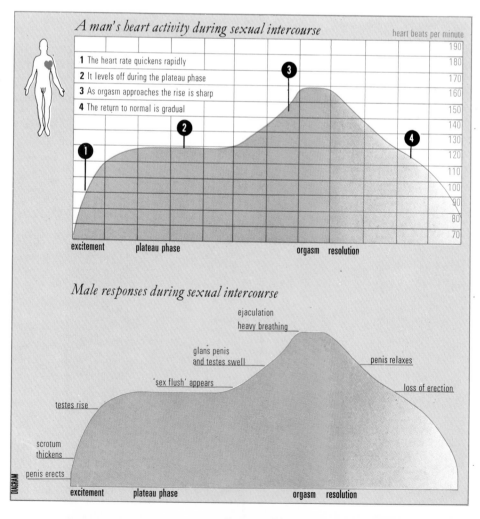

A man's heart activity during sexual intercourse

heart beats per minute

1 The heart rate quickens rapidly
2 It levels off during the plateau phase
3 As orgasm approaches the rise is sharp
4 The return to normal is gradual

190
180
170
160
150
140
130
120
110
100
90
80
70

excitement   plateau phase   orgasm   resolution

Male responses during sexual intercourse

ejaculation
heavy breathing
glans penis and testes swell
penis relaxes
'sex flush' appears
loss of erection
testes rise
scrotum thickens
penis erects

excitement   plateau phase   orgasm   resolution

During intercourse the gradually increasing sexual tension in both male and female is reflected by mounting blood pressure and heart rate. The man's pulse quickens rapidly in the phase of excitement, becomes steadier in the plateau phase, then soars to a peak at the climax of the sexual act—orgasm.

of her partner. She, too, begins by making the steep ascent of the excitement phase. During this period, vasocongestion leads to the erection of her nipples, with some slight increase in the size of the breasts. The veins that cross the skin of the breasts may also become more prominent as blood rushes into these organs.

Late in the excitement phase, the skin of whole areas of the body becomes much darker as a result of vasocongestion; Masters and Johnson call this reaction the 'sex flush'. Far more constant, and more marked in women than in men, it may even, in some cases, look as intense as the rash caused by measles. This lasts through the succeeding plateau phase and terminates rapidly at the moment of climax.

Before the plateau phase, however, besides the changes in breasts, nipples, and skin, the process of excitement results in vasocongestive changes in the female genital organ itself. The inner lips of the vagina (the labia minora) and the clitoris swell slightly, and may change in colour. The outer lips (the labia majora) draw back, as if to make access to the vagina easier. Most important of all, the vaginal walls (and, to a much lesser extent, certain glands near the vaginal opening) pour forth a lubricant moisture, without which there would be little pleasure in intercourse for either man or woman.

Now (and only now) the woman is ready for her partner to enter. During the excitement and plateau phases, the vagina relaxes, deepening considerably to accommodate the penis. At the same time, the womb is drawn upwards, allowing more room for the head of the penis in the upper part of the vagina.

The plateau phase is accompanied by further changes in the breasts; in a woman who has never suckled a child, they can increase in size by anything up to one-quarter, though this is not usually so in mothers who have breast-fed their babies. The pigmented ring around the nipple (the areola) swells so much that the nipples themselves no longer stand out.

Again, no words can satisfactorily describe the orgasm which follows. Some authorities think that it is a more intense experience in a woman than in a man, but since no male has ever undergone a female climax (and vice versa) we shall never know if this is true. Certainly, a woman's orgasm may sometimes be a quite shattering experience, in which consciousness is virtually lost for a short period of time. The same woman may, however, also have 'minor' orgasms, which are merely pleasant and enjoyable, but without the same quality of an emotional earthquake.

In any case, all climaxes will be accompanied by rather similar general bodily reactions: the muscles tense and the body arches (just as a man's does) and the toes curl up. The woman's face is drawn into a tense grimace, similar to an expression of extreme pain, for this is the most ecstatic moment of all.

Now comes the phase of 'resolution', or recovery—and one of the more striking differences between the responses of male and female. In a woman, the resolution phase may be very short indeed—perhaps only a few seconds—after which she may have another orgasm. It is not unknown for some women to experience perhaps 20 orgasms in a row—although this is very unusual, as well as very exhausting. More commonly a woman reaches just one, two, or three climaxes.

Many women are perfectly satisfied with just one climax, after which, their pent-up emotions released, they rapidly 'descend' from the peak of ecstasy to normal. In yet other women, orgasm is not reached at all, and only the plateau phase of enjoyment is attained.

In men, the phase following ejaculation is different. After the peak is reached, there is a 'refractory period' during which a further climax is impossible.

By one of Nature's curious tricks, this refractory period is very short in teenage boys, but lengthens greatly with age. This means that a younger man is able to achieve more than one climax during a 'session' of love-making but the average man of, say, 35 will not usually find it as easy to have intercourse twice in a night. Of course, a great deal depends on the degree of direct stimulation applied to the penis by a woman during love-making. Unfortunately, many men do not realize that a gradual change in their sexual powers is completely normal. They think back to the days when they were readily capable of renewed intercourse only a short time after a climax, and they conclude that something is wrong with their 'virility'.

Nothing could be further from the truth. While the ability to have repeated intercourse in a single night gradually lessens, it is compensated for by a steadily increasing control, which makes sex immensely more enjoyable to both man and woman.

In addition, the increasing knowledge of love technique (and of a woman's body) that the older man acquires, should certainly make him a better lover than he was as a youth. No one need worry about the effect of age on his or her ability to enjoy the act of love, or, indeed, to give enjoyment. One encouraging finding by research workers has been that, contrary to earlier belief, older men and women have very similar responses during intercourse to those of their younger counterparts. There is no dramatic change in physical response with increasing age. The scientific research done by Masters and Johnson shows quite clearly that a well-attuned couple can look forward to enjoying physical love together far into old age.

DAVID DELVIN

In the woman the pulse speeds in a similar way as sexual excitement grows, but the increase tends to be smoother, and after the climax, the return to normal is more rapid. However, a woman may experience more than one orgasm. The variation in response in women is greater than in men.

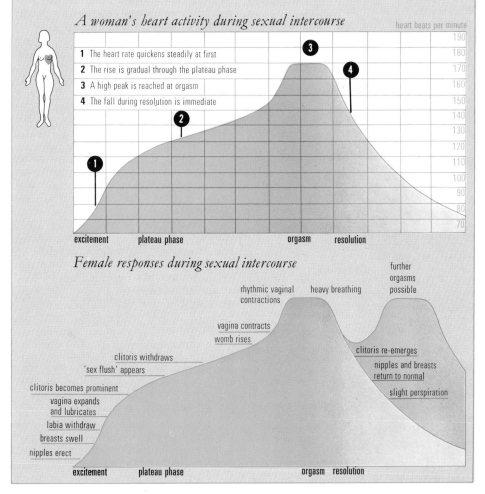

A woman's heart activity during sexual intercourse

heart beats per minute

1 The heart rate quickens steadily at first
2 The rise is gradual through the plateau phase
3 A high peak is reached at orgasm
4 The fall during resolution is immediate

190 180 170 160 150 140 130 120 110 100 90 80 70

excitement   plateau phase   orgasm   resolution

Female responses during sexual intercourse

further orgasms possible
rhythmic vaginal contractions
heavy breathing
vagina contracts
womb rises
clitoris re-emerges
clitoris withdraws
'sex flush' appears
nipples and breasts return to normal
clitoris becomes prominent
slight perspiration
vagina expands and lubricates
labia withdraw
breasts swell
nipples erect

excitement   plateau phase   orgasm resolution

Female orgasm—what is it?

Orgasm, the culmination of sexual intercourse, is the highest form of sexual satisfaction.
Virtually every woman is capable of experiencing it. Here, a doctor explains what orgasm is.

Orgasm, once, was something that nice women didn't have. They were supposed to grit their teeth and suffer through sexual intercourse. Enjoying sex was for 'loose women'. The work of Sigmund Freud, Wilhelm Reich, Karen Horney, and other psychiatrists in the late 1920s showed the repressed neurotic nature of such feelings. Women became aware that they had been denied, and denied themselves, the pleasure and fulfilment of sexual love. As this awareness was handed down to succeeding generations, sex lost many of its fear-inspiring and forbidden aspects.

But doctors who wrote manuals to help young couples understand these powerful impulses often incorporated a great deal of misinformation with the advice. Just as food was the natural end of hunger, and water of thirst, they wrote, so orgasm was the culmination of sexual desire. Unfortunately, they imagined an inherent difference between the sexes and felt that the male must reach climax sooner and more easily than the female: orgasm for a woman would be a luxury, not a natural end to sexual intercourse. They did not consider the psychological strains this attitude imposed on women capable of orgasm but condemned rarely to reach it.

People wanted and needed a better understanding of their sexual lives. The breakthrough of Dr. William H. Masters and Virginia E. Johnson in the 1960s extended the work done by such pioneers as Freud and Kinsey into the field of sexual physiology. Their first book, *Human Sexual Response*, although written for physicians in specialized technical language, was a best-seller for months. Because of their work, a more exact understanding of the changes in men and women during sexual intercourse was generally available.

The idea of orgasm for women as a luxury was cast aside. Any sexually responsive woman could achieve one or more orgasms from sexual intercourse or masturbation. Moreover, this was not only possible and natural, but desirable as the highest form of sexual satisfaction.

Some experts believe that the most important work done by Masters and Johnson was the scientific investigation of orgasm and the new understanding of how couples could help themselves achieve it. By measuring and recording the physical events of the climax, they could define it clearly enough to be recognized by any woman or any man. They removed the aura of myth and mystery surrounding the female's orgasm by making this information available. These facts have lowered the psychological barriers which prevented many women from experiencing orgasm and enjoying sex.

Orgasm differs from woman to woman because of different physiological, psychological, and socio-cultural conditions. Yet there is both qualitatively and quantitatively enough similarity in the range within which orgasm occurs to allow generalization from the data collected by scientists. Even allowing for possible errors because some information was gathered in a laboratory and, therefore, in an artificial situation, there is no denying the magnitude of the discovery.

Orgasm, for both sexes, is a total physical bodily response. For the female, as in the male, there is a short time span, lasting between two and four seconds, just before her climax begins, when she can subjectively feel that orgasm is about to occur. What she feels is a simultaneous spasm of all the small muscles in her pelvis which surround her vagina and uterus. Some scientists think that this spasmodic contraction of all the pelvic muscles may be similar to the contractions of the prostate gland and seminal vesicles in the male during the period when he feels he is about to ejaculate.

As a woman moves from the pre-stage to actual orgasm she may begin to clutch at her partner, losing herself in the increasing sexual tension. The muscles in her face can contort into what might appear to be an expression of pain. The muscles of her arms and legs contract involuntarily and her toes curl up as if they were clenched like a fist. Very often she will also tense her abdominal musculature, lifting her body completely off the bed. This moves her pelvis into position so that the clitoris

The uterus and vagina

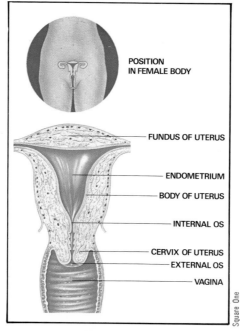

POSITION IN FEMALE BODY

FUNDUS OF UTERUS

ENDOMETRIUM

BODY OF UTERUS

INTERNAL OS

CERVIX OF UTERUS

EXTERNAL OS

VAGINA

Square One

presses against her partner's pubic bone achieving maximum pressure and contact, and thus maximum pleasure.

If the involuntary smooth muscles, such as the diaphragm, tighten, this may produce groaning or the prolonged holding of breath compared to the very rapid rate of respiration which preceded orgasm. These two signs may last only a few seconds, or if orgasm is sufficiently strong, continue 30 seconds or longer.

There are invisible manifestations of orgasm, very similar to the pre-orgasmic spasm of the muscles in the pelvis and sexual organs. These can only be observed when special electronic sensing and recording instruments are attached to the sexual organs. A scientist watching these machines can see the changes from the norm which reveal that orgasm is occurring.

Orgasm is signalled by rythmic contractions which begin in the lower third of the vagina—the *orgasmic platform*—which by this stage is suffused with blood. The entire vaginal barrel is interwoven with fibres of involuntary smooth muscle, and probably the contractions spread quickly through these muscles to the other two-thirds of the vagina. If orgasm occurs at the same instant for both partners during intercourse, then the contractile waves in the vagina will occur every 0.8 seconds, and the first three to six will coincide exactly with the ejaculatory contractions of the penis in the male climax.

With other means of attaining orgasm, or when climax is not simultaneous, the vaginal contractions still occur, and can often last longer. If there are more than six contractions the intervals between them lengthen and their recorded number and intensity is a direct measure of the intensity of the orgasm. Thus, the written record from the machine is evidence of exactly how pleasurable and powerful an orgasm is. This has been proved by participants correlating the judgement of their experience with scientific facts.

The wave-like contractions quickly spread from the vagina up to the *uterus*, or womb, almost simultaneously with the onset of orgasm. The uterine contractions are slower and much more irregular than those of the vagina. Beginning at the *cervix*, or lower third of the uterus, the contractions spread upward to the *fundus* to include the entire body of the uterus.

During climax, the rectal sphincter and the sphincters of the bladder and urethra also contract involuntarily. In some women this can result in small amounts of urine being passed during orgasm. It is normal, however, and nothing to be alarmed about. Generalized contraction of the small

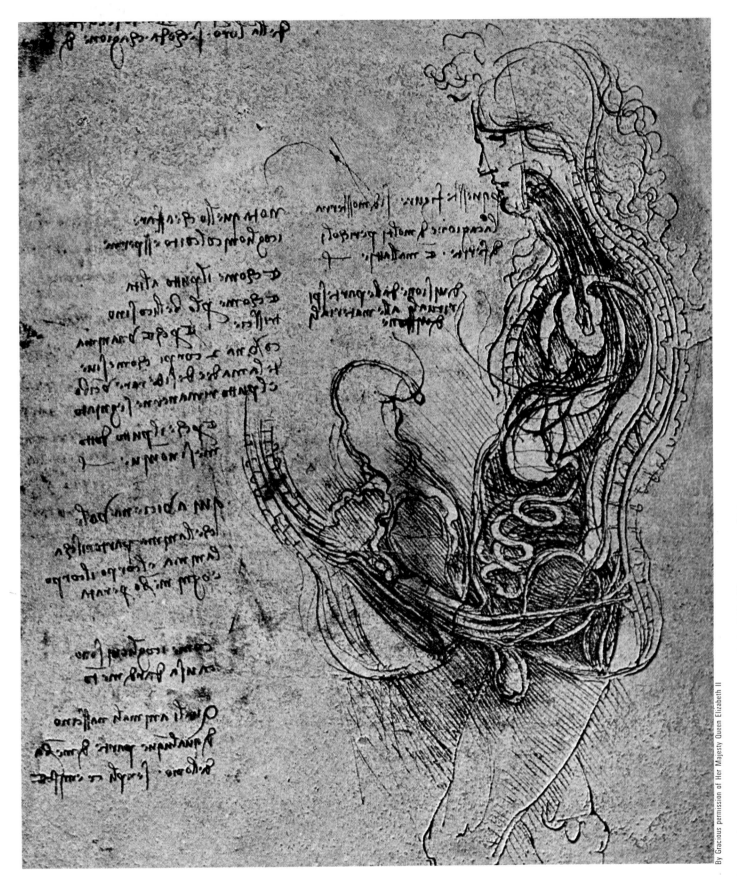

muscles of the pelvis and *perineum*, the sexual area between the thighs, occurs in much the same way as during the pre-orgasmic spasm.

Arteries and veins in the pelvic area also constrict because the smooth muscles controlling the size of these blood vessels contract involuntarily. The woman may experience a warm feeling of the entire body, the 'sexual flush', as the small blood vessels of the skin relax and bring more blood and heat to the surface of the body. The skin may turn a reddish colour, and may even appear to develop a rash: the entire body blushes.

At the same time, the heart pumps blood much faster, a condition known as *tachycardia*. While a rate of 72 beats a minute is average, during orgasm the heart beats at a rate between 120 and 180

This interpretation of intercourse by the Italian artist Leonardo da Vinci in the late fifteenth century is correct in all but one aspect: people at that time thought that there was a direct link from the womb to the breasts. Medical science has shown this to be false, chemicals in the bloodstream form the only connection. (This detail is reproduced by the gracious permission of Her Majesty Queen Elizabeth II.)

11

a minute, and sometimes even higher. The rate of breathing is also faster, between 30 and 40 breaths a minute, compared to a normal 12. And the blood pressure rises, producing *hypertension*. With the end of orgasm, these all return to normal within a few minutes.

Other sexual areas of the body important in love-making—the breasts, clitoris, and the major and minor *labia*, or lips, which cover over the entrance to the vagina—are less specific in their reactions. As yet scientists do not fully understand reactions in these areas during orgasm.

The clitoris retracts during the plateau phase just preceding orgasm, and withdraws under its hood. This continues during the following climax. While the woman may feel a throbbing sensation in her clitoris, there is little evidence of any rhythmic contraction similar to the penis during the ejaculation phase of the male climax—despite the fact of their being analogous organs.

During orgasm the breasts show a *detumescence*, or decrease in the swelling of the areolar tissue which surrounds the nipple. This occurs only if orgasm is taking place, and Masters and Johnson feel that it may signal the resolution phase, or the beginning of the end of orgasm. It is identified by a constricted corrugated appearance around the nipple immediately after climax. If orgasm has not been achieved, the detumescence is much slower to appear and there are no corrugations or wrinkles on the tissue. The nipples, however, remain rigid and erect during orgasm.

Nor is there any evidence that the Bartholin's glands play a specific role in orgasm. These small secretory glands located on the inner surface of the minor labia are unable to secrete more than a few drops of fluid and this rules against there being any outpouring of fluid by the female at climax. Stories of female ejaculation as a sure indication of female orgasm have been passed down through generations. More likely, what was thought to be the fluid of female ejaculation was a mixture of male seminal fluid and vaginal secretions leaking from the vaginal opening as the penis decreased in size after climax.

Additional to penile ejaculation and vaginal uterine contractions there are two major differences between the male and female orgasm. The first is that a woman is quite capable, immediately after completing one orgasm, of moving directly into another, or a whole series one after another. This is termed *multiorgasm*. A woman is capable of multiorgasm if she can keep her sexual excitement above the level of the plateau phase at which she started her climax. To do this, she can take advantage of the fact that the penis loses its erect state very slowly after the male climax, or that during masturbation she can maintain sexual sensation for as long as she wishes. Her partner can help by delaying his climax until she has definitely entered hers.

The second difference is that a woman is able to extend the orgasm period much longer than a man. While the male climax usually lasts only a few seconds, a woman can experience a series of rapidly recurring orgasms with no decrease in sexual excitement until they are ended, or one longer extended orgasmic experience. This condition, known as *status orgasmus*, can last from 20 seconds to more than a minute.

In the laboratory, it can be identified by a heart rate of more than 180 beats per minute, and a longer duration than in a single orgasm of the rhythmic contractions of the pelvis. Status orgasmus seems to occur more often in the laboratory than in the bedroom. This may be because, when the woman is masturbating or using one of the machines which mimics sexual intercourse, she is not preoccupied with her partner's pleasure.

One theory now banished forever by scientists like Masters and Johnson is the postulation by Sigmund Freud that there are two types of orgasm: a 'clitoral' orgasm, which Freud termed an immature sexual response, and a 'vaginal' orgasm, which he considered a mature sexual response. We now know both sexual organs are involved in the climax. There is no evidence to show any physiological difference among orgasms whether they are induced by intercourse, manual manipulation of the clitoris during masturbation, or by rubbing the breasts until climax, when there is no direct stimulation of either clitoris or vagina.

But there is more to the orgasm than just pleasure. During primitive eras it may have served the necessary function of increasing fertility. Orgasm may stimulate the ovary into releasing another ovum at a time during the menstrual cycle when this would not normally happen. Perhaps, to increase the possibility of conception taking place, orgasm can act as a trigger to release an ovum at a time when sperm would be more certainly present to meet it.

Because of modern scientific investigation no woman can afford to pretend to have an orgasm. She must see herself as an equal partner in love-making. While she may not reach orgasm every time she has sexual intercourse, this should not be a cause for worry. What is important is that she realizes that she is free to enjoy sex.

STEPHEN LEVIT

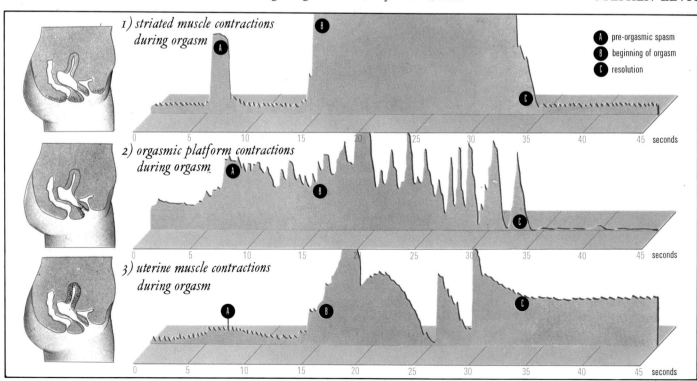

1) *striated muscle contractions during orgasm*

A pre-orgasmic spasm
B beginning of orgasm
C resolution

2) *orgasmic platform contractions during orgasm*

3) *uterine muscle contractions during orgasm*

Researchers into reproductive biology, investigating female orgasm, have measured contractions of the vagina and uterus, and the surrounding muscles. These charts relate the intensities of the different contractions to the three stages of orgasm.

The truth about multiple orgasm

An understanding of female orgasm has emerged from recent scientific investigations. We now know that women can experience several orgasms during a single act of intercourse—something that few men can achieve. But is multiple orgasm the ultimate in sexual pleasure?

The way people feel about sexual pleasure is closely connected to social attitudes current in their culture. But social attitudes have a way of becoming dogma.

If you tell a man he is inferior, treat him as if he were no more than a domestic animal, it is likely that he will soon become what you say he is. Sociologists and psychologists call this a 'self-fulfilling prophecy'. In the same way, Victorian mothers told their daughters that women did not enjoy sexual experience and when these girls married they found that this seemed to be true.

Reflecting the prejudices of their day, nineteenth-century investigators found no 'lady' who would admit that she received pleasure from sex, when they examined the sexual lives of the wives and daughters around them. It was an easy step to the scientific proclamation that women do not achieve sexual gratification. Women who did were often thought to be mentally ill.

Havelock Ellis, the great English sexologist, was the only major Victorian figure to disagree. As a result his books were censored, he was harrassed by the police, and ignored by his scientific peers. Yet Ellis, who read widely, knew that women *did* express their sexual pleasure in societies where it was acceptable. Histories of the voyages of Captain Cook showed that women in the South Sea Islands of the Pacific were frankly sensual, and that few of them remained virgins beyond the age of puberty. Ellis had also read the fifteenth-century erotic classic of the Orient, *The Perfumed Garden*, which made several references to female orgasm.

Around the turn of the century women began to take a dedicated interest in determining their own lives. With the rise of the Suffragette and birth-control movements, women wanted to know more about sex. By the 1920s, militant women's groups were reading Freud along with Marx. Soon after, they started opening family-planning clinics in industrial cities with facilities for sexual instruction and marital counselling.

As women realized that they, too, could have sexual pleasure other problems began to develop. Not only were men wary of the 'new female', but modern myths arose from the Freudian psychological interpretations that were then current. Wives began to worry about the *type* of orgasm they were having. Was it an immature

sexual response, as Freud described the 'clitoral orgasm', or was it the more mature 'vaginal orgasm'?

Not until the 1960's did sexologists understand that Freud was wrong. New scientific evidence became available, proving that every orgasm in women is 'clitoral'—initiated in the inch-long female organ that corresponds to the penis. The American sexual researchers, Dr. William Masters and Mrs. Virginia Johnson, demonstrated that this small organ located between the outer lips of the female genitalia, the *labia majora*, just under the pubic bone, was the most sexually sensitive part of a woman's body.

They also discovered that a woman is capable of having more than one climax during any single sexual episode. This phenomenon, called *multi-orgasm*, will occur during the moments just after climax if the female continues to receive effective sexual stimulation. Instead of returning immediately to the pre-excitement phase at which they started sexual activity, certain women will begin again the rise in tension which leads to orgasm.

Unfortunately, the multiple orgasm may well be on its way to becoming one of the major sex myths of the second half of this century. A good deal of misapprehension about this phenomenon has already appeared. Along with the desire to achieve simultaneous orgasm, the multiple orgasm has almost become a sexual status symbol in the West.

In the minds of uninformed people, these phenomena are assuming the magical status that the vaginal orgasm had for twenty years, beginning in the 1930s, when so many women wished to achieve something which we now know never existed. Many marriages suffered because wives felt guilty about their own sexual capabilities, or blamed their husbands for being inadequate.

Multiple orgasm is not a one-way passport to sexual happiness. Some of the women in the Masters and Johnson survey who reported multi-orgasmic experiences were, in fact, sexually frustrated women, for their husbands were incapable of ejaculating inside the vagina. Although these men could often maintain the thrusting penile movement of sexual intercourse for as long as an hour, the wives remained psychologically dissatisfied even after many orgasms.

One can best understand multiple orgasm as a variation of normal female responsiveness. Almost all women have the physical capacity to achieve it, while virtually no males do. However, other factors—psychological and social—may interfere and prevent this form of climax even though the couple have a happy and satisfactory sex life.

The body's response to sexual stimulation can be divided into four stages, similar in males and females. The rise in sexual tension begins with the excitement stage when the penis erects and the vaginal walls become covered with lubricating droplets. The second phase, known as the plateau stage, carries the couple through increasing levels of excitement, up to orgasm.

During orgasm, the man's sexual organs contract and expel semen, a mixture of seminal fluid and sperm, out through the end of the penis. The contractions continue at full force over three to four ejaculations before diminishing in power. This process slows until the final contraction of the penile urethra terminates the climax.

Immediately afterwards, the third stage, the *refractory period* begins, overlapping the final, or *resolution*, phase. During this time the man loses his full erection and his penis becomes limp and flaccid, a process called *detumescence*. This phase lasts from about half an hour to many hours, depending on the age and physical condition of the man in question.

The penis remains relatively insensitive to sexual stimulation during this time and manual or even oral caresses are unlikely to have any effect. However, it is possible for a few men to experience a form of multiple orgasm. If such a man keeps his penis inside the woman's vagina after his climax detumescence may not occur. And if he remains sexually aroused, continuing the thrusting movements of intercourse, infrequently he can return to a second orgasm.

Most men do not experience this, and few find the second orgasm a pleasurable sensation so near in time to the first. Sexual gratification in the male seems to be closely related to the amount of semen which is ejected, rather than the number of times this occurs. Since the seminal fluid cannot be replenished quickly, pleasure is reduced with successive orgasms.

The female orgasm lasts slightly longer than the male's. It consists of rhythmic

Percentage of women experiencing multiple orgasm					
under age 15	20	30	40	50	60
16	12	14	15	14	12

Experience of multiple orgasm at age 30						
1—2 orgasms	2	2—3	3	4	5+	total
5	3	2	2	1	1	14

The Kinsey Report claimed that many young men are capable of experiencing more than one orgasm in a single sexual episode, but their powers show a marked decline with age. Older women, on the other hand, frequently experience multiple orgasms. Laboratory experiments, such as those of Masters and Johnson, have since shown that a large proportion of women of all ages can have multi-orgasmic experiences, and instances of up to fifty orgasms in one hour have been recorded. Kinsey's figures show only the number of women who experienced multiple orgasm; those with the physical capability would be many more.

contractions of the lower third of the vagina and the smooth muscles of the uterus, followed by sexual sensations which spread in waves over the entire pelvis.

When, after six to twelve contractions, the orgasm ceases, the woman also enters a resolution phase. There is, however, no refractory period like the man's. If the woman continues to be aroused and sexually stimulated, she can quickly return to the plateau phase levels of sexual tension and move on to another orgasm.

As long as her level of sexual excitement does not drop below that of the plateau phase, this process can be theoretically maintained until the woman becomes physically exhausted. In practice, other factors usually intercede. During intercourse, when the male has had his orgasm he may not further stimulate the female. Additionally, the wife may be so preoccupied with her husband's feelings and reactions that she neglects her own.

For this reason most women only achieve the multi-orgasmic state when they masturbate. In the solitary situation when she can control the rate and level of sexual arousal to suit herself exactly a women is much more likely to concentrate on meeting her own sexual needs. Many women are able to experience three or four orgasms in these circumstances.

Another way of bringing about multiple orgasm is to use the caresses of foreplay. Some women, who are deeply aroused by oral manipulation of the clitoris and vulva, can have one or many orgasms when their partner stimulates them in this way. If the woman also has an orgasm with intercourse after this she can easily experience more than a single climax.

In contrast with men many women experience the second or third orgasm as the more exciting. Because these follow rapidly after each other the sensations tend to merge and the woman perceives succeeding climaxes more as a continuous process than they in fact are.

Masters and Johnson identified a very rare form of multiple orgasm in their sexual laboratory which they termed *status orgasmus*. This lasts for up to a minute, with all the physical manifestations of orgasm, including a rapid heart rate, and heavy breathing. In addition, the uterus and or-gasmic platform in the lower portion of the vagina rhythmically contract during the entire time of status orgasmus.

In this case, the woman only returns to the plateau level of sexual excitement for a brief instant before rebounding into the orgasmic state. Thus, what is in actuality a series of four to six orgasms in rapid succession, is experienced as one drawn-out continuous climax.

The American team of investigators found that this occurred more easily when a woman used the artificial coition machine in their laboratory than when a couple had intercourse. Perhaps this was because the woman was able to indulge her own fantasies without concerning herself with her partner, while still receiving the sensations of intercourse. She could then allow her emotions free rein.

Many women have noticed that they feel more sexually aggressive during the days which just precede and just follow the menstrual period. They may experience successive orgasms more easily with intercourse on these occasions than during the middle of the menstrual cycle.

In addition, obstetricians have become aware that a noticeable rise in sexual desire occurs during the second trimester of pregnancy, from the fourth to the sixth month. Women demand more sexual experience in these twelve weeks than is usual for them. Their level of response is also increased. In one study, wives reported that they became orgasmic or multi-orgasmic during pregnancy when they had never been so before. Greater sexual responsiveness during pregnancy is probably due to the increase in size of the pelvic blood vessels, contributing to the generally increased flow of blood in response to erotic stimulation. In addition, the fear of unwanted pregnancy ceases to play such an important part, for the pregnant woman can see her swelling abdomen by the fourth month.

It is important to understand that orgasm and multiple orgasms are not always easily achieved. Because most girls are educated to control their erotic desires they often do not respond to their full capacity until many years after they have become sexually aware and experienced. Unlike men, who reach their sexual peak during their late teenage years, most women do not become fully sexually mature until their late twenties.

Women are also more sensitive to external influences. For example, once a man feels the sensations of orgasm begin—three or four seconds before his ejaculation—he will continue his climax regardless of other stimuli. Women, however, are more easily distracted, and the feelings they identify as their climax will stop if any disturbance interferes.

Thus, before a woman can achieve multiple orgasm other than by masturbation, many conditions must be met. She must have a particular partner who arouses her erotically and satisfies whatever individual psychological needs she may have. Usually she will previously have experienced orgasms. In addition, her male partner must be a skilful and experienced lover, able to withhold his own ejaculation until the woman has had at least one orgasm and is on the threshold of the next.

A good deal of practice is necessary to create these circumstances in addition to love and mutual trust. But even with these conditions, it may be impossible for a couple to achieve multiple orgasm during sexual intercourse.

However, a sexual relationship is not something which can be measured numerically. Its success is a matter of quality and not quantity. No marriage which has failed in its other aspects can be saved by adding to the number of orgasms.

If a couple wishes to improve their sexual relationship, tenderness and consideration for each other's desires and feelings are far more important than the intricacies of sexual technique. Spontaneity is very important in a couple's sexual development.

Love-making, like any other experience, is a learning process. It should not be treated as a routine chore. No harm can come from using variations of position, oral caresses, or any other gesture of love, which bring the other partner pleasure.

But there is no mystical formula in the multiple orgasm that will bring the ultimate sexual experience. Women should not be victims of the belief that there is something wrong with them if they do not experience it. Each sexual episode should be cherished for what it is, at the moment that it exists.

STEPHEN LEVIT

Female sex organs

Compared with a man's external sexual organs, those of a woman are unobtrusive —indeed almost unnoticeable. Within the body, however, the picture is reversed, reflecting the vastly more complicated role which the female plays in the process of producing children. In a sense, the male is a mere accessory in reproduction, and with the act of intercourse his physical involvement ends. A woman, by contrast, must not only produce eggs, or *ova*, for spermatozoa to fertilize, but be prepared to provide nourishment and protection for a fertilized egg for some nine months afterwards, as it grows through the stage of embryo and foetus into a fully-formed baby.

The external sexual organs, or genitalia, in the female are known collectively as the *vulva*. To each side, extending downward and backwards from the *mons veneris* (mount of Venus), the pad of fatty tissue over the pubic bone in front, are two folds of skin called the *labia majora* (greater lips). These folds meet and join below, between the legs, at the *perineum* or area immediately in front of the anus. Their function is to protect the openings of both the urinary and reproductive systems, which lie between them. From the age of puberty, hair covers the mons and the outer surfaces of the vulva. The inner surfaces are moistened by a number of sweat and sebaceous glands.

Between the labia majora lie the more delicate *labia minora* (lesser lips), which vary greatly in size from individual to individual. At the front they meet and join above the *clitoris*. The clitoris is the equivalent in the female of the penis in the male. It is very much smaller, and does not have a passage for urine, but has a very similar structure, and both penis and clitoris develop from the same tissues in the embryo. Like the penis it is well supplied with blood, becomes erect during sexual excitement, and is the most erotically sensitive area of the body, being responsible for much of the woman's physical pleasure during sexual intercourse.

Below the clitoris lies the opening of the urinary passage, or urethra, and below this again the vaginal opening. Behind the

The breasts

Fashions come and fashions go. Sometimes it is the legs that are the focus of woman's sexual attractiveness to man. There have been fashions emphasizing the slimness of the waistline, or the fullness of the hips, or the roundness of the buttocks. But there have been few episodes in the history of fashion when the breasts have not figured in a woman's armoury of come-on signals to her mate.

In fact, a woman's breasts have become, according to some scientists, primarily sexual signals. Certainly, their biological role of providing milk for feeding the young child is assuming less and less importance in these days of bottle-feeding. Yet the fact remains that milk-production is the fundamental reason for a woman having breasts at all. The sexual role of the breasts is unique to man; the milk-production function is common to all mammals. The very name *mammal* comes from the Latin word for breast—*mamma*. And it is this function that governs the breasts' anatomical structure.

At the tip of the breast, the nipple is the outlet from which the child sucks its mother's milk. Surrounding it is the *areola*, an area of darkened skin the size of which—like that of the nipples themselves—varies from woman to woman. So-called virgin breasts—that is, those of women who have never been pregnant—have areolae only a little darker than the surrounding skin. But one effect of pregnancy is to darken and enlarge the areolae; they never return completely to their original colour.

The nipple itself is not, in fact, one outlet but 15 to 20, each one the opening of a duct that brings milk from one part, or lobe, of the breast. The ducts branch like the roots of a tree, collecting milk produced in tiny glands called *follicles* or *alveoli*. Each breast has thousands of these. Between them, and making up the bulk of the breast, is fatty tissue. Supporting the whole structure is a network of connective tissue. This maintains the firmness and shape of a young woman's breasts. If the connective tissue should stretch, perhaps through having to support the heavy weight of large breasts or simply through age, then the breasts will tend to sag.

It seems largely a matter of luck how large a woman's breasts become. In the early teens, female sex hormones, *oestrogens*, poured into the bloodstream by a girl's ovaries stimulate the breast tissue, that has lain dormant since birth, into growth. These undeveloped nipples, and areolae, and the primitive system of milk ducts are the same in pre-pubescent boys and girls. It is simply the difference in hormone chemistry between them that makes only the girl's breasts grow. Oestrogen injections (whether given for medical reasons or as part of an attempt at a 'sex-change') can make a man's breasts develop in just the same way. One of the common side-effects of taking the contraceptive pill (which contains synthetic oestrogens) is to stimulate breast growth.

The size of women's breasts is difficult to explain in biological terms. Certainly many other mammals, including man's nearest relatives, the apes and monkeys, manage to produce a quite adequate enough supply of milk to nurse their litters with proportionately far smaller breasts. But when you consider the sexual role of the breasts, their size begins to make more sense. To put the argument simply, if men find women with large breasts sexually desirable, then these women will tend to receive more sexual advances than their less well-endowed sisters. They will, all things being equal, tend as a result to have more children. And these children, if they are girls, will tend to inherit their mothers' characteristics. In this way, large breasts will gradually, over many generations, tend to become a standard female characteristic. It is an example of evolution by so-called sexual selection. (The term *large breasts* is used here to mean anything more than the very flat-chested development of our ape-like ancestors. Even poorly-developed women have 'large' breasts by this definition.)

But this argument begs one basic question: why should men find large breasts sexually attractive and stimulating? Dr. Desmond Morris, author of *The Naked Ape*, suggests that it is a case of the breasts mimicking the buttocks. When a female ape invites a male to mate with her, she presents her behind to him in a characteristic mating posture. As with almost all mammals, the male mounts his mate and inserts his penis into her from behind, and it is the rear view of her buttocks and genitals that triggers this mounting behaviour.

Dr. Morris suggests that at some time in man's evolutionary past, as part of the transition to the characteristically human upright stance, our ancestors reversed the ape-like mating pattern. Men and women began to have intercourse face to face. But already, he suggests, the buttocks had become much larger and more fleshy than those of apes. If the male had learned to respond sexually to the female buttocks, then some equivalent signal would be needed from the front of the female body to initiate face-to-face mating. If man had already lost his apish body hair, then prominent, fleshy breasts would fulfil this need very well.

In the same way, Dr. Morris believes that the red, fleshy lips of humans, much more prominent than those of monkeys and apes, mimic the labia minora (the inner lips of the female genitals), which become bright red and swollen when a woman is sexually aroused.

Thus, the breasts are sexually stimulating because they trigger off in a man primitive instinctive responses that once, in pre-human times, followed a more ape-like invitation from his mate. So it is no coincidence that the breasts of a woman should develop just at the age of sexual maturity.

If this line of argument is accepted, then it is easier to understand the other functions of the breasts in sexual activities, as opposed to child-rearing. It is only natural that the sexually-responding male should pay particular attention to his partner's breasts, fondling and stroking them. The female's erotic response to this would become a virtually universal human characteristic in exactly the same way as the enlarged breasts themselves—by sexual selection. Thus the breasts have become erogenous zones where stimulation heightens a woman's feelings of sexual desire.

The responsiveness of women's breasts varies widely. In almost all women, their stimulation—usually centred on the nipples and areolae—can help in the arousal stage of love-making, during the foreplay that precedes intercourse itself. But some women respond far more strongly. American sex-researchers Dr. William H. Masters and Mrs. Virginia E. Johnson found that three women out of their study group of 382 could bring themselves to orgasm simply by manipulating their breasts.

Masters and Johnson also questioned a group of 101 women who had just borne children on their sexual feelings and responsiveness. Out of this group, 24 successfully breast-fed their children for at least two months, and it was these women who had the most intense and rapid return of desire for sexual intercourse after childbirth. They found that suckling their babies itself aroused them sexually, often to the so-called plateau level that immediately precedes orgasm. In three cases, women experienced orgasm purely as a result of breast-feeding, without any other stimulation. (In many women, the increase

19

in breast sensitivity to erotic stimulation in fact starts much earlier in pregnancy.)

The sexual role of the breasts is emphasized by the changes they undergo as the woman rises through the level of sexual feeling to the final surge of orgasm. These changes were also observed both during love-making and masturbation by Masters and Johnson. The most obvious of them—and one that occurs early in a woman's arousal—is the erection and enlargement of the nipples. They may increase in length by nearly half an inch and in diameter by nearly a quarter of an inch. This enlargement often occurs more quickly in one nipple and is most rapid if the breasts are directly stimulated. It is caused partly by the contraction of muscle fibres within the nipples, and partly by the breasts becoming engorged with blood (just as engorgement causes the erection of a man's penis). The latter reaction also makes the breasts as a whole get larger— perhaps by as much as a quarter—as arousal reaches the peak of orgasm. As a result, they project more firmly and roundedly from the chest.

In the higher levels of sexual arousal, the areolae around the nipples become engorged with blood, making them darker and swollen. The final effect of vasocongestion (engorgement with blood) is the appearance of the so-called sex flush, a reddening of the skin that centres on the breasts. This becomes most intense just as the woman is on the brink of her climax. It disappears rapidly as the feeling of relief following orgasm sweeps over her. At the same time, the swelling of the areolae subsides, and this may make the nipples appear to become erect again. All that is happening, however, is that the subsiding areolae allow the still-erect nipples to show more fully once again. Within a minute or two, the nipples, too, return to their normal, unstimulated size, but enlargement of the breasts may not subside

for five to ten minutes after orgasm ends.

The role of the breasts as come-on signals from the woman to her mate is obviously boosted by their becoming larger and firmer when she is excited sexually. It also makes sense of women's perennial attempts to increase the power of this endowment. Brassieres cover the breasts and then increase their size and emphasize their shape. Many women attempt a more permanent increase in breast size, using creams, massagers, and other bust-development aids. Few are successful, even the hormone creams containing oestrogens. The reason is that, unless prescribed by a doctor, these creams are not allowed by law to contain more than a very small amount of oestrogen, in case they encourage such troubles as breast cancer. But even carefully controlled and medically supervised oestrogen treatment will not always increase the breasts' size.

One remedy that is usually successful— although few women are prepared to go that far—is plastic surgery, involving the insertion of wax, plastic foam, or silicone oil under the skin of the breasts. It seems to be popular in Japan, where Hollywood's influence has made many young women ashamed of their characteristically small breasts. Otherwise, the only guaranteed cause of bust enlargement is pregnancy— again a somewhat extreme step to take.

This enlargement, due to a great increase in the body's hormone production, is one of the first signs of pregnancy, and a woman may feel a tenderness and tingling in her breasts within three weeks of conception—only a week after missing her first menstrual period. It is caused by the breasts getting ready to feed the newborn child. The follicles grow and the bustline as a whole may enlarge by several inches over the whole nine months. A well-designed bra is essential if the extra weight is not to stretch the supporting tissue, allowing the breasts to droop permanently.

Perhaps the greatest fallacy about the size of breasts is that which makes women strive to achieve firm, rounded, and symmetrical breasts. All breasts droop; that is, they have a concave, hollow curve on the top surface and a convex curve on the bottom. The degree of droop varies, of course, but the breast profile which resembles half a lemon is a myth. The bustline produced by a carefully designed bra may be extremely stimulating to the male, but it is an artificial creation. And when the art directors of 'girlie' magazines need to produce the same effect in their nude models, they have to resort to adhesive tape. (And, for good measure, they often use pregnant or nursing women as models.)

When a woman in the early stages of pregnancy is aroused sexually her breasts often feel extremely tender. This is because they are already enlarged due to pregnancy, and the further enlargement caused by sexual stimulation can be quite painful. The pain is often centred on particularly engorged nipples and areolae. From about the third month to delivery, sexual arousal causes less breast discomfort. By now, they have become more permanently enlarged, and they grow no more as a result of sexual stimulation. The nipples and areolae still become erect and engorged, however. The same pattern occurs when nursing mothers are sexually aroused, but mothers whose milk-production has been suppressed show little breast-reaction to sex, except for the erection of the nipples, for up to six months after giving birth. In contrast, nursing mothers often lose milk as they reach their climax; it may even spurt uncontrollably from the nipples.

The breasts are, then, as much concerned with sex as with child-feeding, and it is their sexual role that has been most influenced culturally. Although the breasts have usually been well in evidence, only rarely have fashions bared the whole breast. Women of the ancient Minoan civilization wore elaborate jackets cut to emphasize their naked breasts, and there was the short but startling topless craze of the mid-1960s. Even in the outwardly staid Victorian era, some ladies drew attention—in private—to their mammary gifts with gold nipple-jewellery. But women have usually left something to male imaginations, being content with areola-grazing décolletage, a fully covered but bra-boosted profile, or a braless, natural shape that is covered to a greater or lesser extent. As one academic wrote at the time of the topless fashion, 'It is a question not so much of morals as of tactics to consider at what stage in the proceedings (the breasts) are to be deployed to the best advantage.' Those sentiments are not far from Dr. Desmond Morris's view of the breasts as 'signals to initiate mounting behaviour'.   MICHAEL WRIGHT

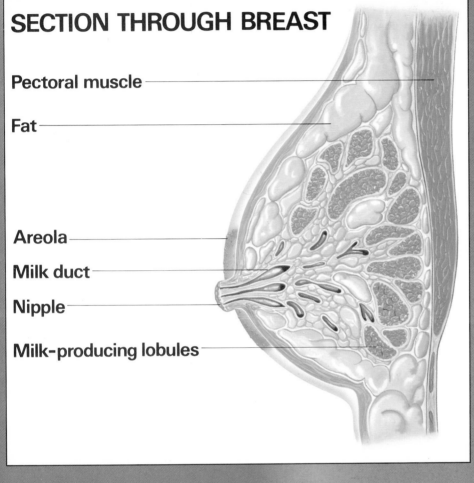

SECTION THROUGH BREAST

Pectoral muscle

Fat

Areola

Milk duct

Nipple

Milk-producing lobules

Square One

John Garrett

The clitoris

The Greeks, of course, had a word for it. What we today call the *clitoris* they named *kleitoris*. Our word obviously originates from theirs, but what is more interesting is that the root, in turn, of this Greek word is *kleis*, which means *key*. The ancient Greeks obviously believed that the clitoris was the key to a woman's sexuality, a view that has been firmly held ever since.

The clitoris is a vital—possibly the most vital—part of a woman's sexual anatomy, for two reasons: first, stimulation of the clitoris—through touch and pressure—is the most important way of arousing feelings of sexual pleasure in a woman. Second, these feelings of pleasure seem to her to be centred on her clitoris. (This is true even if she is aroused by caresses to other erogenous zones or simply by erotic thoughts.)

The clitoris lies towards the front of a woman's vulva, at the apex of the vestibule, into which the vagina and urethra, or urine duct, open. It can be felt as a small lump of tissue where the two labia minora, the inner lips, join, about one to one and a half inches in front of the vaginal opening. In fact, the labia minora form a hood, or *prepuce*, over the top of the clitoris, and in

some women also join behind it to form the *frenulum*.

These folds of skin may almost completely cover the head, or *glans* of the clitoris—which is the only part of it that is ever exposed. The glans is normally about a quarter of an inch in diameter and is set on the shaft of the clitoris, which can be felt beneath the skin just above the glans. The whole organ is normally about an inch long, but there is great variation in clitoral size. The glans can vary from an eighth of an inch to nearly a half inch in diameter,

and the shaft can be long and thin, short and fat, or anything in between.

Since ancient times, in both highly-developed and primitive cultures, people have realized the similarities between the penis of a man and the clitoris of a woman. Some African tribes justify removing a girl's clitoris at puberty (female circumcision) by saying that it initiates her into womanhood by removing the last vestiges of manliness. There is some basis to this reasoning (although it does not, of course, justify female circumcision) for the penis and clitoris are equivalent organs. A de-

veloping embryo in its mother's womb has a small lump of tissue between its legs before its sex can be determined. In a male embryo, this develops into a full penis; in a female, it remains small and becomes the clitoris.

There is a major difference, too, in that the penis carries the urethra, while the clitoris has no opening. But the structure of the clitoris is similar in other ways to that of the penis. Its shaft consists of two rods of tissue, closely linked, known as the *corpora cavernosa*. These, like the equivalent parts of the penis, can become engorged with blood during sexual excitement. This enlarges the clitoris but, unlike the penis, it cannot become erect. The two corpora cavernosa bend and run backwards and sideways to join the pelvic bones on either side of the vagina. They are covered by a pair of muscles and, when these contract, blood in the corpora cavernosa cannot readily escape, which leads to the engorgement. The mechanism of male erection is very similar.

Another muscle joining the clitoral shaft, on the underside, is the equivalent of that which rhythmically contracts during a man's orgasm and propels semen out through his penis. This muscle, the *bulbospongiosus*, runs back from the clitoris, and divides in two, passing either side of the vagina. During orgasm, it contracts rhythmically, causing regular contractions of the outer part of the vagina. The final connection to the clitoris is a ligament which joins the upper part to the pubic bone above it. This keeps the clitoris in its normal position hanging over the entrance to the vagina.

Because it is an organ that detects sensory stimuli, the clitoris has a rich supply of nerve fibres which can carry signals to the brain. Fibres from the whole of the clitoris and the nearby parts around the vaginal entrance combine to form a single nerve. Among these fibres are tiny structures, called Pacinian corpuscles, which are very sensitive to pressure. When stimulated, they send a flood of nerve signals to the brain. The corpuscles occur throughout the clitoris, but they are closest together in the glans. Women differ widely in the total number of these corpuscles in the clitoris, and this may explain differences between women in clitoral sensitivity.

In spite of the similarities between the clitoris and the penis, they respond quite differently in sexual stimulation, whether it comes through intercourse or masturbation. For one thing the clitoral response is much slower. Whereas erection of the penis is the first sign of a man's sexual excitement the equivalent enlargement of a woman's clitoris occurs much later—long after lubricating secretions appear in the vagina. Clitoral response is quickest if it is itself stimulated by stroking, slowest if stimulation is elsewhere, such as the womb or breasts.

Nor does the clitoris increase in size to anything like the extent of the penis. In all women there is a slight increase in

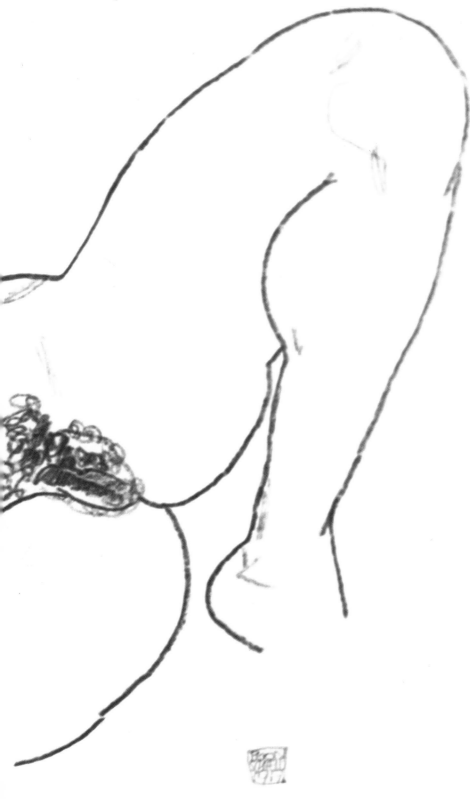

Egon Schiele, *Reclining Nude*/Marlborough Fine Art

23

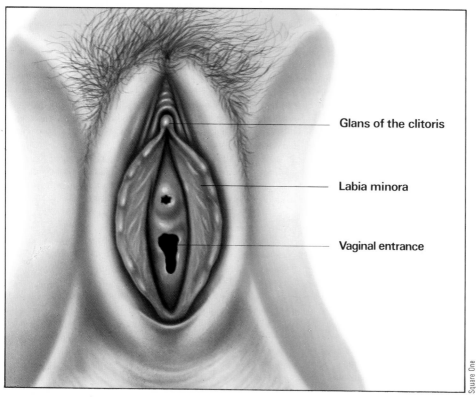

Glans of the clitoris

Labia minora

Vaginal entrance

size by the clitoral glans, enough to bring it into close contact with the folds of skin around it and so increase stimulation of its nerves. More than half of all women have no greater clitoral 'erection' than this; but in others the glans may increase to as much as double the normal size. Whether or not this happens, the shaft of every woman's clitoris becomes engorged with blood and grows thicker as a result of sexual excitement. In some it also grows longer.

When sexual stimulation brings a woman to the *plateau* phase of excitement, just before the explosive climax of orgasm, the clitoris is pulled up under its hood, completely out of sight. If this should happen while a woman's sexual partner is stimulating her by stroking the clitoris, he may stop, and this can be extremely frustrating for the woman. Pressure on the clitoral area continues to stimulate her, even if the clitoris has withdrawn out of sight and touch.

That the clitoris always withdraws before orgasm shows the fallacy of the view that direct stimulation of the clitoris is the key to success in bringing a woman to a climax in love-making. Even with the glans exposed, such direct stimulation is extremely difficult in many love-making positions, and completely impossible in some. In fact, direct stimulation is almost always unnecessary. Movement of the penis in and out of the vagina pulls on and releases in turn the labia minora. This rhythmic tugging is transmitted to the clitoris and stimulates it just as effectively as direct contact or pressure. It takes place in every love-making position so long as the penis fully penetrates the vagina, the only exception being where childbirth injury has considerably widened the vaginal opening.

In exactly the same way, it is a fallacy that direct pressure on the clitoris itself or stroking its glans is the only form of foreplay that will arouse a woman before making love. When women masturbate—and most do at some time or another—they hardly ever touch the glans of their clitoris directly. Many women do rub or press on the shaft of the clitoris, but most never do so. Instead, they stimulate the clitoris indirectly, by touching nearby parts. They may prefer pressure on the *mons pubis*, the swelling just above the vulva, or stroking of the labia minora. To them, touching the clitoris itself may bring discomfort. Whatever technique a woman prefers the amount of pressure she uses can vary widely. Some women rub or press on themselves quite strongly; others use a feather-light touch.

A woman discovers by trial and error the technique that suits her best and her partner will be most successful in arousing her if he follows the technique she herself uses in masturbation. The man should not be too self-confident to ask; the woman should not be too modest to tell.

Another fallacy is that differences in clitoral size and position influence a woman's capacity for sexual pleasure. There are African tribes whose girls spend hours massaging the clitoris and labia in order to make them larger. They do this from a very young age, so that these parts have grown considerably by the time the girls reach puberty. Their aim is to increase their ability to enjoy sex.

Research in the United States by Masters and Johnson has shown that this is nonsense. A woman with a small clitoris, or one that is placed high up, where direct stimulation is difficult, is just as likely to have intense sexual feelings, and to reach a powerful orgasm every time she makes love, as a woman with a clitoris that is large or in a low position. Conversely, she is just as likely to have a poor sexual response and infrequent orgasm. In exactly the same way, the amount by which a woman's clitoris expands as a result of sexual stimulation bears no relation to her ability to achieve orgasm.

But perhaps the greatest clitoral fallacy of all concerns the supposed difference between clitoral and vaginal orgasms. Many people, both experts and ordinary men and women, believe that an orgasm achieved by means of a manual stimulation of the clitoris (whether by the woman herself or by a man) is somehow different from one occurring as a result of the penis stimulating the vagina. What is more, the vaginal orgasm was long thought to be better and more fulfilling than the clitoral orgasm. Even sexologists perpetrated this idea suggesting, for example, that early sexual experience leads only to a clitoral orgasm, and that a woman needs to learn how to achieve the vaginal kind.

The truth is that there is only one kind of orgasm, and this involves both the clitoris and the vagina. No one has directly observed what happens to the clitoris during orgasm, because it always withdraws completely under its hood. But all the other responses are identical whether a woman is brought to her climax by clitoral stimulation or through full love-making. The most important response is that the outer part of the vagina contracts in a strong spasm, grasping the man's penis, and then breaks into a series of rhythmic contractions.

A woman feels her orgasm in many parts of her body, but the whole experience is focused on these contractions. The overwhelming sensuousness of orgasm means that she feels them as much more than simply contractions, just as a man's orgasm feels much more than a series of contractions propelling semen from his penis. One of the muscle actions that causes the contractions and thus contributes greatly to the experience of orgasm is the bulbospongiosus, which is attached to the shaft of the clitoris and also encircles the vagina. This muscle is involved in all female orgasms.

After the climax the clitoris returns very quickly to its normal exposed position, usually within ten seconds of the last contraction. If further sexual stimulation brings the woman to another orgasm, this again is preceded by retraction of the clitoris under its hood. But if the woman is satisfied and relaxes in the fulfilment of a single climax the clitoris relaxes, too. The blood that poured into it during the early stages of sexual excitement drains away within five to ten minutes and it returns to its normal, unstimulated size.

The clitoris remains engorged much longer if the woman reaches a high level of sexual excitement, but fails to achieve an orgasm. This enlargement can last for hours, contributing to the woman's feeling of frustration. For the clitoris is truly at the centre of a woman's sexuality. Its role has been misunderstood by many, but it really is the key, as the ancient Greeks believed.

MICHAEL WRIGHT

The uterus

'That part of the woman which is called the womb . . . if it becomes unfruitful for a long time turns indignant, and wandering all over the body stops the passages of the spirits and the respiration and occasions the most extreme anxiety and all sorts of disease.' Such was the opinion of Plato, one of the greatest of all the Greek philosophers. He expressed this view four centuries before the birth of Christ, and the idea persisted and was widely believed until less than two hundred years ago. It may seem fantastic to us that such an obvious piece of nonsense was ever believed by anybody, but the history of medical science contains dozens of mistaken ideas, some of them far more ridiculous than this one.

Even stranger, for example, is that before 1600 A.D. no one in Europe had a clear idea of what the human womb or uterus even looked like. One of the greatest anatomists in ancient Rome said that it was an organ with seven chambers. As far as he was concerned it must have looked rather like a set of bagpipes. No one bothered to check for themselves to see whether he was correct and, indeed, the mistake became so widely accepted that for a long time it

would have been heresy to try to have denied it.

Ideas like these obviously held up medical progress. If a woman with an abdominal complaint approached a doctor and he decided that a 'wandering womb' was the cause of her troubles he would do his best to bring it back to its normal position. Since the womb was attracted by sweet smells and repelled by unpleasant ones he would give his patient something revolting to sniff at while he applied some sweet-smelling substance to her vagina. If she happened to be suffering from a ruptured appendix, a gall stone, or a gastric ulcer, such treatment would hardly have done her a great deal of good.

But confused ideas about the uterus have had other more subtle consequences because they have, for centuries, influenced the way that men have thought about women. For example, women have always been considered more prone than men to tantrums and to outbreaks of uncontrolled emotion—in fact to hysteria. The very word 'hysteria' comes from a Greek word meaning the uterus. A woman, they believed, becomes hysteri-

cal simply because her womb moves about in her body. For centuries it was believed that women could not help being unstable: it was simply a consequence of the way that their bodies were made. Plato's opinion must have done as great a disservice to womanhood as any other single idea produced in the last two thousand years.

The reason for much of the confusion is that, unlike the breasts or the clitoris, the uterus is a part of the reproductive system that is usually never visible. Only during a surgical operation (a very hazardous business until less than fifty years ago), or at a post mortem (when the organs may well have become distorted), would a doctor have actually seen the womb that he was so happy to speculate about. It is, therefore, not surprising that just like the process of conception, for example, the uterus became the subject of a great deal of uninformed folklore. Fortunately, today, we have a very clear idea of the structure of the human uterus, of the way in which it functions, of the manner in which it develops, and of the causes and cures of many of the diseases which can afflict it.

The uterus in a woman who is not preg-

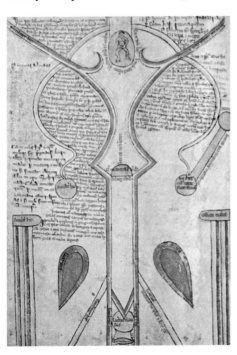

Until scientists of the seventeenth century dissected and studied the human body, and modern surgeons operated on the abdomen, doctors had little real idea of how the uterus

functioned—or even what it looked like. These diagrams from a thirteenth-century English manuscript show what doctors then knew about the female sexual organs, and

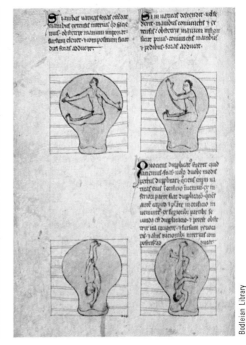

describe the positions a child might present at birth. They embody misconceptions about the uterus which stem from the mistaken theories of the ancient Greeks.

nant is a pear-shaped organ a little smaller than her clenched fist. It lies in the lower part of her abdomen with the bladder in front of it and the rectum behind, and it is held in this position by a number of ligaments. It consists of two different parts, which are continuous with each other. The 'neck' of the pear is known as the *cervix*. It is a tough, thick-walled tube about one inch long which projects into the upper part of the vagina. The narrow canal which runs through it, the cervical canal, has the function of carrying sperm from the vagina into the body of the pear—in this case known as the uterine body or *corpus*. The corpus accounts for the greater part of the uterus. It is a hollow organ about two inches long and just about as wide at its upper region, although it tapers somewhat towards the cervix.

Although the body of the uterus is hollow it would be wrong to think of it as being like a blown-up balloon with a spherical cavity at its centre. In most women the cavity is actually shaped like a flat triangle, because the front and back walls of the uterus lie very close together. It is important to realize this, for if a foreign body, such as an intra-uterine contraceptive device, is wrongly placed in the uterus, so that it forces these two walls apart, it not only causes pain but it is also likely to be rapidly pushed out again. Another fact, that is often overlooked, is that in some women the triangular cavity is short and fat. In others it is long and narrow. Women vary in this just as much as in any other characteristic. Though we talk for convenience about the 'average woman', we have to remember that she really does not exist.

But whatever the shape of the uterine cavity, the wall of the uterus that surrounds it is always made up of the same four distinct parts. The innermost layer is extremely thin: indeed it consists of only one single layer of cells. Inside this single layer is a somewhat thicker area known as the uterine lining or *endometrium* which is in many ways the most important part of the whole organ. The endometrium, however, never reaches a thickness greater than about one-fifth of an inch. The great bulk of the uterine wall is made up of the two outer layers which consist of muscle. These uterine muscles are able to expand and contract very strongly (so strongly in fact that a surgeon's wrist has been bruised by the muscles of the cervix contracting around it). Such contractions are very important in expelling the fully-grown foetus during its birth, but even the uterine walls of a non-pregnant woman undergo rhythmic contractions which, after intercourse has taken place, help to move the sperm up through the uterine cavity and into the fallopian tubes.

The uterus does not stick straight upwards in a vertical plane inside the abdominal cavity even when the woman is standing up. Usually it is tilted slightly

Position of uterus: section through pelvis, seen from the side.
1. Fallopian tube   3. Bladder   5. Rectum
2. Uterus   4. Vagina   6. Vaginal entrance

forwards on the main axis of the body so that it lies along the wall of the bladder. Sometimes, however, this tilting becomes exaggerated and the top of the uterus may be parallel to the ground or may even point downwards. Alternatively, the uterus may lean backwards towards the spinal column. In either of these cases the uterine cavity can become blocked because of the flexion, and some specialists suggest that this may lead to sterility. If the upper part of the uterus does become seriously displaced then the fallopian tubes which join it, one on each side, may also become kinked and obstructed, and again sterility is likely to result. There are several methods of treatment for these complaints, the most effective of which involves a surgical operation to shorten the ligaments connected to the uterus so that they will hold up more effectively.

Sometimes, perhaps because of a series of difficult births, the uterus tends to fall, not forwards or backwards, but downwards so that it bears onto the upper vagina. Occasionally the prolapse, as it is called, is so great that the cervix actually projects out of the vagina. This is a con-

dition which has been known for thousands of years and the ancients, using their ideas about 'the wandering womb', tried to repel the uterus back to its proper position by fumigating the vagina with appropriate substances. Today, we recognize the condition for what it is—a partial or almost total relaxation of the ligaments that hold the uterus in place. Again, the most certain method of treatment depends on shortening the ligaments that hold the uterus there.

What about the functions of the uterus? Even the most primitive civilizations have realized that about once in every lunar month a woman loses a certain amount of blood from her vagina. Indeed great rituals have been built up around this fact. A woman during her menstrual period has often been reviled as 'unclean', and in order to purify herself again she has to go through elaborate ceremonies. But it was only in the last century that a reasonable explanation of menstrual bleeding was found, and even then a lot of confused ideas had to be rejected before the truth was finally agreed

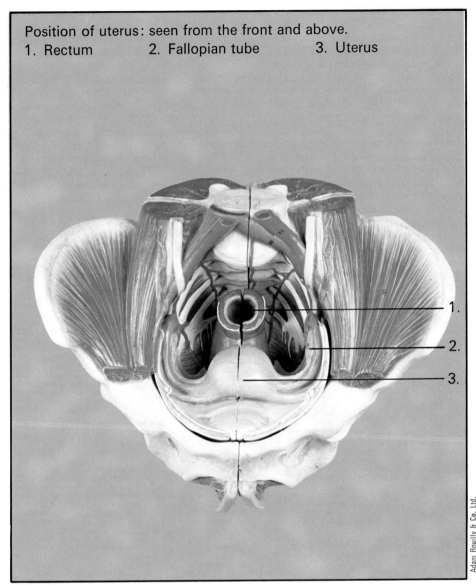

Position of uterus: seen from the front and above.

1. Rectum　　　2. Fallopian tube　　　3. Uterus

Adam Rouilly & Co. Ltd.

Nonetheless, by far the greater part is lost and the process of breakdown is really quite spectacular.

The uterus displays this ability to strip itself down rapidly in another way. During pregnancy a child weighing perhaps seven pounds develops inside the womb. In addition, the same uterus has to contain several pints of fluid in which the developing foetus is bathed. Obviously the organ itself must increase greatly in size during this time. Immediately after birth the uterus weighs about two pounds, although the weight of the uterus before pregnancy begins is nearer two ounces. The return to normal size is another spectacular change.

Its weight is reduced by half within a single week of the baby's delivery, and within only two months the uterus has returned to more or less its normal size. Of course, the uterus of a woman who has had a child is always somewhat larger than it was when she was a virgin. In addition, her cervical canal is also a little wider. For this reason contraceptive devices can be fitted far more easily into the uteri of women who are already mothers.

One fine example of a process of tissue breakdown which is perfectly normal, and which occurs in the majority of girls before they are even born, has to do with the development of the uterus itself. In many species of mammal the uterus consists of two distinct chambers or 'uterine horns'. In some primitive mammals, for example the opossum and kangaroo, each horn may have a separate cervix and even two vaginas may be present. The female reproductive system is therefore quite clearly a 'doubled' structure. It is doubled in exactly the same way in the human female embryo. Two sets of ducts lie side by side, just as they do in the embryos of other animals. In women, however, (and in female apes and monkeys) these ducts fuse together before birth to form a single chamber—the uterine cavity.

This is more than an interesting piece of embryology for it also has practical importance. Occasionally, the fusion is incomplete. In this case the girl is born with a congenital defect of the uterus. The extent of the defect varies. Very seldom will she have two quite distinct uterine horns. More often her uterus will have a partition or *septum* down its centre dividing it, though perhaps only partially, into two chambers. It is very difficult to state how often this happens. Some figures suggest that perhaps one girl in a hundred has such a defect. If she becomes pregnant difficulties might arise, and some women suffering from such defects habitually lose their babies before birth. Today a complete septum can be easily diagnosed, and some of the problems that it would give rise to can, therefore, be averted. But there is no record of any case where a uterus was found with six septa and seven cavities. Though some old wives' tales contain a grain of truth, the seven-chambered womb is not one of them.

CLIVE WOOD

upon. It is unfortunate that a true understanding took so long to arrive at because the process is really very simple. Every month the endometrium grows and thickens inside the uterine cavity. This thickening is brought about by the action of sex hormones which originate in another part of the reproductive tract, the ovary, and which are carried to the uterus through the bloodstream. The main function of the endometrium is to provide a region for the fertilized egg to become implanted. If an egg does implant, the endometrium underneath it becomes transformed into the maternal part of the *placenta*, the organ through which the embryo receives its nourishment.

It seems very likely that the young embryo, at the time of its implantation, sends out a chemical message which maintains the endometrium and prevents it from being broken down. The first thing that makes most women suspect that they are pregnant is that the menstrual period that they were expecting never arrives. But if fertilization has not taken place, or if it has but the egg has failed to implant, no such message is produced. As a

consequence, the ovarian hormones that normally influence the endometrium cease to do so quite abruptly and the tissue disintegrates. It passes out through the cervix as menstrual fluid.

For the biologist, menstruation is a very interesting process. A woman's body breaks down a perfectly normal healthy tissue each month and rebuilds a new one. Usually we think that the breaking down of any tissue in our body is associated with some form of disease, and sometimes it is. But in this case there is nothing abnormal about it. Indeed, the abnormal women are those who do not have regular menstrual periods. Doctors recognize several types of *amenorrhoea*, as this condition in which menstruation is absent is called, and each type may have a different cause. Of course, it is not quite true to say that the *whole* of the endometrium is shed at each menstruation, otherwise from what does the new one develop? What actually happens is that a very small amount of endometrial tissue is retained at each menstruation and the new endometrium is derived from it.

Vagina and muscles

The word 'vagina', as an anatomical term for the first part of the internal genital organs of the female, was used originally as a coarse Roman joke. It is simply a Latin term for the sheath, or scabbard, of a sword. (It is interesting that the male sexual organ, however, did not receive the title of 'sword' which one might have expected from the allusion.) Ignoring the intended humour of the original writer, early anatomists immediately began using the term as an apt technical description for the structure which does 'sheathe' the penis of the male partner during sexual intercourse. Its function, they thought, was merely to do that, so that the male seed, or sperm, could enter the woman's womb and fertilize one of her eggs to produce a child. They regarded the vagina as a simple tube which connected the external female genitalia, the vulva, with the uterus, hidden deeper within the body. That the vagina had the property of great elasticity was also obvious from the fact that during childbirth it became the birth canal through which the baby would be born. But the complexities of the functioning of the vagina remained completely unknown for many hundreds of years, until a few years ago when physiologists evolved techniques to study closely exactly what takes place during every phase of sexual intercourse.

The opening of the vagina lies between the *labia minora* (lesser lips) of the vulva, which normally meet the midline to conceal it. Above, and separated from it by only a short distance, lies the opening of the urethra, where the urinary tract reaches the exterior, while higher still, where the labia minora meet on the pubic arch, is the clitoris. The folds of the labia minora form a hood around the clitoris, and during sexual excitement changes in the state of both the labia and the clitoris occur in a characteristic sequence, so that the appearance is very different from that in the resting state. Like the penis, the clitoris becomes erect during sexual excitement, so that it protrudes from the surrounding hood, while the labia minora increase in width. In addition to expanding to two or three times their normal diameter, and protruding between the *labia majora*, or greater lips, the labia minora also show a very characteristic change in colour, from the normal pale pink to a colour ranging from a deep pink to a bright red or deep wine colour. These changes are visible from the exterior and, simultaneously, changes which are less obvious occur in the vagina itself.

In the normal resting state the opening of the vagina is only seen as a closed orifice, with the front and back walls meeting, so that it has the shape of the letter H, with the middle part forming a slit side to side. From the opening, the tube passes upwards and backwards into the pelvis, behind the urethra and the bladder, and in front of the rectum. On the average, the length of the vagina is some

28

three and a half inches. The front wall is about an inch shorter than the back wall. The width increases slightly from the opening upwards, and the greatest diameter is reached where the uterus protrudes down into the cavity, at the upper end of the front wall. The rather narrower lower portion is called the vaginal barrel, while the expanded upper part is known as the vault of the vagina. The neck of the uterus, or cervix, extends into the vault for about half an inch, and its opening is roughly at right angles to the direction of the vaginal passage. On each side of the cervix the spaces are known as the respective fornices of the vagina. The fornix at the back, the posterior fornix, is deeper than the rest, and lies immediately in front of the front wall of the rectum. It is into this portion of the woman's vagina that the penis normally penetrates during sexual intercourse.

In developing girls, the opening of the vagina is partially closed by the *hymen*, or maidenhead, which is a crescent-shaped membrane, normally broken during the first experience of sexual intercourse, although in many cases it may be torn during the introduction of sanitary tampons. The fact that it is broken is therefore

not necessarily a sign that a girl is not a virgin. Occasionally the membrane may be thicker than normal, in which case it may gradually stretch during continued experience of sexual intercourse, without rupturing. In rarer cases the hymen may have to be cut—a very minor surgical procedure—so that intercourse can take place satisfactorily. Usually all that remains after childbirth are a few small tags of skin at the base of the vaginal opening.

The vagina is composed of two layers, the inner lining, which is soft, pliable, and moist, and an outer, rather thicker layer composed of muscle fibres. The thin lining, or mucous membrane, is thrown up into two ridges on the front and back walls of the cavity, indicating where the two sides of the vagina met and fused early in the development of the foetus. These ridges are known as the anterior and posterior *columns* of the vagina. Extending out on either side from the columns are numerous fine folds or *rugae*, which separate small furrows of variable depth, and give the appearance of many conical projections on the wall. The corrugated effect is most pronounced on the posterior wall, and near the opening of the vagina. In older women the rugae tend gradually to disappear, particularly in women who have borne several children. After the menopause, or 'change of life', the vagina may appear completely smooth, and have no ridges whatsoever.

Outside the mucous membrane, and separated from it by tissue containing numerous blood vessels, lies the muscular coat of the vagina. There are two distinct layers of muscle, an outer layer which consists of fibres parallel to the length of the vagina—the longitudinal fibres—and an inner layer of fibres arranged to form a circular coat. The longitudinal fibres blend at the upper end of the vagina with the powerful muscles which make up the wall of the uterus. It is clear that relaxation of these sets of muscles is necessary for the vagina to show any increase in size, whether during intercourse or during childbirth.

Other sets of muscles which act on the vagina are situated around its entrance, in what is termed the 'floor' of the pelvis, and are responsible for controlling the size of the opening. Linked also are the sphincters, or muscular rings, which are in control of the openings of the urethra in front and the rectum behind the vagina. Two very important pairs of muscles are called the *bulbospongiosus* and *ischiocavernosus* muscles, which pass forward to the region in front of the pubic arch, where the clitoris lies, and, by pressing on the blood vessels leaving the area when they contract, cause the clitoris to become erect. The equivalent muscles in the male are, of course, much more prominently developed, and assist in the erection of the penis during sexual excitement.

In the normal, healthy woman the lining of the vagina in the resting state is pink and moist. A certain amount of moisture is always present, but during

sexual excitement the amount increases many times over, and may become quite a copious flow. Without such lubrication, the entry of the penis during sexual intercourse would be rendered very difficult, if not painful for the woman. The increase in the secretion of fluid in the vagina starts almost immediately with sexual arousal. As the clitoris becomes erect, and the labia minora develop their characteristic colour change, a change can also be seen to take place in the barrel of the vagina. The changes have been observed directly, and photographed by means of special camera equipment placed within the cavity of the vagina itself. Only relatively recently has it been possible to show where the lubricating fluid is produced, and to disprove old theories which had been assumed to be true for many years.

It was long believed that the vaginal lubricating fluid was poured out from the cervix of the uterus at the upper end of the vagina, and flowed downwards when the volume increased during sexual arousal. It was also thought that the pair of small glands, called Bartholin's glands, which have their ducts on the inner sides of the labia minora, on either side of the vaginal opening, were responsible for producing fluid to lubricate the vulva and the vaginal opening during intercourse. Neither of these theories is correct. It has been shown that, in fact, no fluid passes out from the cervix into the vagina during sexual excitement, and that the amount of fluid produced by Bartholin's glands consists of merely one or two drops of material, sufficient to have only a minimal lubricating effect in the vulva. In women who have not borne children, there may only be one small drop of fluid given out by each gland, and this only relatively late in the process of sexual arousal.

The vaginal lubricating fluid, as it is now known, is produced by the walls of the vagina itself. Within a few minutes from the start of sexual response, the walls of the vaginal barrel can be seen to produce numerous droplets of mucoid material—the appearance has been likened to that of beads of sweat standing out on a forehead. As sexual tension increases, the production of these droplets increases, until they finally coalesce to form a continuous, smooth and glistening lining of moisture for the whole of the vaginal barrel. This fluid is sufficient to lubricate the vagina completely for the admission of the penis, and is usually copious within a few seconds. As there are few real glands in the mucous membrane of the vaginal barrel, it seems that the fluid which is observed to 'sweat' from the walls originates from congestion of the numerous veins which form a complex network on either side of the whole length of the vaginal barrel, and surround it completely.

Following the first stages of sexual arousal, other changes take place within the vagina, evidence of the increasing readiness of the organ to receive the penis during sexual intercourse. There is a lengthening of the innermost two-thirds of the vaginal barrel, and also an increase in its width. Whereas in the resting state the front and back walls of the vagina are in contact, during this phase of sexual arousal they become separated, without any conscious control on the woman's part. The vaginal barrel can be seen to expand and relax in an irregular manner in its inner two-thirds, finally becoming distended into a typical balloon shape. In addition to the expansion of the vault of the vagina by distension of the walls, there are changes in the position of the uterus, which moves upwards and forwards so that it protrudes less into the vaginal vault. During this phase, too, the vaginal walls undergo colour changes similar to those seen in the labia minora, and become a darker purplish colour along the whole length of the barrel. The rugae of the mucous membrane also become distinctly flatter as the vagina expands.

In the outer third of the vaginal barrel, there are also changes, and the opening of the vagina relaxes considerably. The membrane becomes distended with swollen blood vessels, so that although the entrance is, in fact, slightly reduced in size, the softness of the surrounding tissues is greatly increased.

When the penis is introduced into the extended barrel of the vagina, the expanded head, or glans, passes the cervix of the uterus, in partners of average propor-tions, so that the thrusts of the penis during intercourse are into the cul-de-sac which is formed by the posterior fornix. Just as there is a normal human variation in the size of the penis, so there are women with vaginas which are either larger than average, or rather smaller. So great is the distensibility and the elasticity of the vagina, however, that provided the woman has reached a sufficiently high level of sexual excitement, a penis of any size can be accommodated, and disproportion in size causes no problems whatsoever during the sexual act.

The first phase of the vaginal response, the excitement phase, is followed by the 'plateau' phase, which in turn leads on to the phase of orgasm, or climax. During the plateau phase, the swelling of the tissues of the entire outer third of the vagina reaches its maximum, and produces temporarily what is termed the *orgasmic platform*, from where the sensations which occur during orgasm will spread. The production of lubricating fluid from the vaginal walls actually decreases during this phase, so that the slipperiness of the vagina is reduced, and the friction between the vaginal walls and the penis increases. A further small increase in the dimensions of the vault of the vagina also occurs during this phase.

At the climax of the sexual act there is a further relaxation of the inner part of the vaginal barrel, but the outer portion, the orgasmic platform, begins to contract strongly and regularly, so that the penis is grasped more firmly. During one orgasm there are between three and fifteen muscular spasms, starting at intervals of less than a second and gradually becoming less frequent and intense. The duration of the contractions varies considerably from woman to woman, and also from one act of intercourse to another. In some women there is an initial strong contraction in the orgasmic platform lasting for two to four seconds before the regular series of contractions starts.

After orgasm, the vagina gradually returns to its normal state. It slowly contracts to its original size, losing the expansion at the inner end. The uterus dips downwards again, so that the cervix reaches the area where the pool of semen has been deposited during the orgasm of the male. The open mouth of the womb is now able to provide a passage for the sperm to swim upwards and fertilize an egg within the body of the womb itself.

It is strange that for so long the vagina was regarded as being simply an inert tube connecting the uterus with the vulva, and that the exact functioning during sexual intercourse was unsuspected. It is only modern developments in the field of investigation which have enabled us to realize just how complex its workings are, and how very much more it is than a simple 'sheath' for the male sexual organ.

DAVID WILLIAMS

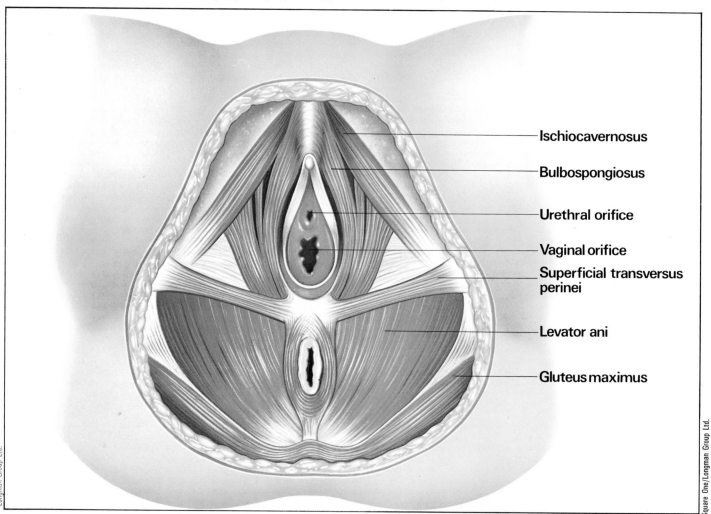

Ischiocavernosus

Bulbospongiosus

Urethral orifice

Vaginal orifice

Superficial transversus perinei

Levator ani

Gluteus maximus

The ovaries

At the turn of the twentieth century August Weismann, a biologist in Frankfurt, described a new and, for its time, quite revolutionary way of regarding the body of any animal, including that of man. Weismann suggested that the body was made up of two quite distinct parts. The great majority of body cells (cells of the brain, heart, liver, and so on) he considered to be different from the small but vastly important collection of 'germ cells' which were passed on from one generation to the next. These latter cells were segregated from the others and played little or no part in the everyday functioning of the body. But when animals reproduced the germ cells suddenly assumed a vital role. Indeed, every part of the offspring's own body ultimately developed from just one germ cell contributed by each of its parents.

Today Weismann's ideas are commonplace. The germ cells are known to be separate from the others. The special organs which contain them are called *gonads*: the testes in a man and the ovaries in a woman. Because they fulfil equivalent functions—and are therefore described by a single term—they might well be expected to be similar. But on examination the two types of gonad appear, at first sight, to be completely different from each other.

Each testis is a small, oval-shaped organ about four centimetres long and two-and-a-half centimetres wide. The ovary is flatter and more almond-shaped than the testis although in its size at least it is rather similar. Where it does seem to differ is in its structure. The inside of the testis is packed full of narrow winding tubes in which the sperm are produced, and its outside surface is completely smooth. A slice taken through the ovary shows that its centre contains blood vessels but no comparable tubes, and its surface, far from being smooth, usually carries a number of lumps and bulges. A further difference is in the position of the two organs. The testes lie in a special scrotal sac outside

In 1672, when Regnier de Graaf, a Dutch anatomist, published this drawing of a dissected ovary, he believed the small lumps he found—Graafian follicles—were human eggs.

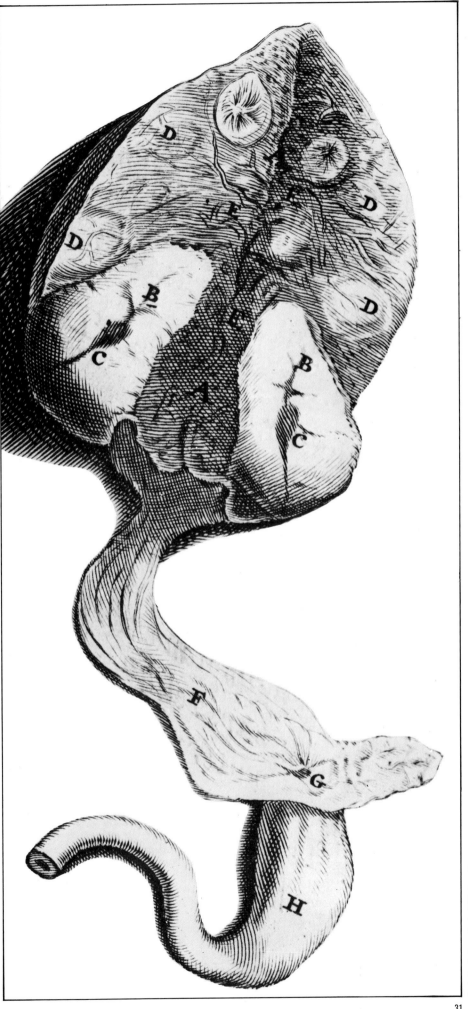

R. de Graaf: *Opera Omnia*, 1677/photo, Thames & Hudson

THE FEMALE REPRODUCTIVE ORGANS.

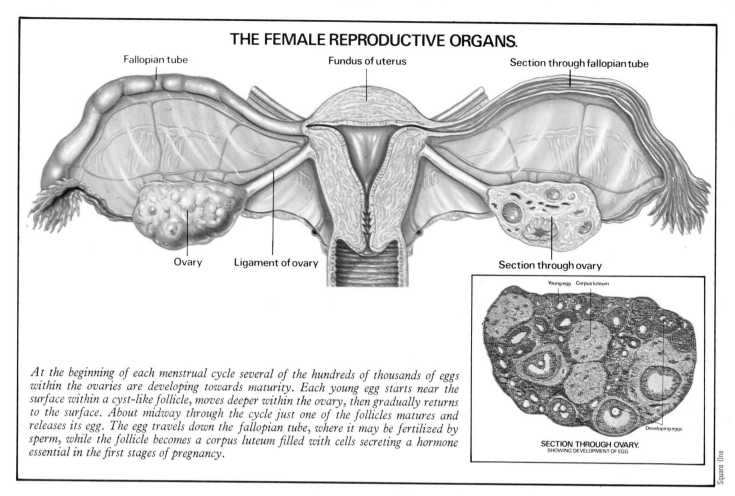

Fallopian tube

Fundus of uterus

Section through fallopian tube

Ovary

Ligament of ovary

Section through ovary

At the beginning of each menstrual cycle several of the hundreds of thousands of eggs within the ovaries are developing towards maturity. Each young egg starts near the surface within a cyst-like follicle, moves deeper within the ovary, then gradually returns to the surface. About midway through the cycle just one of the follicles matures and releases its egg. The egg travels down the fallopian tube, where it may be fertilized by sperm, while the follicle becomes a corpus luteum filled with cells secreting a hormone essential in the first stages of pregnancy.

Young egg   Corpus luteum

Developing eggs

SECTION THROUGH OVARY.
SHOWING DEVELOPMENT OF EGG

Square One

the abdomen. The ovaries, however, lie within the pelvic cavity close to the uterus, where they are suspended by special ligaments.

Despite these apparent differences there are very good reasons for talking about 'the gonads' in general, for they are really extremely similar, at least as far as their development is concerned. They both arise from precisely the same type of tissue in the body of the embryo. If the embryonic gonads are examined during the first seven weeks after conception it is impossible to say whether they will develop into testes or ovaries. The germ cells that they contain are capable of developing into either sperm or eggs in later life, and perhaps the most surprising aspect of their development is that these cells do not originate in the gonads at all. If a human embryo is examined only four weeks after conception the germ cells are found some distance from their eventual destination. They actively migrate during the following weeks to the region where the testis or ovary will eventually form, and there they join up with groups of cells that will play no direct part in producing the children of the next generation.

Once this is realized it becomes far easier to understand the way in which the ovary of an adult woman is put together. It consists essentially of two parts, one inside the other. The centre of the ovary is known as the *medulla*. It contains arteries, veins, and a few muscle fibres, but it plays no part in reproduction. The outer layer is known as the *cortex*. During sexual maturity it is as thick as the medulla, but

later in life it becomes thinner as it loses its ability to function. Scattered throughout the cortex are a large number of rounded cells of various sizes. These are the germ cells which have become embedded in the cortical tissue. It is here that they grow and develop until eventually they are shed as egg cells during the process of ovulation.

The germ cells do not develop at all until a girl reaches puberty—usually when she is between 12 and 14 years old. But from that time until her menopause, somewhere between the ages of 40 and 50, a number of eggs mature each month, although only one of them is usually ovulated. This process of maturation occurs in two stages. First, the egg itself increases in size perhaps one- or two-fold. Even so the egg is so small (one-tenth of a millimetre in diameter) that its growth alone could never account for the raised areas that make the surface of the ovary so uneven. However, the region immediately surrounding the egg cell also expands and the increase in size in this region is altogether more spectacular.

The immature egg cell, as it lies in the ovarian cortex, is closely covered by a layer of other cells. As it matures, fluid starts to appear between these cells and the whole 'envelope' surrounding the egg begins to expand. More fluid accumulates and eventually the egg cell is surrounded by a large fluid-filled 'cyst'. It does not float freely in the fluid. Instead it is attached to one side and the cells which form its attachment are some of those which originally surrounded it. Indeed, even after ovulation

has occurred, and the egg enters the fallopian tube, it still retains a retinue of these cells which are then collectively known as the *cumulus*.

The 'cyst', when fully mature, may stand out from the surface of the ovary by as much as two centimetres. When fluid starts to accumulate round the egg the structure which results is known as a *follicle*. When it reaches the stage of full maturity it is known specifically as a *Graafian follicle*, named after Regnier de Graaf, the seventeenth-century Dutch physician who was among the first to observe it. Because of its relatively large size the Graafian follicle confused early investigators. They assumed that the whole follicle was the egg that would be fertilized. After all, at first glance, it looked not unlike the inside of a hen's egg. Only later was it realized that this relatively large quantity of fluid, as it oozes out of the follicle, carries the very much smaller egg cell along with it into the fallopian tube.

At ovulation, the distended follicle ruptures and the egg is released. But films which have been taken of it rupturing show that ovulation is not an 'explosive' process. The fluid does indeed ooze out carrying the egg, rather than being squirted out in a jet. This shows that the rupture cannot simply be due to the fluid pressure which has been built up inside the follicle. But scientists still have little idea of exactly how ovulation does come about. The most likely explanation is that the wall of the follicle is dissolved by a slow chemical action: that the point of rupture is found to have a smooth rather than a ragged outline also suggests that this is the case.

There is another aspect of ovulation about which little is known. A normal woman has two ovaries and each of them is capable of producing mature eggs. But during each month only *one* egg cell is released from *one* ovary. It is impossible to say from which of the follicles the mature egg cell will come, or even to be sure which of the two ovaries will give rise to it. Roughly speaking, they alternate: ovulation occurs in one ovary one month and in the other the next. But this is only a rough guide. One ovary may ovulate for two or three months in succession before the other one takes over, perhaps for a single ovulation, perhaps for two or three. But what their alternating action does mean is that a woman who has a blockage in one fallopian tube, or who has one diseased ovary, need not regard herself as infertile. Although her chances of conceiving may be less than those of a woman who has two functioning ovaries and two functioning fallopian tubes, she can still become pregnant as a result of ovulation and fertilization on her 'good' side.

Once the follicle has ruptured and the egg and fluid have escaped it might appear that its useful life was over. But this is not so. Within a very short time the cells lining the follicle wall start to increase in number at such a rate that the hollow follicle becomes almost full of cells, many of which carry a whitish-yellow pigment called *lutein*. The whole cell-packed follicle is therefore known as a *corpus luteum*, and it, too, stands out from the ovarian surface. The fate of the corpus luteum depends entirely upon whether pregnancy occurs or not. If it does then the corpus luteum persists right up until birth (although in humans at least, it does not function for the whole of this period). If, however, pregnancy does not occur, then the life-span of the corpus luteum is limited to about ten days. At the end of that time it breaks down and leaves only a few remnants still visible under the microscope. But only a few days after this corpus luteum has regressed another batch of follicles starts to mature in the ovary and the process starts again.

Scientists interested in the fate of the egg cells have actually counted the numbers present in the ovaries at various stages of life. A new-born baby girl has as many as two million egg cells, but by the time she reaches her seventh birthday she has less than half a million and as she approaches the menopause she may have only a few hundred. What happens to them all? Certainly they are not all ovulated; indeed only a very small proportion are. The rest simply degenerate, either during the process of maturation or before. Such degeneration is known as *atresia*, and it presents a problem. Scientists know neither how it occurs nor why. All that they do know is that it represents the certain fate of the vast majority of the egg cells in any ovary.

An even more basic question is what controls the cyclical changes that go on month after month in the ovary. Some women feel a certain amount of pain between their menstrual periods which is believed to be due to ovulation. The ovary must, therefore, have nerves running into it although, even so, every woman knows that ovulation is not under the conscious control of her nervous system any more than is her heartbeat or the rate of her digestion. But the body also possesses a different set of control mechanisms in the form of hormones—chemical molecules which originate in one organ but move through the bloodstream to another where they exert a very profound effect. Insulin is an example of a hormone that most people have heard of and adrenalin is another. The hormones controlling the ovarian cycle have less familiar names. The follicle produces a hormone called *oestrogen* as does the corpus luteum. The latter also produces a second hormone called *progesterone*. These hormones have very marked effects upon a woman's sexual make-up. For example, they are directly responsible for controlling her menstrual periods.

Although the hormones produced by the ovary play a part in controlling the ovarian cycle they are not in full control. They, in turn, are under the control of two hormones produced in the *pituitary*, a small gland at the base of the brain. Since pituitary hormones influence the gonads they are called *gonadotrophins*. But even this is a simplification because the pituitary is itself under the control of a part of the brain called the *hypothalamus* which secretes a range of further hormones. Because the ultimate control comes from the brain it is clear that nervous factors can be involved in controlling the cycle to some extent even though the woman herself may not be aware of them. For example, a sudden shock may delay the arrival of a menstrual period although she certainly has no conscious control over the workings of her uterus.

A vast amount of research work has been devoted to the study of hormonal cycles and the results are often confusing or conflicting. However, many authorities would agree that the sequence of ovarian changes is roughly as follows. The growth of the follicle is stimulated by the presence in the bloodstream of a pituitary hormone called follicle-stimulating hormone or FSH. But FSH alone is not capable of bringing about the final maturation of the egg cell or the rupture of the fully distended Graafian follicle. For this the second gonadotrophin, luteinizing hormone or LH, is necessary. Some days before ovulation a sudden surge of LH occurs in the circulating blood, a surge which is preceded and possibly induced by a surge in the level of circulating oestrogen produced by the follicle itself. Following ovulation, progesterone and oestrogen are both produced by the corpus luteum, but towards the end of the cycle, if no pregnancy has occurred, it breaks down because it has not been fully 'switched on' and the secretion of its hormones falls to a low level. A further batch of follicles is then induced to start maturing and the cycle recommences.

It is absolutely vital that scientists should try to gain an understanding of these subtle hormonal changes, not simply because they pose a fascinating problem for research workers, but also because they have very important practical consequences. For example, why do a girl's ovaries not start to ovulate until over a decade after she is born? Is it because they are in some way 'immature'? Scientists know from animal experiments that the answer is no. If ovaries are transplanted from, say, a rat before puberty into one which is fully mature the newly-transplanted organs start to cycle quite adequately in a short time. In the immature rat they were potentially quite capable of functioning but they did not receive the appropriate stimulus of gonadotrophins from the pituitary.

At first sight, it might appear that in the same way, at the menopause, the pituitary suffers a 'shut-down', leaving the ovary without adequate stimulation from the gonadotrophins, but in this case just the opposite seems to be true. The pituitary in menopausal women secretes large quantities of FSH. Indeed, this hormone is thought to be responsible for the 'hot flushes' experienced during the menopause. In this case it seems that it is the ovary that has become unresponsive and unable to produce adequate amounts of oestrogen. For this reason oestrogen is sometimes given orally to counteract menopausal flushing and discomfort.

Another aspect of hormonal treatment is even more newsworthy. For some women the desire to have children is strong but they nonetheless remain infertile. The possible causes of infertility are numerous but sometimes a careful examination reveals that a woman is not ovulating because of a shortage of FSH or LH or both. It is now possible to extract these hormones (or ones which have very similar effects) from various sources in such a form that they still retain their activity when administered to women.

In recent years in Scandinavia, the United States, and in Britain, too, treatment with gonadotrophins has been in the headlines for one very simple reason. It is extremely difficult to predict just how much of such a hormone preparation is necessary to bring about the maturation and ovulation of just one ovarian follicle. Too little will result in no ovulation, no pregnancy, and disappointment for the patient. Too much will cause perhaps half a dozen follicles to rupture simultaneously. There are usually more than enough sperm in the fallopian tube after intercourse to fertilize such a batch of eggs and the result is a multiple pregnancy. Whether we can ever guarantee to get the dose just right remains to be seen. Some experts would doubt it. We have made great strides in our understanding of the ovary since Weismann put forward his rather tentative suggestions, but it may well take us another 70 years before we can say that we understand it completely.

CLIVE WOOD

The fallopian tubes

Mansell Collection

In 1561, Gabriel Fallopius described the uterine tubes named after him. Today scientists are still studying the role they play in fertility.

The fallopian tubes are the most neglected regions of the female reproductive system. A great many investigations of the vagina have been carried out by doctors and biologists because of its obvious importance: it is where sperm are deposited. The uterus has received even more attention because of its role in pregnancy, and since the advent of oral contraceptives the ovary, too, has come under close scrutiny. But the two tubes which form the connection between the ovary and the uterus—first described by Gabriel Fallopius in 1561 and hence bearing his name—have, by comparison, received very little study. This is surprising for the success or failure of a pregnancy depends just as much on the fallopian tube as it does on the ovary or the uterus. The fallopian tube is responsible for collecting the mature egg as it leaves the ovary, and for transporting it into the uterine cavity. During its passage the most important transformation in the whole sexual process may occur, for it is in the fallopian tube that the egg becomes fertilized.

It may be that the fallopian tubes (which are also known as uterine tubes or oviducts) have received such scant attention because they are not very spectacular in appearance. Some of the textbooks that describe them state flatly that each tube is four inches long. But estimates of their length tend to vary from book to book, and films of the tubes taken in recent years show that they are capable of lengthening and shortening to a considerable degree. If four inches is an average figure for the length of the oviduct, then on average its thickness is rather less than that of a woman's little finger. But the thickness increases further away from the uterus and closer to the ovary, so much so that Fallopius himself compared its appearance to that of a trumpet.

Each tube arises from the upper part of the body of the uterus. The first section of the tube is no more than a narrow channel running through the muscle of the uterine wall. The muscle at this point is half an inch or more in thickness, and the channel which passes through it is extremely narrow—probably no more than a twenty-fifth of an inch in diameter. The first portion of the oviduct arising out of the uterus that is recognizable as a tube is the region known as the *isthmus*. The isthmus is itself quite narrow, and the channel inside it is usually no wider than that running through the uterine wall. It accounts for perhaps a quarter of the total length of the tube.

Almost imperceptibly the isthmus becomes transformed into the longer, wider region known as the *ampulla* which accounts for the remaining three-quarters of the tube's total length. At its widest point the ampulla is three times thicker than the isthmus, perhaps a third of an inch in diameter. The channel which it contains is about five times wider than that in the narrower part of the tube.

The two regions also differ in other ways. The isthmus runs in a straight line away from the uterine body, but the ampulla curves back towards the uterus in such a way that its end comes to lie close to the ovary. The outer wall of the isthmus consists of thin layers of muscle, whereas the muscles in the ampullary wall are far thicker and capable of undergoing wave-like patterns of contraction similar to those observed in other organs with muscular walls, such as the intestine.

But the most striking feature of the ampulla is the end of it adjacent to the ovary. Not only does this widen to resemble the bell of a trumpet, but the bell itself has a 'frayed' appearance, for in this region the ampulla is divided into a large number of finger-like projections known as *fimbriae*. It is often said that one of these fimbriae, which is longer than the others, is actually attached to the ovary, thus holding the open end of the tube in a position of readiness to receive the egg. (Anyone looking at the fimbriated end of the fallopian tube will be struck by its large, funnel-shaped structure, obviously designed for one purpose only—to prevent the egg, once it has left the ovarian follicle, from being lost in the abdominal cavity.) However, there has been much discussion about how the tube succeeds in catching the egg. After all, the egg is extremely small—only one two-hundred-and-fiftieth of an inch in diameter—and it is shed only once a month. Even with a large funnel the chances of losing it are high.

Although opinions on this subject still differ, the most likely answer seems to be that the egg never really has the chance to escape. Close to the time of ovulation, the fimbriae appear to move over the surface of the ovary 'searching out' the one follicle which is going to rupture. Once it is found, they press closely against it. It has been suggested that it is the 'massaging' action of the fimbriae that causes the follicle to burst. Whether or not this is true, the egg, as it leaves the follicle, does come into immediate contact with the funnel-like end of the tube. In addition, currents are set up in the fluid around the egg which ensure that it will enter the funnel.

The lining of the fallopian tube contains many cells which carry a tiny, whip-like hair known as a *cilium*. When these cilia beat together, currents are produced within the tube which move materials up or down. Ciliated cells are particularly common in the fimbriated region, and their action undoubtedly helps to ensure the safe arrival of the egg into the ampulla. Indeed, to illustrate this effect, some most interesting film has been taken in the oviduct of the rabbit. Eggs, coloured for easier recognition, were placed in the vicinity of the fimbriae and their movement studied through a microscope. Slowly they became attracted by the ciliary beat and then, as they came into closer range, they were wafted into the tube.

But the lining of the fallopian tube is not made up entirely of ciliated cells; there are, in addition, numbers of cells whose function is to secrete fluid. The lining of the tube is not smooth such as the inner tube of a bicycle tyre. Instead, it is thrown up into folds which resemble more closely the tread of that same tyre. In the isthmus, the pattern of these folds is fairly simple. The lining is arranged in four ridges so that if the tube is cut open its central cavity is seen to have the form of a cross. In the ampulla, however, these ridges start to become sub-divided, and at the fimbriated end the divisions are very complex, producing a delicate lace-work pattern when seen in cross-section.

The purpose of throwing the lining into such complex folds is obvious. It greatly increases the surface area available both for the ciliary and the secretory cells, thus permitting the inside of the oviduct to undergo much more activity than would be the case if it were smooth-walled. However, the folds can become too complex. If they do, there will not be enough space available to move materials up and down within the fluid-filled cavity.

The fallopian tube performs two quite different tasks, and at first it is difficult to see how it can do them simultaneously. It collects the egg and moves it down towards the uterus, while at the same time it allows sperm to move upwards. Indeed it must assist, rather than simply allow, their movement, because without any help the sperm would never be able to swim against the relatively powerful currents flowing downwards towards the uterus. The movement of the egg is easiest to explain. The ciliary action of the tubal lining may be important, but the regular waves of muscular contraction are probably the principal force moving the egg from the ampulla down to the uterine cavity.

The movement of the sperm is still not fully understood. The most likely explanation was made as long ago as 1931, when it was suggested that the complicated folds or baffles in the tubal lining might sometimes be so close together that they produce small, closed compartments, separated from the rest of the tubal cavity. The beating of the cilia within these compartments will set up circulating currents with a movement of fluid up one side of the compartment and down the other. It is within these currents that the sperm are carried. Since each compartment is only a temporary structure, sperm can be carried from one to the next until they eventually reach their destination. In time they may even be wafted out of the fimbriated end of the tube and into the abdominal cavity.

The complicated folds of the tubal lining can sometimes become so elaborate that they completely block the cavity. If fertilization of the egg is prevented by such a blockage it will obviously lead to sterility. Because the ovaries produce eggs alternately, blockage of just one, although it lowers the chances of conception, will not make it impossible. However, if the sperm are capable of moving up through the tube but the pathway of the fertilized egg is then blocked, a quite different situation can occur. The egg may become implanted within the wall of the tube itself causing a condition known as *tubal pregnancy*.

The frequency of this complaint varies widely from one nation to another. It seems less frequent in white than in non-white races, but on average, perhaps one in two hundred pregnancies will occur with the embryo developing in some part of the fallopian tube. For a time it may be impossible to diagnose the condition because the woman will show all the normal signs of pregnancy. Eventually, however, she will experience sharp stabbing pains on one side of her abdomen. The foetus will have grown too large for the narrow confines of the tube, and the latter will be on the point of rupturing, if it has not already done so. This is a surgical emergency. The abdomen must be opened and usually the entire pregnant tube is removed. If rupture has occurred then the bleeding must be stopped and a massive transfusion may be necessary. Happily, the death rate from tubal pregnancies is falling (at least according to figures published in the United States) mainly because of earlier diagnosis and a more adequate transfusion service.

Sometimes the blockage may have been caused by some disease which has a particular effect on the fallopian tubes. Gonorrhoea is probably the most common. If such a condition blocks both tubes completely then infertility will result. Perhaps a quarter of all women who attend an infertility clinic suffer from such a complaint. The doctor will decide whether the patient's tubes are completely blocked by using one or two methods. With the technique known as *hysterosalpingography*, a fluid opaque to X-rays is introduced into the uterus and X-ray pictures taken to see whether it has entered the tubes or spilled through into the pelvic cavity. If so, there is clearly not a total blockage. However, some gynaecologists point out, the mere introduction of the fluid can sometimes cause the tubes to shut tightly in the region of the uterine wall and so the process may not always be wholly effective.

The alternative procedure is known as *insufflation*. A gas is blown under pressure into the tubes and any resistance to its free passage (any marked 'back pressure') is taken as evidence of a block. Sometimes these diagnostic procedures will actually be curative themselves, removing any blockage that might have been present. Often, however, surgery is required to remove the blocked portion. Even then there can be no guarantee of fertility and the risk of tubal pregnancy is high.

Surgery on the fallopian tubes is now being carried out with increasing frequency, not to remove a blockage and hence restore fertility but with the completely opposite intention of sterilizing women. Sometimes there are medical reasons for this. A woman who has had a number of Caesarean operations, or a woman who has a heart disease, is an obvious candidate for sterilization. But this process is sometimes carried out for purely contraceptive purposes, too.

For the patient who has to undergo a Caesarean section, the ideal time for tubectomy (as the sterilizing procedure is known) is while she is still on the operating table. There are many different ways to perform this operation and much depends upon the preference of the individual surgeon. But in most forms of sterilization ligatures are tied around the tube, and a considerable length of it—perhaps an inch—is removed completely. For the patient not undergoing abdominal surgery for some other purpose, the tubectomy represents a special operation and she will be in hospital for a week.

However, a different method of performing some abdominal operations has recently been gaining popularity. It employs an instrument known as a *laparascope*, and, instead of the usual type of incision necessary for 'conventional' surgery, using this instrument requires only two small round holes to be made in the patient's abdomen. The advantage of the method (in which the tubes are blocked with a special electric cautery and subsequently cut) is that the patient can go home and return to her everyday life very much sooner.

Even so, because the chances of reversing a tubectomy are slight, some women prefer to avoid sterilization. They would rather have a means of birth control that leaves them unaffected once they decide to give up using it. Ideally too, it would save a great deal of trouble if the contraceptives women use did not have to be taken every day, but only after intercourse when they are exposed to the risk of pregnancy. In short, what they might want is a 'morning-after' pill, and the development of such a pill is now well under way. It is particularly appropriate to consider it here because it very probably affects the fallopian tube.

Morning-after pills consist of a hormone called oestrogen which is active when taken by mouth. The pill is taken once a day for three days following intercourse. In at least one published set of results no pregnancies at all were observed following its use. The way the pill works is not clearly understood. It may alter the uterine lining so that the fertilized egg could not become implanted even if all other conditions were perfect. However, oestrogens can greatly increase the waves of muscular contraction responsible for moving the egg through the fallopian tube. In such a situation the egg will reach the uterus very rapidly. It will arrive too soon for the uterine lining to accommodate it, and will be either destroyed or expelled through the vagina before it has a chance to implant. One effect of the morning-after pill would be to blur the distinction between contraception and abortion: when she takes it, a woman will not know whether she has conceived or not, and the egg cell has no chance to develop.

The fallopian tube is thus as important from the point of view of contraception as it is for the enhancement of fertility. Its neglect up to now is therefore doubly regrettable.

CLIVE WOOD

In each menstrual cycle, after one ovary ovulates, the fallopian tube sweeps the egg towards the uterus. If sperm have reached the tube after intercourse, conception may follow.

THE INTERNAL SEXUAL ORGANS IN THE FEMALE.
SEEN FROM IN FRONT AND ABOVE

1. FIMBRIAE   2. AMPULLA   3. ISTHMUS   4. OVARY   5. CLITORIS
6. LABIA MAJORA   7. BLADDER   8. UTERUS   9. FALLOPIAN TUBE

Square One/Scheltema & Holdema

Menstruation

Man, it has been said, differs from other male animals in only two respects: he drinks when he is not thirsty and he makes love all the year round. In the same way it might be said that woman differs from the female of practically every other species (except the apes, to which we are most closely related) because once in every lunar month she menstruates, that is she suffers a loss of blood from her vagina. For centuries the process of menstruation has fascinated medical men, although their notions of what it is all about have frequently been very wide of the mark. For example, the early Greeks knew well enough that the 'male seed' that had to be placed in a woman's body for a pregnancy to occur was contained within the seminal fluid. But if some 'female seed' were also necessary, what could it possibly be? They reached the reasonable, but totally wrong, conclusion that it must be the menstrual fluid. In some ways the two seeds combined within the uterus and a child was the eventual result.

Some 2,000 years later, as recently as the nineteenth century, the medical profession had still not solved the problem of why menstruation occurs, although many of them were quite convinced that women during their menstrual periods were strictly to be avoided—they would contaminate all that they laid hands upon.

A book could be written on man's attitude to menstruation and on the way that this idea of uncleanness has led him to regard women. In the twentieth century, however, interest in menstruation should centre not so much on the superstitions of the past as on the state of knowledge *now* about the process of menstruation, knowledge that should reassure modern women that the process is no more mysterious or distasteful than any of the body's many other functions.

Menstruation is a process which depends upon the activity of at least two separate organs—the ovary and the uterus. The ovary has a double role to fulfil within the body. Its most obvious purpose is to produce the eggs without which no pregnancy would ever occur. But its 'secondary' function is just as important because, without the hormones that the ovary secretes, a woman would never conceive. In fact, her reproductive system would not even pass beyond the stage of puberty. Hormones have been called the 'chemical messengers' of the body and those which the ovary produces and which control menstruation are called *oestrogen* and *progesterone*. They have important effects on many different parts of a woman's body, but perhaps the most striking effect that they have is on

the lining of the uterus—a layer of tissue known as the *endometrium*.

If samples of endometrium are removed from women at different times of the month, quite clear differences can be seen between them. Shortly after menstruation the tissue lining the uterine cavity forms a thin layer and only small amounts of it can be recovered for examination. But under the microscope it is clear that the tissue was growing rapidly before it was removed and so it is not surprising to find that a second sample taken, say, midway between two menstrual periods is thicker and obviously more fully developed. A third sample, taken a few days before menstruation, has a different appearance. It is thicker again than either of the other two and it also possesses a large number of glands. Finally, if a sample is taken during menstruation itself (a procedure which is usually avoided if possible) it will be found to consist of pieces of tissue debris mixed with blood, with little real form or structure.

It is, therefore, clear that the endometrial tissue lining the uterine cavity goes through a series of changes between one menstrual period and the next. The period necessary for all the changes to occur is known as the menstrual cycle. Menstruation causes the destruction of the greater part of the endometrium, but the small quantity that remains has the ability to grow very rapidly to replace what has been lost. Because of the rapid growth and proliferation of such tissue this part of the cycle is often known as the *proliferative phase*. It lasts for roughly half of the cycle's total length. A sample taken in the second half of the cycle has secretory glands, and so this part of the menstrual cycle is normally known as the *secretory phase*. The cycle ends when this secretory tissue breaks down, only to start again once the blood and debris have been cleared from the uterine cavity.

The ovaries, too, go through a series of cyclic changes. The surface of the ovary carries a large number of small 'cysts' of various sizes. These are the *ovarian follicles* and each one contains an egg. In the middle of the cycle one follicle develops which is full of fluid and very much larger than the others. It stands out from the surface of the ovary and it may be as much as two centimetres in diameter. This follicle is on the point of rupturing to release into the fallopian tube an egg ready for fertilization. Later in the cycle the cavity of this follicle becomes filled with whitish-yellow cells and because of their colour the structure is known as a *corpus luteum* (a 'yellow body'). If the egg is fertilized, the corpus luteum remains visible in the ovary

right through pregnancy and up to the time of birth. If not, however, it lasts for about ten days, after which time it starts to regress.

With the knowledge of hindsight it is difficult for some scientists today to understand why it took the medical men of the past so long to realize that the changes in the ovary and those in the uterus were merely two different aspects of precisely the same cycle. The answer may lie partly in the fact that the idea of a hormone was not clearly expressed until 1889 and hormones, of course, form the basis of the whole menstrual process.

The developing follicles secrete oestrogen and it is oestrogen that causes the endometrium to proliferate. At the end of the proliferative phase the follicle ruptures and ovulation takes place. But if the fertilized egg were to come into contact with the endometrium in the proliferative phase it would not be able to implant. Such a tissue cannot go through the complicated set of changes necessary for implantation to occur. However, while the egg is moving down the fallopian tube and into the uterus (a process which takes about a week) the endometrium comes under the influence of the corpus luteum—a gland which secretes both oestrogen and progesterone together. This combined hormonal action converts the proliferative endometrium into the secretory stage. It is in this latter condition that the uterine lining is able to accommodate and implant a fertilized egg.

Once implanted, the egg probably sends a hormonal message (which we do not as yet understand) to the corpus luteum, which makes it grow and secrete even larger quantities of hormone. But if no egg implants no message is received and the corpus luteum breaks down. The endometrium then receives no hormones at all and in this state it cannot persist. It also breaks down (or at least the greater part of it) and leaves the body in the form of menstrual fluid. However, as menstruation ceases another follicle is starting to develop in the ovary. Oestrogen again starts to influence the remnants of the uterine lining and the proliferative phase of the next menstrual cycle then begins.

Throughout her reproductive life, from the age of puberty to the menopause, a woman undergoes a succession of such cycles. It is interrupted only by pregnancy and delayed for perhaps a further three to six months after birth especially if the woman decides to feed her child at the breast. It is usually estimated that a women who bears no children will experience about four hundred menstrual periods during the span of her sexual maturity.

The length of this span depends, of course, on the age of puberty. In Europe and America the first menstrual period occurs, on average, when girls are about twelve-and-a-half years old. However, this is only an average figure and menstruation occurring even a year or two earlier is not at all abnormal. What does seem to be happening is that the age of puberty is constantly falling. Girls now menstruate several years earlier than they did in the last century.

The appearance of the first menstrual flow need not coincide exactly with, the time at which a girl is capable of becoming pregnant. There is evidence, for example, to suggest that for the first few cycles an egg does not actually leave the follicle. In other words, the first few cycles are *anovular*. It is even said that in some societies girls of this age are allowed to have sexual intercourse, although they rarely become pregnant until they are somewhat older.

If menstruation always proceeded regularly and without discomfort it might never have given rise to half of the bigoted attitudes that now surround it. Fortunately, most menstrual disorders are not very common. They may be due to disorders in other glands of the body, to congenital defects or even to changes in the inheritable chromosomes that are found in every one of the body's cells.

By far the commonest menstrual defects are the tension and depression that precede and accompany menstruation in many women and the pain that is often experienced during the menstrual flow. Despite many years of research scientists are still not quite certain about the cause of either of these complaints. Premenstrual tension is important—because it means that many women must spend time off work. It can be treated to a large extent by the use of drugs

Menstrual pain is experienced to some degree by perhaps one woman in every two, although it varies greatly in its severity from one woman to the next. Often it can be relieved with aspirin or some similar pain killer, but occasionally an operation is required. The operation is called *dilatation*. It consists quite simply of widening the mouth of the uterus—the region known as the *cervical canal*. It was practised as a method of bringing relief long before there was any good explanation of why it should do so. Doctors now think that it destroys some of the nerve fibres that are responsible for carrying the pain messages from the uterus.

Another cure for menstrual pain has double significance because it gives the chance to cure the pain and practise contraception by the use of only one form of medication. One of the characteristics of an anovular cycle is that it is rarely painful. For this reason, a cure that is sometimes used for painful periods is the oral contraceptive. Eliminating the ovulation, the function of the contraceptive pill, often eliminates the discomfort, although bleeding still occurs each month when the pills are discontinued. Indeed, some women who have very irregular menstrual cycles are also 'put on the pill' simply to make them bleed at reassuringly regular intervals.

And this brings us to one of the greatest myths of all time—the myth of the woman who, without any form of medication, experiences completely regular cycles. The doctor who is naive enough simply to ask his female patients, 'Do you have regular periods?' will, in the great majority of cases, receive an affirmative reply. The patient likes him to think that she is normal in this respect, and indeed she may quite sincerely believe that she does menstruate at absolutely regular intervals. But if she were to follow the progress of her periods with a calendar for twelve months she would probably be surprised. The most 'regular' women may easily deviate by a day or two from one cycle to the next.

Women also differ from each other in the duration of their cycles, which is perhaps the principal reason why the rhythm method of contraception has a high failure rate. The 'textbook' duration is one lunar month or 28 days, but numerous studies have shown that women can deviate widely from this figure and still regard themselves as normal. The limits of normality have been set rather arbitrarily, at 23 to 35 days. Any woman whose periods fall within this range probably has little or nothing to worry about, even though she may know no one else whose periods are as frequent, or infrequent, as her own.

A great deal is now known about the physiology of the uterus and much can be done for the patient whose periods are painful, irregular, or non-existent. But in this connection it might perhaps be pointed out that if periods which have always been fairly normal suddenly stop altogether the most probable single cause of the patient's condition is pregnancy.

CLIVE WOOD

THE MENSTRUAL CYCLE

From early in the menstrual period graafian follicles in the ovary are maturing under the influence of FSH. Oestrogen secreted by the follicles causes build-up of the uterine wall. Ovulation of one mature follicle depends on the balance between FSH and LH. After ovulation, the follicle, now the corpus luteum, produces progesterone, which alters the lining of the uterus still further; this now becomes thicker and contains well-developed glands. When hormone production stops, this lining breaks down, menstruation occurs, and the cycle starts again.

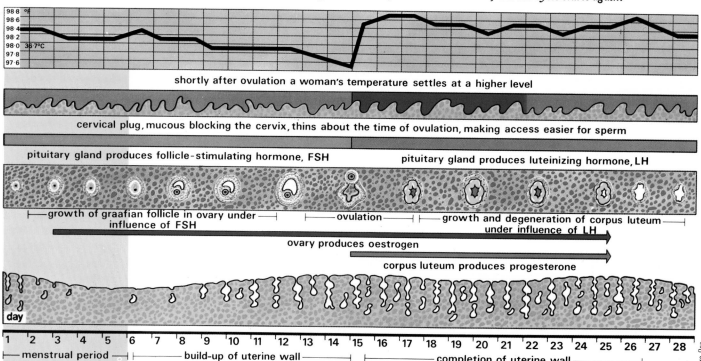

shortly after ovulation a woman's temperature settles at a higher level

cervical plug, mucous blocking the cervix, thins about the time of ovulation, making access easier for sperm

pituitary gland produces follicle-stimulating hormone, FSH   pituitary gland produces luteinizing hormone, LH

growth of graafian follicle in ovary under influence of FSH — ovulation — growth and degeneration of corpus luteum under influence of LH

ovary produces oestrogen

corpus luteum produces progesterone

day

1 2 3 4 5 6 7 8 9 10 11 12 13 14 15 16 17 18 19 20 21 22 23 24 25 26 27 28

menstrual period — build-up of uterine wall — completion of uterine wall

Square One

Conception and misconception

At each act of sexual intercourse a normal man deposits about 300 million sperms into a woman's vagina, and intercourse may occur many times in a week. But at each ovulation a woman's ovary usually releases only one egg into her fallopian tube, and the shedding of an egg from the ovary occurs only once in every month. Whether or not this egg will make contact with a sperm and whether the sperm will be able to penetrate inside the egg and fertilize it, depends on a large number of factors.

An early misconception: around 1750, Gauthier d'Agoty, an anatomist and artist, claimed to have developed an embryo in a glass of water into which sperm alone had fallen.

For this reason conception is a chancy business. Indeed, some specialists, knowing how much can go wrong with the process, have expressed their amazement that it ever happens at all.

On the other hand, many young couples, anxious to avoid a pregnancy, might claim that, unfortunately, conception is the easiest thing in the world to achieve. If we take an overall view we can see that both attitudes are right in their own way. Relatively few acts of intercourse actually lead to pregnancy but some of those that do may be extremely inconvenient. It is only natural for any woman with an unplanned pregnancy to imagine that conception can happen very readily indeed.

What are the facts? How often does conception actually take place and how does it take place? And what of all the stories that one hears about conception being impossible under certain conditions?

What do we really mean when we talk about conception? The word may seem obvious enough, but in the past it has meant different things to different people. To some of the early Fathers of the Catholic Church a foetus was considered to be 'alive' only when the mother started to feel it moving inside her uterus. These 'quickening' movements as they are called do not occur until about halfway through pregnancy, so by their reckoning conception was quite a late event.

Today we would all agree that conception occurs a good deal earlier than this, but there is still disagreement about the precise moment when it takes place. It seems likely that a large number of fertilized human eggs, perhaps up to a third of them, never become embedded in the wall of the uterus. In other words, perhaps thirty per cent of all the eggs that are fertilized are defective in some way and for this reason they never implant. This is perfectly normal—it is probably a mechanism that the body has developed to minimize the number of defective children who are born. If implantation in the uterus does not take place then menstrual bleeding occurs at the normal time. There is no missed menstrual period and the woman never knows that she has been 'pregnant'. In a sense, of course, she has not, and some biologists believe that because these early 'miscarriages' are so common we should not say that conception has occurred until the egg has implanted and the first signs of pregnancy have become apparent.

But others disagree. To them the

whole essence of conception is the fusing together of two quite distinct cells, the sperm and the egg, to form a single fertilized egg-cell. What happens to it afterwards is not important. There is no need for us to take sides in this argument. Both points of view have something to be said for them. But our interest here is with how the sperm and the egg come together. It is with fertilization. Clearly no child was ever conceived without the fertilization of an egg, so we are probably justified in using the two terms to mean more or less the same thing.

The human sperm is only one-twentieth of a millimetre long. Compared with its size the distance that it has to travel in order to reach the egg is enormous. The semen that is ejaculated during sexual intercourse normally forms a pool in the upper part of the vagina. Sperm from this pool has to pass through the cervical canal into the uterus; through the uterus up to a narrow duct known as the utero-tubal junction; through this junction into the fallopian tube and finally two-thirds of the way up the tube to the region where, if ovulation has recently occurred, there will be an egg ready for fertilization. All these regions of the female reproductive system are different from each other and so it is not surprising to learn that sperm behaves differently in almost every one of them.

Sperm were only discovered in the late seventeenth century and the first drawings ever made of them appeared in 1679. The most striking thing that impressed their discoverer was that they showed very active swimming movements. Because of this people assumed for a long time that the sperm simply swims, entirely under its own power, to its destination, the egg. But further investigations showed that this could not possibly be so. The human sperm only swims at the rate of a few millimetres per minute and even then its movements are random. It does not swim in a straight line for long. The chances of it reaching the egg unaided are therefore very slight. In fact, for the greater part of its journey, it has an 'assisted passage'. The assistance is provided by the female reproductive tract.

The first boost that the sperm receives is in its journey through the uterus. The uterus is one of the most muscular organs in the body and at certain times in the menstrual cycle, particularly at the time of ovulation, its walls undergo regular rhythmic contractions. The act of intercourse seems to increase these contractions still further. Semen also contains a powerful, uterine-contracting chemical called prostaglandin.

In this situation any material placed in the lower part of the uterus will be transported to its upper region. Animal experiments, in which radioactive fluids are used to trace the sperm's movement in the uterus have shown this very clearly. From the cervix to the fallopian tube the sperm are rapidly but passively carried along.

They are also carried along once they are

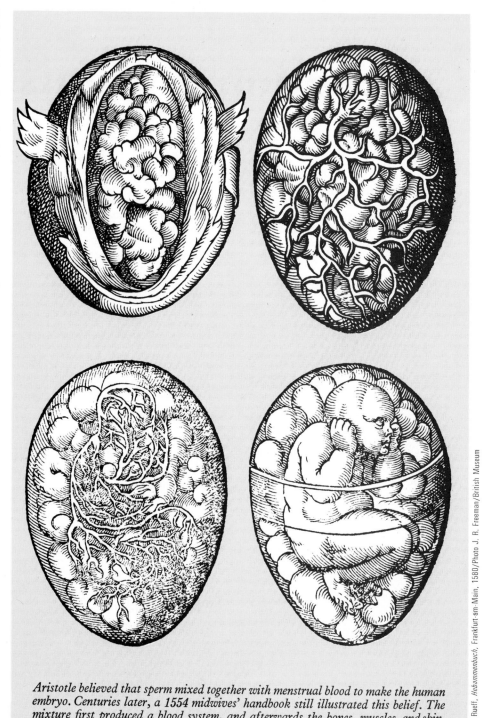

Aristotle believed that sperm mixed together with menstrual blood to make the human embryo. Centuries later, a 1554 midwives' handbook still illustrated this belief. The mixture first produced a blood system, and afterwards the bones, muscles, and skin.

Jacob Rueff, *Hebammenbuch*, Frankfurt-am-Main, 1580/Photo J. R. Freeman/British Museum

inside the fallopian tube itself. Various factors are operated by the tube to set up currents in the fluid that it contains. It is these fluid currents that carry the sperm towards the region of the egg. But why do sperm swim at all if their movement is passive? Is their own motion of any importance? The answer is certainly yes. It is because of their own movement that they can pass through the cervical canal. Their swimming movements are also essential to get them through the utero-tubal junction. And finally, and most important, their movement is necessary for fertilization.

From the viewpoint of the biologist fertilization is the very essence of sexual reproduction. A great deal of scientific research has been devoted to it, especially in the last ten years, although there are still many questions that remain unanswered. By some means, that we still do not understand, the sperm burrows its way into the substance of the egg. Its head and tail become separated from each other and after undergoing a series of changes the head fuses with a part of the egg that looks rather similar to itself. With this fusion the contributions that the mother and father make to the future embryo are combined together. The fertilized egg now has within itself a complete 'blueprint' for the production of another human being. If it experiences no mishap, a baby, who in some ways resembles both of its parents, will be born nine months later.

But initially its development is slow. The egg-cell starts to divide to produce a ball of smaller cells and as it does so it moves down through the fallopian tube and enters the uterus. About a week after fertilization the egg makes contact with the lining of the uterus and, if everything goes right, it implants itself into the uterine wall. It goes on dividing and must do so many times, for the body of an adult human being, which it is eventually destined to produce, contains no less than 10 million million single cells and all of them are derived from one small portion of the developing egg. Once implantation has occurred, by whatever definition we choose to employ, a child can truly be said to have been conceived.

For centuries, man has been interested in conception. He has wanted to know how it happens and how he can interfere with it, either to make his wife more fertile or to stop her from having children altogether. But the process goes on inside the woman's body, entirely hidden from his view. He therefore had to guess what was happening and often his guesses were wrong. Indeed, there can be few aspects of human reproduction that have acquired such a rich folklore of mistaken ideas and widely quoted half-truths as this one has. And the process has been going on for thousands of years. Both Homer and Aristotle were convinced that a mare did not need to be covered by a stallion to become pregnant. She could be impregnated just as well by the wind if it were blowing in the right direction. The ancient Egyptians believed that vultures could conceive in the same way and for centuries the eggs laid by a hen that had never seen a cockerel were known as wind eggs.

It might be thought that once sperm were discovered the confusion about conception suddenly came to an end. But rather than resolving a controversy, their discovery created a new one. One group of biologists was so impressed with the sperm that they decided it must contain the entire embryo within itself. Drawings of the time show a complete little man—the *homunculus*—coiled up in the sperm's head just waiting to reach the uterus where it could grow and develop. But another group was less impressed. To them it was the uterus that contained the whole and entire embryo. The sperm was only needed to stir it up and hasten its growth. It had no essential role to play and it certainly made no contribution whatever to the embryo's development.

It is easy to be amused by the mistakes of the past, but we still have our share of fallacies about conception, even in this enlightened age. Take for example the idea that a woman can only conceive if she experiences an orgasm. The notion is based on the belief that sperm can only get into the uterus if the uterine contractions suck them in from the vagina, rather like a pair of bellows sucking in air. This 'insucking' is thought to occur only as a part of the sexual climax and hence with no orgasm there is no conception. The belief depends on so many fallacies that it scarcely warrants serious consideration.

The seventeenth century saw the 'homunculus' within the head of the sperm, believing the embryo to be a formed individual which simply grew.

Nikolaus Hartsoeker, *Essai de Dioptrique*, Paris, 1694/Photo Thames & Hudson

There are hundreds of women in the world who have never experienced an orgasm in their lives. Some of them have not even read enough about it to be able to describe it to their daughters.

Slightly less unreasonable is the belief that a woman cannot conceive while she is lactating. This idea is based on the observation that women who keep their babies at the breast often start to menstruate rather later than women who bottle-feed their babies immediately after birth. There is some scientific justification for this idea, because lactation does tend to delay the return of regular cycles of ovulation for some time after the baby is born. But although this is a *general* truth that applies if we are considering a large number of women, for any individual woman it is impossible to say just how long her ovaries will take to return to normal. She may start to ovulate just as soon as her sister who is bottle-feeding. For her to use lactation as a form of birth control is therefore extremely unsatisfactory. She may be lucky or she may not. But to go further and imagine that suckling makes conception *impossible* is entirely wrong. It cannot be justified either by science or by everyday experience.

Many women are concerned to know whether the position in which they experience sexual intercourse is likely to affect their chances of conception and it is certainly true that the positions most likely to result in pregnancy are those in which the woman lies on her back. In these cases the pool of semen in the vagina is in contact with the mouth of the cervical canal and the entry of sperm into the uterus is made easier. But this is not to say that any position that does not allow deep penetration of the penis into the vagina will not result in conception. In many cases even shallow penetration can lead to pregnancy. For the couple always to have intercourse standing up, or with the woman on top, is therefore no guarantee against conception. Nor can a woman be sure of avoiding pregnancy by jumping up and down or urinating after intercourse in an attempt to dislodge the semen. Even the vaginal douche is unsatisfactory because it cannot wash away sperm that have already become lodged in the cervix. Indeed, statistics show that douching is one of the least satisfactory of all methods of birth control.

And just how likely is it that a woman will conceive from a single act of intercourse, assuming that she takes no contraceptive precautions? Obviously it depends on the time that she chooses to perform the experiment. At the middle of the cycle the chance is very high. During the time of menstruation it is very low. But it is possible to calculate an average figure, a probability that can be applied to the average woman without our knowing exactly what stage of the cycle she has reached. The figure turns out to be three per cent. That is to say only about one act of intercourse in every thirty will result in a conception.

To many this seems amazingly low. Surely, they think, that hasn't been our experience. Possibly it has not, but conception is a chancy business. And the figure is not really as low as it may seem at first sight.

Let us imagine a couple who were married at twenty-five and who had a normal sex life until the wife reached the menopause. Let us assume that just once in every month, to give their life a little more zest, they deliberately avoided using any form of birth control for just one act of intercourse. On his forty-fifth birthday, if he feels like describing the fruits of his experience, the father would be able to gather his five children together and advise them all to be more cautious than he had been.

CLIVE WOOD

Infertility in women

Discovering the cause of a couple's inability to conceive is rather like solving a crime. Only very rarely is the reason—and thus the action to be taken—blindingly obvious. In most cases a doctor in a subfertility clinic has to search painstakingly for clues, considering every aspect of the problem and weighing all the possible influences. He has to examine both partners, because often the man and the woman each have some slight disorder that probably would not matter if the other partner were more highly fertile. Even if the doctor discovers what he thinks is the cause of their failure to conceive, he must continue his investigation, for there may still exist some other factors which contribute to the couple's subfertility.

It is a task that needs doggedness on both the doctor's part and that of his patients, for the tests and examinations may spread over many months. This is especially true of examinations of the woman, because the female reproductive system is far more complex than the male, and plays a much greater part in bringing a new life into the world. Any defect in a woman's reproductive system may drastically lengthen the odds against conception. Neither is it a static system, for numerous subtle changes take place during the menstrual cycle and their disturbance can easily prevent conception. And because they are so subtle these disturbances may be difficult to detect.

For these reasons most doctors investigating subfertility prefer to thoroughly check the man's fertility first—although prior to this they will usually have carried out some preliminary investigations on the woman. Although different groups vary widely, out of every 100 couples examined, about 20 are found to owe their infertility mainly to some malfunction in the man, and about 30 to a malfunction in the woman. In the remainder either both are involved or there is no apparent cause for subfertility.

The effort and delay involved in carrying through a subfertility investigation mean that the couple need to be extremely determined in their desire for a child. Most doctors feel that this is an advantage. For while every couple should have the right to bear children this right is also a responsibility. When a doctor becomes involved in the decision, the responsibility becomes partly his too. Because of this he must be as sure as possible that both partners genuinely want a child, and that it is not merely a last-ditch attempt to save a crumbling marriage. He must also ensure that the woman is physically fit enough to go through with the pregnancy. This does not mean that he will refuse to help a woman who, for instance, has diabetes or high blood pressure, but he will explain the possible dangers to her and be ready to give her any extra care she may need if and when she becomes pregnant.

A woman consulting a doctor at a subfertility clinic will probably first be given

The desire to reproduce is one of man's strongest instincts, and so it is not surprising that the subject of fertility has been one of art's most recurrent themes. This bas-relief, which dates from the first century A.D., is a Roman depiction of the fertile earth.

a general medical check-up, and be questioned about her general health, her sex life, the regularity of her menstrual periods and so on. This may often provide an immediate clue to the reason why she has been unable to become pregnant. For example, any extreme irregularity in her menstrual periods suggests that her ovaries are not producing ova (eggs) regularly. Or she may show signs of an under- or over-active thyroid gland which can affect fertility. The doctor will probably also take a blood sample to check for any Rhesus incompatibility with the woman's husband. (Although this does not prevent fertilization it may cause stillbirth or deformity.) A blood sample can also be used to carry out a Wassermann test for syphilis. The doctor may inquire about the couple's relationship and home circumstances too, for quite often a woman has been able to conceive as soon as she moved from under the eye of her mother-in-law into a home of her own!

A vaginal examination is another important part of the early check-up. This can reveal a number of possible causes of subfertility. The doctor will, for instance, look for signs of a vaginal infection; the woman herself may or may not have been conscious of a discharge. In any case, the doctor will probably take a smear from the vagina to check for this. This examination will also reveal if the cervix, the entrance to the womb, is at an unusual angle, or has too small an opening, for this can also cause subfertility.

After these preliminary examinations the woman is usually asked to come back for a *postcoital test* about 14 days after the start of her next menstrual period. This is one of the simplest and most important tests in a subfertility investigation. The woman will be told not to have intercourse for a few days before she is due to attend the clinic, but to have intercourse with her husband during the night before the test. At the clinic the doctor uses a small syringe to take several samples of fluid from her vagina. He takes one sample from the wall of the deepest part of the vagina, one from the entrance of the cervix, and a third from within the cervical canal.

Examination of these samples under a microscope shows how well the man's sperm have penetrated the cervix, the first major obstacle on their path to fertilize the woman's egg. This tells the doctor a great deal about both partners—whether, for example, the man is producing healthy sperm, and whether the conditions inside the woman's vagina are favourable to these sperm. Normally, the cervix produces large amounts of clear, fluid mucus about midway through the menstrual cycle which the sperm can easily penetrate. But if the mucus is infected or too sticky, it forms a barrier to the sperm. The doctor can see the sperm with his microscope, and can observe how active they are, as well as noticing any harmful organisms that might be present.

Infections of the vagina can be treated with drugs, such as antibiotics. If there is no sign of infection, but the mucus is too thick and tacky for the sperm to penetrate, the doctor may suspect a slight hormone disorder, perhaps a deficiency of oestrogens. Oestrogens are female sex hormones produced by the ovaries and, among many other things, they are responsible for producing the clear, thin mucus at about the time an egg is released from the woman's ovaries. If the amount of oestrogens in the woman's body is too low the cervical mucus remains thick; so the treatment is to give the woman small doses of oestrogens for a few days in each menstrual cycle.

This may completely cure the whole subfertility problem, or it may be only one part of an effective cure. For after passing through the cervix into the womb the sperm must then be able to penetrate the fallopian tubes, which link the womb and the ovaries. Fertilization must occur in one or other of these tubes, shortly after the egg is released, in order that the fertilized egg has enough time to develop on the journey to the womb and is ready to become implanted. Obviously, if the tubes are blocked in any way, neither the sperm nor the egg will be able to pass through them. Even fallopian tubes that are not blocked may have disorders that prevent conception. For example, the rhythmic contractions of the tubes—known as *peristalsis*—which combined with the wafting motion of tiny hairs inside them carry the egg from the ovary to the womb, may not function properly.

Disorders of the fallopian tubes probably account for one in every four cases of subfertility. There are many possible disorders, including infection by tuberculosis or gonorrhoea. The tubes can become infected following an abortion or even after douching. And scar tissue formed as a result of abdominal infection (such as appendicitis), or surgery can also block them. Psychological tension may close the tubes by tensing the muscles around them. This can cause subfertility in a couple with a mother-in-law problem or where the wife has a fear of intercourse or perhaps

—deep down—of childbirth. Some psychologists have suggested that similar tension can close the cervix, which also results in preventing the passage of sperm.

Testing for blocked fallopian tubes began in the 1920s, and was the first major contribution to scientific subfertility investigation. There are two main methods of testing for this, one using X-rays and the other gas. The gas method is known as *insufflation:* it is the simplest method, and so is generally used first. Carbon dioxide is blown under gentle pressure through the cervix into the womb. A pen on the doctor's apparatus records the gas pressure on a moving sheet of paper. If the tubes are clear the pen draws a zig-zag line which represents the normal peristalsis, or contractions, of the tubes. Poor peristalsis is shown by blunted peaks. If the tubes are blocked the pen will record a much higher pressure. In many cases, a peak of high pressure will be followed by a normal tracing. This indicates that the tubes were blocked but that the gas pressure has cleared them, and is often enough to cure subfertility completely.

Insufflation is sometimes carried out at the same time as the postcoital test. The woman feels only a little discomfort, and needs no anaesthetic, although the doctor may give her a sedative to calm her. The gas, blown through the fallopian tubes, passes through the abdominal cavity and is soon absorbed into the blood stream and breathed out. (Carbon dioxide is, in fact, the gas our lungs expel when we breathe.) Until the gas has all been absorbed, the woman will probably feel some slight disfort similar to indigestion—and perhaps slight pain. This can be reduced if she remains lying down for a few minutes after the test.

Although insufflation often shows up a blockage—and may even cure it—it cannot reveal abnormalities that prevent fertilization if the tubes are not blocked. But an X-ray test can. It is more complicated than the usual X-ray, however, because the fallopian tubes and the womb are both too soft to show up on any X-ray film, and so, to outline them, a liquid that will not

Too little of the hormone that stimulates the ovaries to produce ova can cause subfertility. Though injecting this hormone can rectify this, it may also result in a multiple birth.

43

allow X-rays to pass is injected through the cervix into the womb in the same way as the carbon dioxide gas in insufflation. If the womb and the fallopian tubes allow the liquid to pass, their internal outline shows up clearly on the fluorescent screen of the X-ray machine, and a series of photographs is then taken to record the progress of the liquid.

This technique can reveal many possible causes of subfertility, including distortion or kinking of the tubes, their distension with fluid, infection of the tubes or womb, failure of the womb to develop properly at puberty, and various kinds of tumours, cancerous or benign, as well as straight-forward blockage. Like insufflation, the X-rays are completely harmless and involve little discomfort. And like insufflation they can themselves sometimes restore fertility. One reason for this is that the liquid injected is sometimes an antiseptic and may clear up any slight infection. It may also remove any sticky mucus partially blocking the tubes and can even stimulate the movements that transport the egg.

If the various tests show that the tubes are blocked or distorted, regular insufflation may eventually restore fertility, or the doctor may decide after making further tests that surgery is needed. This can involve opening the blocked ends of the tubes or removing scar tissue. In some cases kinks in the tubes or a part of one tube may be removed and the remainder joined to the womb. If necessary the surgeon will use a piece of plastic tubing to keep the tubes open. The success of this type of surgery varies widely, depending partly, of course, on the exact nature of the disorder being treated. Where everything is favourable more than 60 per cent of patients later successfully bear children. But in some conditions there is a much lower success rate, although this is increasing as surgeons gain more experience in this field.

No amount of surgery on the fallopian tubes will, however, be successful unless the woman's ovaries are producing eggs, and this is often extremely difficult to detect. As the human egg is only just visible to the naked eye, trying to find it is far more difficult than looking for a needle in a haystack. So indirect tests must be used. The most basic is to check whether the woman is having normal menstrual periods; if not, she is probably not ovulating (producing an egg) either. But even if her periods are regular, she may not produce an egg each month—or at all. In fact, most women occasionally have an eggless month.

Keeping a temperature chart for several months will usually show if an egg is being released. This involves the woman taking her temperature each morning before getting up. Within two days or so after ovulation—usually about 14 days after the start of the last period—the temperature jumps about $\frac{3}{4}°$F and stays raised until the next period starts. However, confirmation that the woman's ovaries are producing eggs may be needed. A vaginal smear test or a microscopic examination of a little tissue

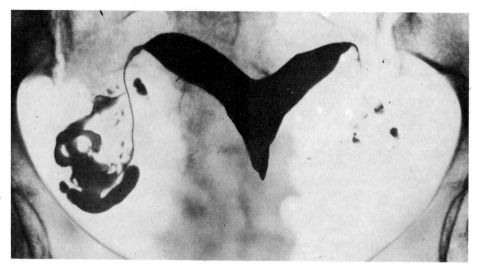

If a special liquid is injected through the cervix into the womb, X-rays can trace its progress and reveal whether the fallopian tubes are blocked or if any other abnormalities exist.

scraped from the wall of the womb will show conclusively whether the changes that accompany ovulation have occurred. Or a drop of cervical mucus can be put on a glass slide and warmed; if ovulation has taken place, it may form a typical pattern rather like a fern as it dries. A final check is to test the woman's urine for a substance called *pregnanediol*, which is only present after ovulation.

No method of detecting ovulation is conclusive, but merely an indication. But if the woman is apparently not ovulating—as is the case with about one in 20 women examined at a subfertility clinic—the doctor must obviously discover why this is before he can decide on the best treatment. The menstrual cycle—including ovulation—is controlled by a delicate interplay of several different hormones circulating in the woman's blood stream and the balance can easily be upset. Indeed, deliberate and controlled interference with this system is the basis of the contraceptive pill. It is possible to treat some cases of subfertility, where, for example, a woman can conceive successfully but has a miscarriage, by using drugs similar to those in the contraceptive pill, but in a different way. Also, the pituitary gland at the base of the brain sometimes fails to produce enough of the hormone that stimulates the ovaries to produce ova. Injections of this hormone can cause ovulation. When this is too successful sextuplets or quintuplets are born, although with experience it may be possible to avoid these multiple births in the future.

Disorders of the ovaries may themselves prevent ovulation even when the hormones are working normally. One causes of subfertility is the so-called Stein-Leventhal syndrome in which the ovaries are covered with tough cysts which prevent the egg being released. The ovaries may be twice the normal size and look like ping-pong balls to the doctor when he looks inside the abdomen with an instrument called a *culdoscope*. This disorder can be corrected by surgery, and in as many as 80 per cent of patients fertility is restored.

Another disorder that can cause subfertility and which needs surgery to correct it is known as *endometriosis*. This occurs when small pieces of tissue from the lining of the womb—the *endometrium*—attach themselves to other parts of the reproductive system and start growing there. They may form chocolate-brown cysts on the ovaries and fallopian tubes, and these bleed at the same time as the womb lining, at menstruation. These cysts, if they are widespread, can cause severe premenstrual pain, and have to be removed. Although this is a difficult task, provided every one is cut out, there is a very good chance of fertility being restored.

With so many possible causes of subfertility, it is not surprising that the doctor's investigations can take a long time. Even after exhaustive tests and many visits to the clinic no apparent disorders may be found in either the woman or her husband that account for their inability to have children. In a very few cases it is discovered that the woman is simply allergic to her husband's sperm; antibodies in her body cause them to clump together so that they cannot swim. The only 'treatment' is to use a condom for several months when having intercourse, so that the sperm never touch the woman. Then her allergic reaction may die down and allow her to conceive when her husband stops using a condom.

There are probably many causes for subfertility that doctors have not yet discovered, perhaps because they involve only extremely subtle disorders in the functioning of the reproductive organs. Whether or not doctors discover further causes of subfertility, and learn how to treat them successfully, the childless couple have an ever increasing chance of conceiving simply because existing techniques are continually being improved. Although curing subfertility is likely to remain a lengthy process its success amply repays the effort involved for both patients and their doctor. For doctors seldom receive such deep and sincere thanks as from a couple whose wish for children has been fulfilled.

MICHAEL WRIGHT

Physical changes in pregnancy

During pregnancy a woman experiences remarkable physical changes—overshadowed only by the new life within her.

The average human pregnancy lasts 280 days. During that time a woman experiences the most profound physical changes that she is ever likely to encounter during a normal healthy life.

During pregnancy a woman gains about 20 to 25 pounds in weight. The amount of water in her body increases by some ten pints. Her shape is completely transformed and her whole psychology may alter. During this time, not only her uterus but also a number of other important organs undergo considerable alteration. Some of these changes revert to normal once birth has taken place. Some changes, however, will persist and the physical state of the woman who has borne a child remains in some ways permanently different from that before she conceived.

Over the centuries pregnancy has been regarded with a sense of wonder. It has been considered an almost magical event. Poets have marvelled at the 'miracle that happens every day' and the detailed scientific investigations of medical men in the nineteenth and twentieth centuries have confirmed that the body is capable of adapting itself to pregnancy in a truly remarkable way.

For the vast majority of women the first indication of pregnancy is the missing of an expected menstrual period. It can be an alarming sign in cases where the pregnancy was neither planned nor wanted because, by the time that the period has been missed, the egg is quite deeply implanted in the uterine lining. It cannot be dislodged by any simple do-it-yourself procedure, despite old wives' tales which suggest the contrary. Menstruation fails to occur simply because the egg, once it has implanted, is able indirectly to prevent the normal monthly breakdown of the uterine lining.

The lining of the uterus, like several other tissues in the body, is affected to a very large degree by the sex hormones which are circulating in a woman's blood. Indeed, the normal menstrual cycle can be divided into two parts. In the first part, before ovulation, the lining is increasing

John Hillelson

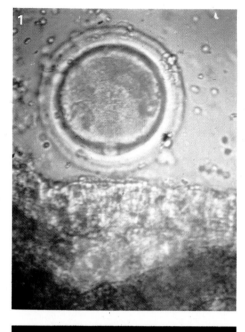

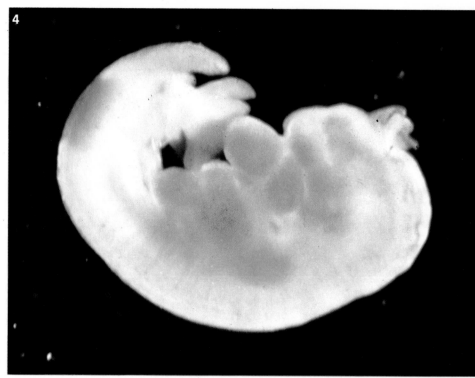

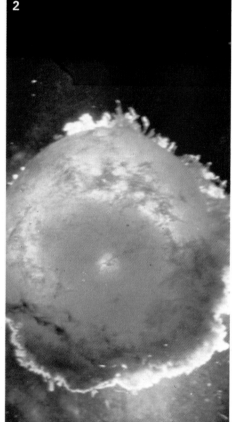

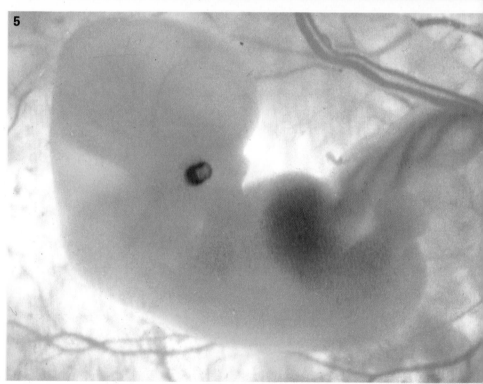

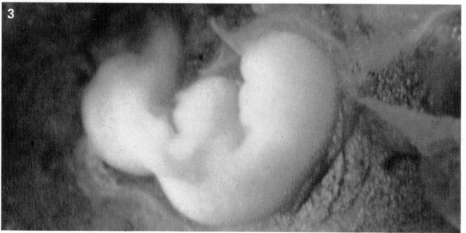

Life begins when an egg released from an ovary meets a sperm from a male. The fertilized, single cell measures 1/250 inch in diameter—but carries hereditary characteristics from both parents. Its sex is already determined. Within six hours the cell begins to divide and redivide, doubling in number every 12 hours. The growing ball of cells reaches the uterus about five days after fertilization and, less than a week later, implants into the uterine wall. **2** By the fourth week the amniotic sac, which protects the developing embryo, has formed. **3** At this stage primitive organs are already apparent in the 1/6 inch long embryo. **4** At five weeks, and 1/4 inch, more sophisticated organs start to appear. **5** Between seven and eight weeks the embryo reaches an inch in

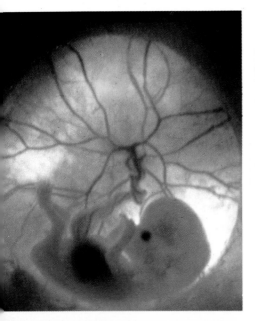

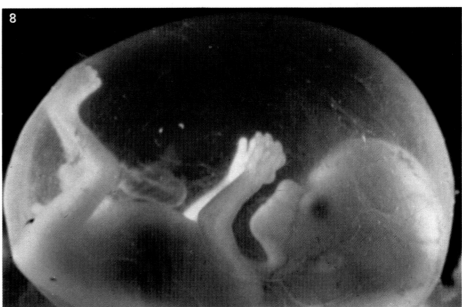

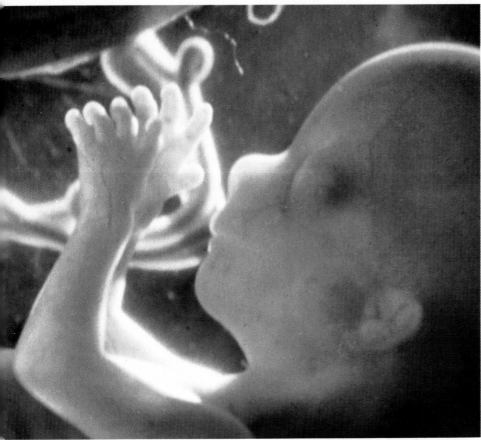

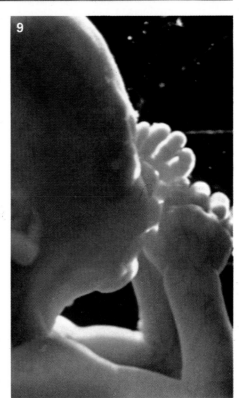

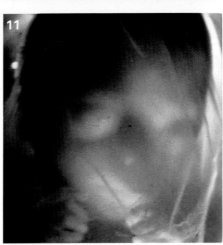

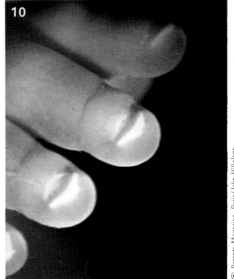

length and the foetus, as the developing organism is now called, is recognizably human. **6** By 11 weeks the foetus has grown to three inches and all the major organs are present. **7** Between 12 and 16 weeks its height virtually doubles **8** and towards the end of this period the poorly-coordinated movements that the mother will feel later as quickening begin. **9** The sucking reflex that ensures that the new-born baby can feed is well-established by 18 weeks. **10** At 20 weeks the nails—and fingerprints—are fully formed. **11** And from 28 weeks the infant, which now weighs over two pounds and is ten inches in height, could live if born prematurely. By about 40 weeks the child will have grown to about 20 inches and over six pounds.

in thickness because it is influenced by the hormone *oestrogen*. In the second half of the cycle the lining is influenced by both oestrogen and *progesterone* and it starts to secrete materials which may be important for the nourishment of the fertilized egg before it has succeeded in implanting.

At the end of the majority of menstrual cycles, in which fertilization has not occurred, the lining of the uterus breaks down simply because hormone production ceases. The part of the ovary which normally produces these substances, a structure known as the *corpus luteum*, has a limited life-span of eight to ten days. At the end of that time it disintegrates, and, as a consequence, so does the lining of the uterus. In some way, however, the fertilized egg, almost immediately after implantation, is capable of prolonging the life-span of the corpus luteum and hence of the tissue which lines the uterine cavity.

It seems likely that the very young embryo itself produces a hormonal message which prevents the 'switching off' of the hormones from the ovary. Such an effect has to happen because, if it did not, the lining would break down and be expelled, taking the newly implanted egg with it.

Because it is the missing of the period that first indicates that conception has occurred, neither the woman nor her physician have any way of knowing precisely when fertilization or implantation took place. It is usual, therefore, to date a pregnancy from the onset of the last menstrual period, and the doctor's notes about the pregnancy record the date of this LMP. Measuring the duration of pregnancy in this way introduces a slight error as far as the true age of the embryo is concerned.

Ovulation and fertilization will have occurred about two weeks after the LMP, and implantation itself about one week later still. However, as pregnancy proceeds, this two-week error becomes progressively less important and, indeed, compensation is often made for it. The traditional method of predicting on what day the child will be born is actually to add nine calendar months and five days to the date of the last menstrual period.

One in 20 women will have her child on exactly that day and about two in every five will deliver within one week on either side of it. Like every other aspect of pregnancy the actual duration varies from one individual to the next. But doctors generally agree that variations may well occur of up to about 30 days either way and so pregnancies from 250 to 310 days are considered normal.

Missing the expected menstrual period is only the first of the body's reactions to pregnancy. As the pregnancy progresses many additional bodily changes become apparent. They are signs that the woman's body is adapting to the need to nourish and protect the foetus.

One of the most striking of the early transformations that occur in the pregnant woman is the change in the breasts. Very early in pregnancy, sometimes even before the menstrual period is missed, the breasts may feel full or tender. Perhaps the

woman will notice a prickling sensation within them. As pregnancy proceeds the breasts become larger. In addition, veins become readily visible beneath the skin, and the *areola* region, which surrounds the nipple, becomes darker, especially in brunettes.

In the areola region there also develop a number of small, pale, raised spots. After the third month of pregnancy it is often possible to squeeze out of the nipples small quantities of a fluid known as *colostrum*, a forerunner of the milk these glands will secrete after delivery.

The type of pigmentation seen in the breasts is also seen in other areas of the body. For example, in some pregnant women, a dark line appears down the middle of the abdomen. The same deposition of pigment on the face may lead to a sun-tanned appearance which may be largely responsible for the suggestion that some women seem to bloom during pregnancy.

However, this blossoming is not entirely without discomfort. In the early weeks it is common to find women suffering from nausea and vomiting, especially in the mornings. There have been many speculations about what actually causes morning sickness and nearly as many different treatments for it have been suggested. However, there is still no general agreement about what actually produces the symptoms. One opinion is that the hormone which the young embryo is thought to produce and which is responsible for stimulating the corpus luteum may itself cause this nausea. Another suggestion is that the balance of the sex hormones themselves is considerably altered very early in pregnancy and that it might be this change which is responsible for the sickness. At a later stage there may still be vomiting and heartburn caused by the escape of some gastric juice upwards out of the stomach.

Another result of advancing pregnancy, again for reasons which are not understood, is that a woman may experience what medical specialists refer to as 'perversions of appetite'—the desire to eat coal, strawberries out of season, or some similarly unlikely food. She may yearn to drink anything from cocoa to champagne. The basis of these desires is probably psychological, although some scientists feel that the hormonal changes of pregnancy may upset the senses of smell and taste. Certainly pregnant women often do show other psychological reactions, such as sleeplessness and irritability, although often these have underlying physical causes.

An obvious outward sign of pregnancy is weight gain which is related to the changes in the woman's shape. At first the weight gain is relatively slow. During the first three months the pregnant woman might gain only about two pounds. But in the next three months she will gain perhaps five times this amount, and the increase in her girth begins to be apparent. The further gain, between six months and birth, will be similar. To some extent the change in the pattern of the mother's weight keeps

pace with the increased growth of the foetus, although the foetus itself accounts for only a part of the total change in maternal weight. But behind such obvious changes a battery of less obvious developments is taking place which is actually responsible for the visible changes.

The physiology of a pregnant woman undergoes a far greater modification than at first sight seems apparent. For example, a considerable part of the weight gain is accounted for by an increase in the volume of body fluid which, in turn, is mainly an increase in the volume of the blood. At about 34 weeks, when this reaches its maximum, the volume of blood plasma is one and a half times greater than it was before the onset of pregnancy. In this situation, some of the blood components tend to become diluted.

If the woman is not receiving sufficient iron, the concentration of her red blood cells decreases. Even when she has been supplied with an adequate quantity of iron this may occur if, because of digestive difficulties, she is unable to absorb it properly. Most doctors will explain to a pregnant woman the need to take adequate quantities of iron and hence to avoid the very common condition sometimes known as 'pregnancy anaemia'. Interestingly enough, with other minerals such as calcium, magnesium, phosphate, chloride, and indeed iron itself if it is available in adequate quantities, the pregnant woman can actually store more than enough for the needs of both herself and her foetus. The stored material is retained so that it can appear in the milk during the period of lactation that usually follows birth.

The increase in blood volume means that the heart is called upon to work somewhat harder—from the twentieth week of pregnancy until birth the amount of blood pumped a minute increases by about 30 per cent. Usually, however, there is no consistent increase in blood pressure. In the later part of pregnancy the heart is actually displaced slightly from its normal position by the pressure which the expanding uterus exerts upon the diaphragm. A similar effect, in which the diaphragm exerts pressure on the lungs, would lead to a decrease in the volume of air taken in at each breath if it were not for the fact that the chest also enlarges in circumference during pregnancy.

These changes that go on in a woman's body during the period of pregnancy result from the need to accommodate the changes occurring in the growing foetus and the transformations taking place in the uterus.

Immediately after conception the newly fertilized egg is less than one two-hundred-and-fiftieth of an inch in diameter, whereas the average infant at birth is 20 inches or more in length and weighs over six pounds. But the process of growth and development that it goes through is not steady or continuous. Indeed it can be divided into two quite separate phases.

From implantation until the end of the second month the egg goes through the *embryonic* phase of its development. From being a small, undifferentiated ball of cells it develops a head and body together with limbs and all the internal organs (liver, kidneys, blood system) that it will require in later life. Its eyes and ears also develop and it produces for itself, at a very early stage of its development, a membrane filled with fluid—the *amniotic sac*—within which the whole of its development takes place.

By the end of the second month the embryo is obviously and unmistakably a small human being although it is only just over an inch long. During the following months it grows more rapidly, but its length increases faster than its weight for a considerable time. For example, halfway through pregnancy, at the end of the fifth month, the foetus is about half the length that it will be when it is born, but it has only reached about one-sixth of its birth weight.

Acceleration in the growth of the foetus is also reflected in the expansion of the uterus to accommodate the foetus and the amniotic fluid which surrounds it as well as itself increasing in volume. At 12 weeks the uterus is still very small, little higher than the top of the pubic bone or the pubic hair. By about 18 weeks the fundus, the uppermost part of the uterus, is midway between the pubic bone and the navel and it reaches the same height as the navel in about week 20. For the next 14 weeks or so it continues to rise higher so that by week 36 it is in contact with the diaphragm. From then until the time of birth, however, the fundus descends a little.

This increase in the height of the uterine body, the cause of the obvious increase in abdominal size, leads to an alteration in the position of the fallopian tubes, which come to lie parallel to the sides of the uterus rather than at right angles to it.

The vagina too undergoes some alteration. Its walls become more congested with blood vessels and so it takes on a reddish or even violet coloration. To some extent this is also true of the labia at the vaginal entrance. The cervical canal becomes filled with a thick mucus plug which perhaps serves to prevent infection entering the uterine cavity. So active are the mucus-secreting glands in the cervix that they often lead to a vaginal discharge which is quite characteristic of pregnancy.

Of the changes during pregnancy the majority—the change in blood volume, heart beat, respiration, and so on—return to the pre-pregnant state shortly after birth.

But some effects are not so reversible. Pigmentation changes often remain. The uterus remains somewhat larger than it was before pregnancy, and the breasts may also retain some of their increase in size. In general, however, it is true to say that most of the body systems return to normal within a few weeks or months after delivery. And these reverse reactions are almost as remarkable a set of changes as those of pregnancy itself.   CLIVE WOOD

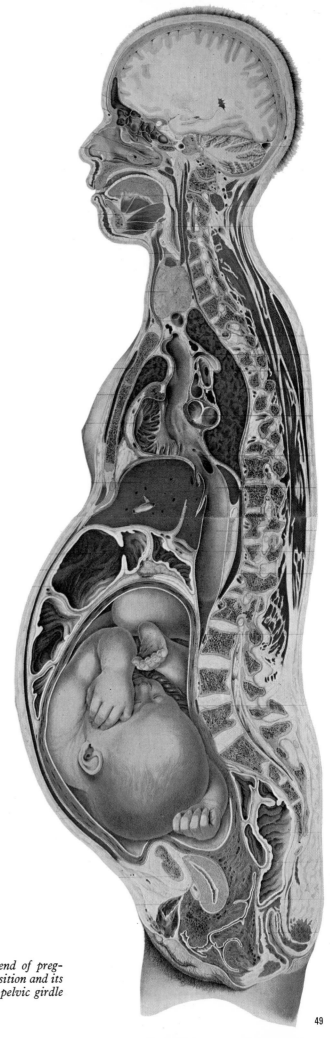

In most cases, towards the end of pregnancy the infant reverses position and its head fits into the mother's pelvic girdle ready for delivery.

The menopause

Women worry about the menopause. They fear that it signifies not only loss of fertility, but loss of vitality and attractiveness. What happens to a woman's body during the menopause?

The end of a woman's fertile life—but not her sexual life—is commonly called the 'change of life' or menopause. Another term sometimes used by the medical profession is the 'climacteric'. After the menopause a woman is no longer able to bear children. The reproductive period of her life, which began with the onset of menstruation, is over, whether she has borne children or not.

For some women who have given birth to numerous children the arrival of the menopause may be a source of relief. No longer is it necessary to worry continuously about the possibility of becoming pregnant yet again, or to concern oneself with methods of contraception. For other women, of course, the event is one of some sadness. The woman who has not borne children now knows her last chance is past and that she can never become a mother.

For all women the menopause is a time charged with emotions of one sort or another, and a great proportion of the troubles which arise during 'the change' are due to difficulties in adjusting to a new outlook on life. Some women adapt rapidly. Others are beset with psychological disturbances, although usually of a minor degree, for several years. Many of the disorders are purely psychological, in that there seems to be no underlying reason for the changed workings of the body to cause them. But there is no doubt that it is the alteration in the body's chemistry, and the disturbance of the complex hormonal balance, which triggers off a certain, very small number of upsets.

When and why does the menopause occur? And what exactly happens to the body during the menopause?

Although women vary widely in the lengths of their fertile lives, the average age for the onset of the menopause is 45 years old. There seems to be a correlation between the time of puberty and the coming of the menopause, but not the correlation that one might think was natural. Women who have a late puberty are in fact likely to have an earlier menopause, and thus a reproductive life which is shortened at both ends. This is not invariable. Many women go through the menopause as early as the late thirties, while others remain fertile well into their fifties.

Very occasionally, in the condition known as 'precocious menopause', a woman's fertile life will stop as early as the late twenties or early thirties. Unfortunately, there is as yet nothing that can be done to prevent this happening, or to reverse

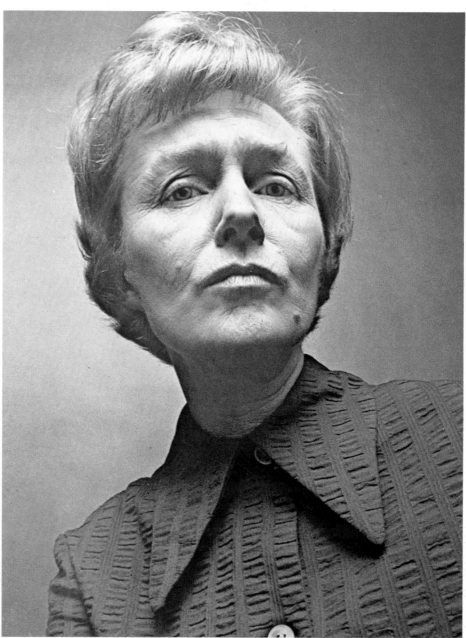

the process when it has happened. It is possible, however, to administer hormones afterwards to replace those whose absence is responsible for some of the unpleasant features of the menopause in such young women.

At the other end of the scale, there are undoubtedly women who remain fertile into their fifties. One woman in Los Angeles is well-documented as having given birth to a baby daughter at the age of 57 years, in October 1956. However, when a South African grandmother claimed to

A woman who is overwhelmed by anxiety and depression during the menopause will find that this is reflected in her appearance.

have borne a child at the age of 58, in 1969, investigation by medical authorities interested in such an unusual occurrence uncovered a hoax. In general, claims to child-bearing in a woman as old as this are regarded with extreme scepticism.

By definition the menopause is said to have occurred when there has been complete and permanent cessation of men-

John Garrett

But the woman who is secure and confident will easily cope with any minor symptoms and look forward to a new phase of her life.

today is generally several years longer than was that of their grandmothers.

The cessation of menstrual periods may take up to a year to be confirmed, and the menopause may begin in several different ways. At the simplest, the regular monthly periods just stop. An expected menstrual period fails to come along, and no period ever occurs again. In some cases, the interval between the periods, normally 28 days or so, becomes gradually longer and longer, until eventually they no longer occur. In other women the amount of the menstrual flow may gradually dwindle until the flow ceases entirely.

The menopause is not normally accompanied by heavy or irregular bleeding, as many women imagine. In the years immediately preceding the menopause there are sometimes upsets in the regularity of the periods, and very occasionally the waning effects of the body's hormones produce an alteration in the lining of the womb, the endometrium, so that on occasion bleeding may be heavier than normal. These effects may sometimes be remedied by the administration of additional hormones. However, any irregularity or increase in the amount of bleeding in an older woman is regarded by doctors with grave suspicion. If the menopause does not happen in one of the three ways mentioned a woman should report it to her doctor immediately.

If all is well the menstrual periods never occur after the menopause. There should be no more vaginal bleeding. If bleeding does reappear suddenly after a couple of years this is not simply menstruation which has returned, but bleeding due to an abnormality of the womb which requires treatment. There are many abnormalities of the womb which are easily corrected, but every woman should remember that after menopause cancer of the womb occurs quite frequently. Any delay in seeking advice about bleeding of the womb after the menopause is asking for trouble. Bleeding does not necessarily indicate cancer, but it is essential that the cause is ascertained as soon as possible. The earlier cancer is diagnosed the better are the chances of success in treatment.

Why do the menstrual periods cease at a certain age? The answer to this is not yet really known. One could imagine that if all the follicles in the ovaries which are responsible for the release of the egg cells, or ova, into the fallopian tubes at the time of each period, were used up, then it would be logical for the menstrual periods

struation. An interval of some six to 12 months during which there has been no menstrual flow (and, of course, when it has been proved that the woman is not pregnant) is, in general, necessary to establish the fact. During the past 50 years or so there seems to have been a gradual tendency for the menopause to occur later in life. At the turn of the century women noted the cessation of their periods on average some three or four years earlier than their daughters and granddaughters do today. Exactly why this should be so is not known, but it is thought by some authorities to be due to the gradual improvement in health of the population in general, and to an improvement in nutrition. The increase in the age of women going through the menopause has, of course, a parallel in the decrease in age at which menstruation now first occurs in girls. Taken together these facts mean that the fertile life of women

51

to stop. But this is not so. At the time of birth all the follicles which are later to be released from the ovaries are already present. But there are in fact so many of them that at the release-rate of just one a month only a small fraction would ever be released during a lifetime. The menopause seems to be caused by the aging of the other bodily systems rather than simply by the ovaries becoming worn out.

The ovaries are, of course, under control of other endocrine organs, particularly the pituitary gland, the 'master gland' situated at the base of the skull beneath the brain. The pituitary is responsible, by means of the hormones which it releases into the blood stream, for the control of the whole of the menstrual cycle. The hormones which mediate control are known as gonadotrophins, and under their influence the ovaries are stimulated to produce mature follicles once every month and to release them into the fallopian tubes. Under their influence, too, the ovaries produce quantities of the hormones called oestrogens, the important female hormones which act on the tissues of the body to produce the typical bodily characteristics of the female. Other oestrogens are produced by the adrenal glands, situated above the kidneys on each side of the body. These glands are also governed by the secretions of the pituitary gland.

What apparently happens at the menopause is that the pituitary gland 'shuts down' the supply of gonadotrophins entering the blood stream, so that the ovaries are no longer stimulated to produce and release follicles. At the same time the amount of oestrogens secreted by the ovaries is reduced. It is these oestrogens which are responsible for the normal growth of the endometrium during the monthly cycle. Because the ovaries do not release follicles, and the endometrium does not grow to its normal thickness and is no longer shed from the wall to produce the typical bleeding of the monthly period, the menstrual periods cease, and fertility ends.

It is known that in some 50 to 70 per cent of women the ovaries carry on producing oestrogen in small amounts, as do the adrenal glands, for as long as 10 or 15 years after the menopause. These small amounts are presumably not sufficient to cause growth of the endometrium, but are just sufficient to alleviate some of the effects of sudden total withdrawal of oestrogens from the blood stream and the tissues. Thus they have the effect, during the years following the menopause, of allowing the body to adapt to conditions without oestrogen.

When the ovaries have degenerated, and are no longer producing follicles or the normal amounts of oestrogen, the 'feedback' mechanism starts to function. This mechanism balances the amounts of gonadotrophins released by the pituitary gland and the level of oestrogen in the blood. The pituitary now responds by increasing the amount of gonadotrophin it releases in response to the lowered level of oestrogen in the blood stream. By assessing the amount of gonadotrophin in the blood stream (this is done by measuring the quantities excreted into the urine), it is possible to diagnose whether the menopause has occurred.

Most of the symptoms which occur at the menopause are caused by the upset of the balance of hormones. So, too, are the other changes in the body, which may not be noted, and may cause no discomfort, although definite changes have occurred in the tissues. When the menopause occurs, not only is there a decrease in the amount of oestrogen which is secreted by the ovaries and the adrenal glands, but a decrease in the amount of the male hormone, androgen, which, although the person is female, is also secreted in small amounts by the adrenals. The androgen is responsible for regulating the way in which protein from the food which is eaten is built up into the protein which forms the structure of the body itself. Reduction in the amount of androgen which is circulating alters the metabolism of the body slightly, so that rather more protein in the tissues is broken down. This is called catabolism.

The tissues which are mainly affected by this increased catabolism are the bones, the muscles, and the skin. In addition to the normal changes which come with age, therefore, and because in any case women of middle age are likely to be less fit and active, there are such changes as muscular flabbiness, thinning of the skin, and the development of wrinkling. There may also be changes in the texture of the nails and the hair. Changes in the structure of the bones lead to a slightly increased tendency to fracture after a fall. The latter changes are due to lack of oestrogen, which has a function in bone formation, as well as to reduction in androgen.

As a result of the lowered amounts of oestrogen, the genital tract also gradually undergoes changes. The lining of the vagina becomes thinner and less developed, and there may be an increased tendency for infection to obtain a hold. But it is not only in the mucosa of the vagina that these changes can be noted. Similar degeneration is also seen in the mucosa of the nose and mouth, and even in that lining the stomach. But these changes may themselves produce no symptoms and may not even be noted.

The symptoms which most women associate with the menopause are the so-called 'hot flushes' which are often experienced. These are simply transient feelings of heat, accompanied sometimes by a visible blushing of the skin, usually occurring in exposed areas of the body, such as the face and neck, but sometimes spreading over the whole body. This is sometimes accompanied by profuse perspiration.

These phenomena are due to the lowered levels of oestrogen circulating in the body. Oestrogen normally has a role in keeping the body cool by causing the expansion of small blood vessels in the deeper layers of the skin, so that more blood passes into the skin and is cooled by the air passing over it. When insufficient oestrogen is available to cause this response to anything which causes the body to become overheated, an alternative method of cooling must be employed. Under the influence of the nerves in the skin the more superficial blood vessels suddenly expand. Because these are the vessels which normally cause blushing, the whole skin suddenly becomes pink, and may feel hot and perspire so that the heat is dissipated.

Hot flushes can be caused by excitement, exercise, eating, or emotional tension, all of which cause an increase in the amount of heat produced by the body. Such factors as warm weather, excessive clothing, or bedclothes which are too heavy, which hamper the normal loss of heat from the body surface, may also cause hot flushes.

After the menopause another change in the physiology is the increased susceptibility of women to suffer from disorders of the circulation. Normally men are far more likely to have coronary trouble up to the age of 45 than women. Some medical authorities believe that the increased incidence of coronary heart disease after the menopause may also be due to the lowering of the levels of oestrogen in the body. It is possible that during the earlier years the presence of the hormones has a protective action which prevents atherosclerotic changes in the blood vessels. Once the menopause has reduced the protective action of the circulating hormone, women would then be as likely as men to have circulatory troubles. This topic is, however, still controversial.

To avoid the occurrence of coronary heart disease in women after menopause, regular administration of oestrogens may be undertaken in the future. However, there are doubts whether men could safely undergo the same sort of treatment. In fact, it has been found that men who have been given prolonged treatment with oestrogens to control cancer of the prostate have actually had an increase in the incidence of coronary disorder. More research must be done before the situation becomes clear.

Very few of the symptoms of the menopause can be definitely attributed to actual change in the body's physiology. Far more numerous are those which arise because of psychological disturbance. They include nervousness, irritability, headaches, insomnia, inability to concentrate, spells of anxiety and depression, and an overall decline in the normal feelings of mental and bodily well-being. Such disturbances naturally affect some women more than others. Only a very small proportion of women need psychiatric help to see them through, but for these women the menopause may well be a traumatic experience.

However, most women, with understanding from their friends and family, can easily cope with the minor psychological problems. Happily, for the great majority the menopause merely marks the end of their fertility and passes with little disturbance.   DAVID WILLIAMS

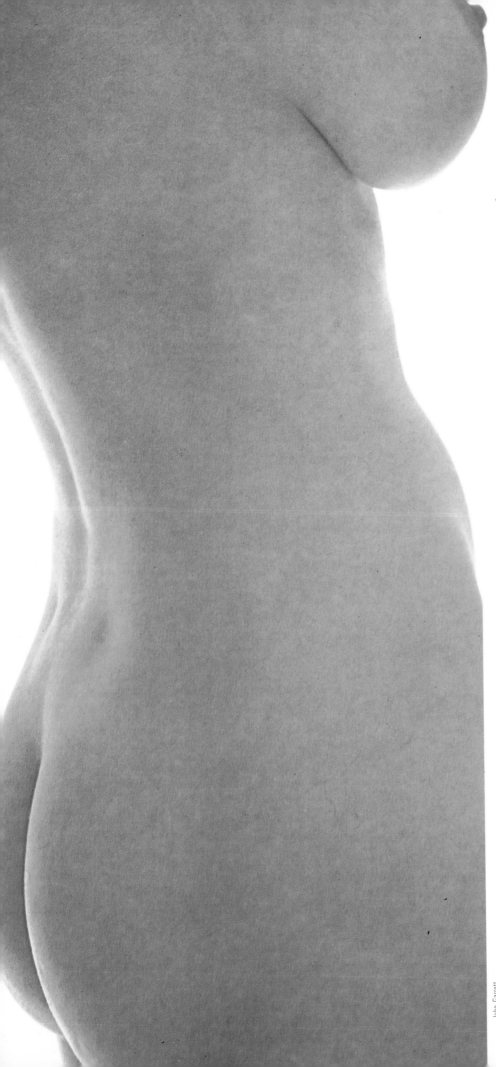

John Garrett

Female disorders

Some conditions affect women only—those which are treated by the gynaecologist. What, for example, causes excessive menstrual pain? And what is cystitis?

Gynaecology literally means 'the study of women'. But, rather than dealing with every aspect of the female sex, gynaecologists confine themselves to studying the medical disorders of women. Indeed, there is an even narrower limitation—gynaecologists concern themselves mainly with afflictions which are related to the female genital tract.

While this might seem to be a very narrow field of specialization, in fact it is vast, because the consequences of the reproductive role of women are widespread throughout the body, and reproduction cannot be regarded as a function of the genital tract alone. It is, therefore, very difficult to define precisely the boundaries of a gynaecologist's work, or to specify what exactly 'female disorders' are.

Certainly, diseases of the female genital tract come within the province of the gynaecologist, but what about diseases of the female breast? The breast is essentially part of the reproductive system, but is generally thought of as being in the domain of the general surgeon. On the other hand, diseases of the urinary tract in women are more likely to be dealt with by a gynaecologist than by a general surgeon.

It is also extremely difficult to separate upsets of the female endocrine system from other hormone disorders, and to say that they should be dealt with by a gynaecologist rather than an endocrinologist. And it is clear that the responsibilities of the gynaecologist are not simply passed on to an obstetrician as soon as the patient becomes pregnant. Another point is that a gynaecologist cannot dissociate himself from male disorders on occasion, as when considering the problems of poor fertility in a marriage. The distinction between the different specialists who are likely to be called in, in any one case, may seem academic, but it is extremely important in practice. It is essential that a woman with an illness should be treated by a doctor who has relevant training and experience in that particular field.

Among the most common problems which a gynaecologist is called upon to deal with are those which result from disorders of menstruation. This is surrounded by more misunderstanding, myth, folklore, and old wives' tales than possibly any other field in medicine, and it is important to note that misunderstanding itself can generate menstrual problems.

The *menarche*, or the start of menstruation, usually occurs when girls are between 10 and 16 years old. It is rare outside these limits. The menstrual cycle which is then established is sometimes irregular for the first few years, at its most regular during a woman's twenties, and then more likely to be irregular until the *menopause*, or change of life, which occurs in the late thirties to fifties. The period, or interval during which there is a loss of blood from the vagina, has a normal range of duration from about two to seven days, and the total loss of blood during this time is usually from 20 to 60 millilitres. On the average the length of the cycle is about 28 days, but it varies in different women from three to six weeks. In most circumstances, variations do not constitute a serious problem, but sometimes treatment may be appropriate.

The start of menstruation is only one facet of broader changes which occur in girls during puberty, but, of course, it has an especially dramatic effect upon a girl's outlook. If menstruation starts much earlier than the age of 10, or indeed if any of the other changes of puberty appear before this age, then medical advice should be sought. In particular, if bleeding from the vagina occurs without there being any of the signs of puberty, a doctor's examination is advisable. Usually this sort of disorder is dealt with, not by a gynaecologist, but by a specialist in children's disorders—a paediatrician. Very often the cause is found to be an infection which has invaded the vagina. Before puberty, the lining of the vagina is very thin and especially liable to such infection. But when the infection has been controlled by the use of appropriate antibiotics, or perhaps small quantities of female sex hormones, more trouble is unlikely.

When a girl fails to have her first period by the age of 16 or 17, the problem is very often more complex, because there may be disorder of the hormone changes which normally occur in the body at the age of puberty. On the other hand, there may be some underlying structural abnormality of the genital tract.

One simple anatomical abnormality which can delay the appearance of menstrual periods (called *primary amenorrhoea*) is the presence of a membrane across the opening of the vagina, so that blood cannot escape. There is, of course, a natural membrane at the entrance to the vagina, the hymen, which is present at birth. Normally however, this has a small opening. In the condition of *imperforate hymen* however, the membrane is complete.

The hymen may simply be a very thin layer of tissue, which is easily broken, but in a few cases it develops as a complete and tough layer of tissues. A girl with this condition, who does not appear to be menstruating, is in fact doing so, but the blood released from the lining of the womb is being dammed back behind the hymen, and cannot escape. This is likely

to cause discomfort at the time of each menstrual period, and of course the blood gradually builds up and will eventually cause continuous pain. This condition, called *haematocolpos*, can usually be treated very simply when it has been diagnosed. A gynaecologist will cut away the excess tissue at the entrance to the vagina—a straightforward, minor operation.

The cause of failure to menstruate may not be so easy to discover. In some unfortunate instances it is the result of a much more serious abnormality of the structure of the genital tract. The uterus, for instance, may have failed to develop at all, although the ovaries are present. In this case the girl shows all the signs of puberty, which are governed by the hormonal actions of the pituitary gland and the ovaries, but fails to lose blood from the missing uterus. On the other hand, the uterus may be present, but the ovaries themselves missing. In this case there is no menstrual bleeding, and none of the signs of puberty. It is thus fairly easy to distinguish between absence of the ovaries and absence of the uterus.

It is far more difficult, however, to discover *why* the genital tract has failed to develop in the normal way. The gynaecologist has to find out if the uterus is absent because the patient only looks like a female, and in reality has a male genetic structure. This sometimes occurs in the unfortunate cases of intersex conditions. Such a person may possess not ovaries, but male testes, to the secretion of which the body has failed to respond, so that the patient is apparently neither one sex nor the other.

The pituitary gland, which controls most of the other endocrine glands of the body, may itself be at fault. Thus a girl may be born with normal ovaries, uterus, and vagina, but the stimulus from the pituitary gland may be missing or inadequate. This may simply be a condition of 'delayed puberty', if the stimulus is later forthcoming. It is an interesting problem for the gynaecologist to determine whether amenorrhoea at this age marks a delay in puberty, and is a condition which will right itself in due course, or whether there is another underlying cause which no amount of hormone treatment can correct.

If puberty seems to be exceptionally delayed it is simple enough for a doctor to administer hormones which are missing from circulation, and in this way induce a patient to menstruate. But there is no point in doing this if the only result is bleeding from the uterus. For there may well be a more serious underlying abnormality—because fertility depends not just upon bleeding, but upon the release of fertile eggs from the ovaries into the fallopian tubes with each menstrual cycle. Amenorrhoea of this type, therefore, demands a series of investigations into the whole working of the genital tract before the most appropriate course of treatment can be decided on.

After the periods have become established at the menarche, there are other symp-

toms which may pose problems for the gynaecologist. The cycle itself may be abnormal in several ways. The amount of blood lost at each period may be excessive, or the periods may occur at too frequent intervals, or the duration of each period may be too long.

The term *menorrhagia* is given, rather loosely, to any condition in which a woman bleeds excessively during the menstrual cycle. As women vary considerably from one to another in the amount of blood which they lose with each period, it is hard to define what is really 'normal' for any individual. It is, in any case, difficult for a woman to estimate with any accuracy how much blood she is losing.

If a gynaecologist does decide that a woman is losing too much blood (and this can lead to serious anaemia if unchecked), then he is again faced with the problem of deciding at which level the basic fault in the system lies. As with amenorrhoea, the problem may be hormonal, due to inadequacy of control by the pituitary gland, or the ovaries, or there may be something wrong with the uterus itself.

Two types of condition are commonly the cause of menorrhagia. There may be a swelling of the lining of the uterus, in the form of a lump or lumps, which protrude from the wall into the cavity of the uterus. These are usually benign tumours of the sort known as fibroids. The growths interfere with the normal working of the uterus, and so cause excessive bleeding. If the fibroids are small they can be removed by simple surgery. If they are very large, and have caused considerable distortion of the uterus then it may in some cases be necessary to perform a hysterectomy, the removal of the whole uterus. The gynaecologist has to decide the appropriate procedure in each case, always considering the patient's age and whether she has already had children.

Another common cause of menorrhagia, when there is no physical abnormality, is psychological stress. A woman may have an underlying fear of becoming pregnant, there may be overwhelming family problems, or there may be other emotional problems which manifest themselves in this way. No amount of surgery will help in this case, and the gynaecologist will have to refer the patient to someone better able to deal with such emotional difficulties.

A common surgical procedure which is undertaken by gynaecologists for diagnostic reasons or as a form of treatment, is dilatation and curettage, commonly called D and C. This involves gently dilating or stretching the cervix (the neck of the uterus) with special dilators of graded sizes, and scraping the lining, endometrium, of the uterus. Not only is this procedure valuable in diagnosis—examination of the scrapings of the lining under the microscope may reveal several different disease processes—but the procedure sometimes cures certain conditions. And it is not always certain why. This procedure is frequently used in the treatment of menorrhagia.

Menstrual disorders can also be treated, in some cases, by the administration of hormones. Because the level of hormones in the blood stream is responsible for the menstrual cycle, a hormonal abnormality can produce different menstrual disorders, including menorrhagia. With the powerful drugs now available, a gynaecologist can put right many hormonal irregularities, and control the working of the ovaries virtually at will, thus imposing an artificial menstrual cycle. Pills allied to those used as oral contraceptives are often used in this way, to control the length and the frequency of bleeding at the periods.

Another disorder of menstruation is that in which bleeding occurs, not only at the periods, but at some time between them. This is called *intermenstrual bleeding*, which is occasionally accompanied by abdominal pains. This may be due to slight bleeding from the uterus at the time of ovulation, in which case it is of no significance. However, unless it is proven that this is the case, this symptom should be regarded seriously, and probably due to a disorder between the lower end of the vagina and the upper part of the uterus.

This should always be thoroughly investigated by a gynaecologist, to make sure that there is no malignant growth at any level in the genital tract. In particular, of course, a specialist will be on the lookout for cancer of the cervix. Any woman who notices bleeding from the vagina at any time when it is not to be expected should consult her doctor. Bleeding is sometimes noticed immediately after sexual intercourse. This again, called *postcoital bleeding*, is significant, and usually means that there is a lesion, which could be malignant, between the cervix and the opening of the vagina.

Discomfort, and sometimes mental depression, are noted by many women before or during the onset of the menstrual period. This is termed *dysmenorrhoea*. There are two different forms which are generally recognized. *Primary dysmenorrhoea* is the term used to describe menstruation which is painful from the menarche, or in the first year or two. This is due in some way to ovulation, and if ovulation is suppressed —using sex hormones similar to those used in the contraceptive pill—the pain can be controlled. However, the sex hormones are extremely powerful, and if a doctor can alleviate his patient's discomfort with less powerful, pain-killing drugs he will always do this.

The other form of dysmenorrhoea, *secondary dysmenorrhoea*, is that which develops, not at the onset of the regular monthly periods, but in later years. This may be due to psychological factors or it may be caused by disease of the pelvic organs. Again, it is the responsibility of the gynaecologist to discover the underlying cause and to treat it accordingly.

Sometimes the menstrual periods cease long before they would be expected to do so at the change of life. This is called *secondary amenorrhoea*, and requires careful examination to find the underlying cause. Rarely, a woman ceases to have

Venus/Capitolini Museum, Rome/Scala

periods in the late twenties or early thirties because the ovaries have no more ova to release during ovulation. This is a condition for which there is no remedy, and it means that a patient has become irreversibly infertile.

More commonly, secondary amenorrhoea is due to stress—it was noted in women in prison camps, but may also be seen in women who undergo such mental stresses as going to university, or taking a new job. The treatment lies more in the province of the psychiatrist than anyone else, and the condition is not serious.

As a cause of death in women, cancer of the cervix of the uterus is second only to cancer of the breast. Cancer can affect any part of the female genital tract, but malignant growths of the vulva and the vagina are rare. Cancer of the cervix is more common, and is important because it can be so readily detected by routine examinations, and even discovered before it has actually established a hold on the

tissues. This is one type of cancer where early warning is possible, and can be prevented in very many cases from progressing to an incurable stage. The examination is very simple, consisting of the removal of a very few cells, scraped painlessly from the cervix during an examination. These are then examined under a microscope for abnormality. The outlook in each case depends upon the stage at which the malignant change is detected— without exception, the earlier the better. Treatment is usually by radiotherapy, but sometimes surgery is used.

Cancer of the uterus itself may produce irregularities in the pattern of menstrual bleeding. Quite commonly it occurs in patients of menopausal age, and may be missed in the early stages because the patient attributes menstrual irregularity to the change of life. To make sure that nothing is amiss, most doctors, therefore, encourage all women of menopausal age to report any irregularity of their periods. These tumours are inclined to grow more slowly than cervical tumours, and the outlook is therefore better than in the latter. Because many tumours are resistant to radiotherapy they are generally treated by surgery.

Among the disorders which concern the gynaecologist are many which affect not the genital tract, but the closely associated urinary tract. A number of these are due to chronic infection of the urinary system—kidneys, ureters, bladder, and urethra. The symptoms which a gynaecologist comes across most frequently are those concerned with lack of control of the act of urination. This is termed *urinary incontinence*. In *urge incontinence* a patient who has the urge to pass urine is unable to control it, and must pass urine immediately. It may be due simply to faulty bladder habits. Again, it is often due to excess irritability of the bladder, which may be caused by *cystitis*, an infection of the bladder by bacteria.

Cystitis is an extremely common complaint among women, which sometimes causes great distress. The symptoms include a painful and frequent desire to urinate, which in some cases can seriously interfere with social activities. A number of different bacteria may be responsible and most respond to treatment with antibiotics. In a few cases, however, the disease can persist despite all efforts and become a severe problem.

These disorders are but a few of those which affect the female sex, and which come into the care of the gynaecologist. To deal adequately with all of them, as medical knowledge rapidly increases, and the range of drugs and other modes of treatment expands so rapidly, would really need a 'super-gynaecologist'. As it is, there is a tendency for these 'specialists in women's disorders' to have their own particular specialities within the field. The years to come may well see a radical change in the whole system, if each disorder is to receive the most appropriate treatment at the earliest possible opportunity.

DAVID M. H. WILLIAMS

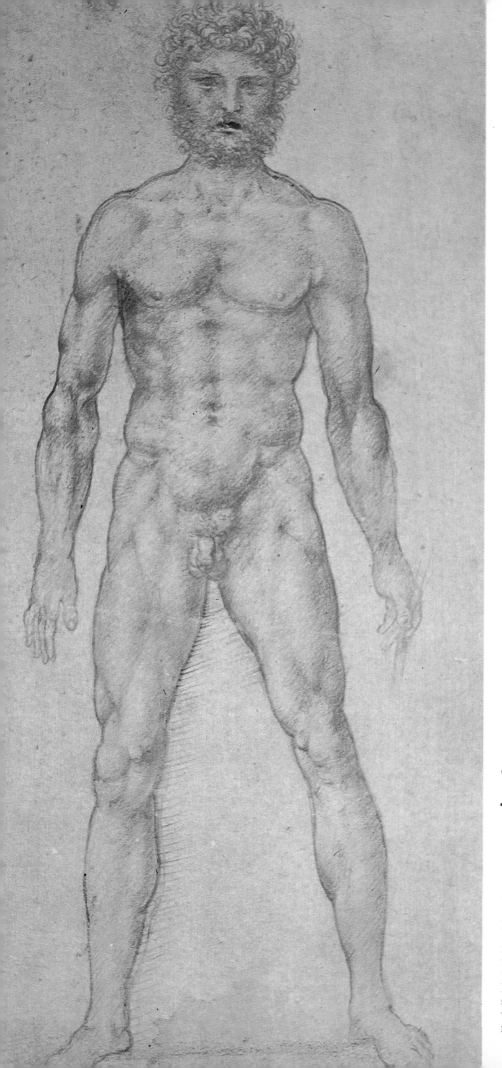

Male orgasm — what is it?

The psychological excitation of orgasm is the climax of the physiological processes that occur during sexual intercourse. Here a doctor describes what happens in a man's body during orgasm.

For a man, as for a woman, orgasm, the climax of sexual intercourse, is a total bodily process involving more than just the sexual organs. While differences exist, there are many similarities in the climaxes of both men and women. Orgasm is essentially the same for both sexes because the human body is similar, apart from sexual differences. Yet these anatomic differences and psychological details have separated the sexes since prehistoric times.

Because tradition has assigned different roles to men and women—the hunter and the hunted—the male orgasm is less bound up in myth and mystery than the female. Perhaps this is because a man's external sexual organs are more visible than a woman's and their dual functions take place more openly. Sexual and excretory functions are combined in one organ, the penis, whereas the vagina and urethra in a woman are distinctly separate. As a result, custom has not demanded of the male the false modesty and passive demeanor imposed on the female.

But greater visibility may contribute to the misunderstandings and apprehensions that most men feel in their sexual life. The myth that sexuality depends on penis size and virility, often imposes superhuman demands upon the male which can result in increased vulnerability if he is not knowledgeable about sex and worries unnecessarily.

Tradition has left the male with a heavy burden. At the risk of having his virility challenged, he must be aggressive, boastful, and the initiator of 'sexual conquest'. Even the terminology of sexual relationships is dominated by the masculine point of view. Intercourse is consummated by 'penetration', never by 'envelopment', a man 'conquers' a woman if he is a 'real man'— if he is not, then he is 'subdued' by her.

Like most responsibilities, the traditional male sexual role of aggressor and dominator has drawbacks. The man whose psychological frame of mind leads him to prefer other roles may find himself a sexual outcast, shunned by men and women whose limited understanding rejects all but traditionally played parts. He may be called a 'sissy' or an 'old woman', although his virility, desire, and potency are as strongly heterosexual as any other man's.

Potency and impotence loom large in the mythology of male orgasm. Before a man can have an orgasm, or even have sexual intercourse, he must get an *erection*, whereas a woman is always capable of having sexual intercourse. Erection is the state of sexual excitement during which the spongy tissue of the penis fills up with blood, causing it to become hard. Erection is part of the generalized sexual vasocongestion, in which vessels distend as they fill with blood, of sexual excitement and climax. To be potent, a man must be able to keep the penis erect until orgasm occurs, yet he has no conscious control over the erection of the penis.

If a man cannot get or maintain an erection, then he has a condition called *primary impotence*. If his climax comes very quickly, within 30 seconds of placing his penis inside the vagina, then he suffers from *premature ejaculation*, a form of secondary impotence.

Impotence can be considered analogous to frigidity in the female. Though they are different physiological phenomena and no woman can be impotent, these conditions often have similar psychological roots. For example, impotence may be caused by a fear of sexual relationships resulting from a childhood experience, or from an unresolved sexual conflict such as the *Oedipus complex* of a man who has never outgrown the sexual love he had for his mother when he was a child. The result of frigidity or impotence is the same: the inability to experience an orgasm with a partner which

is the ultimate pleasure of sexual love.

Orgasm in males is both a specific and a general phenomenon. It includes many of the same physiological reactions that occur during the female orgasm, for the male climax divides naturally into the same psychological, sociological, and physiological components. The differences are specific— as the male and female have obvious anatomic dissimilarities, orgasm affects different organs and its outward manifestations also vary slightly according to sex.

As an example, just at the point of orgasm, the male is unlikely to experience *carpopedal spasm*, the involuntary contraction of the muscles in the feet making the toes curl, which occurs commonly during the female orgasm. He is, however, more likely to experience this if he is lying on his back underneath the female.

Secondly, before climax, during the plateau excitement phase that precedes it, the penis secretes an emission which is not ejaculation. This small emission of mucous droplets may contain moving viable sperm cells capable of fertilizing an ovum. The mucus is squeezed out involuntarily from the *urethral meatus*, the opening at the tip of the penis. Thus, it is possible for the male to impregnate the female without having a complete ejaculatory climax.

At one time, doctors thought that this fluid might be important for lubricating the *glans*, the knob of flesh at the end of the penis. This was because the fluid is produced by the Cowper's glands located in the pelvis near the prostate gland. The Cowper's glands are the male equivalents of the Bartholin's glands located on the minor labia, the inner lips of the female's sexual organs, and they believed the Batholin's glands helped to lubricate the vaginal opening. However, physicians now think the amount of fluid produced to be too small to have this lubricatory effect.

Physicians now understand that the pre-ejaculatory emission appears most often when, during the mounting sexual excitement, the male voluntarily controls his urge to have a climax. Because a woman needs more time to achieve orgasm than a man, the male must repress his urge to have a climax a number of times during sexual intercourse, while the woman constantly moves towards orgasm.

When masturbation or fellatio (oral sex) are the means of gratification for the man, then the pre-ejaculatory fluid is not likely to appear for he is less inclined to delay orgasm. The purpose of this emission is unknown. While some scientists feel that it helps ensure conception, the union of sperm and egg, many more feel that this emission needs further investigation.

As orgasm becomes imminent during sexual intercourse, its inward and outward manifestations appear. The rate of breathing increases to become panting, or *hyperventilation*. Rates between 40 and 50 breaths per minute are not uncommon, as compared with the normal range of about 12 to 16 breaths per minute.

The rate at which the heart pumps blood

also increases, a condition known as *tachycardia*. The heart rate increases in direct proportion to the level of sexual tension, so that the heart is contracting most rapidly just at the point of orgasm. While the normal level is 72 per minute, a pulse between 110 and 180 is very common, and may even be faster if sexual tension is sufficiently high. Measurements of the blood pressure show that it, too, increases at orgasm, a condition known as *hypertension*: the pressures at which the valves in the heart open and shut are elevated.

The possible effects of increased heart rates and blood pressure are more important in men than women, because the male is more prone to heart attacks. Doctors are unsure whether the increases in pulse and blood pressure are harmful or beneficial to the man who has already suffered a heart attack, or whether they increase the chances of a man having a 'coronary'. But they do agree that the lower a man's presexual heart rate, the less it will rise during sexual excitement. This fact reinforces current medical opinion that maintaining good physical condition during life is important for preventing heart attacks, for the healthier a man is, the lower his heart rate.

The outward manifestations of the imminence of orgasm can be seen, if the man is on top of his partner, as the rate of his thrusting in and out of the vagina increases, and he begins to penetrate even more deeply. He clutches at his partner and, just before the moment of orgasm, he thrusts forward as hard and deep as he can. Subjectively he feels that he can no longer voluntarily control whether or not he will have a climax.

This point in the sexual cycle is the period of *ejaculatory inevitability*, and occurs two to four seconds before the actual ejaculation. During the time of ejaculatory inevitability, all the secondary sexual organs are involved in expelling seminal fluid into the prostatic urethra. This is the first stage of the male orgasm. During this time all the muscles in the male pelvis contract involuntarily, similar to the spasm which occurs in the female during climax.

The *spermatozoa*—sperm cells—are moved through the *vasa efferentia*, or emptying ducts, from where they are stored in the testes, up into the abdomen through the *epidydimis* and then into the *vas deferens*, another conducting tube. From there, the sperm move into the *ampulla*, where they are momentarily stopped, prior to ejaculation. Scientists believe that the involuntary contractions of these tubes that begin simultaneously with orgasm propel the sperm through the ejaculatory duct and into the urethra.

Simultaneously, *seminal fluid*, which carries the sperm into the vagina, is being produced by the prostate gland which surrounds the male urethra. During the period of ejaculatory inevitability, the prostate contracts regularly, and rhythmically squeezes out the mucus which forms the basis of seminal fluid. The *seminal vesicle*, another secondary sexual organ in the male, also empties its contents into the prostatic urethra, contributing to the formation of the seminal fluid at this time.

As the seminal vesicle discharges, the spermatozoa stored in the ampulla are also forcibly ejected into the prostatic urethra. Now the seminal fluid mixes with the sperm cells. At the same time, the *urethral bulb* at the base of the penis behind the scrotum involuntarily increases in size and volume in preparation for the forcible ejection of fluid during the second, or ejaculation, stage of orgasm.

A split second before ejaculation, the internal sphincter muscle of the urinary bladder involuntarily contracts. This reflex serves two purposes during orgasm. It prevents seminal fluid and sperm cells from being forced into the bladder and tightly seals the passage along which the ejected fluid flows, ensuring that the liquid under great pressure travels in only one direction. In addition, no urine can escape from the bladder when the more powerful muscular spasms of the second stage begin.

Stage two of the male climax begins at the moment during the ejaculatory process when the external sphincter muscle of the urinary bladder relaxes, directly in opposition to all the other muscles in the pelvis. The nervous mechanism controlling this action is not understood, but it permits the seminal fluid to move from the prostate urethra into the channel within the urethral bulb.

When sufficient fluid is in the bulb, it contracts. This forces the seminal fluid out in the same way that squeezing the rubber bulb at the head of a medicine dropper will force the fluid through the glass tube. As the urethral bulb contracts rhythmically, the *bulbospongeosus* and *ischiocavernosus*, two large muscles in the floor of the pelvis, undergo involuntary spasm. They add their power to the action of the urethral bulb, and make the ejection of fluid down the urethra even more powerful. The force developed by the muscles is sufficient to hurl the fluid and sperm 12 to 24 inches if there is nothing to stop it.

These rhythmic contractions of the male secondary sex organs occur at intervals of 0.8 seconds, about three or four times.

Thus, sufficient fluid and sperm are expelled to ensure conception; and it is ejaculated a sufficient distance to aid the spermatozoa on their long journey to meet the ovum in the female's *Fallopian tube*, the passageway between ovary and uterus.

After three or four hard contractions the expulsion process ebbs. Less fluid is driven out as it is used up, and the contractile movements of the muscles diminish. This point marks the beginning of the *resolution phase* of male orgasm. The sensations felt by a man during resolution are different from the powerful stimulus of climax. Anaesthesia has developed along the urethra, so that the male can, no longer estimate the amount of seminal fluid he expels.

The longer the time span between orgasm for the man, the more seminal fluid is expelled in ejaculation. The greatest portion of seminal fluid is forced out during the first three or four strong contractions, and seems related to the amount of sexual pleasure the male experiences. Women who have experienced multi-orgasms state that the later orgasms are the most pleasurable. Almost invariably, men report directly opposite preference in the sensations. They choose those first contractions after a long period of abstinence as the most enjoyable. After three or four orgasms, most males reported a decrease in sexual pleasure. Only a few say they preferred the 'exquisite sensation' of pain and pleasure mixed.

Multi-orgasm is impossible for the male. The ejaculatory phase of orgasm is followed by the *refractory period* which coincides with resolution, and lasts from twenty minutes to several hours, depending on the man's age, the length of time since his previous orgasm, and the degree of sexual excitement he experiences. He is unable to achieve or maintain an erection during the refractory period.

Previously exciting sexual movements such as rubbing against the glans of the penis, are now felt by the man as acutely uncomfortable sensations. Further sexual motion will be difficult for him, and his partner may suffer if she is in the middle of her own orgasm or just about to achieve climax.

Men usually prefer to lie quietly after orgasm, either resting the penis inside the vagina, or withdrawing it immediately after ejaculation. The location of the penis determines the length of time over which the two stages of *penile detumescence*, or loss of erection, occur.

The first stage is early in the refractory period of the resolution phase, and the penis decreases in size from full erection to a state 40 per cent larger than the normal flaccid organ.

Although the first stage often passes within a matter of seconds, it can be prolonged if the man has delayed ejaculation a number of times by voluntary control. If the penis remains in the vagina longer than five minutes after ejaculation, it will remain erect for some time. The second stage, when the penis returns to normal size, can then be delayed indefinitely. If sexual excitement is kept high enough at this point, some men can begin thrusting movements again, and although initial sensation is low, they can move to a second orgasm. Unfortunately, science is unable to explain why this is possible sometimes, and not at other times.

If the male withdraws his penis from the vagina immediately after ejaculation, or if he stops masturbatory movements after climax, the first and second stages of detumescence will pass very quickly. Any action or movement involving the conscious mind with other than sexual thoughts, such as urinating, getting up and moving around, or even lighting a cigarette, will increase the rapidity with which the penis returns to normal size.

While the male experiences orgasm with nearly every sexual experience, he still has in common with the female a great deal of freedom to discover. For the man, sexual liberation lies in moving away from outmoded and traditional, almost reflex, sexual rigidities. By escaping from the traditional roles, he can free himself and enjoy the gratification of an unrepressed sexuality.

STEPHEN LEVIT

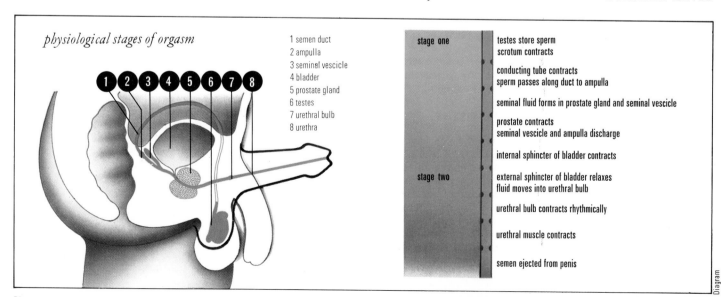

physiological stages of orgasm

1 semen duct
2 ampulla
3 seminal vescicle
4 bladder
5 prostate gland
6 testes
7 urethral bulb
8 urethra

stage one

testes store sperm
scrotum contracts

conducting tube contracts
sperm passes along duct to ampulla

seminal fluid forms in prostate gland and seminal vescicle

prostate contracts
seminal vescicle and ampulla discharge

internal sphincter of bladder contracts

stage two

external sphincter of bladder relaxes
fluid moves into urethral bulb

urethral bulb contracts rhythmically

urethral muscle contracts

semen ejected from penis

Male Sex Organs

The sheer visibility of the male genitals conceals both complexity and efficiency. This article makes clear the complicated functioning of the male reproductive system.

Michelangelo: David/Bargello, Florence/Scala

When our distant ancestors first crawled out of the sea, over 300 million years ago, they faced formidable problems. The most vital to the survival of their kind concerned reproduction. This was because their predecessors had depended on the water for success in mating and producing young —just as aquatic creatures do today. Female fish, for example, lay their eggs in the water while the male, swimming behind, deposits his sperm over them. With luck, an egg will be fertilized by a sperm, and—provided that it is not eaten by some other inhabitant of the deep—will eventually form a young fish. It is a chancy business, but such a vast number of eggs and sperm are produced that there are plenty of young.

The first land animals were amphibians —creatures not unlike present-day frogs, toads, and newts. But they only half-conquered the land, because they returned to the water to lay and fertilize their eggs in the same way as fish. It was only with the reptiles, birds, and mammals (the latter including Man) that the higher animals developed methods of reproduction completely independent of water. Reptiles, birds, and the most primitive mammals laid eggs with hard shells to prevent them drying out. Higher mammals kept the egg within the mother's body until it was well-developed. This last method is, of course, how human beings reproduce.

Most of the changes connected with this development are evident in a woman's sexual anatomy and physiology. She, after all, has to harbour the developing child and eventually give birth to it. The man's role is, in contrast, extremely simple. He has merely to produce sperm and deposit it within the woman's reproductive system so that it can fertilize her egg.

It is for this task that evolution has designed the male sex organs—and it is an extremely efficient piece of functional design, even though complicated by the necessity for some sections to double as a urine-transport system. The part that actually produces sperm consists of the two *testes*, or *testicles*. These also make the male sex hormones which cause the various bodily changes of puberty. The part that transports the sperm into the woman's vagina is the *penis*—and this, of course, is also used to get rid of urine. There is a system of ducts to carry sperm from the testes to the penis, and these include storage spaces. This is because the testes produce sperm continuously, not simply at the moment of orgasm when they are expelled through the penis. Finally, the male sex organs include a number of glands which produce the fluid in which the sperms live and swim.

Most important of all these parts are the testes. They lie outside the main body cavity, in a wrinkled bag of skin called the *scrotum*. The testes first develop within the body cavity, and normally descend into the scrotum at around the time of birth. If this does not take place—a condition known as *cryptorchidism*—and is not corrected by surgery early in life, the man will be completely sterile.

Inside, the scrotum is divided in two —one half containing each testis. A small ridge on the outside marks the division. In most men the left testicle hangs a little lower than the right, but both are moved up and down by a system of small muscles. These are the *dartos* muscles (attached to the inside of the scrotum) and the *cremaster* muscles (attached to the testes themselves). In the cold, these muscles draw the testes close up to the body; in warmth, they relax and the testes hang lower.

This complex arrangement is necessary because the testes can produce sperm efficiently only at about 35°C (95°F)— rather below the normal body temperature. If their temperature is too high, not enough sperm will be produced, and the man may be unable to become a father. It is said that tight trousers, jockey-style pants, or even much time spent riding a bicycle can interfere with sperm production. The built-in cooling system of a kilt is, on the other hand, claimed to promote fertility.

Each testis is divided into about 250 small compartments, and these contain tiny, tightly-coiled tubes known as *seminiferous tubules*. There are more than 800 of these, and each is more than two feet long. This is where the sperm develop, being produced in hundreds of millions every day. The tubules join together and open into a slightly wider tube which winds over the surface of each testis. This is the *epididymis*, which is also tightly coiled, and is nearly 20 feet long. The name *epididymis* is derived from Greek, and means *on top of the twin;* the testes are, of course, the twins.

The production of new sperm in the seminiferous tubules pushes those already formed into the epididymis of each testis. They stay here for some time, maturing for perhaps a fortnight before being ejaculated or, otherwise, dying. The epididymis leads directly into another tube, called the *vas deferens*, which is about 18 inches long and surrounded by thick muscular walls. Together with blood vessels and nerves, the vas forms the *spermatic cord*. The spermatic cord from each testis takes a roundabout route to reach the base of the penis, resulting from the descent of the testes from the body cavity. It runs over the front and top of the pubic bone, loops over the ureter (which carries urine from the kidneys to the bladder), turns, and finally runs down behind the bladder.

The last parts of the two vasa deferentia are wider than the rest, forming sperm storage areas called the *ampullae*. After joining the ducts from the two small glands called *seminal vesicles*, the vasa deferentia enter the round *prostate gland*. Within this, the two ducts join and enter the *urethra*. This is the tube extending from the bladder along the penis. Yet more glands empty into the urethra below the prostate. These are known as *Cowper's* and *Littré's* glands.

These various 'accessory' glands provide lubrication for the tip of the penis during intercourse and also provide the fluid in which the sperm lives. This fluid supplies food and oxygen for the sperm, without which they cannot swim. In fact, it is not until they are ejaculated that sperm start the tail-thrashing movements that propel them along. Sperm and the various glandular secretions together make up the *semen*. The chemical composition of the glandular secretions is so characteristic that chemical tests revealing their presence on clothing can be used in court to support an allegation of rape.

Among the chemicals produced by the prostate gland are a number of substances known as *prostaglandins*. These stimulate contractions of the muscles of the woman's womb and may play a part in helping the sperm to travel up the female reproductive tract. Research has also shown that purified prostaglandins can be used to induce an abortion by generating muscular contractions of the womb.

The penis, as already mentioned, carries the urethra to the outside world. When used for urination, it is most convenient if the penis points downwards and is soft, or flaccid. But a flaccid penis is not very suitable for placing sperm deep inside a woman's vagina. So when a man is sexually excited he has an erection. His penis grows larger, stiffens, and points upwards—and becomes much easier to insert within his partner.

The ability of the penis to become erect is due to its structure. It contains three columns of porous tissue. At the top and sides are the two *corpora cavernosa*, which are attached to the pelvic bones at the base. Underneath lies the smaller *corpus spongiosum*, which also forms the acorn-shaped *glans* at the head of the penis. Blood vessels open into all three columns of tissue, and when a man is sexually excited, blood pours rapidly into them. But the vessels leading away are almost completely shut off, with the result that the spongy tissue becomes engorged with blood. It expands, rather like a balloon being blown up, and causes the penis to become erect.

Basically, erection is an automatic action caused by nervous signals from the spinal cord. But many things can set off these signals, including stimulation of the touch receptors on the penis itself. Conscious thoughts are extremely important, and a sight or smell can induce an erection without any physical contact being involved. On the other hand, messages from the brain may inhibit an erection, too.

One of the results of erection of the penis is to uncover the glans. In men who have not been circumcised, a fold of skin—the *prepuce* or *foreskin*—covers this when the penis is flaccid. The skin of the glans—particularly where it joins the shaft of the penis—has many sensitive nerve receptors. Signals from these, caused by friction between the penis and the inside of the vagina, eventually bring a man to his orgasm.

Before this stage is reached, a small quantity of fluid is produced by the Cowper's and Littré's glands. This not only moistens the glans and improves the sensations from it, but also prepares the urethra for the passage of sperm, neutralizing any chemicals in it that might harm the sperm. Finally, involuntary nerve signals cause the muscles around the vasa deferentia, the prostate gland, and the seminal vesicles to contract, propelling sperm and the glandular secretions into the urethra. A series of contractions from the muscles around the spongy tissues of the penis drive the semen along the urethra and out. At the same time, muscles contract to shut off the duct to the bladder, preventing the sperm going the wrong way or urine being ejaculated.

Circumcision—removal of the foreskin—is one of the oldest ritual mutilations in the world. It is carried out in numerous cultures, both primitive and advanced. In some, it is regarded as a religious duty; in others, it is a mark of manhood. But it has hygiene advantages, too, for in uncircumcised men a secretion called *smegma* may collect under the foreskin if washing is not regular. If this becomes infected, the painful conditions of phimosis or balanitis will result. There is also some evidence to suggest that circumcised men almost never get cancer of the penis; nor do their wives seem to develop cancer of the cervix (the neck of the womb). As a result of these supposed benefits, circumcision has become a routine for boy babies in many areas.

The widely-held belief that circumcised men are better able to satisfy their sexual partners seems much more doubtful. The idea is that constant rubbing of the exposed glans on clothing in every-day life dulls its sensitivity. The result is said to be that the man takes longer to reach his orgasm, and is more likely to bring the woman to hers. American researchers Masters and Johnson refuted this claim, however. They found no difference between circumcised and uncircumcised men in their speed in reaching a climax.

Another increasingly common operation—performed on adult men—is that of *vasotomy*, in which the vasa deferentia are cut and the two ends tied off. The result is that sperm cannot reach the penis from the testes, and the man is thus sterilized. There should be no effect on his sex life, unless it is psychological, for the production of male sex hormones and the man's ability to have and enjoy sexual intercourse are unaffected. In fact, he will notice virtually no difference, for the secretions of the various accessory glands will still be ejaculated at orgasm. Only the sperm will be missing—which makes vasotomy one of the most effective methods of contraception.

So far, this article has dealt with the male sex organs as they are in an adult. How do they develop at puberty, and how does a child come to have male rather than female characteristics? The basic difference between men and women is found in the tiny nucleus of each of the millions of the cells making up their bodies. These contain the *chromosomes*, the person's hereditary material—the set of 'instructions' he inherits from his parents that give him his own set of personal characteristics.

Among them are a pair of sex chromosomes. All women have a matching pair of so-called X chromosomes. A man has one X and one different chromosome—a Y. This Y chromosome first has an effect on the foetus about seven weeks after conception. Until then, the sex of the foetus can be discovered only by examining the chromosomes under a microscope. The anatomy of male and female children is at that stage identical. Between the legs is a slit with a small knob of tissue at the front end. Within the body, the sex glands are primitively formed, and they are identical in a boy and girl.

Then in the seventh week, a male child's sex glands start to grow rapidly—somehow stimulated by the Y chromosome. Then—most important of all—these embryonic testes start producing *androgens*, the male sex hormones. It is these that

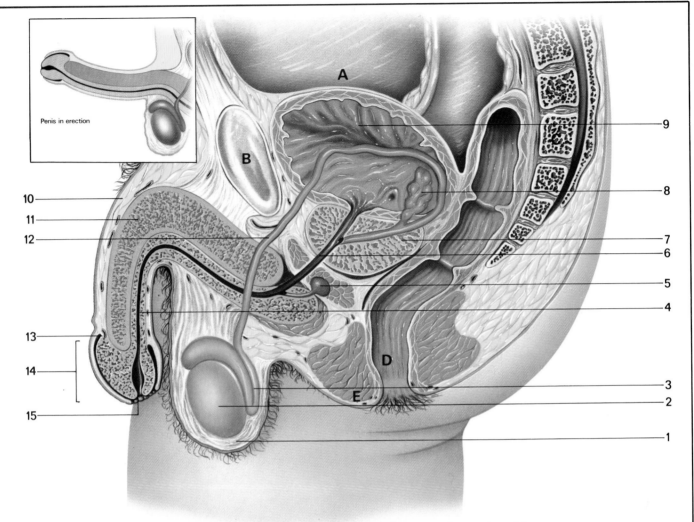

External and internal male genitals: section through pelvis, seen from the side.

A.Peritoneal cavity   **B.**Pubis   **C.**Vertebral columm (coccyx)   **D.**Rectum and anus   **E.**Perineum

1. Scrotum   **2.** Testis   **3.** Epididymis (a. head, b. body, c. tail)   **4.** Corpus spongiosum (unpaired)
5. Cowper's gland   **6.** Urethra   **7.** Prostate   **8.** Seminal vesicle   **9.** Urinary bladder   **10.** Penis
11. Corpora cavernosa (paired)   **12.** Vas deferens   **13.** Coronary sulcus   **14.** Glans   **15.** Urethral orifice

Penis in erection

cause the external male sex organs to develop. The two sides of the slit join to become the scrotum, and the knob develops into the penis. Later, the testes will descend.

This process needs the male sex hormones to push it in the male direction. If for some reason, the developing testes fail to produce androgens—or if, as in the case of a female child, they do not develop at all—then the external sex anatomy will take the female form, with the knob becoming the clitoris and the slit the vulva. The sex glands will remain in the body as the ovaries.

The male sex hormones play just as vital a part in the second major sexual development, puberty. Stimulated by hormones secreted into the bloodstream by the pituitary gland (which is at the base of the brain), the *interstitial cells* of the testes, which lie between the seminiferous tubules, start producing large amounts of androgens when a boy reaches the age of about 12. The result is the breaking of the voice, growth of facial and body hair, enlargement of the penis and the testes themselves, the start of sperm production, and general body and muscular growth—all the male secondary sexual characteristics.

Throughout history, the possession of testes has been associated with masculine characteristics. The word *testis* is Latin for *witness*, and it is said that only those having testes could give evidence; eunuchs, who were castrated before puberty, could not. (The word *testify* comes from the same root.) But it is not merely the possession of testes that confers masculinity; it is the sex hormones produced by these organs. Eunuchs failed to develop at puberty because they had none of these hormones; a boy accidentally castrated today can be given injections of androgens to make his puberty occur artificially.

But without such treatment the eunuch retained a high-pitched voice and small penis. His body hair was similar to a woman's. However, some did experience sexual desire, and could probably have an erection—if the penis remained. So the ladies of the harem guarded by eunuchs may not have been as safe as their masters supposed.

Castration after puberty is not as drastic in its effects. It does not cause loss of the sexual characteristics already acquired, and the problems are more psychological than physical. The sex life need not suffer, and androgen injections can counteract effects caused by a lack of male hormones. However, hormones cannot enable a eunuch to have children.

Although the testes are just one of the male sex organs, they produce the sperm without which the woman's egg cannot be fertilized. However, the ducts that carry sperm from the testes to the penis, the penis which transports the sperm in to the vagina, and the glands that produce the fluid essential for the sperms' movement there—all these are male sex organs. Each is indispensable to the process of reproduction.

The testes

They comprise less than one thousandth part of the body's weight, yet their effect is out of all proportion. For, in both his mind and in reality, a man's potency is rooted in his testes.

The testes or testicles, the pair of seemingly insignificant organs which hang below the penis, produce not only the sperm which may unite with human eggs to create new life, but also produce the hormones responsible for the development and functioning of a man's penis, for his deep voice, his muscle power, his beard, and his characteristic personality.

The testes are loosely covered by the scrotum or scrotal sacs. The scrotum, which is partitioned into two, is strengthened with muscle fibres and other sinewy, fibrous cells. Within it the testes themselves can be felt as a pair of firm, compact masses. Each testis is about an inch wide and two inches long and surrounded by a discrete covering called the *tunica vaginalis*. This is a double layer of membrane similar to the one enveloping all the internal organs. Inside the tunica vaginalis lies the testes' main protective coat, the *tunica albuginea*, a dense tissue layer impregnated with tough fibres.

Linking the testes with the abdomen is a thick cordlike structure called the *spermatic cord*. In it is a tube, the *vas deferens*, which eventually leads to the penis, blood vessels, nerves, and muscles.

The vital sperm-making role of the testes is carried out, behind the tunica albuginea, by hundreds of tubules tightly coiled together, called the *seminiferous tubules*. They number nearly 1,000 in each testis and each is over two feet long, making a total length of about a quarter of a mile. Unlike those of the lower animals like fish and amphibia, a man's testes can make sperm continuously, which means that the human male is constantly prepared to fertilize the ovum.

The development of spermatozoa, a process called *spermatogenesis*, starts in the *germinal epithelium*, the tissue lining the wall of every tubule. There, the potential spermatozoa are round cells called *spermatogonia* with large central nuclei which house the genetic material.

When a boy reaches puberty, the spermatogonia in his seminiferous tubules begin to divide many times and in doing so give rise to large numbers of cells called *primary spermatocytes*. Like all other cells in his body, the nuclei of a man's primary spermatocytes contain 46 chromosomes. That is, they contain 23 *pairs* of strands, made up of the genetic material DNA.

At the time of his own conception, one member of each chromosome pair came from his mother and one from his father. Before a man can himself father a child, the 23 pairs must separate, giving each spermatozoon just 23 chromosomes, each derived from the material of one pair, so that when these combine with 23 chromosomes from an egg at the moment of fertilization the correct number of 46 will be restored.

The *reduction division*, cutting the chromosome number from 46 to 23, is called *meiosis* and takes place in the next

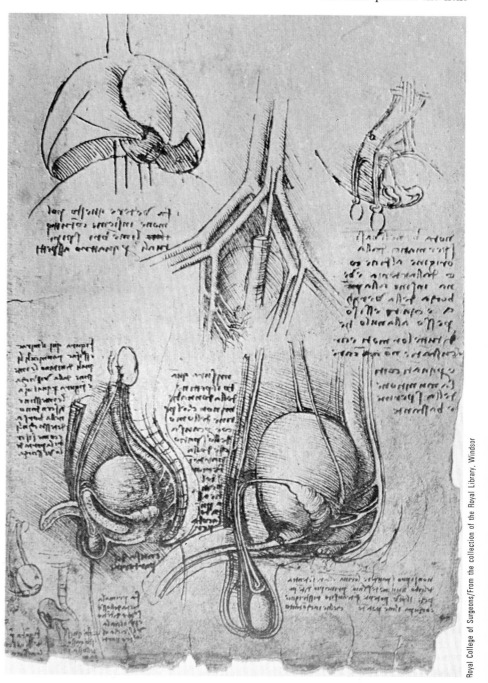

Leonardo da Vinci's annotations—in mirror writing—on his sketches of the sexual organs reveal that, at the end of the fifteenth century, he understood that the testes played a part in the formation of seminal fluid. He did not know that they produced minute organisms, sperm.

step in sperm production. Each primary spermatocyte splits into two *secondary spermatocytes*, halving its chromosome number as it does so. One secondary spermatocyte will contain the X sex chromosome, the other the Y sex chromosome, thus giving subsequently two types of sperm. Then comes another division, duplicating each chromosome as it takes place, so that each primary spermatocyte is the originator of four new cells, each given the name of *spermatid* and each assured, through the mechanism of meiosis, a unique genetic composition.

Newly-formed spermatids are not capable of bringing about fertilization. Each must go through a maturation process throughout which it is nourished by large, elongated *Sertoli* or *nurse cells* which lie attached to the inner wall of the seminiferous tubules.

Gradually, the squat spermatid grows longer. Its diffuse nucleus becomes smaller, denser, and moves to one end of the cell. With this formation of the sperm head, the bulk of the cell substance, the *cytoplasm*, is cast off into the testis where it is destroyed and the final whole takes a tadpole shape.

The nearly-mature spermatozoon lies with its head attached to a nurse cell, its tail hanging down into the centre of the seminiferous tubule. The head is a flattened oval four thousandths of a millimetre long and two thousandths of a millimetre wide. Within the head, occupying over 90 per cent of its volume, is the nucleus. At the very tip is the *acrosome*, a small part of the cell which, through its biochemical action, helps the sperm penetrate the egg.

Behind the head of the sperm is the *middlepiece* which contains the *mitochondria*, small bodies which break down carbohydrates and provide the energy for movement. The whiplash sperm tail itself, at an average length of forty thousandths of a millimetre, is some 10 times longer than the head. Composed of eleven separate fibrils, two centrally placed and surrounded by the other nine, the tail of the sperm gives it its exceptional swimming power.

Some 45 days from the time when it was a spermatocyte, the sperm is mature. By this stage it has floated off the nurse cell, down the seminiferous tubule, and into a single, much larger, tube the *epididymis*. Connecting the two are tubes known as the *vasa efferentia*. Within these are millions of minute hairs called *cilia* which move to and fro in waves and, as they do so, push the not-yet-mobile sperm along. It is in the epididymis that the sperm attain their motility. And it is along the 15 to 20 feet of coiled and counter-coiled epididymis that sperm are stored until needed in a reproductive role.

Sperm production is a steady process and it is unrelated to the frequency of ejaculation. If ejaculation does not take place, through abstinence or inability, the sperm stored in the epididymis die, are removed by the process used to get rid of all foreign bodies in the human system, and replaced by new, more active ones. If orgasm takes place more than once or possibly twice a day however, the number of spermatozoa in a man's ejaculate decreases rapidly. The testes cannot keep up with the body's demands. It takes five to seven days to get back to a normal count of between 200 and 400 *million* sperm ejaculated in each orgasm. This aspect of sexual physiology helps to explain how couples can try too hard to have a baby. By having sexual intercourse every night they reduce the sperm count so much that fertilization is unlikely because there are simply not enough sperm present.

In men, and all other mammals, the left testis is larger than the right—in humans by about a quarter of an inch all over—but the left testis has no measurable superiority in sperm-producing power. If necessary, because of accident, disease, or a fault in development, one testis can competently do the work of two.

For the testes to function normally, it is not even necessary for there to be a clear passage between them and the tip of the penis, though any blockage will mean, of course, that sperm cannot escape into the female. If the two vasa deferentia, one leading from each sperm-storing epididymis to the exterior, are blocked or cut, as they are in the operation for male sterilization, spermatogenesis continues unhindered. If, however, the deeper-lying ducts, the vasa efferentia, are blocked or tied, the back pressure on the testes is so great that the germinal epithelium is destroyed and no sperm can be made.

Two factors control sperm production in the testes. The first depends on the position of the testes outside the body. For sperm to be manufactured, the temperature of their environment must, within the bounds of individual variation, be between 29° and 36° Centigrade (84° to 97° Fahrenheit), that is, at maximum, 8°C or 14°F below the normal, internal body temperature. The external scrotum, which should be cool to the touch, ensures the right low-temperature surroundings. But wearing tight underpants, or even riding a bicycle, may increase the temperature of the testes too much and inhibit their powers.

Some researchers have suggested that heating the testes in some way might be a feasible method of contraception, and in fact raising the temperature of the testes above that of the body rapidly injures the germinal epithelium, producing temporary sterility.

The cremaster and dartos muscles, joining respectively the testes and scrotum to the lower part of the abdomen, assist in keeping the testes at the right temperature. By relaxing with heat and contracting with cold, they draw the testes just near enough to the body to remain thermally constant. In extreme cold, the testes may appear to have left the scrotum completely.

The second factor controlling sperm production comes from the blood supply

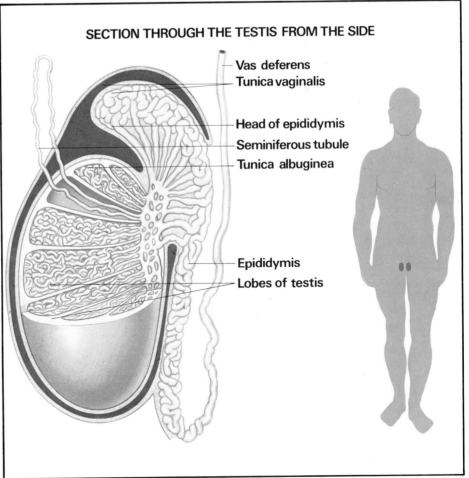

SECTION THROUGH THE TESTIS FROM THE SIDE

- Vas deferens
- Tunica vaginalis
- Head of epididymis
- Seminiferous tubule
- Tunica albuginea
- Epididymis
- Lobes of testis

Square One

to the testes. In the blood, chemical messengers called *hormones* are transported to the testes, and the testes also produce a hormone of their own which the blood stream carries round the body. Without the presence of a hormone, the germinal epithelium within the seminiferous tubules can produce only spermatogonia and Sertoli cells.

The all-important chemical trigger which initiates the change from spermatogonia to sperm cells comes from the pituitary gland at the base of the brain which produces a *gonadotrophic hormone* (the name means 'acting on the gonads or sex cells') called *follicle stimulating hormone*, FSH. This chemical is also made by women but in different quantities. Also acting on the testes is another pituitary gonadotrophic hormone known as *interstitial cell stimulating hormone*, ICSH. This hormone affects the cells—called interstitial cells—which fill the gaps between the honeycomb of seminiferous tubules. Under the influence of ICSH, these cells manufacture a male hormone or androgen known as *testosterone*.

Testosterone, in common with other sex hormones, is a *steroid* and as such has a characteristic chemical shape which can be thought of as a skeleton of carbon atoms in which four hexagons and one pentagon are joined together. At puberty, before testosterone is produced, the two gonadotrophic hormones cause the testes to grow, although relatively their enlargement is not as great as that of the penis.

But testosterone has wider powers. It is testosterone that brings about penis enlargement, produces the 'breaking' or deepening of the voice caused by the growth of the larynx or voice box, the appearance of axillary and pubic hair, the beard, and moustache, and the rapid enlargement of muscles in arms, legs, and torso.

Testosterone also plays an important part in producing erection and therefore in successful intercourse. If given to a man whose testes are imperfectly developed, testosterone can bring about successful erection, formerly impossible; should too much be administered, it can produce priapism, a state of more or less continuous erection. Yet men who secrete normal amounts of testosterone, but are nonetheless impotent, are unaffected by additional injections of the hormone. Testosterone is powerless to overcome the strength of the unconscious will whose seat is in the higher centres of the brain. Unlike women, most men go on producing normal amounts of hormones until they die. Fertility, therefore, dependent on the testes, is not doomed with the onset of middle age.

In the embryo the testes start to develop at a site just behind the kidneys. To begin with, the potential testis is exactly the same as the potential ovary. It consists of a *genital ridge* of tissue called *primordial germinal epithelium* in which the very first sex cells are formed. By six weeks from conception, cells are grouping together, growing, and elongating inwards to form the *sex cords*.

Only some seven weeks after fertilization do seminiferous tubules begin to develop from the sex cords, for it is only then that the sex chromosome make-up of a boy, the XY pairing common to all men and determined at conception, begins to make itself felt. Gradually, the seminiferous tubules become well defined, the vasa efferentia form, plus the epididymis, and the sex and urinary systems join up.

On the outside of the foetus is a slit, towards the front end of which is a small knot of tissue. Under the influence of the Y chromosome which stimulates the production of male hormones, the sides of the slit enlarge and join to make the scrotal sacs. The knot becomes the penis.

By the time an embryo is eight to ten weeks old, the testes are formed as two firm, regular shapes each joined to the base of the scrotum by a long strand of folded tissue, the *gubernaculum*. Although they will go on growing inside the abdomen, they will not descend into the scrotum until a few weeks before birth, or even after delivery. First, an appendix-like tube, the *vaginal process*, pushes down into the scrotum. This tube is formed of the *peritoneum* tissue lining all the abdominal organs. Next, the testis moves down from behind the pubic bone so that it is behind, but touching, the vaginal process, the gubernaculum shrinking in length in compensation. Finally, the vaginal process on each side curves round the testes and forms the envelope, the tunica vaginalis.

At any stage, this development process can be diverted and abnormality will then result, although this happens to only a small proportion of boys. Even after the testes have descended, two small channels remain open between testes and abdomen. Normally, each is just large enough for the vas deferens, nerves, and blood vessels to pass through. If too wide, or if the closure is weak, the abdominal contents may get pushed out through the opening, a condition called inguinal hernia.

Undescended testes, as well as making a boy infertile because they remain in an environment too hot for sperm production, are dangerous because the condition can lead to disease later in life. Other matters too can go wrong in testis development. If the hormone production in the foetus is deficient the testes will be small and permanently incapable of manufacturing mature sperm. Some, but not all, men with this abnormality suffer it as part of a set of symptoms known as Klinefelter's syndrome which is due to an extra X chromosome—making them XXY genetically.

A child may be born possessing both testicular and ovarian tissue—either mixed in 'ovotestes' or as separate testes and ovaries, one on each side of the body. These true intersexes are very occasionally able to function as men, but are most usually sterile.

Throughout the ages, people have recognized the importance of the testes and taken steps to protect them. Medieval armour bore a protective codpiece to shield the genitals, soldiers in the first world war padded their trousers with saucepan lids to ward off shrapnel, and modern sportsmen wear plastic or metal 'boxes'. The law too reflects this concern. The Assyrians, more than 1,000 years B.C., laid down penalties for harming a man's testicles and modern statutes make it illegal for a woman to wilfully damage a man's testes in anything but self-defence.

Men's concern about their testicles results not only because injury can be exceedingly painful—even a light touch, though erogenous to some men, can hurt—but also from the need to assure their masculinity. For the testes are the seat of masculinity.

RUTH GARDINER

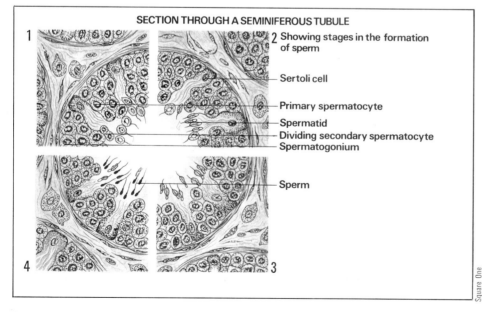

SECTION THROUGH A SEMINIFEROUS TUBULE

1

2 Showing stages in the formation of sperm

Sertoli cell

Primary spermatocyte

Spermatid

Dividing secondary spermatocyte

Spermatogonium

Sperm

4 3

Sperm develop in the 1,000 feet of coiled tubule in each testis—this section is 40,000 times life size. **1** *The spermatogonia divide to produce primary and then secondary spermatocytes.* **2** *These split into spermatids which* **3, 4** *then shrink to the final tadpole shape of the sperm.*

Penile size and female satisfaction

One man believes he can satisfy any woman, another fears he may be sexually inadequate. Both think sexuality depends on penis size. What relation does this have to successful love-making?

No man can be a perfect lover every time he has sexual intercourse. But some men's concern about their sexual adequacy produces needless anxiety that affects their readiness to approach women as well as their performance. Ignorance is the basis for many of these fears, which can cause psychic damage and prevent people from attaining sexual happiness.

One myth that affects virtually every male at some time in his life concerns the size of the penis. One of the most common sex games played by young boys is to compare the size of their genitals. In some cases, a man who wrongly links genital size with sexual potency may come to believe that his penis is smaller than average and will misguidedly fear that it is not large enough to give sexual satisfaction to his partner. This belief may extend to a feeling of general inferiority and handicap him in all his relationships.

For any man who feels this, or any woman who thinks it about her partner, the result can be tragic—unfortunately so, because most of the beliefs which people have about penis size are completely false. Regardless of sex, class, economic status, or educational background, people can be woefully misinformed in matters pertaining to their sexual organs.

This has been true even of physicians —whose responsibility it is to supply information to the public. A study undertaken in the 1950s by the psychiatry department of an important American medical school showed that doctors suffered the same delusions as the public they were treating for sexual problems.

Concern about penile size is common to many societies. Statuary unearthed by archaeologists studying such ancient cultures as pre-Columbian Mexico matches the folk art produced by primitive societies still functioning today; all their fertility symbols have exaggerated sexual organs. During Renaissance times, upper-class dandies frequently wore cod-pieces to magnify the appearance of their genitals. Similarly, some Australian tribesmen decorate and stretch the penis. Like some civilized men of today, they endow the penis with a magical importance.

The power of the penis has been invoked through fertility symbols which exaggerate the size to increase the potency of the magic. This statuette of the god Bes, found at Ephesus, belongs to the Roman period.

Culturally, this preoccupation with the size and power of the penis has localized the male role as that of an active initiator of sexual activity, whose duty it is to provide the female with sexual satisfaction. The possibility of failing to provide this satisfaction can, therefore, leave a man with unspoken fears. For he has to acknowledge that if his partner is unsatisfied she might look elsewhere for gratification, implying an excuse for infidelity, or he must negate her right to sexual pleasure to rationalize his own feelings of inadequacy. These 'fears of inadequate performance' have created a breeding ground for sexual fallacies to grow. Wrongly, and perhaps egocentrically, the male felt that, since the source of his sexual stimulation and satisfaction lay in his penis, this was true for the woman as well. The penis became the indicator by which all things sexual were judged and superstitions about the relations between penis size and sexuality sprang up.

A common penile myth is that a man's libido and potency are directly propor-

tional to the size of his genitals; that is, the larger the penis, the more powerful the sex drive and the greater the ability to achieve and maintain an erection.

Libido is the psychiatric term describing the amount of sexual drive a person has. This sex drive is a complex combination of inherited instincts, hormonal urges, and psychological feelings, both conscious and unconscious. Each of these factors influences the libido, but the size of the penis plays no direct role in libido.

The libido can, nonetheless, be influenced by what a person sees. For example, a child's accidental or intentional viewing of his or her parents in the act of sexual intercourse (the 'primal scene' as it is called by psychiatrists) can have a profound effect. The young man may come to hate his father for being able to make love to his mother with the result that he turns from women to men as the objects of his sexual desire. Similarly, a girl, hearing her mother moaning from sexual pleasure during intercourse, may interpret wrongly, and have a diminished libido in adult life because she falsely believes sex to be extremely painful.

A man's libidinal drive may also be lessened as a result of an insufficient amount of male hormones, a situation often arising after testicular or adrenal gland diseases. Also, if during puberty insufficient hormones are manufactured by these glands, the penis may fail to develop sufficiently. However, such a circumstance is extremely rare.

Libido, and hence potency, the ability to achieve and maintain the penis in an erect state until after orgasm and ejaculation, is not affected by the size of the penis. However, difficulties with potency are primarily psychological. A form of impotence can be caused by a man believing that his penis is too small to be able to satisfy a woman. This performance fear has no basis in fact.

A man with a smaller than average penis might be extraordinarily potent. His sexual desire is probably as strong as that of a man with larger sexual organs; nor is his virility, a term meant to describe his 'hairy-chested' self-image as a sexual satisfier of women, to be impugned.

Virility, however, may be a poor term, for in its connotations the word embodies many of the myths which society has fostered. For example, while many people believe homosexuals to be small, delicate, and effeminate, they are often men whose 'virile' appearance is never questioned. All those men who believe themselves to be extraordinarily virile are not always good lovers. Their 'Tarzan' self-image can lead these men to be rough when gentleness is called for, or unfeeling and uninterested when sensitivity is required. A skilful and considerate lover treats a woman as a woman, and not as a wrestling partner whom he wants nothing more to do with after intercourse.

These self-proclaimed virile men are often great believers in another myth concerning the penis: that penis size is directly proportional to the skeletal and muscular development of the body. This falsehood follows naturally from the myth about libido and potency. Because these men believe that potency and desire are directly correlated to penis size, they also imagine that the tallest, strongest men have the biggest sexual organs. But this belief also is totally untrue. Although short men may worry about this, genital size has one of the least constant relationships to body size or muscular strength. A tall, strong man can have a small penis, and a frail, short man can have large genitals.

A loose corollary, also false, of the mythical relationship between body stature and penis size is the old wives' tale that nose size is an indication of penis dimension. According to this superstition, a man with a prominent nose has similar genitals.

Penis size does not play any part in determining whether or not a man will be

Alan Burns

66

fertile, or whether his children will be male or female. The manufacture of sperm is controlled by one set of cells within the testes, the two egg-shaped organs contained within the scrotum. Male hormones, which are also produced by cells in the testes, have no control over which sex determinant chromosome a sperm cell will contain, although lack of male hormones during puberty or adult life can reduce the number and amount of sperm produced. Neither does hormone production affect penis size, unless an outflow of characteristically female hormones occurs during puberty.

Many of the false beliefs about the size of the penis result because there are two normal states of the penis. The first is the flaccid, or non-erect penis. The second is the erect penis. Erection occurs when, as a result of reflexes triggered off by sexual arousal, the hollow, honeycombed tissue of the two *corpus cavernosa* bodies along the top or dorsal part of the penis, and the spongy tissue of the *corpus spongiosum* below fill with blood.

The average length of the penis in the flaccid state is between three and three and a half inches. In the erect state, penis length usually increases another two to four inches. But penises which are small in the flaccid state increase in size far more than larger genitals, often doubling their length. Those organs which were larger in the flaccid state, between three and a half and four inches long, grow proportionately less with erection, adding only two or two and a half more inches in the erect state. In this way the difference between the large and small penis lessens with sexual arousal. The average erect penis is between five and a half and six and a half

inches long from its base to the very tip.

The vagina is not a rigid, hollow tube, and this further blurs the distinction between the large and small penis. The vaginal barrel is like a piece of soft corrugated rubber hose, which has collapsed upon itself. It is extremely adaptable and capable of accommodating any size penis. During childbirth the vagina stretches so the head and body of an infant will be able to pass through. Once sufficient lubrication develops during the first stages of sexual intercourse, the vagina stretches just enough to hold the penis firmly.

During the excitement phase of intercourse, when the penis has been inside the woman for some time, the upper two-thirds of the vagina expands. The penis and vagina both lose some sensation at this point. But the lower third of the vagina, the 'orgasmic platform', does not dilate, and so feelings in this area do not decrease. A penis, regardless of its size, can manoeuvre in the outer vaginal area during this time and heighten the woman's sexual excitement.

Moreover, the primary centre for a woman's sexual sensitivity is the clitoris, an organ about an inch long located at the juncture of the major labia. When a woman becomes sexually aroused both the clitoris and its protective hood fill with blood and swell. During intercourse, while the penis is moving within the vagina, the minor labia are stretched and released. The hood of the clitoris is attached to the minor labia, and the alternate tension and relaxation stimulates the clitoris, although the penis has no direct contact with it. Another important sexual sensation for the woman comes from the direct contact

which her clitoris makes against the pubic bone of her partner. Clitoral stimulation is the most sexually exciting sensation for the majority of women, and vaginal sensation, even in the sensitive outer third, is secondary.

This destroys the major penile myth, that the larger a man's penis the greater sexual satisfaction he is able to give his partner. Size makes absolutely no difference to female satisfaction. An abnormally large penis can even cause a woman more discomfort than pleasure, because striking the penis against the vaginal part of the cervix can be painful. Yet if she enjoys this sensation, perceiving it as a mixed feeling of pleasure and pain, a change of position, such as lifting the woman's thighs into the air or placing a pillow under the small of her back, allows the normal penis to touch the cervix.

For the woman, too, psychological feelings are often more important than physiological effects. A man rarely achieves sexual satisfaction without orgasm and ejaculation, both almost totally physiological reactions. Many women are different. Although capable of orgasm, they do not always find it essential. Sexual satisfaction for a woman can arise from being with someone whom she loves and enjoying his body. A woman's climax is bound to her psychological state and the more profound joys of orgasm may need practice and familiarity as well as love.

Unless, out of ignorance of the actual facts, a woman believes that a large penis guarantees increased sexual pleasure, and her psychological arousal depends solely upon this myth, penis size makes little difference to the excitement of sexual intercourse. STEPHEN LEVIT

Shiva, one of the chief deities of Hinduism, is symbolized by the lingam, or phallus, which becomes a focus of worship. The

variation among these Indian votive objects emphasizes the diversity in penile size—but endows each with equal effectiveness.

Circumcision: facts, myths, and prejudices

The world's most widespread operation is shrouded in mystery and misapprehension. Are there medical, as well as religious, reasons for circumcision? Does it affect sexual performance?

On the wall of an Egyptian tomb at Saqqara is a painting, dating from 2400 B.C., showing a boy being held while a priest circumcises him. Earlier written descriptions of the circumcision operation indicate that it was already well established in Egypt by 4000 B.C., which makes it one of the oldest surgical operations known to man. Yet no one knows how it originated, and few know why we continue it today. What is circumcision? Is it necessary? Or is it the unkindest cut of all?

The penis of an uncircumcised man has a loose fold of flesh called the prepuce or foreskin which covers the end of the organ in its normal state. During erection this skin folds back, exposing the glans penis. Circumcision consists of pulling this loose fold of flesh as far forward from the end of the penis as it will go and then cutting it away. After the cut has healed the knob of the penis remains permanently exposed giving it a characteristic appearance.

At various times in history the operation has been practised in most parts of the world; only the Mongol, Hindu, Finnish, Hungarian, and Germanic peoples have remained uncircumcised. It is still regularly performed by Jews, Muslims, the Australian aborigines, and other native tribes as a traditional rite. The operation has also undergone periods of popularity in most Western countries.

The first known references to male circumcision appear in Egypt where it was a requirement of the priestly class, the nobility, and royalty. (Even today the wealthier classes are more drawn to circumcision than others.) But old as the custom is, it is probably antedated by female circumcision.

Female circumcision is the surgical removal of the external lips of the sexual organ and sometimes the removal or mutilation of the clitoris. Once widely practised in many parts of the world including the Sudan, Egypt, Malaya, New Guinea, Australia, Latin America, and even Southern Europe, it is now declining. Female circumcision in Moslem countries appears to have been carried out—usually when the girl was between two and five years old—not so much for religious reasons

(Mohammed specifically discouraged the extensive mutilation that the operation sometimes involves) but in the belief that a circumcised woman made a more faithful wife. The British passed legislation outlawing the operation in the Sudan in 1926, but cases were numbered in the thousands in the 1950s and still occur despite the spread of education and propaganda against the practice. The effects are physical (possible loss of orgasm being one) rather than psychological.

The most likely theory about the origin of circumcision in both men and women is that it represented a blood offering to the gods and was connected with fertility, either of the person making the offering or of tribal lands. Some peoples buried the blood and the severed portions of the organ in the ground. Among the ancient Egyptians circumcision was carried out when the boy was between six and 12 years old. Moslems are circumcised shortly after birth, and others at about the time of puberty. For Jews, it represents the fulfilment of a covenant between God and Abraham requiring that every male child should be circumcised. The operation is carried out with great ceremony on the eighth day after birth in the presence of the boy's father and ten other men. The conditions of the operation are strict: there is on record a case where British prison authorities allowed a Jewish baby to be brought into a prison hospital so that the operation could be performed before his father who was being held there.

In those societies where the operation is performed at puberty, as among the Australian aborigines, the ritual concerns the discarding of childhood and initiation to manhood. There circumcision marks the acceptance of adult responsibility, social position, and sexual rights, and the way a youth tolerates the operation is therefore considered important. Since circumcision has such ancient origins it is often carried out with a knife made of sharpened stone, even when a metal one is available. The operation can be brutal, the pain intense, and death from shock or loss of blood is not unusual. Some tribes of Australian aborigines add to the pain and the risk

by not only removing the foreskin but by making a slit on the underside of the penis, thus opening part of the urethra, the tube through which urine and semen passes. It was at first thought that the purpose of this was to provide a primitive form of birth control; that the semen would fail to ejaculate from the end of the penis, and instead be lost from the gash underneath. Against this there is the argument that the uneducated Australian aborigine made no intellectual connection between the act of sexual intercourse and conception, and, therefore, could not have attempted this surgical form of contraception. The reason for this additional

IOANNES
BELLINVS·

operation remains shrouded in mystery.

Societies which, for centuries, have practised circumcision for religious and ritual reasons now advance another reason —apart from profound emotional significance—for carrying out the operation: hygiene. On the inner layer of the foreskin there are a number of glands which secrete a thick substance called smegma. Excessive accumulation of smegma can cause irritation and a penetrating odour. To cleanse this area properly the foreskin has to be pulled back and washed. If, through ignorance or lack of opportunity, this is not done, then irritation and odour result.

The hygiene argument made circum-cision acceptable to societies which did not require it as a ritual, and by the early twentieth century it had become a common operation in Anglo-Saxon countries, particularly Britain and the United States. The case for circumcision was given a further boost by research in the mid-1960s into the incidence of cancer of the penis and of the cervix or neck of the womb. It was known that in India the Hindus, who do not circumcise ritually, suffer a significantly higher rate of cancer of the penis than Moslems who practice ritual circumcision between the ages of 10 and 12. Further research produced statistics which showed that the rate of cancer of the penis is low in

Jesus was circumcised on the eighth day after his birth in accordance with Jewish law, as shown in this painting by Giovanni Bellini. The custom is as old as the Hebrew race, for it was given as a covenant to the aged Abraham, who had previously been childless but fathered Isaac as a result of his agreement with God. According to the Bible, God told Abraham that circumcision would mark future generations of his family as a race apart—the chosen people. But many other groups in the Middle East and elsewhere also circumcise their children. It seems probable that the custom originated as a practical means of preventing discomfort and disease in primitive and unhygienic conditions.

69

Jewish men and cancer of the womb equally low in Jewish women. Could smegma be a cancer-causing agent? And if so, since Jewish men did not deposit smegma in the vaginas of their sexual partners, was this the reason for the lower rate of cancer of the penis and of the womb among Jews?

It was several years before it could be shown that the theory was not as promising as was first believed. Further research showed that the rate of cancer of the penis in circumcised but non-orthodox Jews was roughly the same as uncircumcised Gentiles. In other words, it was only the orthodox Jew who had the lower cancer rate and a factor other than circumcision appeared to be involved although it is as yet unknown. The British expert on circumcision, Dr. Douglas Gairdner, says: 'The smegma cancer case remains unproved. The evidence is neither black nor white and what has so far been presented is enormously complicated.' Research therefore goes on.

What other reasons can be advanced for performing the operation on non-ritual grounds? Until 1949 it was thought that a condition known as 'tight foreskin' existed which could cause discomfort and even fever in an infant. Then Dr. Gairdner published his now famous work 'The Fate of the Foreskin', in *The British Medical Journal*. Dr. Gairdner showed that in the womb the whole of the penis, including the foreskin, develops from a single bud. At birth the foreskin and the end of the penis are united. During the early years of life the foreskin and the penis slowly separate, the process being completed sometime between the first and the third year. It was obvious, therefore, that a tight foreskin could not exist at birth. Well-meaning attempts by the doctor, nurse, or mother to push back the foreskin of a baby were wrong, therefore, and could tear the delicate union between the foreskin and the end of the penis. This tear could heal by scarring and cause the foreskin to adhere permanently to the penis, thus creating the very condition it was desired to prevent and requiring circumcision to correct. Dr. Gairdner suggested that the correct advice for the mother of a newborn baby boy was to leave the foreskin strictly alone so that the natural separation was not interfered with.

Dr. Gairdner's paper came out in Britain at about the time the National Health Service started. Before then the operation was a common one in middle-class families and the family doctor was happy to earn a little extra money for performing it. Once he had to do it as part of a complete medical service he

began to have second thoughts as to whether the operation was really necessary. Dr. Gairdner's paper gave him the rationale he needed. Much the same situation occurred in the United States, where the operation had become part of the American culture until a change of attitudes called its necessity into question.

Are there any arguments that can still be advanced in favour of circumcision? Firstly, the operation does occasionally become necessary in adult life and when performed then causes considerable pain and emotional strain. It is important to avoid sexual excitement for some time afterwards in case the rush of blood to the penis causes haemorrhage. Secondly, it has been argued that the exposed knob of the penis in an uncircumcised male becomes toughened, is therefore less sensitive during intercourse, and thus endows its owner with much-envied sexual staying power. This is difficult to prove and has been ridiculed as propaganda put about by the circumcised to gain an unfair advantage over their uncut brethren. There is also an aesthetic point to be considered. Some doctors believe that women who know the difference find the circumcised penis less attractive. Some have said that they find the unfolding of the foreskin as the uncircumcised penis becomes erect a sexually stimulating sight.

The arguments against circumcision are many, but a number of them are fallacious. Circumcision does not cause a traumatic shock from which an infant never recovers. A leading psychiatrist says: 'There is no evidence whatsoever that the operation has any effect on a child's psychological life.' Equally, there is little evidence that boys are circumcised at the behest of their mothers because of Freudian reasons concerned with penis envy. In fact it is more likely to be the father who requests the operation, especially if he was circumcised himself. So, although no figures are kept as to the number of males circumcised, it is possible to say what type of person is most likely to have been circumcised: he will come from a higher social class, he will have been born before the second world war, have gone to a private school, and his father will have been circumcised.

The arguments against circumcision which have some weight begin with the fact that it is physically an unnecessary operation. It carries the risk of complications serious enough to have caused 16 deaths in Britain in 1949, the year Dr. Gairdner published the results of his research. Apart from complications, the danger of mutilation must be considered. Even when the operation is performed by

people the parents believe to be experts, matters can sometimes go wrong. In a case in 1968 the English High Court awarded £12,500 damages against a *mohel* (a Jewish practitioner of circumcision) who had, it was claimed, 'maimed the child for life'.

In Britain, the Ministry of Health offers no guidance on circumcision at all and leaves the decision to the individual doctor. It will allow the operation under the National Health scheme only if medically necessary and not as a ritual or as a routine operation. National Health hospitals tell parents requesting the operation that they will have to arrange to have it done privately. Health insurance schemes, which operate in Britain, America, Australia, and other countries, adopt the same attitude. That is they will cover the operation if, and only if, it is felt necessary on medical grounds. The best summary of current medical attitude is contained in a letter written to a general practitioner in 1950 by the famous British paediatrician, the late Sir James Spence. The letter, little known to the layman, but cherished in the medical world, reads:

'Your patient of seven months has the foreskin with which he was born. You ask me, with a note of persuasion in your question, if it should be excised. Am I to make this decision on scientific grounds, or am I to acquiesce in a ritual which took its origin at the behest of the arch-sanitarian Moses?

'If you show good reason why a ritual designed to ease the penalties of concupiscence amidst the sand and flies of the Syrian deserts should be continued in this England of clean bed-linen and lesser opportunity, I shall listen to your argument; but if you base your argument on anatomical faults, then I must refute it.

'The anatomists have never studied the form and evolution of the preputial orifice. They do not understand that Nature does not intend it to be stretched and retracted in the temples of the Welfare Centres or ritually removed in the precincts of the operating theatres. Retract the foreskin and you see a pin point opening, but draw it forward and you see a channel wide enough for all the purposes for which the infant needs the organ at that early age. What looks like a pin point opening at seven months will become a wide channel of communication at 17.

'Nature is a possessive mistress and whatever mistakes she makes about the structure of the less essential organs such as the brain and stomach, in which she is not much interested, you can be sure that she knows best about the genital organs.'

PHILLIP KNIGHTLEY

Sexual capacity

Exactly as individual physiology and appetite for food vary from one human being to the next, so does the appetite for sexual activity, and the need of an outlet for sexual tensions. An obsession on the part of the male about this appetite, and the ability to fulfil his desires at least as well as his fellow men, has led to the building up and fostering of a mythology about sexual capacity rivalled only by that woven around the size of the sexual organs and virility.

A lack of understanding about the nature of the sexual drive, and misconceptions about what constitutes a 'normal' sex life when it comes to satisfying this drive, has led to much human misery. Hearing tales of feats of sexual athleticism in the bedroom has convinced many men that, because their own abilities in this direction are pale by comparison, they are not succeeding as lovers or, indeed, as men. Fear of this lack of virility can undermine any sexual relationship, and may lead to depression or continuous anxiety, with harmful results.

The sexes differ in their capacities for love-making because of the very different roles which their bodies play in the act of sexual intercourse. The male has the more active role and, at the same time, finds it easier to obtain sexual satisfaction and experience orgasm. The female, cast in the passive role, is very much reliant on the male partner to provide her with complete satisfaction, although she is able to experience many more orgasms than he if the conditions are right.

By strange convention, a man able to take part in many acts of sexual intercourse within a relatively short time is admired, whereas a woman who desires prolonged or often-repeated intercourse is tagged with the unjust label of 'insatiable'. A man who pursues an exaggeratedly active sex life is likely to become something of a hero, following in the footsteps of Don Juan or Casanova, while a similarly vigorously sexual woman is mislabelled a nymphomaniac, and classified with Messalina of ancient Rome, or Catherine II of Russia. In both male and female cases the exaggerated amount of sexual activity is very often due not to abnormally increased sexual desires but to normal sexual desires which

No one has a 'normal' sex life. Sexuality varies so greatly that near-abstinence for one is satisfaction for another.

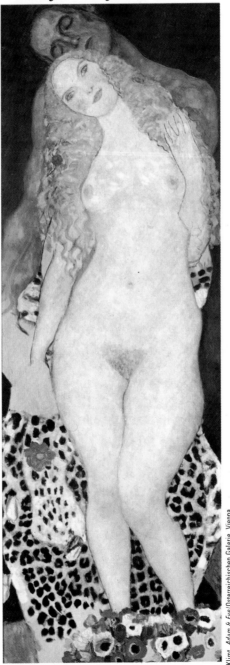

Klimt, *Adam & Eve*/Österreichischen Galerie, Vienna

have not been satisfied, and so have mounted for lack of a proper outlet.

No worldwide studies have been carried out on statistics of varying sexual vigour, but many self-appointed authorities have felt able to comment on supposed sexual differences. The author Mantegazza stated, in 1885, 'Negroes are mighty lovers, possibly the first of the human family in this respect.' He held also that 'polygamous peoples, owing to greater exercise of their sexual organs, have stronger ones, and are, so to speak, more ready for the fray'. Turks, Arabs, and Hindus, because they 'expend as a rule less strength in intellectual struggle, and have at the same time in their harems and zenanas a luxurious assortment of females, are in a position easily to outdistance us, when it comes to bedroom joustings'. This point of view persists in the common misconception that coloured peoples have much larger genitals than races of European stock, and so are better lovers. This fantasy, many psychologists believe, is responsible to some degree for maintaining an irrational fear of coloured peoples which exacerbates racial prejudice. Even if the myth of genital size difference were true, this would have no implications about sexual capacity. There is no relationship between the size of the penis and sexual drive or capability.

To establish what should be regarded as normal sexual activity in human beings Alfred C. Kinsey and his fellow workers undertook monumentally large studies in the United States between the 1940s and the 1960s, enquiring into the sex lives of many thousands of men and women. From the figures they amassed it is possible to draw a picture of the sex life of the average man and the average woman, but it is extremely difficult to equate or compare the two sexes in terms of sexual capacity because of the different natures of their experiences.

For a man it might be sensible to measure sexual performance by the number of orgasms experienced over a given time—weeks or years—but such data would not be comparable with figures for the number of orgasms experienced by a woman, because the significance of orgasm is so different. Nevertheless, the number of orgasms is some indication of sexual performance, even if it does not take into account sexual activity which stops short of orgasm—an experience more likely to be had by a woman than a man.

Kinsey identified the chief ways in which orgasm may be achieved as masturbation, nocturnal dreams, petting, intercourse, and homosexual relations. While there are certainly people who reach orgasm every time in only one of these forms of sexual activity, most people rely on two or more sources of sexual outlet. Some people may even experience all these forms of activity within a relatively short period of time, although this is, of course, rare.

Surveys found that an average man between adolescence and the age of 30 experiences roughly three orgasms a week, with the rate gradually decreasing with age. However, the differences in the sexual behaviour of men at the extremes of the samples of people questioned is vast, far exceeding the differences which are normally expected as part of human variation in, for instance, body form or ability. Thus, in Kinsey's study, at one end of the scale was one person who, although apparently perfectly fit physically, had ejaculated only once in the course of 30 years. Other people had average frequencies of 10, 20, or more orgasms a week for very long periods of time, while one man had averaged 30 orgasms regularly every week for over 30 years. Between him and the man who had only one orgasm in the same period the difference was over 45,000.

Although the average number of orgasms for a man during one week is three, a reasonable proportion, 7.6 per cent, of men experience seven or more orgasms a week. Age and educational background make a noticeable difference—men under 30 outnumbering those over 30 by four to one, and people with a university education are relatively rare in this group. The people in the group are, of course, mainly married men with an established pattern of sexual behaviour; intercourse at night and first thing in the morning is quite usual—especially in people of the lower rather than the higher social levels.

There are many men who ejaculate regularly more than once every time that they have intercourse. Most men occasionally ejaculate more than once, but there are a few for whom this is a regular occurrence. Very few men are able to ejaculate more than four or five times

during one sexual act but cases are on record of as many as twenty ejaculations in a few hours (this was in a teenage boy). To the average person this would seem impossible and many physiologists have doubted the veracity of the report. However, in some men the glands secreting the seminal fluid *can* work at such a rate and, as well as orgasm, ejaculation is possible. One 39-year-old man claimed to have averaged more than three orgasms a day from the age of 13, and was still able, on occasion, to experience six to eight orgasms.

Sexual capacity in the male reaches a peak during adolescence and, thereafter, declines very gradually into old age. The initial drop is the steepest and after the twenties the changes are much slower. At the age of 50, the average number of orgasms experienced during one week is only just under two, compared with the three of the early twenties, and is still around one when the seventies are reached.

The gradual decline of sexual capacity which accompanies ageing is part of the general picture of loss of physical and physiological powers spread out over the years. For men there is no menopause or 'change of life' to signal the end of useful reproductive life; sperm are produced in the testes probably for as long as a man lives. Gradually the functioning of the sex organs declines, accompanied by 'psychological fatigue' when it comes to sexual activity—very gradual loss of interest and boredom with too much repetition of the same experience. There is a waning of interest in erotic stimuli, and it takes longer for the penis to reach the erect state. The length of time during which an erection without ejaculation can be maintained also decreases, from the several hours which are possible in the adolescent to five or six minutes in the 65 to 70-year-old. The ability to have multiple ejaculations also declines with advancing age; after about 40 years most men have completely lost this ability.

A man's sexual capacity can also be affected by functional impotence which should be distinguished from the simple waning of sexual ability and inclination which gradually appears with age. Impotence may manifest itself in many ways; it is most commonly the inability to have an erection, despite the presence of the appropriate erotic stimuli, but it may also be premature ejaculation. Both forms nearly always have psychological causes,

but this does not make the problem any less serious. Most men, in fact, experience impotence on occasion and are afraid of it. This very fear of being impotent on a special occasion can itself cause sexual difficulties. Thus a vicious circle is set up which may be very difficult to break. Constant anxiety about impotence—of not being a 'whole man'—can become an obsession.

For women the situation as regards sexual capacity is completely different, if by capacity is meant ability to take part in sexual intercourse. There is no female equivalent to obtaining an erection as a prerequisite of intercourse and, potentially, a woman is able to respond to her partner at any time. Because no part of her reaction corresponds to the ejaculation of semen from the penis, a woman's orgasm is not necessary to fertilization. However, a woman is potentially capable of achieving orgasm in every act of intercourse or masturbation (provided that the stimulation is appropriate) and she is more able to experience multiple orgasms than is a man.

Kinsey found that a married woman has on average about three and a half orgasms a week between the ages of 16 and 20. This drops to about two and a half orgasms a week at 30 years, and to one orgasm a week at 60 years. Unmarried women, who are less likely to have continuing opportunities for intercourse and tend to masturbate less than men, reach orgasm on average between once and twice a week. The maximum, of course, is far higher. Kinsey interviewed women who experienced 29 orgasms a week between the ages of 20 and 40, and women of 50 who reached orgasm 18 times in a week. Masters and Johnson have found that a woman is more capable than a man of retaining a high level of sexual excitement over a protracted period and of achieving more than one climax. They suggest that a woman may enjoy three or four orgasms, particularly during more easily-prolonged masturbation.

In the past, society has attached great importance to the erection of the penis and to sexual prowess as a means of survival of the human race. With increasing knowledge we should be able to end the identification of sexuality with stamina and realize that the capacity for intercourse is just another attribute which distinguishes one individual from another, neither advantageous if great nor disadvantageous if small.

DAVID WILLIAMS

72

Male disorders

To a man, disorders of the genital organs can be among the most worrying of all because they may affect his sexual functioning. What are these conditions and how do doctors treat them?

Angelo Visconti/Institute of Art, Siena/Scala

To any man who gave it thought, it might seem unfair that there should be no distinctively named class of medical specialist to whom he could turn for advice about any specifically *male* disorder. A woman can consult an obstetrician, a specialist well versed in the whole intriguing process of childbirth, or a gynaecologist, whose work is devoted to specifically female problems. There is no equivalent 'andrologist' to deal with the hazards of being born male, despite the many afflictions that only a male can suffer.

Disorders which affect the male reproductive organs, and which can, therefore, interfere with a normal sex life, may be due to abnormalities which have been present from birth (congenital abnormalities), or they may develop later in life as a result of damage or infection (acquired abnormalities).

As a foetus develops within its mother's womb its sexual characteristics gradually become more and more pronounced, and many weeks before birth it is possible to distinguish a male from a female child. Whether a foetus develops into a male or a female depends, of course, upon the sex chromosome pattern of the fertilized ovum. If the fertilized ovum contains two XX sex chromosomes, the child will develop gonads of the female type, ovaries, while if the pattern is XY, the gonads will be testes and the genital tract should develop along male lines.

Sometimes, however, the development of the genital tract and the formation of the sexual organs proceeds abnormally, often due to disturbances of the balance of hormones in the child's body. Such disturbances may lead to the formation of 'intersex' children. Thus, although the testes are present together with the normal XY chromosome pattern of the male, a child may be born with purely feminine external genital organs, look exactly like a female—and be reared as a girl. This intersex state is usually discovered at puberty, when the expected menstruation does not occur and the breasts fail to develop. There is, unfortunately, little that can be done, and the individuals are encouraged to carry on living as women. Intercourse is often possible, although child-bearing is not. This form of intersex is very rare.

Rather more common forms of male intersex are those in which testes are present, but the external genitalia are not pronouncedly either male or female, but half and half. A boy born with a small penis and the condition known as hypospadias, in which the urethral opening is not at the tip of the penis as is normal,

73

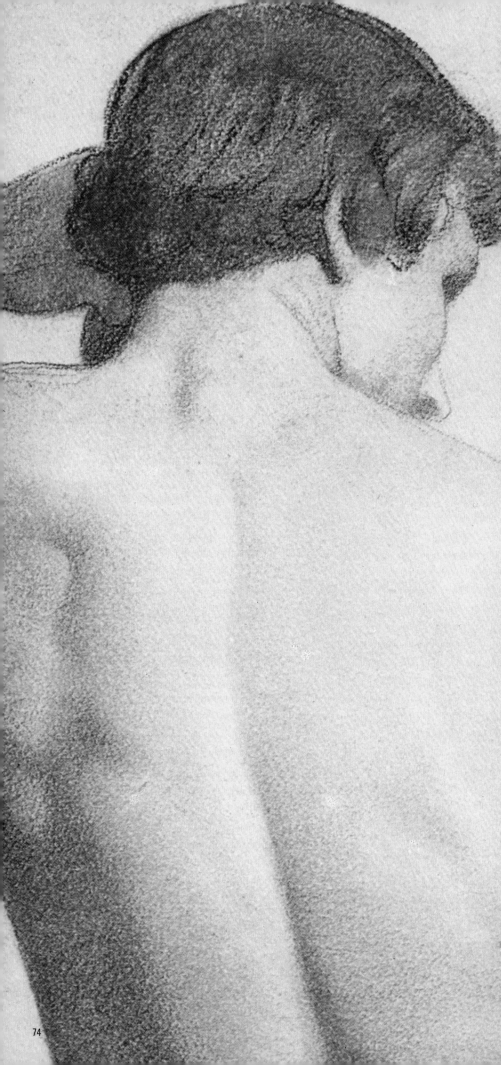

but lower down, is often mistaken for a girl. Careful examination is necessary to reveal the true sex of the individual.

Needless to say, it is vital to diagnose the state of affairs as early as possible in infancy. A policy of waiting to see how such a child develops is likely to have disastrous effects on the emotions of both the growing child and his parents. The changing of a sexual role in adolescence or even adult life is psychologically very disturbing. In most cases some form of surgical correction will enable these unfortunate boys at least to look more like their own sex, even if a normal sex life as a man cannot be guaranteed.

More common than these intersex conditions, in which the very sex of the child may be in doubt from external appearances, are congenital abnormalities of the male sexual organs in which the urinary parts of the urogenital system are displaced. In the male, the urinary system leads to the exterior through the same route as that traversed by spermatozoa during sexual intercourse. There is no separation of the sexual and excretory functions as there is in the female, who has a vaginal opening concerned only with sexual functions and a separate opening for the urethra. In the male there is a common duct through which both urine and seminal fluid pass, according to the circumstances, and which has its opening at the end of the penis, the male sexual organ. Any disturbance of the lower urinary tract in the male is, therefore, likely also to disrupt sexual function.

The processes of development of the male urinary tract sometimes go astray so that the urethra, instead of opening at the end of the penis, opens in an abnormal situation lower down the penis. If the opening is on the upper surface the condition is known as epispadias, if on the lower surface, down towards the scrotum, as hypospadias. Both of these conditions, if uncorrected, clearly upset sexual functions, as well as proving embarrassing and awkward during the very ordinary process of passing urine.

Fortunately, modern surgery is usually able to correct these conditions, even if it means a spaced series of operations on the penis to restore a proper channel. Hypospadias and epispadias are normally detected early in a child's life, but it does happen that boys grow into adulthood without undergoing the treatment which could render them functionally normal.

Another major fault of development of the male genital system is the failure of the male gonads (testes), to appear in their proper place, the scrotum, as growth proceeds. The testes develop in the abdominal cavity of the foetus, high up beneath the kidneys, and are then drawn down into the scrotum, the pouch beneath the penis, some time before birth.

Occasionally this process of 'migration' of the testes is interrupted, so that one or both may fail to appear in the scrotum. This is an important developmental abnormality, because for a testis to function normally in adult life, and to produce normal spermatozoa, it is essential that it be kept at a slightly lower temperature than that of the body. Occasionally, also, an undescended testis becomes cancerous. Every effort is, therefore, made to induce a testis which has not descended to follow its proper path. Hormones have been used, but it is very often necessary to resort to surgery if, by puberty, the testis has not descended into its rightful place. However, the presence of both testes is not necessary for fertility, and there are many men who have apparently only one testis who have fathered children.

Congenital abnormalities which are likely to cause difficulties in the male sex life are fortunately relatively rare. Much more common are the disorders which may afflict any normally developed male. The male genitalia, unlike the female, are predominantly outside the body, and, therefore, more prone to physical damage. Any blow in the 'groin', as the genital area is euphemistically and inaccurately termed, has agonizing results because of the extreme sensitivity of the testes. So well supplied with nerves are these organs that pressure of any sort generates pain. A violent blow to the testes has even been known to cause death from shock, so overwhelming can the pain be. Possibly this rich nerve supply is present to provide a continuous reminder of the importance of keeping the testes, which have a life-giving function, out of harm's way.

Apart from the pain which is produced by the physical violence of, for instance, a kick, or the impact of a hard-thrown ball, there is the danger of permanent damage. Severe bruising of the tissues of the testis causes bleeding from the ruptured small vessels into neighbouring structures, and the whole scrotum is likely to become grossly swollen. If there is serious disruption of the blood supply because of haemorrhage, the vitality of the testes is threatened. Although recovery may apparently occur, testicular function may be lost so that the male becomes infertile.

Damage so severe is fortunately infrequent. The majority of incidents, although the effects may persist for many weeks, leave little permanent reduction in function. It is only rarely that damage is so serious that removal of the testis by operation becomes advisable. Besides being well supplied with nerves the genital organs are also well endowed with a blood supply, so that healing is relatively efficient.

An accidental occurrence that has usually no apparent outside physical cause is torsion of the testis. This sometimes occurs spontaneously, when the testis on one side twists so that the spermatic cord, which supplies it with blood (and also carries seminal fluid into the genital tract) becomes constricted, or strangulated.

The condition sometimes occurs at intervals, being followed by spontaneous recovery. There is sudden severe pain in the testis and usually a sickening abdominal pain, which may be accompanied by vomiting. If the testis does not 'untwist' spontaneously, it may be necessary to perform a small operation to make it do so. The surgeon will probably make an anatomical correction at the same time, so that the condition does not recur. If the condition is left without treatment the pain and swelling may disappear after a while, but the testis becomes atrophied and useless.

More common than these defects, which result from accidents, are those which are due to infections of the genital tract The word 'mumps' raises terror in the minds of many males, because of the sterility which this is supposed inevitably to confer on any adult man who contracts the disease. Certainly inflammation of the testes (orchitis) may be one of the unfortunate complications of an attack of mumps in a man, but it is extremely rare, and, in any case, does not invariably so damage the testes that the person becomes sterile. The chances of an attack of mumps seriously affecting the virility of any man must be about those of him being struck by lightning. A much more serious threat is posed by bacteria which are likely to infect not the testes themselves, but the lower end of the genital tract, the urethra, leading from the bladder to the end of the penis and lined with sensitive tissues.

The urethra in the male is roughly eight inches in length, extending from the exit of the bladder, where it is surrounded by the specifically male structure, the prostate gland, down to the base of the penis, and then along the length of the penis to its tip. In the female, of course, the urethra is very much shorter, and infections which gain a hold on its tissues are more likely to spread upwards into the bladder and so cause cystitis. Because of the extra length of the male urethra, inflammation of the tissues which form its lining (urethritis), is relatively more serious. Infections which cause swelling of the urethral lining naturally impede the flow of urine from the bladder during urination, and give rise to both pain and difficulty in this act. There are several different species of bacteria which commonly cause urethritis, but certainly the most important are the gonococci, responsible for the venereal disease gonorrhoea.

Gonorrhoea is a disease which afflicts not only the urethra but also the prostate gland, and on both structures the effects are often serious. In a man who has been infected there is an intense inflammation of the urethral tract. Urination becomes extremely painful and there is an unpleasant discharge of infected material. Treatment of the condition with appropriate antibiotics reduces the risk of permanent damage, provided that the disease is recognized at an early stage. But it has been known for a person who has had just one attack to develop serious symptoms as long as 20 years afterwards.

During the acute stage of the disease the lining of the urethra is destroyed by the infecting bacteria, and the tissues are replaced, not by delicate lining tissues of the same sort, but by emergency fibrous tissue which the body supplies as an immediately available defence. This fibrous tissue, as the years progress, gradually contracts and so causes a narrowing of the normal urinary channel. The result is a 'stricture' of the urethra, an extreme narrowing of one section, which not only causes difficulty in passing urine but is likely to lead to further infection because of the damming-up of urine in the bladder. To a person who contracts gonorrhoea, and thinks little of it because the cure was so simple, this should be a reminder that the effects can be much more serious than they first appear.

The prostate gland, which surrounds the neck of the bladder in the male, may be affected by gonorrhoea. Much more common, however, are the afflictions of the prostate which accompany the process of aging. The prostate is largely made up of muscular tissue. As a man becomes older it tends to increase in size. Very often there are no symptoms, but sometimes the enlargement causes pressure on the urinary channel. The working of the valve which regulates the flow of urine from the bladder is affected. Sometimes there is complete inability to pass urine—the condition of urinary retention—or there may simply be difficulty in commencing the flow.

The cause is usually just an increase in size of the gland, without there being any malignant change. It is often possible to cure the condition by removal of part or all of the enlarged structure. Such surgical treatment may not even require an incision from the outside. Under anaesthetic it may be performed entirely by means of instruments passed up into the urethra through the end of the penis. An electrical diathermy knife is used to shave away the unwanted and obstructing portions of the prostate so that the channel for the passage of urine is left clear. Hormonal treatment, too, may be of use in reducing the size of the prostate.

Occasionally, as in any other part of the body, malignant changes may occur in the prostate and a cancer may form. It is only by a direct examination of the enlarged gland that a surgeon can distinguish between a prostate gland which has undergone simply enlargement, or 'benign hypertrophy', and one which has become cancerous. If a cancerous change is suspected then, of course, the operation for removal of the affected gland must be more extensive.

Perhaps it is the variety of male disorders that has discouraged any attempt to consider them as a whole. No doctor feels competent to treat them all, but each condition falls within the field of a specialist concerned with more general bodily systems. Hormonal imbalances, for example, might be treated by an endocrinologist, while disorders of the urinary system would be treated by a urologist. The male reproductive organs, although obviously vulnerable, are far less complex than those of the female and more accessible to straightforward treatment. As a result, any doctor is able to cope with the simpler disorders and can refer a patient to the proper specialist to treat more serious conditions.   DAVID WILLIAMS

The arousal gap

Too often sexual intercourse fails to satisfy a woman because it takes longer to excite her than her partner. What causes this difference in the timing of male and female sexuality?

Anyone who doubts that men and women in Western society are sexually excited by different forms of stimulation has only to place a dozen women's magazines next to a similar pile of those bought by their husbands. The heroines in women's fiction are attractive, elegant—and intact. They are wooed by tall, handsome heroes, called Nigel or Edward, whose immaculate trousers never lose their crease even after a hundred miles behind the wheel of their sleek sports cars. The ladies in men's journals, by contrast, are physically challenging, scantily clad, and while they may yet retain their virtue the implication is that they would not do so if the right man—the reader of course—were at hand.

Until quite recently to have said this would have seemed flippant. After all, few sexual physiologists have ever regarded station bookstalls as a primary source of scientific information. Textbooks are more usually referred to. But until the publication in April 1966 of *Human Sexual Response*, by William Masters and Virginia Johnson, the textbooks were unreliable. The work of these two investigators, which originated in Washington in 1954 and transferred ten years later to the Reproductive Biology Research Foundation in St. Louis, Missouri, has given us more information about the physiology of sexual intercourse than all the books and scientific papers of previous workers taken together.

One fact of human sexuality that has come over clearly is that most men are easily aroused by purely physical, bodily stimuli; whereas a woman's full sexual response depends far more on her state of mind and on her total responsiveness to her partner. This is not to say that the majority of men are capable of full sexual expression in a situation which is physically or emotionally uncomfortable. However, the initial stages of arousal are more immediate for a man and can be initiated by fewer stimuli—the sight of a nipple or perhaps a thigh or, for our grandfathers, even an ankle. At the very start of sexual excitement there exists, therefore, an *arousal gap* in the responses of the two sexes.

Recently it has become fashionable to regard man as biological material, to consider him as a 'super-ape', whose intelligence distinguishes him from the beasts, but whose body is subject to the same biological rules as theirs. If we understood the rules properly, say specialists in this area, we could understand man far better than we do now. To a large extent this may

be true, as long as we qualify it by saying that man is a *social* ape. The social aspect of his make-up has moulded and modified him as much as any other single influence. It has certainly moulded him sexually and it may even be partly responsible for the arousal gap.

The basic problem in explaining the relatively slow physical response found in most women, compared to that shown in the majority of men, is that it is probably not really a biological effect at all. It seems just as likely to have a social basis when we consider the role that women play during pregnancy and childbirth, the responsibility that they assume in bringing up children and, not least, the way in which for centuries they have been regarded by men, at least in Western communities, as inferior beings.

The female of most species will mate only at certain times. They fight off any male who tries to mount when they are unwilling. But once the right time has been reached females of many different types embark upon the process of mating just as instantaneously as do males. There is no gap apparent in their responses.

Similarly in the human situation. The first stage of sexual excitement in men is, obviously, erection of the penis. In women, as Masters and Johnson have shown, the corresponding change is the secretion of fluid to lubricate the vagina. This was the very first response to sexual stimulation that could be measured in the women volunteers taking part in their study. The flow of secretion could be induced by various forms of arousal and in those women who were suitably prepared it appeared in as little as ten seconds. We might, therefore, quite reasonably assume that for those women who do not respond so quickly—those with a prolonged arousal gap—the delay is caused not so much by physical as by emotional factors which, presumably, have an underlying social cause. In other words, the gap is the product of a woman's psychological conditioning during childhood and not of her biological make-up.

A woman's responses during the later stages of the sexual act tend to confirm that this is so. Masters and Johnson analyzed in detail the physical changes taking place in both the woman's body and in that of her partner during sexual intercourse, and the striking feature of their results is not so much the difference as the similarity between them.

The Missouri workers divided the process of human sexual response into four

phases which they called the excitement, plateau, orgasmic, and resolution stages. Changes which characterized each of these phases could be found in both sexes. For example, the penis becomes erect early in the phase of excitement. Towards the end of the plateau phase its widest and most sensitive region, the *glans*, increases even further in diameter and often becomes darker in colour. During orgasm, muscular contractions along the length of the penis expel the semen into the vagina. The first few of these contractions follow each other at intervals of rather less than one second but the subsequent ones are less powerful and have a longer time interval between them. During the phase of resolution following orgasm the penis loses its erection, usually in a two-stage process, and returns to its former size.

A similar set of changes occurs in the vagina. Sexual stimulation in the excitement phase causes the production of vaginal secretion, the function of which is obviously to lubricate the vaginal barrel and make penetration easier. The vagina starts to increase both in length and in diameter and its walls often take on a darker purplish colour in much the same way as the glans penis. In the plateau phase, the region of the vagina nearest to the cervix continues to increase in volume but at its other end the vagina starts to contract to form the 'orgasmic platform'.

During orgasm, a set of rhythmic muscular contractions occurs in the region of this platform. The first few waves are separated from each other by intervals of a little under a second, although the later ones are less powerful and less regular. During resolution the vagina returns to its normal size, again as the result of a two-stage process. The orgasmic platform first relaxes and increases in diameter, then the rest of the vaginal barrel contracts to the size that it was before sexual stimulation began.

The similarity between the sexes is even more apparent when we look at the individual as a whole. One of the most characteristic changes occuring during intercourse in both men and women is an increase in muscular contraction in several different regions of the body. In the plateau phase both participants start to lose control of many of the muscles in their face, hands, and legs. This leads to a tight clinging to the other partner together with the type of facial expression that film-makers have used as a most blatantly obvious indication that the heroine was losing her virtue. During the orgasmic phase voluntary control of these muscle groups is lost completely, but during resolution the muscular spasms rapidly relax, usually within a period of five minutes if a satisfactory orgasm has been experienced. The same type of change—a build-up through the excitement to the plateau phase to reach a peak at orgasm, followed by a fairly rapid resolution—is also seen in the alteration of blood pressure and heartbeat experienced during intercourse in both sexes.

However, the fact is well known that men and women do not show *identical* patterns of sexual response and any scientific investigation that did not show up such obvious and frequently experienced differences would have failed somewhere. The work of Masters and Johnson certainly did not fail in this respect and, indeed, it threw considerable light on perhaps the most basic single difference between male sexuality and that in the female, an effect that can be best described as an arousal gap in reverse.

Following orgasm a certain length of time has to elapse before a man can ejaculate again. During the phase of resolution he enters a *refractory period*, when no amount of sexual stimulation can evoke another orgasm. Despite his wishes, the man's body returns to the situation that it was in during the early excitement phase and he must pass again through the phases of later excitement and plateau before he can experience a second orgasm. But a woman, during the phase of resolution, if she continues to receive sexual stimulation, need not fall below the plateau phase of arousal. She is, therefore, capable of experiencing a number of orgasms one after the other without having to go through the whole response cycle. It is most important that couples should realize that this difference exists in their physical make-up; for a failure to understand it can lead to emotional tension which might eventually put their relationship in jeopardy.

It is just as well known that individual women show rather different patterns of response and again the work of the St. Louis investigators has been extremely valuable in explaining these differences. The most common cause of individual variation is simply one of timing. Some women go through the whole cycle of response, particularly the excitement phase, far more rapidly than others. Again, it seems likely that conditioning is important here. The woman whose previous sexual experience

has been unsatisfactory may well build up psychological barriers which prevent her from responding normally to the kisses and caresses which would excite other women. But if she can become sufficiently relaxed and receptive she will go through precisely the same stages of arousal as any other woman, and she will show a very similar pattern of physical changes, even though they may take longer to complete.

The truly frigid woman is far rarer than might be imagined. What the woman who fails to achieve orgasm needs is patience and understanding on the part of the partner. If he hurries the whole process, and if he dissociates intercourse from affection, he may only serve to make her problem worse.

Understanding this is all the more important because men, and especially young men, can achieve orgasm very quickly. This is largely because they go through the excitement phase in a matter of seconds. A girl on a calendar or on an advertisement may be all the stimulation necessary. Their whole cycle of sexual responses, including the refractory phase, is telescoped into a very short period. If the physical changes which they experience are analyzed, they are found to consist of an abbreviated version of the pattern found in men of middle age or older. But if the whole cycle is completed before their partner has left the excitement phase, she at least will regard the experience as a failure.

Premature ejaculation is one of the commonest causes of sexual disharmony. It is what most men think of when the term 'arousal gap' is mentioned. But the solution to it is not the one that many of them imagine. It is not for their partners to race through the cycle at a speed that few of them can attain. Rather, it is for the man himself to slow down and to prolong the stages of excitement and plateau prior to a mutual orgasm. And this delay can be learned. It requires practice together with patience and understanding on the part of both partners, but clinics exist where advice on the problem is given and their number will undoubtedly grow.

Followers of the fashion of considering man as a sophisticated ape like to speculate on the reasons why mankind has adopted such a unique pattern of sexual behaviour, for unique it certainly is. Even in the species to which we are closely related, animals such as the gorilla and the chimpanzee that have a menstrual cycle, mating occurs only at specified times during the cycle. The human female, however,

shows no particular preference and she is almost equally receptive at all times. In addition, our own species is the only one which has turned copulation into a fine art. It is rare to find any mammal which prolongs the process of mating beyond a few minutes. The boar may take a quarter of an hour but then he produces half a pint of semen. The stallion and the bull are quicker and the buck rabbit ejaculates almost instantaneously. In all of these species there is clearly no intention on the part of the male of gratifying the female, and the process is got over as quickly as possible.

It has been suggested that this unseemly haste is necessary because two animals locked in a sexual encounter present a likely target for any predators that may be in the vicinity. Man, however, solved the predator problem fairly early in his evolution. Indeed he himself became the principal hunting animal on the landscape. After solving that problem he then had the leisure to take his most pleasurable activity —sexual intercourse—more seriously, and to prolong it in order to derive from it the maximum possible degree of enjoyment. It was also suggested that in so doing he was able to strengthen the emotional bond that joined him to his mate, and thus produce a more stable system of pairing for the rearing of children than exists elsewhere in the animal world.

These are suggestions and indeed they are certainly no more. Many zoologists would reject them outright, but others would quote the existence of the arousal gap to justify such ideas. The timing of sexual arousal even in modern man does not correspond in men and women—that is to say, even now couples have to work to reach orgasm simultaneously. This might possibly be a way of strengthening the ties between two individuals to the extent that they cease to want to find another partner.

One final theory is even more controversial. Does the fact that a woman will at least entertain the idea of intercourse at any hour of the day or night, rather than simply during one or two seasons of the year, mean that she has evolved to a position of sexual superiority over the females of other species? Does it mean that she can be more sexually selective? Are we indeed seeing women's liberation at a biological level, a liberation which has been going on for hundreds of generations? It would be interesting to hear the views of women biologists on this matter for few males would have the temerity to express any definite opinion.   CLIVE WOOD

Infertility in men

Men have always had fertility symbols and gods whom they supposed would promote fertility if treated with reverence. Today, of course, men look to doctors and scientists for help in this direction. Why are some men infertile? And how successfully can male infertility be treated?

'Be fruitful and multiply and replenish the Earth.' The commandment comes from the Old Testament of the Bible, but it is echoed by almost every religion and culture. Man's foremost duty is to beget heirs, whether to ensure a comfortable old age, to provide ancestor-worshippers after death, or merely to continue the family name. Indeed, the desire to breed is one of man's strongest instincts, and he has reinforced it through the ages with prayers, sacrifices, fertility rites, and charms. Many religions have had a god or goddess with the sole job of promoting fertility.

Today, some people would say that man has been too fruitful. With the world's population growing at an ever increasing rate, and likely to double in the next 30 years, our planet seems likely to burst at the seams. There are dire warnings that the population explosion is the greatest threat to mankind's survival. The only hope of salvation seems to be in the more widespread use of contraception aiming not merely to stabilize the birth-rate, but to reduce it. To this end scientists in laboratories in many countries are striving to discover cheaper, simpler, and more effective contraceptives.

Other scientists—often in the same laboratories—are trying to find ways of combating infertility, of helping the childless to conceive. This may seem paradoxical, if not irresponsible. But what is the basic purpose of research into the control of conception? It is simply to allow a man and woman to decide freely whether and when they wish to bear children. Very few people advocate compulsory contraception. So if people are to be persuaded voluntarily to limit the size of their families surely they should be allowed help where nature has apparently denied them any choice in the matter? In fact, preventing conception and promoting it are two aspects of the same problem. This is emphasized by the fact that advice on fertility and infertility is often given in the same clinic. For if an unwanted child can weaken the relationship between a man and a woman so, too, can the inability to conceive.

Infertility is a problem that concerns a great many people. Estimates vary and the figures certainly differ from country to country and group to group, but roughly out of every 100 couples who are using no form of contraception about 65 will conceive within six months, another 20 within a year, and five more by the end of a further year. But about 10 couples will fail altogether in their attempts to start the family they desire. In addition, it is reckoned that some 20 per cent of couples fail to conceive as many children as they want. This inevitably puts a strain on many marriages. A relationship can become particularly bitter if one partner starts to blame the other—whether openly or secretly—for their failure to conceive.

The fact is that no one is 'to blame' for the inability to bear children. It is usually an accident of nature that neither partner can help and so neither partner should feel guilty about it. Furthermore, in most cases the man and the woman both contribute to the failure to conceive. For it takes two to

This papyrus painting shows the Egyptian deities in the act of creating mankind.

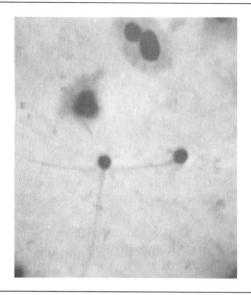
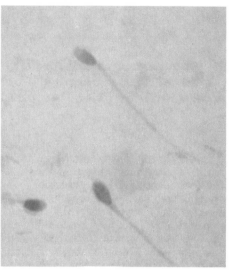

*A doctor investigating subfertility will, before reaching any conclusions, want to carry out an analysis of fresh semen from the man. The sample, delivered to the doctor within two hours of ejaculation, is tested in various ways, for it will tell him a great deal. If a large proportion of the sperm are abnormal in appearance **right** rather than normal headed **far right**, the chances of them fertilizing the woman's*

beget children and, considering the complexity of the process of conception, the surprising thing is that most women become pregnant as easily as they do.

First, the man must produce enough healthy, fertile sperm and the woman must produce healthy, fertile ova (eggs). The couple must have intercourse at the right time and under the right conditions. The sperm must be deposited correctly within the woman during intercourse. The conditions within the woman's reproductive system must allow the sperm to reach the egg and the sperm must be capable of making the journey. The egg itself, once fertilized, must be able to reach the womb, become implanted in its wall, and grow into a healthy baby.

Failure can occur at any one of these stages, but rarely does this result in complete inability to conceive. For fertility is not a black-and-white subject; people do not fall simply into fertile or sterile categories. There are a large number of intermediate stages and this is why doctors prefer to talk of *subfertility* rather than *infertility*. A couple who are both highly fertile will usually conceive very quickly and, if they want to, frequently. If only one partner is highly fertile then the chances of conception are lower but still relatively high. If both are subfertile then there will probably be considerable delay before they start a family. Only very occasionally can one or both partners be said to be completely infertile. For this reason help from a subfertility clinic is often successful in aiding a childless couple.

About half of those couples who seek and accept the advice of a clinic succeed in conceiving. This may require considerable determination by both partners, involving interviews, medical examinations, and extensive tests. The doctor may then be able to give the couple advice on the frequency, timing, and positions of intercourse to give the best chance of conception. He may suggest minor surgery for the husband, the wife, or both. He may conclude that artificial insemination—either by the husband or by a donor—is the answer. Or, in a few cases, he may tell the couple that adoption

is the best course for them to take. Whatever the treatment it is liable to take months rather than weeks or days—although in a few cases a simple piece of advice may be enough. Not surprisingly, many couples drop out and decide to 'leave it to nature'. On average, however, only one in eight of these will succeed in conceiving.

It should again be emphasized that subfertility is a problem for both sexes. Traditionally in a childless marriage it is the wife who is considered barren, and even today it is usually she who first approaches her doctor or a clinic. Indeed, many wives will plead with the doctor not to involve their husbands. Yet in well over half of all subfertile marriages, whether or not his wife contributes to the problem, the cause of it is found to involve the husband. The misunderstanding arises because both husbands and wives confuse infertility with impotence. Many husbands asked to attend a clinic for fertility tests feel their virility is being questioned.

This, of course, is complete nonsense. A man with an immense sexual appetite may be subfertile because the semen he ejaculates when he has an orgasm contains very few sperm. However, a man with a low sex drive may, on the few occasions he has intercourse, produce highly fertile sperm. For this reason a medical examination of both partners, and a semen test, is the routine first stage in any subfertility investigation.

There are two kinds of semen test and doctors vary in their preference or order of conducting them. The usual first stage is known as the *postcoital test*.

The man's wife is asked to attend the clinic or surgery one morning about halfway through her menstrual cycle (that is, about 14 days after the start of her last period), having had sexual intercourse with her husband some time during the previous night. She is told not to douche or bathe before attending. Using a pipette (a small pipe) or a syringe, the doctor will remove samples of fluid from various parts of her vagina and cervix (the entrance to the womb). Examination of these under a microscope will tell him a great deal about both partners.

It will, for example, show if any and how many sperm have reached the entrance to the womb, the first stage on their marathon journey to fertilize the woman's egg. If there are sperm present the doctor will estimate how many of them are moving and how many are abnormal in appearance. Abnormal and immobile sperm are both possible causes of subfertility. But before coming to any conclusions the doctor will probably want to carry out an analysis of fresh semen from the husband.

This involves the husband collecting a sample of semen in a clean glass or plastic jar. He cannot use a condom to catch the semen, since chemicals in the rubber may harm the sperm. The man can either masturbate to produce the sample or have intercourse with his wife and withdraw as he reaches his climax. The Catholic church forbids both masturbation and withdrawal, but allows the use of a condom washed clean of its spermicide and pricked with a pin so that some semen can escape into the woman's vagina. Enough normally remains in the condom for the doctor's later examination, although a sample produced into a jar is much better. However it is obtained the sample should be produced after three days' sexual abstinence and delivered to the doctor within two hours.

The sample will then be tested in various ways. A technician will measure its total volume, the number of sperm per millilitre, and the proportion of immobile or deformed sperm. Doctors believe that the quality of the sperm is more important than the quantity but, in any case, the clinic will want to examine several samples over a period of time before reaching any conclusions. The value of this test is that it offers clues which, combined with others from the man and woman, may show where the reason for their failure to conceive lies.

Suppose, for example, that the postcoital test shows no sperm in the upper part of the woman's vagina, although seminal analysis shows that the man is producing healthy sperm. The doctor may suspect that the couple's technique in love-making is at fault. His routine medical examination may actually have already shown this. About one

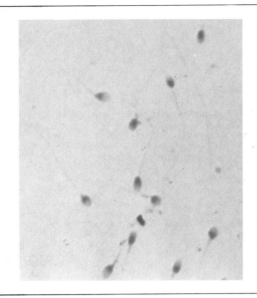

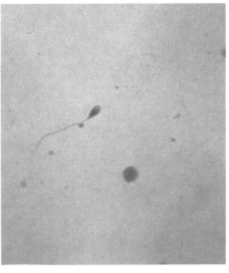

*egg are reduced. The technician testing the sample will also estimate how many sperm are moving, as immobile sperm can cause subfertility too. He will then measure the number of sperm per millilitre to see whether there is a normal number **far left** or noticeably less **left**. The results of these tests can reveal the reason for a couple's inability to conceive, and indicate the best form of treatment.*

in every 20 women attending subfertility clinics is found to be a virgin. Questioning by the doctor may reveal that the woman has great fear of intercourse and that she suffers from a vaginal spasm every time her husband tries to have sexual intercourse with her, with the result that he never manages to enter her.

Amazing as it may seem some wives—and their husbands, too—do not even realize that they are virgins. A doctor in one clinic discovered that a couple had practised anal intercourse for the entire 12 years of their marriage without realizing that this was the cause of their failure to conceive. Another woman complained that her husband found it difficult to penetrate; he had, in fact, been attempting to enter her urethra (urinary passage) instead of her vagina.

For subfertile couples the best position for intercourse is for the woman to be on her back and the man above. She should hold her legs up round her husband's hips, and keep her legs up for some time after her husband withdraws—up to 20 minutes if possible—to keep as much semen as possible within her vagina and give it the greatest chance of penetrating the cervix. In those cases where the woman's womb is at an abnormal angle—a fact that would be discovered during the doctor's examination —the couple may be advised to have intercourse with the woman face down, and for her to remain lying face down afterwards for a little while.

Couples whose love-making technique is correct may fail to start a family because they do not have sexual intercourse at the most fertile time of the woman's cycle. In a woman who has a reasonably regular 28-day cycle this is usually about 14 days after the start of a menstrual period, but it can vary substantially. The doctor may advise the woman to keep a temperature chart in order to find out when her egg is released, for this is the most fertile time of her cycle. To do this she takes her temperature immediately after she wakes up each morning, before getting out of bed. Within a day or two *after* ovulation, the temperature rises by an average of $\frac{3}{4}$°F, and stays raised until the next menstrual period begins.

Some couples still fail to conceive, though the woman keeps such a chart, because they have intercourse just once on the day of apparent ovulation. Other couples have intercourse as frequently as possible in the hope of conceiving, but this does not guarantee conception either. On the contrary, it can quickly deplete the husband's reservoir of sperm and thus lessen the amount of sperm in each ejaculation. The best chance of conception results from an in-between rate of love-making, every two days or so during the week of ovulation. Then it is quite likely that a sperm will be ready to fertilize an egg as soon as one is produced by the woman's ovary. Orthodox Jews, who must not have intercourse until seven days after menstruation, may encounter a problem if the woman's cycle is unusually short, because she may be ovulating within the period of abstinence. If the rabbi will not waive the abstinence rule, the doctor may use hormones to delay ovulation. Also, for conception to take place, the man's semen should wet the entrance to the womb as it is ejaculated. The normal instinct is for the man to thrust his penis deeply into the vagina as he reaches his climax and this usually ensures wetting the cervix. But if a couple have been using withdrawal as a method of contraception the husband may find it difficult to break this habit. He may ejaculate while only partially penetrating the vagina—either through ejaculating prematurely or because lack of lubrication makes full penetration difficult. Clearly, too, complete or partial impotence—which almost always has psychological causes— also makes it difficult to conceive normally. In all these cases medical advice or psychotherapy may solve the problem, but artificial insemination with the husband's semen (AIH)—either at a clinic or by the couple themselves at home—may be used to bring about conception.

Disorders can also occur in the testes themselves, affecting the production of sperm. For example, an injury, or excessive exposure to radiation, can damage the testes. Among the more serious disorders are mumps after puberty, which can infect the testes and cause sterility, and late descent

of the testes. The testes normally descend from within the abdomen to their normal position in the scrotum before or soon after birth, but if this is delayed until after puberty total sterility will result. Even if the testes descend after the age of six they may be unable to produce as many sperm as they should. The reason for this is that only in the lower temperature outside the body cavity can the testes fully develop, and late descent is evidenced by the testes being unusually small and soft.

Further, fully-developed testes must remain a few degrees below the normal body temperature if they are to maintain full sperm production. A high fever— from malaria, for example—can raise their temperature enough to cause temporary subfertility. Tight trousers or jockey-type underwear, which hold the testes close to the body, may possibly reduce the number of sperm produced, and this may show up in a seminal analysis. Wearing looser underwear will probably increase the sperm count, but a Scotsman's kilt is claimed to be the best garment for promoting the testes' sperm production.

Sometimes swollen veins surround the testes in a warm blanket of blood. This is known as a *varicocele*, a clinical disorder which raises the temperature of the testes. The swelling can be corrected by simple surgery and in suitable cases there is an 80 per cent chance that fertility will be restored. This is, in fact, the only instance of male subfertility where surgery has a really good chance of correcting it.

There are many things that can make a man subfertile, and only a full investigation at a clinic can discover whether any of these exist in a particular person. However, many men are shocked at the suggestion that they perhaps contribute to their failure to conceive. In fact, one subfertility clinic worker has estimated that one in three men refuse to attend for tests, some even pretending to their wives that they have been to the clinic when they have not. It is a great pity that prejudice and misunderstanding should stand in the way of success in bringing happiness to a childless marriage.

MICHAEL WRIGHT

81

Misconceptions about sex

'Can I get pregnant from kissing?' a young girl might ask innocently. But, frequently, adults also harbour such misconceptions. Is there any truth in today's sexual myths?

Sex and reproduction—the very concepts are shrouded in layers of myth and superstition. In the days when the survival of a community depended on the availability of enough willing hands for hunting, farming, or simply building shelter, the gift of new life must have seemed truly supernatural.

Fertility was a blessing, barrenness a curse. The very nature of the sexual act—with its intense feelings, both physical and emotional, and the way in which it was sometimes followed after nine months by the birth of a new being—set it quite apart from other human activity. In few actions is the separation of cause and effect so great and yet so important. It is no wonder that primitive man gave pride of place to his gods of fertility.

And once reproduction had been raised to the level of the supernatural, the path was wide open for strange ideas and misunderstood coincidences to become established beliefs—and from there to be accepted as facts. Thus a whole body of myths and misconceptions grew up around sex. Many of them are bizarre-sounding to modern sophisticates, but many are still widely believed. For it is not only primitive tribal religions that are preoccupied with fertility. The whole Judaeo-Christian tradition behind Western civilization has a similar interest.

Added to this is the fact that the process of reproduction is a 'taboo' subject —thanks again largely to the Judaeo-Christian background. There has always been a sense of shame, or modesty, in the Western world with regard to sex. Education and the new, franker atmosphere are sweeping away some of the cobwebs of false beliefs, but, for many people, sex is still something they prefer not to talk about, except possibly in euphemisms or dirty jokes. In such a secretive atmosphere facts have little chance against hearsay and fantasy. Indeed, so pervasive was this atmosphere of secrecy surrounding reproduction, that no one seriously tried to uncover many of the 'facts' about sex until the middle of the twentieth century.

Other factors have, of course, played a part in generating sexual legends. The use of sex appeal in modern advertising and 'pop' culture has helped to create a false picture of successful sexual behaviour. At the root of some myths lies a fear of pregnancy and childbirth, often nurtured by mothers whose own experiences date back to a time when childbirth was a far more hazardous occurrence than it is today. Prejudice and simple sexual rivalries and jealousies are also sometimes involved. But probably the greatest blame lies in simple ignorance, which is particularly dangerous when educators—especially parents and teachers—are involved.

Ignorance can only be corrected by straightforward, clearly presented truth, but even so there are pitfalls because many misconceptions about sex have just a small germ of truth in them. One example lies in the various versions of the 'safe period' theory which forms the basis of the rhythm method of family planning. The facts are that most women reach a peak of fertility about 14 days before the start of their next menstrual period. It would seem to follow then that most women are unlikely to become pregnant if they have sexual relations immediately before, during, or immediately after their menstrual period.

However, the truth is that, quite apart from the problems arising from irregular periods, and the impossibility of knowing in advance when the next menstruation will start, there are no absolute fertile and safe periods. A woman is *unlikely* to conceive during a menstrual period, but it is not impossible. She might become pregnant at literally any time in the month. In fact, some women are believed to sometimes release an extra ovum (egg) late in the cycle, just before their period starts. If fertilized, this could lead to pregnancy. Thus, although the 'safe period' may be a period of negligible fertility, it is a misconception to talk about the 'impossibility' of impregnation at a particular time of the month.

A similar misleading idea concerns the possibility of conception while a mother is breast-feeding her child. The fact in this instance is that a woman is generally sterile for about six weeks after childbirth and the first ovulation (release of an egg) is generally delayed the longer she breast-feeds. Again, there is no absolute protection, but the act of suckling (rather than lactation or milk-production) does seem to alter the woman's internal hormonal

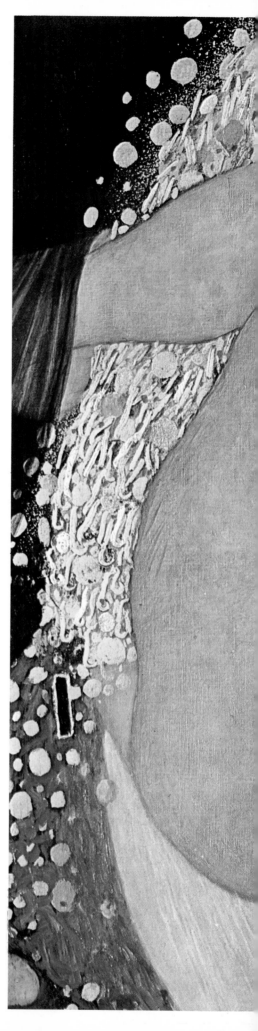

According to the Greek myth, Danae, imprisoned in a tower, was impregnated by Zeus in the form of a shower of gold. Such early myths reveal a superstitious awe and fear of sex.

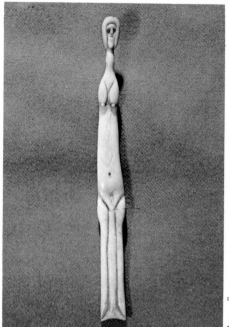
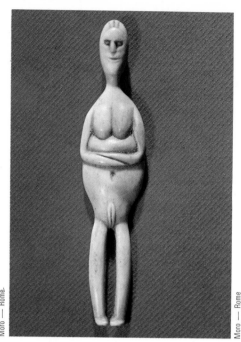

Michael Holford

Moro — Rome.

Moro — Rome

balance and tends to prevent ovulation and menstruation. But, as with the 'safe period' theory, there is no certainty in this practice. Once menstruation has begun again, the woman should certainly take other contraceptive precautions. Even so, the first ovulation following childbirth may take place before the first menstruation. As a result, the woman may become pregnant again without any warning.

There are all sorts of false beliefs about the situations in which a woman can, or cannot, become pregnant. One of the commonest notions is that conception will occur *only* if the woman has an orgasm. This is complete nonsense, and, in fact, she can conceive even if the *man* has no orgasm, for the fluid seeping from the penis before ejaculation often contains a few sperm. But, again, there is a logical reason for such a belief to arise. Some evidence does exist showing that if a woman does have an orgasm—particularly if she has not had intercourse for some time —this may cause the release of an egg even if it is not the normal time for her ovulation. Thus an orgasm may, in some cases, encourage conception. But any strong emotional stimulus may have the same effect—including having sexual relations for the first time. So another common idea— that a woman cannot conceive the first time she has intercourse—is also false.

There is an opposite belief, too—that promiscuous women and prostitutes are less likely to become pregnant than women with normal sex-lives. As a Scandinavian saying puts it, 'No grass grows where many people tread.' The most likely explanation for this observation is, of course, that promiscuous women and prostitutes take careful contraceptive precautions. And, secondly, they are more likely to catch a venereal disease, and VD is a common cause of infertility. But there is an intriguing possibility that, once again, the belief has an element of fact. Experiments with mice have shown that if newly-pregnant females mate with new partners, their first

pregnancies mysteriously disappear, and they conceive again by their new mates. Women are not mice, of course, but there is just a chance that the same thing might happen. Implantation of a fertilized egg in the womb is, after all, a chancy occurrence, and little is known about possible influences on it.

Still other beliefs are much more clearly false—for example, that a girl can become pregnant through kissing. Such a notion is simply the result of inadequate sex education, as is the idea that pregnancy can result from swallowing semen. There is, of course, only one way of becoming pregnant. Sperm must enter the vagina, travel through the woman's reproductive tract, and fertilize one of her eggs, which must then become implanted in the womb.

For this to occur, the man's semen does not necessarily have to be deposited within the vagina. If he ejaculates outside the vagina, but close to its entrance (following withdrawal or 'heavy petting'), there is a chance of impregnation. This can happen if the girl's hymen is intact, for even virgins have an opening in the hymen. However, it is virtually impossible to become pregnant from, for example, semen on a lavatory seat.

On the other hand, to believe that pregnancy cannot result if the couple have intercourse standing up, or if the woman urinates or sneezes afterwards is simply to court disaster. Nor do vaginal deodorants have any contraceptive effect, as some women may think. And the idea that men have a menopause, like women, after which they are sterile, is completely false. Many men have fathered children when well into their 80s.

If the normal act of love-making inspires so many misconceptions, it is not surprising that unusual or 'abnormal' intercourse should also do so. Perhaps as a result of lingering Victorian ideas, many people still consider anything other than quick, straightforward sexual intercourse —in the dark, with the woman on her back and the man above her—to be 'perverted'.

Amulets believed to affect fertility have been carried by women for centuries. **Above left** *This Cycladic stone fertility figure dates to pre-Greek times.* **Centre** *These medieval amulets, made of bone, protected the owner's chastity and* **right** *promoted fertility.*

Sex educators and marriage guidance counsellors have tried for years to convey the message that *anything* a couple may do to increase the pleasure of their sex life, so long as it is acceptable to both partners, is perfectly natural and normal. Yet still, people believe that oral sex is wrong, or that it indicates homosexual tendencies; that only perverts want to make love in daylight, in the open air, in the bath, or in unusual positions; or even that any pleasure gained from seeing the other partner nude is disgusting.

Perhaps the most ridiculous belief of this type is that a child conceived in a rear-entry intercourse position will grow up to be a homosexual. It probably arises from associating rear-entry intercourse with anal intercourse. They are, of course, quite different, and, in any case, it is a myth that all male homosexuals indulge in anal intercourse. Many never do so and most do so only infrequently.

Ignoring the strong evidence that homosexuality is far more a result of environment and upbringing than of heredity, the position of intercourse at the time of conception can have no conceivable effect on a child's characteristics. The inherited traits—including physical appearance and sex—are determined in the instant of fertilization, when sperm penetrates egg. The child's characteristics depend on which sperm wins the race for fertilization and that is a matter of chance. Any one of the 200 million or so sperm in a single ejaculation could be the winner and nothing the couple do while having intercourse can influence this.

In the same way, nothing the mother does during pregnancy can influence the sex of her child in any way. Once it is conceived its sex is decided.

A closely related and equally false but widespread belief is that the unborn child can be 'marked' if something frightens or shocks its mother. In particular, many people believe that the child will have a birthmark in the shape of whatever caused the shock. Often a parent of a child with a strange birthmark will later 'remember' the incident that 'caused' it. Certainly the mother's health, diet, smoking habits, and so on can influence her child's development, but in a more general way—its birth weight may be affected, for example. Some diseases (such as German measles) can cause deformities, but there is no truth whatsoever in the birthmark theory.

There is one aspect of heredity, however, in which the result of the 'sperm race' is not the only important factor and where a well-known, old wives' tale does have some basis. It has long been known that a higher proportion of male infants are born after a war. It happened after both world wars, and the theory is that it is Nature's way of compensating for her losses on the battlefield. Scientists are distrustful of attributing things to Nature, however. A more logical explanation seems to be that fewer male children die before birth during and after wartime.

It is a known fact that many more males than females are always conceived—that is, at the stage of sperm fertilizing egg. But more male than female embryos fail to implant themselves in the womb and more males, again, are aborted or stillborn.

This immense stone phallus appears on the Dionysian Sanctuary at Delos, where festivals once celebrated the mysteries of reproduction.

As a result the number of male babies born alive is normally only slightly greater than the number of females. Something in wartime conditions seems to upset this natural balancing act. One plausible idea is that, in wartime, people tend to marry young, and young mothers lose fewer children before birth. Thus fewer boy babies are lost. There are other suggestions, all having a more logical basis than the idea of a mystical and benificent act of Nature.

Of all the myths and misconceptions surrounding sex, perhaps the most alarming are those concerned with sexual health. Venereal diseases, in particular, are the focus of various quite dangerous false notions. It is understandable, of course, since VD is even more unmentionable than sex itself. But one result of this has been the rapid spread of serious disease through simple ignorance.

VD is most frequently spread by direct contact with the sex organs of a diseased person, particularly during sexual intercourse. Anything that reduces contact lessens the chances of infection, of course, and the original sheaths or condoms used as long ago as Roman times were originated to prevent infection as well as conception. But to believe that it is impossible to catch a venereal disease if the man wears a condom is a dangerous illusion.

Some other curious ideas have grown up around this subject. There is a belief, for example, that if a man has intercourse with a virgin, he will rid himself of a venereal infection. Certainly, he will 'give away' the infection, for the girl will probably contract it, but this will not alleviate the man's own condition—any more than giving someone else a cold cures one's own cold. Also, it must be stressed that vaginal deodorants give no protection against VD, any more than they offer contraceptive protection. On the other hand, the old horror story told to countless children that it is possible to catch VD from lavatory seats is probably exaggerated, if not actually false. As already mentioned, the vast majority of VD cases are contracted during sexual intercourse.

Other health aspects that give rise to sexual misconceptions concern supposed 'dangerous times' or situations for sexual intercourse. Many people believe, for example, that sex during a woman's menstrual period is harmful. This idea dates back thousands of years. The Romans believed it, and orthodox Jews are still not permitted to have sexual relations for several days after menstruation. In fact, no harm can come of it. The menstrual flow itself is quite harmless, and the woman can suffer no damage from love-making at this time. The only governing factor is the couple's own desires.

Nor is intercourse usually harmful during pregnancy, as many people suppose. Couples should obviously be careful not to put too much pressure on the woman's body and not to thrust the man's penis too deeply into the vagina. And they should stop if the woman feels pain, or if spotting or bleeding occurs. Finally, it should be remembered that if a woman has an intense orgasm in the last few weeks before the expected date of delivery, labour itself may begin. Otherwise, sex during pregnancy is probably very good for the couple's relationship during this rather long period. However, these generalizations do not apply to all women—particularly those prone to miscarriage—and the advice of the woman's own doctor should always be followed.

One other situation in which a doctor's advice is vital occurs when either the man or the woman has heart trouble. 'Coital coronaries' are something of a joke, but they are not, in fact, common. Nevertheless, someone with a weak heart should always get expert advice on when and how frequently they may have sex. The great danger is not from over-exertion, but from heightened blood-pressure and heart-rate. As he or she approaches orgasm, even a passive partner's heart-rate and blood-pressure reach double their normal levels. On the other hand, the anxiety and frustration that may arise if a heart patient is denied all sexual activity may be even more dangerous. It is a question that both partners should discuss openly with a doctor.

As can be seen there is hardly any aspect of sex where misconceptions, half-truths, and outright myths have not left their mark. The only antidote is open, frank, and truthful education. It has worked wonders in the field of general health—there are very few people today who believe that tuberculosis is caused by 'foule aires', for example. Perhaps the greatest benefit that the 'permissive' age can bring is that of sweeping away the cobwebs of sexual misconceptions.

MICHAEL WRIGHT

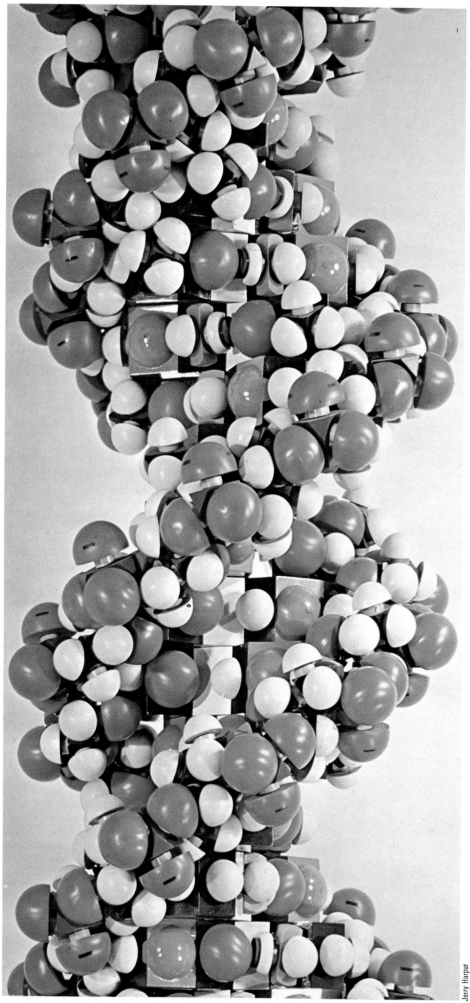

The physiology of heredity

What are the mechanisms in the body that control heredity? By finding the answer to this scientists hope to enable man to control the traits he passes on to his progeny. This article discusses what is now known about the workings of man's genetic structures.

One of the most obvious features of family life, and one which is always just a bit surprising, is that children when they are born all tend to look alike; but as they grow older they develop a remarkable resemblance to their parents. In primitive societies and even more so in the 'sophisticated' Western world, after a birth the relations play the game of 'child-spotting'. 'Oh,' they exclaim, 'he has his mother's eyes, but the chin is definitely his father's, and there's a lot of his grandmother's side in him!' So fully is this resemblance to one's forebears appreciated that when a woman gives birth to a child who looks neither like her husband nor herself the occasional whispered remark is likely to be made about her trip to Boulogne or about the friendly disposition of the new milkman.

Almost as obvious as this immediately physical inheritance from one's parents is the fact that particular aptitudes tend to run in families. For four generations the family that produced Johann Sebastian Bach was at the forefront of Western music. At least a dozen distinguished composers shared this same surname. In England, in the century and a half which began in 1830, the Darwin family produced no less than ten Fellows of the Royal Society —physicians, astronomers, and engineers, as well as Charles Darwin himself, the founder of the modern theory of evolution.

When we talk about heredity we are, therefore, describing something that everyone knows about and something which has been accepted for centuries as an unalterable feature of life. As with any aspect of our lives which appears so very obvious, it is not unusual to find that it took a long

DNA has been called the 'thread of life' because it is the substance which carries man's genetic instructions. The model shows its double helical structure.

Jerry Harpur

time before anyone started to question exactly *why* this should be so. Why, for example, should tall parents tend to have tall children? Indeed, why even should white parents have white children rather than black or yellow ones? And there are more subtle questions to be answered, such as why straight-haired parents rarely have curly-haired children; not to mention the problem of why a child, though resembling its parents very closely, is never actually *identical* to them.

Although the scientific study of heredity took a long time to initiate, once it did begin its progress was remarkably rapid. Slightly more than a century separates the original, widely known genetic experiments of Gregor Mendel in his monastery garden in Moravia from the Nobel prize-winning work of Watson and Crick in Cambridge on the 'double helix' structure of the DNA molecule—work which is the key to the genetics, not only of man, but also of most living things. Indeed, because Mendel's original work generated almost no interest in his own lifetime and was only rediscovered in the first decade of this century, it is fair to say that the study of genetics is really only as old as the successful development of aeronautics. It has progressed at approximately the same speed and if we consider its importance to our everyday lives, we can also say that its results have been at least as momentous.

Because of what we know about genetics, we can explain why roughly half of the babies in the world are born male and half female. We can diagnose certain diseases which have a genetic basis and, to some extent, we can treat them. We can advise a couple who are about to marry whether, on the basis of their genetic histories, it would be wise for them to produce children. And we can even look forward to a day when, perhaps, we will be able to alter our genetic make-up and so influence directly (and one hopes for the better) the physical characteristics of our children and grandchildren.

Textbooks on genetics tend to start at the beginning. They explain why a tall sweet pea crossed with a short one always produces tall offspring—a finding which Mendel himself discovered. However, it is much more relevant to start at the end and to describe the results of half a century's research work, rather than the painstaking investigations that led to those results. And the result that is of most crucial importance is that any individual possesses the characteristics that he does simply because of his complement of hereditary factors.

The human body is made up of cells— billions of them in the average adult—and each of these cells consists of two distinct parts. The majority of the cell is a grey featureless fluid-like substance known as the *cytoplasm*. (The very fact that it is a semi-fluid jelly helps to remind us that 80 per cent of our bodies is composed of water.) But within this rather featureless jelly there are a number of more organized structures of which the most important from the point of view of future generations is the cell *nucleus*. The body grows from its conception to its maturity because of two cellular processes. Obviously, the cells themselves grow and, rather more importantly, they also divide. Cell division is a process which has now been studied in a large number of different animals and plants. Using a special type of microscope and a time-lapse camera, it is possible to photograph cell divisions as they occur inside a living organism. It has been found that almost invariably the nucleus divides first and the cytoplasm divides after it. A cell with only one nucleus becomes, for a brief period, a cell with two, and then, shortly afterwards, two quite independent cells are produced.

Many years of detailed observation have shown that it is the behaviour of the nucleus which is of primary importance in the process of cell division. Just before the cell divides it is possible to see within the nucleus a whole collection of thin, thread-like structures which, simply because they can be stained with particular dyes, are known as 'coloured bodies' or *chromosomes*. A very careful examination will show that the chromosomes are actually paired. The number of pairs is constant for almost every cell in the body, but it varies from one species to another. In man there are now known to be 46 chromosomes although the older books stated quite clearly that there were 48—a reflection on how difficult it was until recently to observe them with complete accuracy. Normally, before a cell divides each one of these chromosome pairs produces another identical to itself. The pairs then migrate in opposite directions and each 'daughter cell' ends up with exactly the same number of chromosomes as the parent cell which gave rise to it.

But there is an exception—one which is vital to any understanding of human heredity. When special cells in the body divide to produce the gametes (either the sperm or the egg) only *one* of each chromosome pair enters the gametic cell. The cells which together produce the future generation, therefore, contain only *half* the chromosomes of the adult organism. Now the study of chromosomes is important for one particular reason. Chromosomes carry the hereditary factors or *genes* which are responsible for every single characteristic that the offspring will possess. For example, hair colour, eye colour, and the presence or absence of diseases such as haemophilia and certain types of

The Darwin family has a long, illustrious heritage. The founding fathers of the family tree, Josiah Wedgwood (notable English potter) and Erasmus Darwin (physiologist and poet), made important contributions in their fields. Their grandson, Charles Robert Darwin, is perhaps the best known of the family—famous for his theories of evolution and natural selection.

He had 10 children, and four of his five sons were prominent scientists: G. Howard, astronomer, mathematician; Francis, botanist; Leonard, eugenist, engineer; and Horace, civil engineer. Although it is difficult to prove that such talent is due solely to genetic inheritance, there is little doubt that it is at least partially responsible.

Josiah Wedgwood (1730-1795)

Susannah Wedgwood (1765-1817)

Emma Wedgwood (1808-1896)

Charles Robert Darwin (1809-1882)

Sir George F.R.S. (1845-1912)

Elizabeth (1847-1926)

Sir Francis F.R.S. (1848-1925)

Erasmus Darwin (1731-1802)

Robert Waring Darwin (1766-1848)

Major Leonard (1850-1943)

Sir Horace F.R.S. (1851-1928)

anaemia are controlled by either one or a small number of hereditary factors. More complex characteristics like height, weight, rate of growth, and the time of the onset of puberty are controlled by the interaction of larger numbers of genes. Indeed, a detailed understanding of exactly how they are controlled is something that we have only recently started to gain. We are, nonetheless, sure that every physical characteristic that an individual displays has some underlying genetic basis. In a sense, therefore, we are all the products of our genetic make-up.

And just what are these genes upon which we are all so dependent; what, for example, do they look like? It is perhaps most convenient to think of each chromosome as a thread upon which the individual genes are strung, rather like a row of beads. Sometimes the thread can be broken (by X-rays or chemical treatment for example) and the results for the next generation can then be disastrous. But, although this analogy is convenient it does not really answer the question. Even when viewed through the most highly-powered microscope, genes do not appear as a series of tiny beads, each one responsible for a particular factor in our make-up.

The prize-winning work on the 'genetic code' has shown that a part of each chromosome is made up of a substance called deoxyribonucleic acid or DNA. It is this substance which is arranged in the famous and much publicized 'double helix' inside the cell nucleus. DNA is itself made up of a number of different chemical components, a group of which are known as purine and pyrimidine bases. The arrangement of a number of these bases constitutes a gene. In other words, hair colour, eye colour, and any other of the physical characteristics possessed by anyone on earth depends ultimately upon the arrangement of a number of very small chemical molecules within the chromosomes of their cells.

Any new individual ultimately results from the fusion of a sperm and an egg; conception involves the bringing together of genetic material from both parents. We would, therefore, expect a child to resemble both of its parents to some degree, for it has the characteristics possessed by both of them. But every one of us has his own unique genetic make-up, and so (with the exception of identical twins of a particular type) every one of us is physically unique. Some biologists would even suggest that the whole purpose of sexual intercourse is to bring together the father's genes in the sperm with those of the mother which are contained in the egg. But in the process the genes get mixed up. There are many millions of possible genetic combinations, and so there will be many millions of unique human beings produced as a consequence of our sexual reproduction.

The factor which decides the sex of our children is deceptively simple; it is merely the possession of a particular chromosome. Of the 23 pairs of chromosomes found in human beings, the members of 22 of the pairs are always identical to each other.

The ability to control hereditary traits might alleviate some crippling disabilities. Haemophilia is a blood disease in which coagulation fails to occur, resulting in excessive bleeding. Its distinctive feature is that it is transmitted by female 'carriers' to some of their offspring. The women are not normally 'bleeders' and the male 'bleeders' do not transmit the disease directly to their children. One of the most famous families in history to have suffered from haemophilia centred on 2 Queen Victoria, who appears to have inherited the defective gene from 1 her father, the Duke of Kent. 3 Her son Leopold, a victim, died at 31 from a brain haemorrhage. 4 Beatrice passed the disease to the Spanish royal family, and 5 Alice to 7 her daughter Alexandra who married 6 Tsar Nicholas II of Russia. Their son 8 Tsarevitch Alexis suffered from the disease.

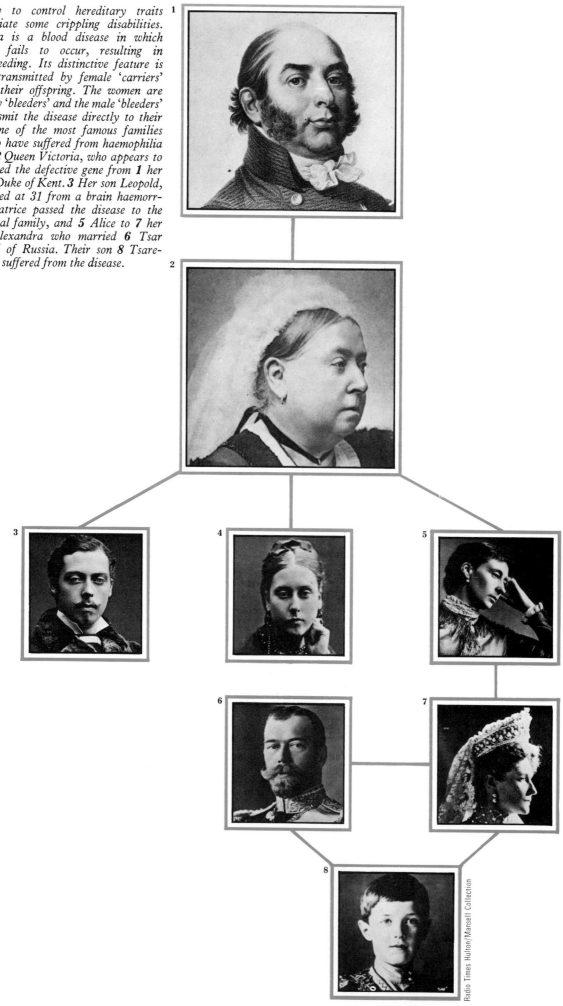

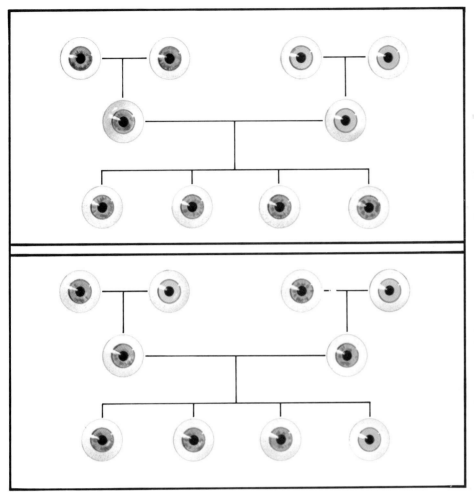

What determines the colour of one's eyes?
Top *The gene for brown eyes is dominant to that for blue eyes, so a brown-eyed and a blue-eyed couple (whose own parents were of pure colour strains) will almost always have brown-eyed children.* ***Above*** *These brown-eyed children will carry a recessive gene for blue eyes, however, and when they themselves have children this recessive blue trait may appear once again.*

They are called the *autosomes* and they control every physical characteristic with the exception of the sex of the individual and those features which depend directly upon his or her sex—sexual anatomy, sex hormones, and so on. In men, however, the chromosomes of pair number 23 are not identical to each other. One is larger than the other and is known as the X chromosome. The smaller one of the pair is known as chromosome Y. But in women the two are always identical. They are both chromosomes of the type X. We now know that it is the possession of a Y chromosome that induces the development of the embryo in the direction of 'maleness'. Indeed, this chromosome has a very powerful masculinizing effect. Occasionally, we find individuals who have not one or two X chromosomes but as many as three or four; and yet the possession of a single Y chromosome may still give them a masculine appearance, although they are never fertile.

When the cells which produce an egg divide and two egg cells are formed each will receive half of the chromosomes from the parent cell. Since the sex chromosomes (as the members of pair number 23 are called) are both of type X in the original cell, every egg cell must contain such a chromosome. All eggs, therefore, have 22 autosomes plus one X chromosome. But when sperms are formed from their sperm-producing cells in the testes, two possible cell types can be produced. When the X and Y members of the sex chromosome pair part company, one will go to one sperm and one to another. Since this occurs completely at random there should be as many X as Y sperms.

A sperm containing an X chromosome is said to be female-directing, but one containing a Y will produce maleness. During fertilization, the union of an X sperm with an X carrying egg will produce a female embryo. However, a Y sperm, if it fertilizes an egg, will result in an embryo having the genetic make-up of 22 autosomes plus an X and a Y chromosome. In other words, the embryo will be male. Fertilization again is random and so there should be, on the average, as many males as females produced at conception.

Over the last 20 years many scientists have been attracted by the idea of separating artificially the X and Y sperms in any sample of semen. The economic advantages of producing, say, only female calves by artificial insemination are obvious, and some parents would like to be able to determine the sex of their children in the same way. The search has, therefore, gone on for some physical characteristic that can be used to separate the two sperm types. Attempts have been made to exploit any differences in weight or electrical charge that may distinguish them. One or two spectacular claims have been made by researchers who thought that they had succeeded. However, not one of these investigations could be repeated by other biologists and, at the moment, we are forced to admit that the artificial determination of the sex of our children still eludes us.

Even more revolutionary are current ideas about altering our genetic make-up by artificial means. After all, if our genes are no more than groups of bases in the framework of a molecule of DNA, we ought to be able to alter their nature by chemical or physical means. In other words, there ought to be scope for genetic engineering to eliminate undesirable characteristics and to substitute 'fitter' ones into the population. Leaving aside any moral problems which this might raise, the scientific problems facing the genetic engineer are enormous. Certainly, we can alter our DNA by a number of procedures. However, we do not know *how* we are altering it, and we still do not know enough about the make-up of the gene to alter it selectively. By applying the 'sledgehammer' methods that we have at present we are likely to do far more harm than good and there are distinguished geneticists who feel that this type of investigation should not be pursued. Others, however, are more hopeful. They believe that enormous as the problems are it is only a matter of time before they are solved. It may take a quarter of a century or more before we can decide whether they are right.

From what has been said, it would seem that every single characteristic in our make-up has a genetic basis. And so it has. But to make such an unqualified statement is rather a simplification of the truth. The other great factor which moulds our lives is, of course, our environment. Over the last half century great arguments have raged on this subject. One school of thought has suggested that our genes alone control our entire character, and hence both past and future. At the other extreme, some biologists and psychologists have pointed to the all important influence of the environment into which we are born. To them, our genetic make-up is an incidental factor. They argue that environment moulds personality by conditioning early reactions exhibited by the infant. It is difficult to prove such a theory, as there is no scientific control. We cannot know what a person might have been like had they matured in a different environment. And so the pendulum has swung from one fashionable theory to the other.

And where does the truth really lie? Almost certainly it is somewhere in the middle. Today, most reputable scientists would be fully prepared to recognize that the environment in which we find ourselves shapes us to a considerable degree. But it can only shape us if it has something to work upon. If 'manners maketh man', our genes have a lot to do with the formation of our manners.　CLIVE WOOD

Contraception

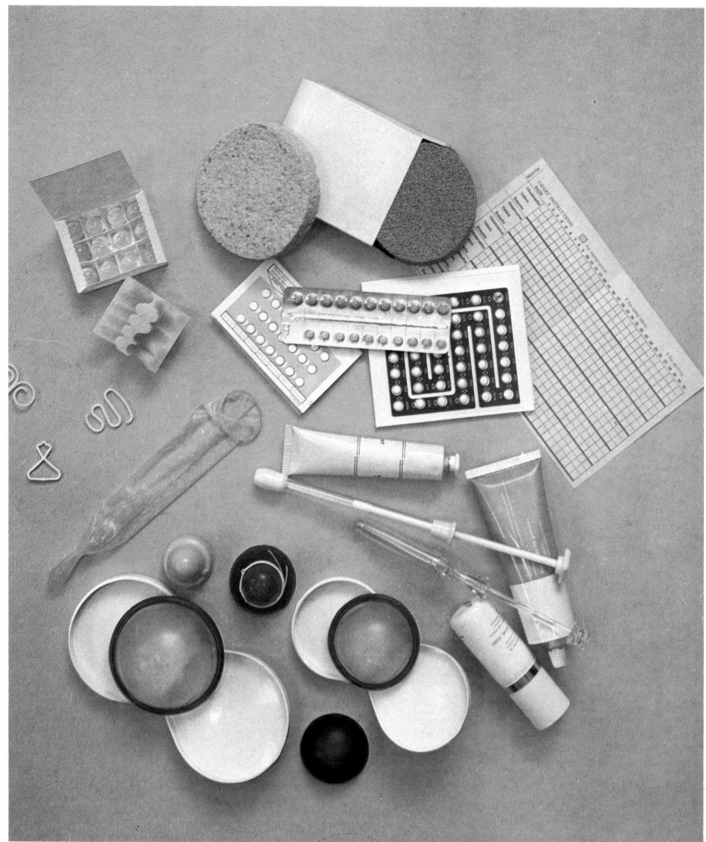

John Banks

Words change their meaning from one generation to the next and the words used by medical men are no exception. In 1929 a book appeared which proclaimed itself with the title *Practical Prevenception or the Technique of Birth Control*. Today, no one would use a term like 'prevenception'. It has become redundant, together with a host of other terms—'birth prevention', 'wise parenthood' and so on—which all basically relate to the same topic. They all refer to the means that we have at our disposal for avoiding the birth of unwanted children.

Today, when we talk about limiting the size of the family we are generally content to use one of two expressions, either *contraception* or *birth control*, and for most people the two terms mean much the same thing—the prevention of unwanted births. Usually, they imply that the birth is being prevented even before the child has been conceived.

But what about expressions like 'family planning' and 'population control'? To most people they again imply the same thing, but there is no good reason why they should. One can plan one's family without using any form of contraceptive. With enough self-control one could limit one's children simply by limiting the number of

*Today, although there are a great variety of mechanical contraceptive aids available, not all of them are effective. (**See Key below**) 1 Oral contraceptives, which must be taken under medical supervision and according to a regular schedule, are most reliable. 2 Intrauterine devices—coils, loops, rings, bows—are inserted inside the uterus by a physician. After the Pill, IUDs give the highest success rate. 3 Condoms are male contraceptives which are reasonably effective and give some protection against VD. 4 Spermicides are chemicals placed in the vagina which kill sperm. Used alone they are not very effective. 5 Diaphragms and cervical caps must be fitted by a doctor and when used with a spermicide are dependable. 6 Sponges are unreliable cervical barriers. 7 Vaginal suppositories, a form of spermicide, are not considered effective.*

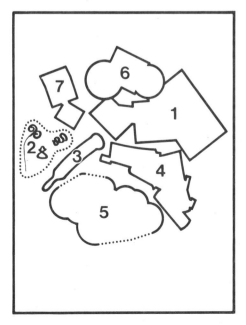

times that one had sexual intercourse. And a government could certainly limit the size of its population by, for example, forbidding all women to marry until they had reached the age of 30.

But when most people use any of these expressions, they are generally thinking about the artificial means that we have at our disposal (caps, jellies, pills, and so on) to prevent an act of conception from occurring. The development of modern contraception has put us in a position where we are capable of completely separating sexual intercourse from conception. But what are these modern contraceptive methods? What are the advantages and drawbacks of each and just how effective is each one of them in preventing the conception of unwanted children?

The effectiveness of a contraceptive is certainly one of its most important features. When a couple decides to use one method in preference to another, they want to have complete assurance that it will safeguard them from the danger of pregnancy. But this is not the only aspect which has to be considered. At least as important is the problem of acceptability. A method which gives 100 per cent protection for one couple may be largely useless for another, simply because they may find it so difficult or objectionable to use that they would rather leave it in a drawer on most occasions and simply hope that everything will be all right. Although this is a statement of the obvious, it is, nevertheless, a fact which is frequently forgotten, often with tragic results.

For every one of the common methods of birth control, many different studies on effectiveness have been published and the striking feature is that the results of these reports differ greatly from each other. But the explanation is simple. The 'best' sets of results were obtained with groups of users who were strongly motivated against pregnancy, who were intelligent enough to know how to use the method, and who were happy enough with it to use it consistently. The 'worst' results came from groups who were either indifferent or who disliked the method altogether. Consequently, they failed to use it properly and the results of such action showed up clearly in the figures.

The proof that a contraceptive has failed is the birth of a child or at least (if the mother decides upon an abortion before the child is born) the occurrence of a pregnancy. Contraceptive failures are, therefore, measured in terms of pregnancies. But the number of pregancies has to be related to something. We would expect it to be low in a convent but higher in a commune. In practice it is related to the number of months or years for which the women in a group have been experiencing regular sexual intercourse and hence running the risk of conception. The traditional way (although not the only way) of describing the effectiveness of any means of birth control is, therefore, in terms of failures (pregnancies) per 100 woman-months of exposure. And since 100 women exposed for a year are roughly

Above *Dr. Marie Stopes (1880–1958) is best known for her passionate campaigns for birth control. In 1921 she founded the United Kingdom's first birth control clinic.*

equivalent for these purposes to 50 women exposed for two years or 200 women for only six months, one can say that a method like withdrawal, for example, shows a failure rate of so many pregnancies per 100 woman-years.

Using this system it is possible for us to compare a whole range of contraceptives from the pill (showing an effectiveness of one or less) to the rhythm method, which when practised carelessly can give a failure rate of over 40. To put the failure rate in perspective, it is usually agreed that a population practising no means of birth control at all will show a pregnancy rate of 80 or rather less.

Withdrawal (next to abstinence, which few people are prepared to consider seriously) is certainly the oldest and probably the most widely practised of all forms of contraception. Although many specialists have little to say in its favour, its failure rate is surprisingly low, usually in the order of 15-20. Many men reject it because they feel that to have to withdraw the penis before ejaculation is really no form of sexual intercourse at all.

To be effective withdrawal (or 'holding back', in which the man deliberately refrains from having a climax) requires some concentration and experience—perhaps making the sexual act less spontaneous and relaxed. The woman, too, may worry about whether her partner will withdraw in time. Some couples find the method a bit messy, since the man normally ejaculates outside the vagina. But withdrawal does have the advantage of costing nothing and of requiring no medical attention or supervision. During the last century and even in this one, suggestions have been made that it causes 'pelvic congestion' and that all sorts of ills from nervousness to cancer will result from its practice. There now seems to be no good medical evidence to support such views, but the possibility certainly does exist that it may set up psychological tensions, at least among certain groups of users. As long as *both*

Int. Planned Parenthood Federation

Population control is a major concern of world governments. **Top** *In India a social worker tells villagers about family planning through the medium of a puppet dressed as a village elder, whose advice is more readily acceptable.* **Bottom** *This Singapore poster contrasts the misery of a large family with the happiness of one which is planned.*

partners are satisfied with it, there is no proof that it is harmful or damaging.

The other principal method that requires no special equipment, other than a pencil and a calendar, is the rhythm or safe period method. This depends upon the principle that the egg, once it has been shed from the ovary, is only capable of fertilization for a short time and once that time has passed, there is no possibility of conception until the next ovulation. The principle, of course, is perfectly sound, but, unfortunately, predicting the time of ovulation proves to be a very difficult task. One method is to record the length of at least the last half-dozen menstrual cycles, to assume that the next will have the same length as the average of the others, and also to assume that ovulation will occur at some fixed time before the onset of the next period. If women always showed perfectly regular menstrual cycles, this principle would be perfectly adequate. Unfortunately, however, the appearance of the next menstrual period is notoriously difficult to estimate. If a woman's periods are irregular (more than eight days' difference in the length of cycles) there may be only one or two days a month on which it is 'safe' to have intercourse. Usually it is necessary to abstain from intercourse for at least ten days in each cycle—a feature which, obviously, may discourage some people from practising it.

In a refinement of the rhythm method a thermometer is used. It is well known that after ovulation the temperature of a woman's body rises slightly (perhaps half of one degree Fahrenheit). Once this temperature rise is detected, it should then be safe for intercourse to occur. However, there are problems. Sometimes a 'false' rise is found which takes place before ovulation. In addition, a complaint as mild as a head-cold can produce a temperature variation which makes the method totally useless. Although the use of the safe period is recommended by the Vatican, leaders in the medical rather than the religious field tend to greet it with far less enthusiasm. Of the two variations, the temperature method is the more effective —14 to 20 per 100 woman-years. The calendar method has almost double the failure rate.

Withdrawal and the rhythm method do not involve the use of any special equipment. But the commonly used contraceptive techniques do and in general, as a result of the equipment, they produce better results.

By far the most common of all the 'artificial' contraceptive techniques in the world is the use of the male sheath or condom. The condom is said to have been invented by Gabrielli Fallopius in the sixteenth century, although his original intention seems to have been the avoidance of syphilis rather than pregnancy. Certainly, today it still has this 'prophylactic' quality and for this reason it has much to recommend it for those who enter into casual sexual relationships.

There is no doubt that when properly used the condom also gives a high degree of contraceptive protection. Figures of about seven failures per 100 woman-years have been quoted, although for select groups of careful users, the figure is almost certainly lower than this. The old story that there is a pinhole in every 100th condom is complete nonsense and, indeed, most modern sheaths are made under very stringent conditions of quality control. For this reason they do not need to be checked for holes and it is very rare for them to break during use. However, condoms may be more effective when used with some kind of chemical contraceptive as well. Probably the greatest source of failure with the condom occurs with those men who allow their erection to subside while the penis is still inside the vagina. In this situation it is not difficult for a certain amount of semen (enough to cause conception) to leak around the rubber ring at the end of the condom and thereby seep into the vagina.

Some couples find the use of a condom an embarrassment, since it can only be put on when the man has an erection, often necessitating interruption of love-play. Of course, with a bit of imagination it is possible to incorporate this into the act of love-making. Another drawback of condoms is that either partner may find that it dulls sensation or feels unpleasant.

In addition to the condom there are washable rubber sheaths made of thicker rubber, which must be washed, powdered, and re-rolled after each use. They may be more effective than the usual condom because they are made of thicker rubber, but this is not necessarily so. As with condoms, they are perfectly harmless, except to a very few people who are sensitive to a particular rubber. One great advantage of condoms or sheaths is that they are easy to purchase, it is not necessary to see a doctor beforehand, and they are useful at times when no other form of contraception is suitable or available. The cost is quite reasonable.

Marie Stopes, however, one of the greatest English proponents of the birth control movement, felt sure that a condom was bound to be destroyed within the vagina during the act of intercourse, and she recommended the use of an 'occlusive pessary'—a mechanical barrier, of which many different types have been designed, which fits inside the vagina and prevents the passage of sperm into the cervix. Probably the most widespread of all such designs is the vaginal diaphragm, or Dutch cap, which fits diagonally across the vagina and blocks off the cervical entrance. However, if used alone such a device may have disappointing results. Today the recommendation is invariably that such a diaphragm should be used only in

conjunction with a spermicidal agent, a cream or jelly which contains chemical substances that will destroy all of the sperm with which it comes into contact. When used in this way, a diaphragm and jelly together are capable of giving a failure rate in the order of seven to ten per 100 woman-years.

However, much depends upon the selection of the diaphragm. It must be the right size to begin with, and it may need to be changed if the woman has children, an abdominal operation, or a weight gain of more than ten pounds. The fitting of such a device can only be carried out by an experienced gynaecologist. Some women may find the procedure embarrassing, but if a woman has previously used tampons, she will probably find the insertion of a diaphragm relatively easy to get accustomed to. Also, there are devices called diaphragm introducers which can facilitate the correct insertion of the cap; these are also useful in withdrawing the diaphragm, a process which some women find a bit messy. To achieve the greatest effectiveness, the cap must be inserted correctly, so that it covers the cervix, and it must be left in place for six to eight hours after intercourse. If a woman has intercourse more than once, she must insert some more of the spermicidal agent. This feature, together with the fact that the cap must be inserted well before a woman expects to make love or she must interrupt love-play to insert it, are the chief drawbacks to the use of the diaphragm. Normally, couples are unaware of the presence of the diaphragm if it has been correctly inserted.

Quite a number of spermicides have appeared on the market which are designed to be used *alone* rather than in conjunction with a diaphragm. These come in a variety of forms from creams, jellies, and pastes that can be inserted into the vagina, to suppositories, which melt after being inserted into the vagina (at least 15 minutes before intercourse) to foaming tablets and aerosol foams. These spermicides differ greatly in their smell and consistency and people must experiment to find the one best suited to them. Some people may find the extra lubrication which these provide an advantage, others may find it a nuisance. Generally, these chemicals have given rather poor results when used alone. Evidence suggests that aerosols used on their own are more effective than some other chemicals. Certain people may find that they are sensitive to certain brands of spermicides—resulting in irritation or soreness, but most brands have been tested to see that they are harmless. Future developments in this relatively simple field of contraception may produce a minor revolution in contraceptive usage.

The two major contraceptive methods currently available—the pill and the intrauterine device—will be discussed at considerable length in the second part of this article. Although they are not by any means the most widely distributed or widely used contraceptives on the market, their

very high degree of effectiveness advocates that they should occupy a special place in the family-planning programmes currently being carried out throughout the world. However, even these methods are not without their drawbacks—which can be measured in terms of cost, difficulty of distribution, and lack of acceptability to a large proportion of the population. These facts in themselves serve to emphasize once more that even a contraceptive which may produce perfect results in the laboratory will often be far from perfect for large-scale use.

And the solutions are far from easy. How, for example, does the government of any developing (or for that matter developed) nation persuade the populace that its numbers are rising too fast, that birth control is a good and even necessary practice, and that they should all be happy to accept it? Coercion is one technique which is certain to fail. It has failed too often in the past, and to try to force couples with regard to their intimate sexual lives is almost certain to lead to rebellion and failure.

First and foremost the government (and with a problem of these dimensions the government is the only possible effective agency) should attempt to persuade its people that a population problem exists—that there are too many people for the amount of land or for the quantities of raw materials available. Very few world governments seem eager to do this, and even in Great Britain, for example, where any number of population specialists are convinced that the islands are overpopulated by nearly one-third, it is easy for certain politicians and economists to turn a blind eye to the problem.

But the problem is even worse in developing regions where every individual, not unnaturally, tends to think in individual terms; he does not see the problems at a national level. Instead his only concern is with those things which immediately affect him and his family. The acceptance of contraceptive methods, then, must be made attractive to the individual; and since attraction most commonly means money, it must be made financially attractive.

Alteration of the tax structure in favour of bachelors and methods of this type have been proposed, but they are only practicable in areas where there *is* a tax structure. Direct monetary payments either to an individual or to a group would seem far more sensible. But they must be coupled, of course, with the provision of free and effective contraceptive methods. And since it can be argued that the means presently at our disposal are not effective or acceptable enough, then we must start to produce a generation of contraceptives which are.

The pill and the coil should be re-regarded only as starting points. After all, they have both been developed in their modern forms for rather less than 20 years. Who knows what a second 20-year-crash-programme in contraceptive technology might eventually bring about, or what its world-wide consequences might be?

Birth control today and tomorrow

It is often thought that because we now have forms of contraception which, if properly used, will give a relatively high degree of protection against pregnancy, the simpler and more 'traditional' methods that have been used for centuries will cease to be useful. In addition, with the vast amount of publicity that oral contraceptives and intrauterine devices (IUDs) have been receiving some people believe that the contraception problem is already solved—that we have no further need to develop new methods of birth control because present methods can satisfy these needs, which would be splendid if true.

But both of these beliefs are based on a fallacy—the fallacy that the pill and the IUD are not only perfect ways of preventing a woman from becoming pregnant, but also that they are simple to distribute, that they have no side effects, and that they are completely acceptable methods of contraception to every woman on earth. If this were so, then certainly we could throw away the condom and the diaphragm, forget about the safe period and withdrawal and, perhaps more importantly, stop any further research designed to produce new and improved contraception for use in the next decade.

Unfortunately, however, although they do, and must, continue to play a vital role in family-planning programmes both in developed and in developing nations, neither the IUD nor the pill, even when both are used in the same programme, will solve our contraceptive problems completely. For many years hence, 'old-fashioned' contraceptives will still be with us and for at least as long we must continue to develop newer and better methods. Why this should be so can best be understood by considering the advantages and the drawbacks of a pill, which is taken daily, and of a mechanical device which fits entirely inside the uterus.

No one is quite sure when IUDs were first used to prevent contraception, nor even how the idea of an intrauterine foreign body first originated. It is often suggested that the practice, apparently still employed by some Arab tribes, of placing a small stone in the uteri of female camels they wished to keep sterile, is actually the original idea which led to the development of an IUD for women. It is an intriguing story, but it probably has no basis in fact.

Although intrauterine foreign bodies were often used in the last century and in the first few decades of this one, certain problems associated with their use led to their becoming extremely unpopular and widely condemned for several decades. One of the main problems with these early devices was their construction. The most common, known as 'stem pessaries', were usually made of metal and consisted of two parts—an upper portion held in the uterine cavity and connected by a stem passing through the cervix to some sort of plate covering the cervical entrance in the vagina. The greatest danger was that the upper portion could easily perforate the uterine wall.

The weight of responsibilities that two parents can successfully balance between them is shown as being near the breaking point in this family-planning poster from Hong Kong.

In the early 1960s the more modern forms of IUDs (which fit entirely within the uterine cavity) suddenly made a re-appearance, and almost overnight they regained a tremendous popularity as a means of preventing conception.

What changed the prevailing attitude? Essentially, it was the sudden realization of the enormity of the world population explosion. The problem led to a re-appraisal of this contraceptive method (and, indeed, of a great many others) and it was realized that the unfortunate reputation which IUDs had developed was not entirely justified.

Within about five years more than a dozen different types of IUDs suddenly appeared on the market and, in the same space of time, they were put into use by the thousand. Now, with ten years of IUD experience behind us, we can start to consider their role more objectively. Undoubtedly, they have a very important part to play in the limitation of family size, but, unfortunately, they have proved to be rather less valuable than at one time was hoped.

The modern IUD comes in several different shapes and sizes (variations of loops, bows, or coils) and is usually made of flexible plastic. To introduce the IUD into the uterus, the doctor stretches it out to a long, thin shape and passes it through the cervical canal—once inside the womb the IUD returns to its original shape. The process of insertion may be slightly uncomfortable, but if the woman is relaxed there should be little pain. If there are no complications such a device can be left in place for several years. No one is quite sure how the IUD works. The woman continues to ovulate normally. One theory is that the IUD may stimulate the uterine wall to produce a substance that inactivates the egg and prevents its probable embedding in the lining.

One risk with the IUD, even with proper medical insertion, is that in some women the device is expelled from the uterus out through the vagina, sometimes without the woman even knowing it. Obviously there is no contraception protection at all in this instance. If a new IUD is put in, it will generally remain in place. But it is recommended that women who have not had children do not use the IUD, since the risk of expulsion is considerably higher for them. Pain and bleeding with an IUD is also more common among women who have not had children. A considerable minority of women, sometimes between 10 and 20 per cent, complain that the pain or bleeding is severe enough to prompt removal of the device. Every woman usually experiences a little discomfort after the IUD is first inserted—this is normally in the form of greater period pains and longer, heavier periods than usual. After a few months these symptoms generally subside, although loss of blood during periods may be slightly heavier than previously. A doctor will have to check the position of the IUD only about once a year after the first few preliminary examinations have been completed. In addition, devices have a thread

attached which hangs an inch or so into the vagina to allow the woman to check the position herself.

Another side effect which occasionally arises is that the IUD can provoke a minor irritation and, subsequently, infection of the womb. In such an instance, the woman might have some pain, even a backache, and probably a discharge of mucus. Medical treatment should be sought at once to consider removal of the IUD. The chances of sterility resulting from an infection caused by an IUD are extremely remote.

Considering these side effects, how reliable is an IUD? When used by women who have ready access to medical care, they are second in effectiveness only to the contraceptive pill. Failure rates between two to five pregnancies per 100 woman years of exposure to intercourse are the figures generally quoted.

However, some pregnancies have occurred even with the IUD in place. In such rare cases the IUD will not interfere with the baby's development or with the birth. It will probably be expelled from the womb during labour.

The IUD has not proven to be as valuable a contraceptive aid as was originally hoped precisely because of the side effects it produces. Most of these effects are easily overcome, but, unfortunately, women are not always willing to be patient in dealing with them. In areas where the doctor has time to explain the reasons for the pain or the bleeding that many women experience, he may be able to persuade them to persist with the method until the transition period is over. However, in developing countries where there is often only one doctor for many thousands of people, the doctor may have no alternative

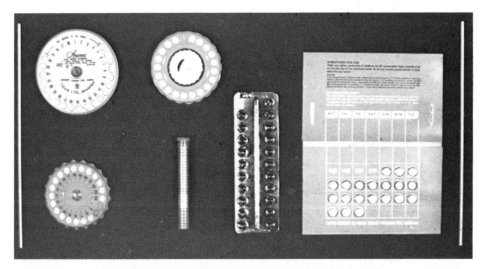

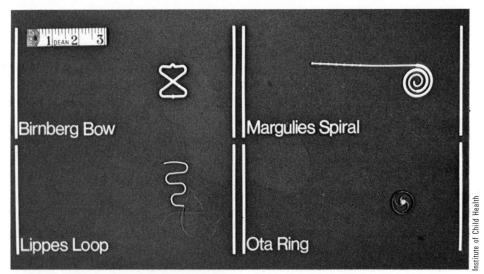

Institute of Child Health

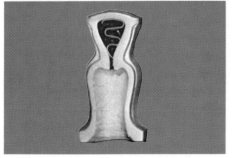

Top Oral contraceptive pills come in a variety of brands and dosages, each with its own container geared to help the woman remember to take the pill for the prescribed number of days. The latter feature is crucial to the success of the contraceptive. Above Intrauterine devices come in a variety of sizes and shapes, and a doctor must decide which is best for each individual. The Lippes loop is one of the most popular IUDs. Left This model cross-section shows its position in the uterus.

Days							0	7	14	21	28		
	0	7	14	21	28							0	7
Take Pill													
Bleeding													

Above *The chart illustrates the normal cycle of pill-taking for the combined pill. The woman must take the first pill of the new cycle after a lapse of seven days, during which time she should experience 'withdrawal bleeding' which is much like a normal period.*

but to remove an IUD if the patient requests it. Also, in such regions, a woman who loses her device is quite likely to become pregnant before she can see a doctor to have another one inserted.

Because of a combination of these factors it has been found in developing countries such as Korea, for example, that the rate of IUD insertions has reached a plateau. They are being lost, either spontaneously or at the patient's request, almost as fast as they can be inserted. They still *do* exert a considerable effect on controlling the birth rate, as indeed they do in more developed countries, but their impact has not been as great as was originally expected.

Clearly, the devices must be altered in some way if they are to become more effective and one way which is now being tried with some success is to add to an ordinary T-shaped plastic IUD a certain amount of metallic copper. The effect of this metal is to lower the expulsion rate, to lessen the bleeding (and hence the request for removal), and also to decrease the number of pregnancies. Interestingly enough, although several theories have been put forward, no one is yet certain precisely *why* it should do so. However, copper IUDs are generating considerable excitement in the contraception world and it is predicted that in the 1970s or 1980s such an IUD is likely to be the most effective, safe, and economical contraceptive available to the public.

Of course, the entire concept of oral contraception will also be undergoing dramatic changes in the not too distant future. The forms of oral contraception presently available are largely the result of research work carried out in the mid- and late-1950s by M. C. Chang, John Rock, and Gregory Pincus. They are basically of two types and both contain a combination of two hormones—an oestrogen similar to that found in the body and a synthetic progestogen which has similar properties to the natural hormone progesterone, but which is far more potent in its action.

In the 'combined pill' these hormones are taken together for a period of about twenty-one days. In the 'sequential' type of pill oestrogen is taken first, followed later in the cycle by a combination of oestrogen and progestogen. In both cases the effect is to suppress the release of the mature egg cell from the ovary and hence to prevent the possibility of fertilization taking place. There are also other 'secondary' effects on the uterine lining and on the mucus that fills the cervical canal. Such pills have been shown to give a high degree of contraceptive protection. With a combined pill used properly, there should be no possibility of pregnancy at all and although the sequential type of pill appears to be rather less effective, its failure rate is still only in the order of perhaps two pregnancies per 100 woman years.

But the key phrase is 'when used prop-

erly' and one of the greatest drawbacks to the use of oral contraceptives is precisely the problem of the way in which they are used. In the first place, most of the pills currently available need to be taken every day. It seems simple enough to remember to do so, but for a surprisingly large number of women the effort is too great. One, two, or more pills are forgotten in each cycle. This applies just as much to women in 'sophisticated' Western societies as it does to those in developing nations. In addition to this simple, but important drawback there are side effects which do considerably lessen the suitability of the pill as a contraceptive for all women.

Some women report having headaches, bleeding at odd times of the month, weight-gain, and feelings of depression when they are on the pill. Often these side effects last only for the first few months of pill-taking and then disappear. Sometimes switching to a different brand of pill (with a different dosage) will cure any ill-effects. On the other hand many women report feeling happier when taking the pill—probably a psychological response to the freedom from worry about becoming pregnant. The only conclusive disorder that has been linked to the pill is the incidence of thrombosis (blood clotting). This incidence is quite small, however, and appears most frequently in women already susceptible to it—a fact which means that it can be prevented to some extent. All things considered, the dangers to a woman's life in the course of pregnancy are considerably higher than those involved in the regular use of oral contraceptives.

When considering the pill there are two problems which apply particularly to developing countries and which Western women are less likely to find difficult. The first is cost. Although the price of a course of oral contraceptives forms a relatively small part of the weekly income of a Western family, in other parts of the world the price is relatively very much higher. The simplest answer would be for governments to buy up huge supplies and to distribute them free to the entire populace. Regrettably, few governments consider this a reasonable course of action but even for those which are prepared to do so, the mechanics of distribution are far from easy. If a country consists of ten thousand villages, each isolated from the next and from the central government, the sheer difficulty of getting adequate supplies to those who need them may well be a principal factor responsible for the failure of a particular family-planning programme.

A number of solutions have been proposed to eliminate these difficulties. The first is for a woman to take a pill, not every day *just in case* she might run the risk of pregnancy, but rather when she knows that she has had intercourse at a time when conception seems likely. In other words, there is surely a place for a 'prophylactic' contraceptive—a 'morning after pill' which she should take to ensure that, although she may have been impregnated, the fertilized egg will never succeed in

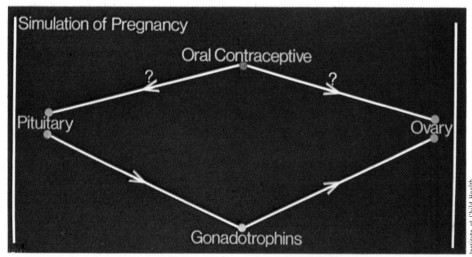

Above *The oestrogens and progestogens in the pill act upon the pituitary gland to inhibit its normal production of gonadotrophins—hormones which affect the activity of the ovaries. The result is that the follicles in the ovaries do not have sufficient hormones to mature and no ova are released. Also, the uterus remains hostile to a fertilized ovum.*

Institute of Child Health

implanting itself in the lining of the uterus.

A good deal of work is currently being done on the development of such a pill. It consists of synthetic oestrogen which is active when taken by mouth. It is taken for two or three days after intercourse and its effect may be either to hurry the egg down the fallopian tube or else to make the endometrium unready to receive it once it enters the uterus. Initial trials on such a product have been very promising, although much more work needs to be done before we can be sure that such an approach will definitely be effective.

A second attempt to solve the difficulty depends upon a quite different principle. If each of the present oral pills gives protection for only a day or so, why not develop one which would give protection for a month or longer? In other words, why not develop a 'once-a-month' pill? Again, work is going on in this area and such a pill might be a practical proposition in the near future. But why stop at a month? The ideal should surely be to produce some contraceptive formulation which will protect a woman for as long as a year.

Here the problem is that the greater part of any substance taken by mouth is likely to be excreted by the body in a fairly short time. The method of application, therefore, needs to be different and an

Below In India, where the population explosion is an enormous problem, the IUD loop is produced, packaged, and distributed as part of the government's birth control programme.

injection is the obvious method that springs to mind. For several years now trials have been carried out in which synthetic progestogens have been injected into women at concentrations intended to prevent them from becoming pregnant (probably by preventing their ovulation) for three months or longer. Sometimes these injections are in the form of Silastic capsule implants. These capsules contain the progestogen which is timed to be released in precise doses (perhaps 20 micrograms per day) into the body. The capsules themselves are placed under the skin of the arm or hip with a hypodermic needle—a relatively painless procedure. In several parts of the world this approach has been well received.

The principal difficulty with most of these forms of oral contraceptive seems to be that of predicting when the woman will resume her normal menstruation. In many cases patients have started to bleed at random and at completely unpredictable intervals, causing them some distress. In other cases the bleeding has been held up for much longer than expected, so much so that it became necessary to take an orally-active oestrogen, which produces a psychologically reassuring 'withdrawal bleeding' very similar to a normal menstrual period.

However, the contraceptive ideal for the future may well have already been discovered, at least in the opinion of some specialists. A group of compounds known as *prostaglandins* have recently been tested to establish their value in bringing a preg-

nancy to an end. They are either injected intravenously or, more simply, placed in the vagina, and in very many cases they cause uterine bleeding irrespective of whether the uterus is pregnant or not. Their value as abortifacients is, therefore, obvious.

But without stretching the terms that we use too far, we might also consider them to be of the utmost value as contraceptives. If a woman were to instill an appropriate amount of such a substance into her vagina just before her expected period and she had not conceived in the interim she would experience normal menstrual bleeding, quite independent of the presence of the drug. However, even if she were pregnant, she would still bleed. To be precise, she would be experiencing an early abortion. But it would be so early that she would have no way of knowing whether or not conception had taken place.

The use of prostaglandins *may*, therefore, give us a method of ensuring that all women who wish to avoid pregnancy experience a perfectly regular pattern of menstrual bleeding without having to concern themselves with what is for some women the important moral question of whether they are inducing themselves to abort. If such menstrual regularity can be achieved, a great step forward will have been taken in solving many of our present contraceptive difficulties. The contraception of tomorrow will be a much safer, simpler, and more reliable process, which every woman should welcome.

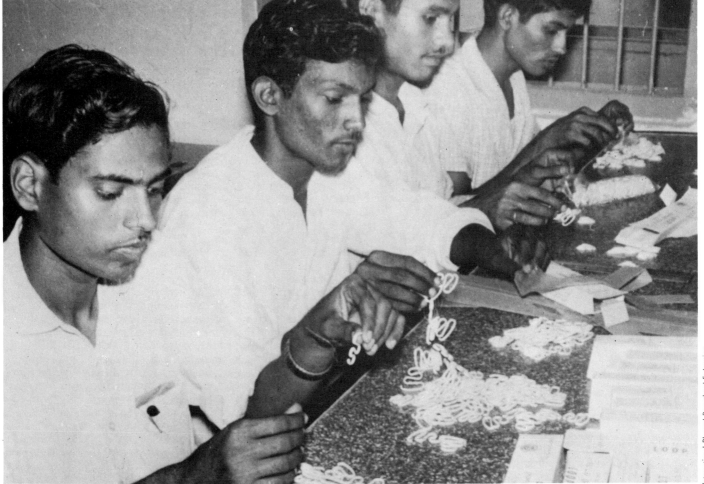

International Planned Parenthood Federation

Permanent contraception

The contraceptives most widely used today have little in common with each other. The condom, the pill, and the intrauterine device, known as IUD, all work on their own individual principles—be it to prevent fertilization, to suppress ovulation, or to inhibit implantation of the fertilized egg. However, they all share at least two common features: They all prevent pregnancy (more or less effectively), and they are all reversible. When a man neglects to wear a sheath or when a woman stops taking the pill or has her IUD removed, the risk of pregnancy immediately rises to the maximum degree possible. The duration of contraception has usually not had the slightest effect upon the woman's subsequent ability to conceive.

But there is another approach to the problem of preventing conception and one which is becoming increasingly popular. Instead of a couple having to use a sheath for each act of intercourse or a woman having to take a pill each day, it is now possible, as the result of a single surgical operation on either the husband or the wife, to give the couple complete contraceptive protection for the rest of their lives. However, the protection that they receive is usually not reversible. That is to say, once they decide to have one or the other of the operations performed the chance that the couple has of producing any more children is rather slight.

For this reason these procedures are often referred to as methods of 'irreversible contraception'. Some would refer to them as *sterilizing* operations, and in the strictest sense the term is an accurate one. However, to most people the idea of sterilization also involves the mistaken implication of castration—removal of the testes or ovaries. Neither of these operations involves the removal of either of these organs and so to avoid confusion the term 'sterilization' is perhaps better left unused. If it is referred to we must be very clear about what it involves and, even more so, about which it does *not* involve.

The 'irreversible' operations are termed *vasectomy* for the man and *tubectomy* for the woman. They are similar in that they both involve the severing of several ducts within the body and they both require the use of an anaesthetic. But they differ somewhat in the way that the operation is carried out and to some extent in the difficulty that the surgeon may experience. Most doctors will agree that vasectomy is the easier of the two operations to perform, and it is this that we will consider first.

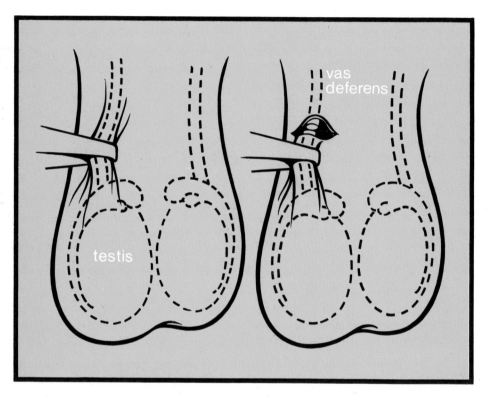

Above In a vasectomy the vital sperm-carrying tubes are exposed by a one-inch incision on each side of the testicles. The tubes, the vasa deferentia, are then cut and tied together.

The sperm, which are produced in the testes, undergo a lengthy journey through the duct system of the male reproductive tract before they ever appear in the ejaculate. They first enter a much coiled and convoluted tube called the *epididymis* which runs down the side of the testis. In the epididymis the sperm probably undergo their final period of maturation and, when fully mature, they enter a wider duct with quite thick muscular walls known as the *vas deferens* or simply the *vas*. Those sperm which move through the full length of the vas eventually enter the urethra, the duct contained within the penis from which they are eventually ejaculated. But the operation of vasectomy severs the vas deferens completely by dividing the vas on each side and tying the ends back. The testicles themselves remain untouched and neither the production of spermatoazoa nor of male hormones (which reach the body through the blood stream, not through the vas deferens) is affected. After the operation sperm produced by the testes can no longer reach the urethra and so the man is effectively prevented from fathering any more children.

Three questions immediately spring to mind about the procedure. The first is what happens to all the sperm that the testes keep on producing? Do they not build up a great deal of pressure behind the point where the vas has been blocked and cause it to distend like a balloon? In the vast majority of cases, when the operation has been properly carried out, the answer is 'no'. The older sperm are absorbed by the vas leaving room for the production of new sperm and 'back-pressure' is rare.

The second question, which leads on from the first, is whether, if this absorption takes place, a man will ejaculate anything at all? The answer is that he will. He will produce almost the same volume of ejaculate as before and, indeed, anyone examining his semen without the aid of a microscope would not be able to tell whether he had been vasectomized or not. This is because the sperm themselves are so small that they contribute very little to the three millilitres or so which is the volume of the ejaculate in an average man; they probably contribute no more than one part in a hundred. The vast bulk of semen is, in fact, the fluid seminal plasma which is produced by the accessory glands of the male reproductive tract—the *prostate* for example. Each of these glands secretes its contents into the duct system at a point 'higher up' than that at which the vas is cut. Vasectomy itself does not, therefore,

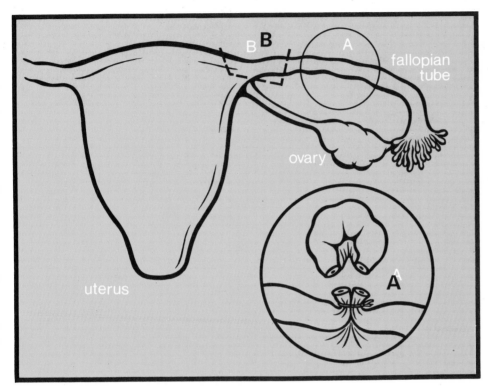

Above In a tubectomy **A** an inch is cut from each fallopian tube and the ends are tied, or **B** a bit of the uterus is removed with part of the tube and the ends are tied and 'buried'.

actually alter their function in any way.

A third question has to do with precisely how the operation is carried out and whether it has any unpleasant side effects. As far as the procedure itself is concerned different surgeons have their own very definite views on how best it should be performed, and many different variations exist. In general, the side effects are few, although this depends to no small degree upon the skill and care of the doctor who performs the operation. Usually, it is performed under a local anaesthetic injected into the scrotum, although some surgeons prefer to use a general anaesthetic. It is normally completed within 15 to 30 minutes, and very often the patient can return to work within a few days. In India, for example, where the number of vasectomies already performed is estimated to be about two million, it is usual for the man to be vasectomized on Friday and for him to return to work on the following Monday.

The surgical technique involved is relatively simple; the object of the operation being to remove a piece of the vas deferens —a length of about an inch or so—from the region inside the scrotum. It is necessary to take out such an apparently large piece simply because the cut ends of the vas have a remarkable ability to join up

again. If they are left side by side they may often do so, and it is, therefore, essential to create a space between them. Since there are two vasa, one associated with each testis, many surgeons like to make two incisions in the scrotum, one on each side. It is possible, however, (and perhaps a little quicker) to reach the vas on both sides through a single incision, but many specialists feel that this will increase the chances of difficulties arising in the post-operative period.

Whether it is approached through one incision or two, a portion of the vas is lifted and cut out, and the cut ends are then often bent backwards on themselves and ligatured in that position to further lessen their chances of rejoining. Every effort is made to damage the blood vessels associated with the vas as little as possible during the procedure, and any minor bleeding that does occur is stopped before the operation is completed. At the end of the process the cut portions of the vas are returned to the scrotum and the skin incision is closed. In the period immediately following a vasectomy a man may feel a certain amount of pain and perhaps a 'dragging' sensation in the scrotal area. A certain amount of bruising in this region is also not uncommon. However, it is rare

for these symptoms to persist for long.

It is of the utmost importance for the doctor to impress upon the patient that he will not become infertile for a number of weeks. Obviously, there are a number of sperm in a position 'upstream' from the point at which the vas has been cut. It is necessary to empty the ducts of these sperm before intercourse without any other form of contraceptive can be considered safe.

Estimates vary as to how long it takes for a man to lose his fertilizing capacity. Obviously, it depends upon the frequency of intercourse or of masturbation. Although eight to 12 weeks is considered normal by some workers in this field, there is good evidence that a sexually-active man can deplete his reserve of sperm much more quickly than this. But rather than trusting to guess work it is usual for the patient to be asked to return to the clinic some weeks after the operation to have a sperm count taken and thus to prove that conception is now impossible.

Again there is no need to guess about the overall effect of the operation on the patient's emotional or mental well-being. A number of surveys have been carried out to assess these effects, of which perhaps the best known was a British survey of rather more than 1,000 men who had had the operation performed. The vast majority of them were pleased with its effects. They were quite prepared to recommend the operation to their friends and they felt it had no adverse effects upon their sexual lives. On the contrary, in many cases it had actually *enhanced* the sexual side of their marriage by removing the fear of an unwanted pregnancy.

When given the choice, most doctors would prefer to solve a family's contraception problems by operating on the husband rather than on the wife. This does not imply that tubectomy is in any sense a dangerous operation, but simply that a longer time is usually spent in the operating theatre and a longer time is necessary for complete recovery. In addition, the busy mother of a large family may simply not be able to find the time to go into the hospital for an operation upon which her health does not (at least directly) depend. For this reason, many tubectomies are performed on patients who are undergoing an operation for a different purpose. The most common instance is that of a Caesarean section, often carried out on a woman who may have passed the age of thirty and who has three or more children.

Tubectomy is nearly always performed

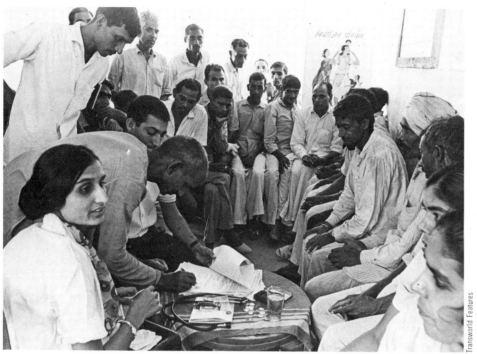

Left *In India family planning programmes are relying more and more on the technique of vasectomy as generally the safest, simplest, and surest method of contraception.*
Above *Financial incentives are often given to encourage participation in the programme.*

under a general anaesthetic, since it is necessary by one means or another to enter the abdominal cavity. The fallopian tubes are exposed and a piece of each is removed, just as is the case with the vas deferens. Often, the cut ends of the tubes are bent back and tied. Again, however, many different versions of the operation exist. In one, the end of the tube closest to the uterus is actually sutured into the uterine wall. The main object of all these variations is to prevent the cut ends from rejoining.

Recently, the whole process of tubectomy (and many other abdominal operations) has been revolutionized by the use of an instrument known as a *laparoscope*. With the use of this instrument only two very small incisions are made in the patient's abdominal wall. Although the time taken on the operating table is much the same as for the conventional method of surgery, the patient recovers and can be discharged from the hospital much more quickly—often within two or three days.

Laparoscopy became possible because of the development of a system known as 'fibre optics'. A thin tube containing many very fine, pliable glass fibres can easily be inserted into the body. By illuminating the fibres and looking down the tube with a special lens arrangement the surgeon is able to see the abdominal organs quite clearly, even though the tube itself may be bent at an angle somewhere along its length. It is possible to insert thin surgical instruments into the body and to manipulate the organs that become visible through the fibre optic system. Only two small scars are left after the operation at the points where the instruments were inserted.

Many tubectomy operations are currently being carried out using this method, and the results have, in general, been encouraging. Certainly, there should be little tendency for the ends of the tubes to rejoin, even though a piece of the tube

is not actually extracted. Instead, a device called a *thermo-cautery*, which consists of a pair of small electrically heated forceps, is used to coagulate a length of the tube and to obliterate its central channel. The ends are then separated by means of a special knife. The coagulation is, of course, quite painless because the patient is anaesthetized, and in addition to deliberately damaging the tubes so that they will not rejoin, it also serves the purpose of stopping any bleeding which might be associated with separating the two ends. The operation becomes effective immediately. The woman will continue to have her normal periods and she may have sexual intercourse without any other contraceptive as soon as she feels fit enough.

The question arises as to whether the 'irreversible' methods that we have considered are really completely irreversible; in other words, can a severed vas or a severed fallopian tube ever be rejoined? The answer is that they *can*, but often at very considerable expense both in time and effort. And even if the reverse operation is a success as far as the ducts themselves are concerned, there is no absolute guarantee that fertility will also be restored.

Estimates of the likely success rate for reversal of vasectomy vary enormously from one medical centre to another. An optimistic figure is about 50 per cent, but there are very few cases in which this rate of success has been consistently achieved. A more realistic figure is probably 10 to 25 per cent, which means that only somewhere between one in four and one in ten of the men who have the operation can expect to have their fertility restored at some future date. The rate for reversal of tubectomy is even lower—approximately only one woman in 20 will find the reverse operation to be successful. For all practical purposes, therefore, to call these methods of contraception 'irreversible' is a fairly accurate description.

And this, of course, gives the clue as to the types of people for whom such operations are likely to be most suitable. Vasectomy and tubectomy are certainly not for the young couple who have so far had no children, unless, because of the state of the wife's health, she has been told that she absolutely must avoid becoming pregnant. But such cases are rare. Nor is it likely to be performed on an unmarried person, except for reasons of health. The operations are also unsuitable for those couples who have had, say two children, and who wish to have more, but seek to delay their arrival for a few years. For such couples an intrauterine device might be more appropriate. The ideal candidates for an irreversible operation are those who are quite sure that they have had as many children as they want during their lifetimes. The absolute number is not important. It may be two or 12. What is important is their firm wish not to have any more.

In general, such couples will probably be over 25 years old. Ideally, they will have discussed the problem thoroughly with each other and will both have come to the conclusion that an irreversible method is appropriate for them. When one partner approaches the doctor, the consent of the other to the operation should be easy to obtain, because they have agreed upon it beforehand. Although permission to perform the operation from the other spouse is not always required, it might constitute grounds for divorce if the other partner did not know of the operation and was not agreeable to it. Sometimes, the doctor may suggest that the husband rather than the wife should have an operation and when the pros and cons of the situation are explained the two may well be agreeable. But whichever one undergoes the surgery, the doctor will explain and the two must fully appreciate that as a couple their fertile days are then over.

CLIVE WOOD

When contraception is a problem

In the West today a wide choice of safe, reliable, birth-control methods is available to the general public. Yet, many couples still have contraceptive problems. What are these problems and how can people be helped to solve them?

Posters, pamphlets, books, and articles in newspapers and magazines have made the public aware of the various methods of birth control from which one can choose. There is concise and well-distributed information about the contraceptive pill, the intra-uterine device (IUD or loop), the diaphragm (or Dutch cap), sheath (or condom), various forms of spermicides, the rhythm method, and vasectomy and tubectomy operations. From a rational point of view there is no reason why every couple should not be able to practise effective birth control. Why then, when information about contraception abounds, does it remain a problem for so many people?

Despite the wide and ever increasing amount of contraceptive information available, it is estimated that only two million of the 10 million women in Great Britain who might become pregnant seek family-planning advice or help from doctors.

Demographers charting the alarming population growth are suggesting compulsory limitations of family size. Concerned doctors are exploring incentive programmes to delay marriage and limit childbearing. Critics of England's Abortion Law claim it is being exploited as a birth control method, and family planners rejoin that abortion should never be thought of as anything but a last resort due to failure of effective contraception. So the controversy surrounding birth control rages as the birth rate rises.

But the crux of the problem of contraception comes right down to the very complex interaction of two unique individuals —the man and the woman whose choice, if any, of contraceptive protection depends on emotional as well as rational factors. It is not enough to know the physical facts of sexual intercourse and reproduction. When a woman goes to her doctor for con-

traceptive advice she is asking for·understanding of her emotional as well as her physical well-being. Usually she cannot easily put this into words. Delicacy, tact, and patience are required on the part of the doctor. Some doctors are trained and sufficiently skilled to put the woman at ease and to recognize her needs as a total human being instead of just as a reproductive unit.

Sybil, for example, had not given sympathetic Dr. Lane much of an opportunity to treat her individually. A well-organized, brisk woman, Sybil was 22 years old, married to an accountant, but still working herself in a smart dress shop. She and Hugh, her husband, wanted to wait until they were financially more secure before having any children. What Sybil wanted now was a simple, safe method of contraception. Hugh had been using sheaths but he and Sybil both had come to the conclusion that sheaths spoiled the spontaneity of intercourse. Sybil then decided that the popular pill was the answer to their needs and she simply asked her doctor for a prescription. Dr. Lane examined her, decided it was safe for her to have the pill, and prescribed the dosage most suited to her. Sybil went away happy.

Eight months later Sybil was back at the doctor's office. The pills seemed to be making her lethargic and despondent, but an even more definite effect was that her sylph-like figure was spreading out of control. Since she prided herself on her neat figure, and her employer felt it was necessary for her to be slim to model the shop's dresses, Sybil concluded that she would like to find another method of birth control rather than try out other dosages of the pill. She had read a great deal of literature on contraception and decided that this time she would try the loop since it, too, was highly effective and did not require any preparation once it had been inserted by the doctor.

When Sybil told Dr. Lane what she wanted, however, she explained that she never prescribed a loop to a young woman who had not yet had children. There is a sound basis for this position. For some as yet unexplained reason, women who have not had children have a considerably higher rate of expulsion of the loop than women who have had children. Frequently, the woman is unaware that she has expelled the loop from her vagina and she continues to have intercourse under the false impression that she is protected. Not until pregnancy occurs does she realize the failure.

For the first time Sybil realized that contraception was a highly individualized problem and not just a matter of leafing through a catalogue and picking the method one thought most attractive. Dr. Lane patiently described the pros and cons of alternative methods. Since Sybil was in the most fertile period of her life she needed a highly effective contraceptive method. This ruled out the rhythm method which is reliable for only a small number of women who ovulate regularly. And to determine whether one ovulates regularly, an accurate record is needed of menstrual periods or morning temperatures over a year's time. Withdrawal or coitus interruptus, besides having psychological disadvantages, has a high risk. The man must have excellent control to withdraw his penis from the vagina before ejaculation. Sybil felt Hugh could not, or at least would not want to, have this demand made upon him. Since, eventually, they did want to have children, both vasectomy and tubectomy, which for all practical purposes are irreversible, were ruled out.

Thus the choices for Sybil were narrowed down to the use of the diaphragm, or cap. Sybil had rejected the diaphragm from the start because it seemed so messy and inconvenient. Having to make preparations before intercourse seemed too premeditated to suit her. But Dr. Lane pointed out that this form of birth control has been popular for many years. It is the most satisfactory

method for many people because it is completely reliable if correctly used, and it has no physical side-effects. She explained in detail how to use the diaphragm in conjunction with a spermicide and, with a diagram, explained to Sybil how it is placed in the vagina to cover the mouth of the womb.

Sybil than climbed onto the examining table and Dr. Lane gently inserted a diaphragm, trying several for size, until she found the one which fitted properly. When it was in place Sybil could not feel it. Dr. Lane removed it and had Sybil re-insert it.

In the unhurried atmosphere of confidence which Dr. Lane had been able to establish with Sybil there was no embarrassment. As one married woman to another they were able to talk about the advantages and disadvantages of available contraceptive methods. Dr. Lane had let Sybil work out her problem, 'try on' various solutions, and eventually settle on the one which may not have answered all of Sybil and Hugh's hopes, but was the best science could offer them at the moment. Dr. Lane asked Sybil to come back in 10 days time with the diaphragm in place to be sure that she had inserted it correctly.

With practice, confidence, and the development of a heightened awareness of Hugh's amorous intentions so that she could insert the cap well before love-making, Sybil will no doubt succeed in using it successfully. Several things are in her favour—her motivation to avoid becoming pregnant is sincere and uncomplicated by any psycho-sexual problems, and she had a sympathetic doctor specially trained in birth-control techniques.

Unfortunately, not all doctors have this special training. Many general practitioners were not instructed in contraceptive methods in medical school and so confine themselves to prescribing the contraceptive pill without giving the patient a thorough examination. Very often a woman who asks for the pill is also asking for reassurance that her vagina is normal, that she does not have cancer of the cervix, or lumps in her breasts. But a doctor who is not trained to recognize those veiled or unspoken anxieties will deal with her problem summarily—and all too often unsuccessfully. If the pill has unpleasant side-effects, the woman simply stops taking it and, while wondering what to do next, may become pregnant. Often her vague uneasiness about sexual matters smoulders and grows out of proportion, sometimes flawing her sexual relationship.

If a woman is truly worried about a specific physical symptom she will usually see a gynaecologist. This specialist in women's diseases is a highly trained doctor, skilled in the physical aspects of female problems. But a gynaecologist is not always trained in the emotional problems related to sex. It is natural for a gynaecologist to be primarily concerned with the proper physical functioning of a woman's body and to view a chosen birth-control method in this narrower context. Even William H. Masters and Virginia E. Johnson in their pioneering work, *Human*

Sexual Inadequacy discussed only physical techniques which might alleviate sexual problems. In their detailed descriptions of foreplay and the sexual act no mention was made of how contraception might be handled—surely a significant omission when so many people are still seeking a more satisfactory answer to this intimate problem.

When sexual problems are severe enough to threaten a marriage or relationship, or to cause anxiety, one or the other of the couple involved may go to a psychologist, a marriage counsellor, or a religious leader, all of whom are equipped to handle emotional problems. Few if any of them are prepared, however, to deal with the subtle but significant and revealing role contraception plays in the sexual act.

The problem Pam had, for instance, was not atypical in its general nature. An attractive, young, biology teacher, Pam was planning to marry James, the popular history teacher in the same school. On the surface Pam seemed an extremely competent, cool, and factually-orientated person. She spoke as though she knew everything about sex. It was reasonable for James to feel that it was the furtiveness and lack of privacy in their first sexual encounters that caused them to be so unsatisfactory.

Although Pam was, in fact, knowledgeable, she was frightened of sex. After several months of marriage their otherwise stable and happy relationship was not physically consummated. However aroused Pam became, she could not allow James actually to penetrate her. He, ever optimistic and loving, hoped that it was only her fear of pregnancy which held her back, since they both knew that under no circumstances could they afford a child at this time. James urged Pam to take the pill so that she could be more relaxed.

Pam, however, had not been eager to go on the pill, because she felt there might as yet be undetermined side-effects arising from its use. She had such a long future need for contraceptive protection that she hoped to wait until she was older if she were to take the pill at all. But James was occasionally impotent because of the strain and tension, and he convinced Pam that she should, at least, talk to a doctor.

Pam decided to go to her local family-planning clinic. There she discussed the problem of what sort of contraceptive method was best for her. She told the doctor that James wanted her to use the pill but that she preferred not to. She did not mention, however, that their marriage was unconsummated. Instead her attitude was one of extreme confidence and 'I know as much as you do, Doctor'. Not until it was time for her to undress and climb onto the examining table did her almost belligerent defences break down. She blushed deeply and, when asked to draw her legs up for the vaginal examination, held her knees tightly together. It was apparent to her doctor that Pam had not come to terms with her sexuality. Trained, experienced, and skilled in such problems, the doctor, over a number of visits, was able to help Pam to regard her vagina as a valid sexual organ and to achieve an emotional as well as an actual acceptance of the penis.

In England the National Health Service Act of 1967, conferred permissive powers on Local Health Authorities to give birth-control advice without regard to marital status. Under this act unmarried as well as married women will be seen free of charge. In the same year The National Council of the Family Planning Association empowered their clinics to advise the unmarried if they wished to and, subsequently, nearly all clinics decided to do so. All of their doctors and nurses are trained in the techniques of contraception. If the local Health Authority does not provide birth-control advice free, the Family Planning Clinic will for a modest annual fee, covering as many visits as are needed. The only extra costs are for the supplies which can be purchased from the clinics—such as pills and diaphragms.

At these clinics a woman can discuss her changing contraceptive needs. No longer must any woman think that she must settle on one method and continue using it for years and years. Some doctors even suggest that it is best for a woman to take the pill for no more than four consecutive years, then stop for a year before starting to take it again.

Counter-indications to the advisability of any contraceptive method should always be considered. Liver complaints or high blood pressure rule out the use of the pill, while irregular menses or extremely heavy menstrual bleeding may be helped by taking it. A woman who has wanted to try the loop may decide to do so after she has had her children. A man may feel no contraceptive is quite right for his wife and seek to have a vasectomy for himself, either privately or at a family-planning clinic. Illness, age, the number of children one has or wants, all enter into the choice of contraceptives.

A change of contraceptive method, however, should never be made as a panacea for sexual problems. A switch from the sheath to the pill to assure orgasm, for example, is fallacious and self-defeating. Sometimes sex before marriage is fraught with frustrations and is, therefore, unfulfilling. The hope of many newly-married couples is that with the proper birth-control method their sexual life will suddenly be all that films and magazine articles have indicated it should be. But the sexual act is as much emotional as physical, and the problems brought into a premarital or marital relationship cannot be solved so simply. Doctors are aware of deeper problems in the relationships of couples who come to them asking for constant change, finding one contraceptive method after another unsatisfactory. At the Family Planning Association men or women with special difficulties are referred to clinics which deal with psycho-sexual problems.

Usually, couples are in some way aware of it if sex has become a battle between them, but they need special help to see sexual difficulties as a symptom rather than a cause. Polly and Richard had very liberal, informed ideas about sex. Before they met and married, both had had several sexual partners, although none had been very satisfactory. Polly, who was 25 years old, had worked her way up as a television scriptwriter, and Richard, 27 years old, was a programme director.

It was a fiercely competitive, fast-paced world in which they worked. The demands were for imagination, creativity, stamina, and success. Richard had done remarkably well for such a young man. Proverbially tall, dark, and handsome, with a light, easy manner, he had been considered a very eligible bachelor and he knew it. Polly, too, had more attention and marriage proposals than she could cope with. She was blonde and willowy, had a great sense of style and saucer-sized blue eyes that belied her tough determination to get ahead. When she and Richard met they realized at once what a stunning couple they made. It seemed inevitable to them that their whirlwind courtship would lead to marriage. Two such well-endowed, success-orientated creatures also expected instant success in their sex life. But they were sorely disappointed.

Richard had in most of his sexual encounters practiced the withdrawal technique and thus acquired a habit of rapid ejaculation outside the vagina. Polly was a self-controlled person who had built up a brittle defence system against her deeper desire to be dependent and protected. She was unable to achieve an orgasm and Richard often suffered from premature ejaculation. Each, without saying so in words, but making it amply clear in their attitudes and actions, blamed the other.

For them sex became a duel and modes of contraception were their chosen weapons. Polly in an elegant scarlet kaftan and Richard in a gold corduroy suit, descended on their doctor demanding a better pill, 'to help her have an orgasm'. The beleaguered doctor had a difficult time persuading them that there was no magical answer to sexual fulfilment, least of all through experimentation with birth-control methods while ignoring the underlying causes for their competitiveness with each other.

In cases such as that of Polly and Richard, it takes a good deal of time for a doctor to help them to work out their problems, and often they must have special help. It is much easier when simple ignorance about contraception is the only obstacle to a successful choice. A doctor can then point out to his patient the exceedingly negligible risks of the pill against the higher risks of pregnancy. He can explain how essential it is to maintain careful temperature records to determine the 'safe' days in the rhythm method, and he can emphasize the need for careful control on the part of the man using the withdrawal technique. He can also demonstrate how correct insertion of a diaphragm is essential for effectiveness, and how refitting must be done after every childbirth or significant weight gain.

Occasionally, a problem will arise with a husband who refuses to let his wife use a contraceptive and will not use one himself. Sex for pleasure as well as for procreation, with the pleasure to be found in marriage or a stable relationship in-

stead of in promiscuous liaisons, is the accepted social attitude today. But should a woman find herself in a situation where her partner rejects all attempts at birth control, it would be wise for her to discuss the problem with her doctor. If the man can be persuaded to go with her on a subsequent visit to the doctor, usually the selfishness of his position can be demonstrated to him, for it is the woman, not he, who runs the risk. A doctor, as professional, emotionally-detached, third person, can explain this better than a distraught woman who lives in fear of bearing an unwanted child.

But the world is still waiting for that utterly simple, perfectly safe for everyone, answer to all our problems, contraceptive. Medical research is constantly being conducted to try to improve or develop new birth-control methods. One method currently being tested in the United States and Mexico is called the Uterine Contraceptive System. This is a soft, flexible, membrane-enclosed, drug packet that is inserted directly into the uterus by the doctor. There it floats freely without causing bleeding or pain. The device contains the hormone progesterone which, in minute amounts, alters the chemical balance within the uterus, just enough to prevent a fertilized egg from becoming implanted, as it must to develop, in the endometrium, or wall, of the uterine cavity. The device contains enough progesterone to be effective for one year.

The Uterine Contraceptive System is indicative of how complicated and widespread the search is for a more perfect method of contraception. Aeronautical engineers from the United States's space programme, who were experts in fluid mechanics, were recruited to design the device since once it is placed in the uterus it must float freely.

If this amazing device proves effective it will add one more possibility to the ever-growing list of reliable contraceptive methods. But new contraceptives and knowledge alone will not answer all the very complex, intensely personal, and intimate problems that arise in the area of birth control. Probably there never will be one simple, safe answer for everyone. Personal needs and temperaments are too diverse. A recognition of the subtleties involved and a willingness to look beyond the purely physical applications by the man and woman, and the advising doctor, is essential to a genuine acceptance and comfortable use of any birth-control method. LAURIE QUILLEN

Abortion

Men and women have always wanted both fertility and sterility, each at the right time and in the chosen circumstances. Planned parenthood should mean parenthood entered into willingly, fully prepared for the sacrifices necessary. What is the role of abortion—and what stresses does it produce?

Abortion is the most expensive form of contraception, mentally, physically, and financially. Every year about 30 million abortions are performed throughout the world. More than 80,000 women ended unwanted pregnancies in England alone in 1970, pregnancies many of which could probably have been avoided.

More than half the pregnancies in Britain are believed to be unplanned. Seven out of ten of these 'accidents' happen because the couple uses no contraceptive measures, not because the method used is faulty. Although proper contraception is preferable to abortion, punishing a couple's negligence by insisting that unwanted children be born is hardly the best solution a society can offer.

Japan and Eastern European countries have the most liberal abortion laws. In Japan unlimited abortion on request by the woman has been legal since 1949. The Japanese cut their birth rate from 34.3 per 1,000 in 1947 to 16.9 by 1961. An abortion is less expensive than a year's supply of contraceptives.

Although women may end pregnancies on demand in the Soviet Union, abortion is not authorized for first pregnancies, on the grounds that it is not good medical practice. There is no social reason why a single woman should have an abortion, since illegitimacy has been abolished and the State cares for the child until a woman can assume the responsibility.

The enforcement of abortion laws in different countries varies more than the laws themselves. In Switzerland, Syria, Honduras, Peru, and Thailand, for example, a woman may have an abortion if the pregnancy endangers her health. In practice, an abortion is fairly easy to obtain in Switzerland, but only two were performed in Thailand in 1963 and four in 1965.

Abortion is strictly prohibited in Belgium and Ireland, while Italy, Austria, the Netherlands, Portugal, and Spain allow the operation if there is a vital danger to the mother. France and West Germany allow abortion if there are medical indications, but again enforcement varies. Some people believe all abortion laws should be repealed, leaving the matter entirely up to the woman and her physician.

There is a common misconception that Scandinavian countries allow abortion on demand. Actually, controls are so tight in Sweden, where abortion was legalized in 1938, that a student association promoted tourist trips to Poland for abortions in 1965. The trips stopped when the Swedish government stated that participants were liable to prosecution.

The most common reason allowed for abortion is a serious threat to the mother's life or to her physical and mental health, from disease, bodily defect, or exhaustion. In 1946 an amendment in Sweden added 'anticipated exhaustion' which might seem like the perfect loophole for liberal abortion practice, but only 11 per cent of all abortions are performed on that basis.

Norwegian law favours social indications: 'When the birth of a child would be a misfortune because of serious or chronic illness of husband or children, alcoholism, criminality, lack of housing, or other specially unfavourable circumstances.' This social consciousness is the reverse of most countries where a therapeutic abortion can

be obtained by the wealthy, but is strictly out of the reach of the poor.

Early criticism that the Scandinavian laws would be exploited is disproved by the fact that the total number of abortions has declined from 6,300 in 1951 to 3,000 in recent years.

In the United States there is no national abortion law. In 39 states pregnancy may be ended to save the life of the mother. In five states it is allowed to save the life or preserve the health of the woman, and three states have expanded the law to include mental health, rape, incest, or the risk that the baby will be defective. Three states prohibit 'unlawful' abortion without clarification.

The State of New York has the most liberal abortion law, enacted in July 1970. There are no restrictions except that abortion cannot be performed after six months of pregnancy.

In 1968, abortion was legalized in England, Scotland, and Wales, 32 years after the foundation of the Abortion Law Reform Association and 16 years after the first Parliamentary bill on abortion was introduced. A woman finally could turn to her general practitioner for help in ending pregnancy instead of seeking the aid of a 'backstreet abortionist' or trying to do the job alone or with the help of a friend.

The Abortion Act of 1968 allows a woman to have a pregnancy terminated by a registered doctor in a National Health Service hospital if two doctors sign a statement that they believe abortion is justifiable. Justification is based on whether a woman's life or her physical and mental health, or the well-being of any existing children, are jeopardized by the pregnancy. Substantial risk that the baby would be born with a physical or mental abnormality serious enough to be a grave handicap also serves as justification. Either risk must be greater than that of abortion.

But the subject is so muddled with myths and moral overtones that objective assessment of risks to a woman is difficult. Even the medical literature is confusing. Reliable statistics cannot be compiled on an illegal operation and the time and experience since legalization of abortion in most countries are too short to yield significant results. Nevertheless, this highly-charged subject evokes reactions ranging from gross exaggeration of the dangers to a complete whitewashing of all risks.

Rumour has it that only illegal 'backstreet' abortions are dangerous whereas an abortion performed in hospital conditions is a perfectly safe, simple operation. The incidence of infection of the womb, pelvic tissues, or blood stream is greater in illegal abortions. Delayed death from haemorrhage caused by clumsy handling of the instruments used or retention of part of the placenta in the womb occurs, often because the woman is afraid to seek medical help after the abortion.

In hospital, complications can be managed efficiently and usually effectively. The most common problems are perforation (puncture) of the uterus with surgical instruments, haemorrhage, embolism (blood clotting), and pelvic infection. Although the operation is not near-fatal, as some opponents of legalized abortion would imply, like all surgical procedures it is still potentially dangerous.

In Sweden five per cent of women who terminate pregnancy before the twelfth week suffer from complications. The rate increases from 15 to 20 per cent for those who wait until the second trimester, or between the twelfth and twenty-fourth week.

Death caused by abortion is less frequent than death from childbirth. In 17 causes of death in British women, abortion is listed thirteenth while childbirth is tenth. In Scandinavia, when the pregnancy is ended legally in sterile conditions before the twelfth week, the death rate is 0.05 to 0.1 per cent, about equal to mortality rates for childbirth. Age increases risk, however. In the age group 35 to 39 years, maternal mortality is twice the national average, and over 40 years old it rises to four times the national mortality rate. After the twenty-eighth week of pregnancy the chances of dying from abortion seem to be about twice the chances of dying from childbirth.

The importance of early abortion is evident. But since the operation must be treated as a surgical emergency it poses problems for already overcrowded hospitals. Each abortion requires a two- to three-day stay in hospital with services of doctors, nurses, and operating-theatre staff. Frequently, because of the delay in getting a bed in hospital, many women still seek illegal abortions.

By the time a woman confirms that she is pregnant, she is usually about six weeks along, leaving her six weeks to find a doctor and get a hospital bed. Some gynecologists who are against abortion on religious grounds will not refer a woman to a doctor who will perform the operation. She may spend two or three weeks looking for a cooperative doctor, even in a country where abortion is legal. With only three weeks left to arrange everything, she is pushing her luck.

After the twelfth week, because the foetus is too large to be removed through the vagina, a hysterotomy must be performed. The doctor must do a caesarian operation, removing the foetus through the wall of the womb. The procedure is more complicated and more dangerous to the woman from a medical standpoint. The operation is not to be confused with hysterectomy which is the removal of the entire womb.

One method used for abortion would solve some of the pragmatic problems by allowing women to have the operation in a clinic as outpatients. Vacuum aspiration, or suction curettage, sucks the contents out of the womb. The entire procedure takes less than five minutes, which is five to seven times less than termination of pregnancy by other methods.

A transparent plastic tube is attached to the suction apparatus. The patient is given an injection to hasten evacuation of

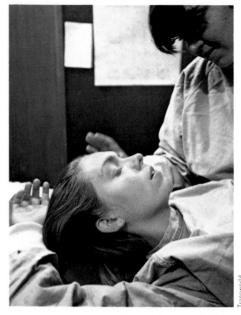

Transworld

Every abortion is an emergency. After a woman discovers she is pregnant she has about six weeks to make arrangements, if she is not to need major surgery. At this stage the operation can be simple—vacuum aspiration, the fastest method, takes less than ten minutes, followed by a few hours' rest. A clinic, especially if it is run as a social service, may try to help the patient through any emotional crisis—and advise on contraception.

the uterus by stimulating muscle contractions. After the bladder is emptied by catheter, she can be given a local anaesthetic or light general anaesthetic. The cervix is dilated, the tube inserted, and, within three minutes, aspiration removes the contents of the uterus. The suction curette is moved up and down, facing all directions within the uterus.

One clinic in the United States does 60 abortions a day by vacuum aspiration. The woman never removes her street clothes. After resting one to three hours in the clinic, she can go home to convalesce, returning to the clinic for periodic check-ups.

Because there is little loss of blood and infection is unlikely, suction curettage is considered the safest method for terminating pregnancy. There should be no danger to the reproductive organs.

The most commonly used abortion technique is dilatation and curettage (D and C). Almost two-thirds of therapeutic abortions are performed through the vagina by stretching the neck of the cervix, scraping out the embryo inside using a curette, a small spoon-shaped instrument. The operation takes about 40 minutes and is done under general anaesthetic.

Another method is the injection of an irritant solution into the uterus which causes the embryo to be expelled. The abdominal skin is anaesthetized and a four- to six-inch needle is inserted slowly into the uterine cavity. Amniotic fluid, which cushions the foetus, is withdrawn and replaced very slowly by a similar amount of sterile solution. Labour generally begins within two to three hours. This

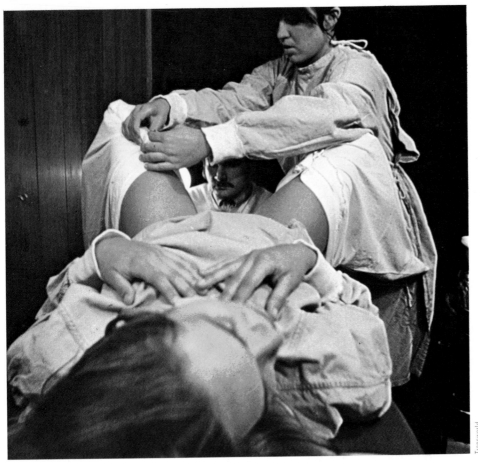

method is usually used for therapeutic abortions and can be done during the second trimester.

These methods are used for legal and illegal abortions. Other illegal methods are varied and most seem to be based on folklore. For centuries women have taken herbs and drugs which are of little value unless the woman tends to miscarry easily. Chemists and surgical stores still sell 'female pills' usually advertised to 'regulate' the periods. The pills contain nothing more then myrrh, quinine, ginger, rhubarb, and cascara. Their only effect is to make the woman ill.

The most dangerous drug used for illegal abortions is potassium permanganate which is inserted into the vagina as crystals, powder, or solution, with a syringe. The substance causes great pain, ulcers, and bleeding. Because of the bleeding the woman thinks she has begun to menstruate. Instead of inducing abortion, however, she can bleed to death.

More strenuous home remedies include cycling uphill, jumping, or falling downstairs Scarlett O'Hara style, or wringing wet clothes with great force. If that does not work, some women try to dislodge the foetus physically by pushing anything from knitting needles and scissors to rubber tubes and wax tapers into the vagina. The most violent method is having someone hit the woman in the abdomen with a board.

If the threat of having an unwanted baby can drive women to such extremes to get rid of it, one wonders why there is so much concern about the 'dreadful psychological after effects' of abortion. According to

one doctor's study, the majority of women who are refused abortion when it is illegal are not glad when they go through with the birth. In considering the psychiatric trauma to any woman, the ill effects of continuing the pregnancy must be weighed against the emotional upset that might result from the abortion.

It is quite easy to dismiss the emotional aspects of abortion by statistics. In a study of 354 women from Scotland who had abortions and their fallopian tubes tied to prevent future pregnancies, one doctor found that only 29 were referred to the regional psychiatric clinic by the family doctor. In only four of these cases was there a possible link between the operation and the referral. In three of those women, the disturbance was trivial.

Dr. M. Ekblad, in Denmark, believes that psychotic and neurotic symptoms are no more common among women who have pregnancies terminated than in the population generally. But in all of these generalizations the individual woman is left out. Only the woman facing the decision to end her pregnancy can honestly appraise her own reaction.

A married woman with three children who decides with her husband's support that a fourth child would cause too much strain emotionally and financially is not likely to suffer guilt feelings. Her motive is a positive one. She is conserving her energy and the family's resources for the benefit of her existing children.

A single woman quite often wants to have a baby by the man she loves. If he is not ready to commit himself to marriage, she

may sublimate her own desires, believing that it is only a postponement. If she does become pregnant, it may be a shock to her when the man suggests, or indeed assumes, that she will have an abortion. The depression she feels after abortion may be masking her anger and disillusionment. Some doctors believe women become pregnant 'semi-deliberately' because they subconsciously want children.

The person left out of most discussions about the pros and cons of abortion is the father. Again generalizations tend to obliterate the individual. The Romans made it a crime for a woman to induce abortion without the consent of the father. The reason, however, was not out of respect for the father's feelings, but because the child was considered the property of the man. Today in Morocco abortion is performed if the woman's health is endangered, but only with permission from her spouse.

Some men want children very much and a man can suffer the after effects of abortion. He may become depressed and feel that his partner's rejection of their baby is a rejection of him personally. Feelings of helplessness may be intensified by the fact that the child is in the mother's body so that the final decision whether it will be born is up to her. But he is unlikely to seek treatment and if he does, he would not be included in statistics labelled 'after effects of abortion'.

While the physical consequences of abortion may be minimized by modern methods in a sanitary setting, the emotional consequences must be considered part of the medical picture. The best and most qualified people to consider these consequences are the man and woman involved.

A psychiatrist who is asked to recommend abortion has the task of assessing the personality of a patient he does not know who is in a temporary crisis. He has to weigh the risk of abortion to her emotional health against the risk of the strain she must suffer by either agreeing to allow the child to be adopted or taking the responsibility upon herself to keep it and care for it—perhaps alone. He must make these decisions without knowing the strength of his patient's personality. The risk of death in psychiatry is the risk of suicide. And despite the common assumption that pregnant women do not carry out threats of suicide, they do.

Regardless of improved contraceptive methods and their wider distribution, pregnancy is still a possibility and termination must be considered. Abortion should not be regarded as a method of birth control, but as emergency treatment for individuals to whom the dangers and disadvantages of continuing the pregnancy outweigh those of ending it.

Until the attitudes towards abortion correlate with society's technological status, women may have to continue having unwanted children. From a medical standpoint, there does not seem to be any reason why a woman who does not want a child should have to bring one into this overcrowded world. SHERRY V. BENN

Venereal diseases

Venereal diseases are diseases passed from one person to another during sexual intercourse. The word 'venereal' derives from the Latin, *venereus*, from Venus, the goddess of love. The most severe are gonorrhoea and syphilis, and it is these two that most countries legally define as venereal diseases or V.D. There are, however, more than a dozen diseases which can be passed on by sexual contact. Today doctors tend to group these infections together under the heading 'sexually transmitted diseases', including such conditions as non-specific urethritis, trichomoniasis, herpes genitalis, and scabies.

Gonorrhoea and syphilis are caught only from an infected sexual partner, and are passed on by sexual activity, heterosexual or homosexual. Some other conditions can be transmitted without sexual involvement, for example, by close bodily contact within a family.

Without medical tests it is impossible to tell whether a person has a venereal disease. A person who practises good personal hygiene could, nevertheless, have a venereal disease. The more sexual partners a person has the greater the risk of infection. Possibly because young people are likely to have more sexual contacts than older people some 60 per cent of all those infected in the world are under the age of 24 years. Other recognizable groups in which the likelihood of infection is higher than average include such people as migrants, servicemen, and seamen, and export businessmen, who travel a great deal or spend long periods of time away from home. People who tend to be promiscuous, such as prostitutes and some homosexuals, also have a greater than average chance of being infected.

Unlike many of the other infections which have plagued mankind, gonorrhoea, syphilis, and most of the other sexually acquired diseases have not been reduced to near extinction by preventative medicine and control measures. Indeed, since the 1950s many sexually transmitted diseases have been increasing in incidence throughout the world, giving rise to mounting concern. The situation is more paradoxical because methods of diagnosis, particularly of gonorrhoea and syphilis, have become increasingly exact and modern treatment gives every assurance of prompt and complete cure, safely and cheaply, to the individual patient.

The incidence of gonorrhoea and syphilis did fall generally throughout the world after the introduction of penicillin during the second world war. But hopes that the use of penicillin and other drugs would control these diseases have not been fulfilled.

In 1963 the World Health Organization reported 53 of 111 countries and areas as showing persistent rises in the incidence of cases of gonorrhoea since 1957. In the early 1960s there were an estimated 60 million cases a year of gonorrhoea, by the 1970s the figure was approaching 180 million. In many areas gonorrhoea has become the second most common infectious disease after measles. Syphilis, too, has been increasing in incidence. In 1954 the World Health Organization reported that there were 20 million syphilitics in the world. A United Nations report, referring to 1967, estimated the number of

the X in sex

Don't let the unknown

factor result in the

hazards of Sexual

Infections

London Borough of Hammersmith Health Education Service.

cases of venereal syphilis at between 30 million and 50 million.

Gonorrhoea is caused by a gonococcus, a bean-shaped bacterium always occurring in pairs, that attacks the mucous membranes setting up an inflammation and causing the production of pus. In both men and women it is primarily a disease of the genitourinary organs, although if untreated it may affect adjacent organs and, rarely, more distant parts of the body.

Infection in adults takes place almost always during sexual intercourse or by genital contact when the affected person deposits natural moisture or discharge containing gonococci on to the genitals of his or her partner. Rarely a person may transfer the infection on wet fingers to his or her eyes. In some cases parents or attendants with gonorrhoea can infect a small girl while attending to the child's toilet needs. And an infected mother can transmit gonococci to her baby's eyes during the birth process.

Non-sexual modes of transmission of gonorrhoea are rare because of the sensitivity of the gonococcus. It dies quickly if deprived of the moisture and warmth of the human body and is highly susceptible to even weak antiseptics. Gonorrhoea cannot be caught from a lavatory seat, for example, because the gonococcus is quickly killed when any discharge dries and cools.

However the new victim contracts gonorrhoea, the incubation period, the time between contact with the disease and its earliest possible detection, is commonly between two and five days and certainly not longer than three weeks.

With few exceptions men with gonorrhoea develop obvious symptoms. They have a discharge of pus from the penis and passing urine gives rise to a slight burning or scalding sensation. Within a week of the start of these symptoms the whole length of the urethra—the tube running from the bladder to the tip of the penis—becomes acutely inflamed. Men are, to this extent, more fortunate than women because the obvious symptoms usually direct their attention to the need for diagnosis and treatment. Occasionally, men who have no symptoms are carriers of gonorrhoea, especially during the incubation period.

Male homosexuals who play the passive role in their relationships frequently develop gonococcal proctitis or inflammation of the rectum, the terminal part of the bowel. Many such men have no obvious symptoms, but those who do complain of discharge from the anus with surrounding irritation. Gonococcal urethritis in homosexuals does not differ from the heterosexually acquired form of the infection.

Complications arise in men who ignore the symptoms or in those where diagnosis or treatment are inadequate and incomplete. Glands at the opening of the urethra or along its length may become involved, leading to the formation of small or large abscesses. The prostate gland which surrounds the urethra at the base of the bladder may be infected and so, occasionally, may the base of the bladder.

Radio Times Hulton

Sir Alexander Fleming discovered the antibiotic penicillin in 1929. Large-scale production began during the second world war. Penicillin is highly effective in the treatment of both gonorrhoea and syphilis.

Gonococci can track along the fine tube which, on each side, runs from the urethra through the prostate gland and around the inside of the pelvic cavity to emerge in the groin and join a testicle. The normal function of this tubing is to carry sperm from the testicle. That part of the delicate tubing which partly surrounds each testicle—there are 36 yards of it—is called the epididymis. Gonococcal epididymitis occurs in one or two per cent of men with gonorrhoea. It gives rise to a red, hard, painful, and tender swelling about the size of a tennis ball. When this inflammation subsides scarring nips the fine tubing of the epididymis and blocks it so that spermatozoa are unable to pass from the testicle. If both sides are involved the man will almost certainly be sterile.

In marked contrast to men, girls and women with early gonorrhoea usually have no symptoms. The few women with early symptoms complain of abnormal vaginal discharge and, in some cases, discomfort on urination—a symptom readily assumed to be cystitis, inflammation of the bladder commonly caused by other organisms. Even the one woman in five who does have these symptoms may regard them as quite unremarkable until she receives notice from a man she has infected. This is one of the most important factors in the spread of gonorrhoea because a woman, unaware that she has the disease, may continue to pass the disease to her sexual partners over a long period of time.

Because the first signs of the disease can be so slight many women fail to seek early treatment, and so complications of gonorrhoea are commoner in women than in men. Abscesses may form at the opening of the urethra or vagina, or menstrual blood or vaginal discharge containing gonococci may run out over the anus and give rise to proctitis.

A far more serious complication of gonorrhoea in women is salpingitis or inflammation of the fallopian tubes. This arises in between five and ten per cent of all women with the infection. Salpingitis occurs when the infecting germ spreads from the neck of the womb up through the womb itself to the tubes which normally carry ova or eggs from the ovaries to the uterus or womb. Both fallopian tubes are always affected simultaneously, although one may be more seriously involved than the other.

Salpingitis can be an acute illness necessitating emergency admission to hospital. The woman experiences severe low abdominal pain and fever, symptoms similar to those of acute appendicitis. In other patients, salpingitis is a sub-acute illness with recurrent and moderately severe bouts of low abdominal pain sometimes more marked on one side than the other. Low backache, occasional high temperature, sickly pallor, general malaise, weight loss, anaemia, and irregular menstruation are common accompaniments. The condition may smoulder for weeks or months to end in a chronic state of pelvic sepsis.

The fallopian tubes themselves eventually develop into bags of pus or become severely scarred, so that ova are no longer able to pass through them and the woman becomes permanently sterile.

In a few men and women, especially women, gonococci may enter the blood stream, circulate, and come to settle in one or more joints, usually the large ones, where they give rise to acute arthritis. Occasionally organisms may settle in the skin, usually around affected joints, and cause a rash of small septic lesions.

Gonorrhoea cannot be diagnosed simply or solely from the sex history of the patient, nor even from consideration of symptoms and blood tests. Laboratory tests, aimed at identifying the gonococci, are essential. Specimens of discharge or moisture from suspected sites, particularly the urethra in the male and the urethra and cervical canal in the female, are smeared on glass slides, dried, stained, and examined microscopically. At the same time similar samples are smeared on biochemical jellies in small flat dishes. These are kept at body temperature and inspected after one or two days. Chemical tests are used to identify organisms growing on the dishes. By determining whether or not gonococci are present the diagnosis of gonorrhoea can be confirmed or denied. Sound and scientific diagnosis in men is usually straightforward, but in women repeated testing is frequently necessary to establish or eliminate the possibility of gonorrhoea.

If the man or woman is found to have gonorrhoea the most effective drug for treatment is penicillin. Where the patient is sensitive to penicillin a wide range of other antibiotics is available. Although, with the passage of time, strains of gonococci have developed some resistance to penicillin, especially in Eastern countries, gonorrhoea can still be cured by one injection of penicillin. The actual dosage used in any area depends on the penicillin sensitivity of the local gonococci. Whatever the drug used, repeated examinations and tests after treatment are essential to assure that it has been successful, and to preclude the possibility that the patient also has another venereal disease such as syphilis.

Syphilis, like gonorrhoea, is a world-wide disease, although its incidence varies widely from one place to another. It may be five to 50 times less common than gonorrhoea, but for those affected it is a much more serious infection, a potential cause of chronic ill-health and even death.

Syphilis is caused by a germ called *Treponema pallidum*, one of a group of coil-shaped micro-organisms known as spirochaetes. Moisture is essential to its survival and for transmisson from one person to another. Like the gonococcus the treponeme dies within a few minutes when drying takes place or when exposed to antiseptic or even soap and water. For this reason, as with gonorrhoea, adults almost always acquire the disease during sexual activity, heterosexual or homosexual.

The first sign of infection is a primary sore, or chancre, which appears where the treponemes first enter the body, usually through some microscopic skin abrasion. In 95 per cent of new victims, therefore, the chancre appears on or in the genitals. In some homosexuals it may appear around the anus or even in the rectum. In a quarter of all infected women the primary sore is on or in the neck of the womb and such women have no immediate indication that they are highly infectious.

There is usually only one primary sore. It tends to be rubber hard, regularly edged, and based with very little surrounding inflammation. It may look painful, but seldom is. Occasionally small, multiple, primary-stage sores appear. For this reason doctors view all genital sores as potentially syphilitic until repeated laboratory tests identify their true cause. In some patients the incubation period before the appearance of the primary sore, usually three weeks, may be anything from nine to 90 days.

The primary sore results from the first stage of the body's attempt to try and prevent the spread of organisms. In the second stage the local glands, usually those in the groins, enlarge, and this may be the first symptom the patient notices. As a rule these defences have little effect and within a week or two the treponemes have entered the blood stream, circulated, and established themselves in every organ of the body. Their presence soon becomes obvious in the skin, causing the appearance of a rash which is at first faint but is soon followed by well-marked, coppery-red, solid blemishes which are usually symmetrically distributed.

The type of rash varies widely according

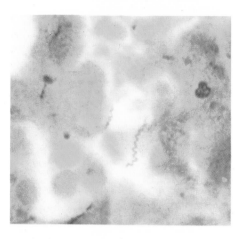

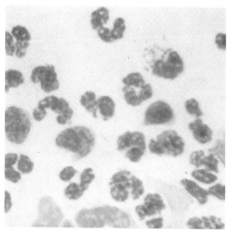

Top *Syphilis is caused by the organism* Treponema pallidum, *a corkscrew-shaped germ less than 1/100 millimetre long.* **Above** *Gonorrhoea results when bean-shaped gonococci invade the cells which line the genito-urinary system causing inflammation.*

to the duration of the infection, the type of skin, the state of personal hygiene, and so on. This is the secondary stage of the disease. The rash is not itchy, but all too frequently imitates other skin diseases and syphilis may go unsuspected as the cause. Lesions in the mouth are common. Undiagnosed and untreated, the rash may come and go. Eventually, usually within four years, the body's defences master the situation. The rash disappears for good and the patient becomes non-infectious.

The disease has now entered the third stage. Although non-infectious to a sexual partner the syphilis is latent or dormant. This stage may last for five to 50 years or even longer.

Between 25 and 30 per cent of undetected and untreated latent syphilitics eventually reveal late or fourth-stage manifestations. These usually occur in chronic, crippling, or killing forms. In the remainder, the disease may die out or become dormant. The majority of late syphilitics develop serious symptoms in the heart and great blood vessels, or in the nervous system, but any organ may be affected. The results are, therefore, usually chronic, syphilitic, heart disease, partial paralysis of the legs, blindness, or syphilitic insanity. Such complications, which may require long periods in hospital, are ex-

tremely costly to the individual, the family, and to society generally.

An expectant mother suffering from syphilis can transmit it, as congenital or hereditary syphilis, to her unborn child, although only after the fourth month of pregnancy. The more recently the mother has acquired her infection the more likely is the foetus to be involved. Even when the mother has had latent syphilis for 10 to 20 years, however, the foetus has only a five in six chance of escaping infection.

The foetus may be so overwhelmed by showers of treponemes into its body that it succumbs to the infection and is miscarried. Succeeding pregnancies may fare better and the child be born alive, but diseased. Like secondary-stage syphilis in the adult, infantile congenital syphilis varies greatly. In some children the signs may be apparent soon after birth. In others, the symptoms are so mild as to give rise to no suspicion of syphilis and it may be years before infection declares itself in the form of inflammation of the eyes or deafness.

In the primary, secondary, or early infantile forms of syphilis the diagnosis can be made by examination under the microscope of fluid from a patient's sores or rash. The finding of treponemes by this method is sufficient to indicate the need for prompt treatment. Where the disease has been present for more than five or six weeks testing the blood for the presence of the body's own antibodies which help fight the disease, the Wassermann reaction test, for example, offers confirmation of the diagnosis. In the latent or third stage only blood tests can detect syphilis.

Many countries give such tests as a matter of course to all pregnant women at each and every pregnancy, and for all donations of blood for transfusions. In some countries they are administered in pre-employment examinations, or prior to marriage.

In cases where syphilis is diagnosed penicillin has still an almost magic quality in its treatment. Cure can be assured for all those found in the primary or secondary stages. Penicillin given to a pregnant syphilitic woman, even near full-term, can practically guarantee a healthy baby. Latent syphilitics can be assured freedom from late complications, and those found with the late forms of syphilis can have the pathological process arrested.

If permanent damage has not been too extensive or severe many such patients improve in general health and are capable of a return to work.

When a syphilitic is found to be allergic to penicillin one of the many other antibiotics can be used with equally good effect. Follow-up and continuing blood tests for a year or two after treatment are essential to ensure that no relapse occurs.

Gonorrhoea and syphilis are the two forms of venereal disease which most people have heard of—and which cause the most fear. But the incidence of other conditions, such as non-specific urethritis, is rising rapidly, and the long-term effects of these sexually transmitted diseases can be dangerous.

As well as gonorrhoea and syphilis there are other sexually transmitted diseases

Besides gonorrhoea and syphilis, which are transferred from person to person almost exclusively through sexual intercourse, there are a number of other sexually transmitted conditions. As with gonorrhoea and syphilis some of these other conditions are rising rapidly in incidence and giving increasing cause for concern.

Non-specific genital infection is becoming a major worry. After penicillin had been introduced, during the 1940s, as an effective cure for gonorrhoea and syphilis, doctors found that a group of diseases that had previously been diagnosed as gonorrhoea did not respond to the same treatment. These conditions result in inflammation of the genito-urinary system similar to gonorrhoea, but they are not caused by the gonococcus organism. In only a small proportion of cases can a cause as yet be recognized, whether it be a parasite, fungus, or bacteria.

The widespread condition non-gonococcal urethritis, inflammation of the tube which carries urine through the penis, is as common among men as gonococcal urethritis. In the few countries which record its incidence there has been a steady increase in the number of cases. In England and Wales, for example, there were 17,000 cases in 1951 and about 51,000 in 1970. In 90 per cent of cases the cause is unknown and the condition is therefore called non-specific urethritis.

Non-specific urethritis usually follows sexual intercourse, after an incubation period longer than that of gonorrhoea. The first signs, a discharge from the penis, discomfort during urination, and a desire to pass water frequently, appear a few days to a month after intercourse. But in some men the symptoms are so slight that they may pass unnoticed for a time.

Most men who are affected, however, consult a doctor or a clinic fairly soon after they contract the infection and treatment with broad-spectrum antibiotics causes the symptoms to disappear. In a small proportion of cases the disease is likely to recur within five years, and in about one per cent of all cases a cure is difficult to obtain.

Between one and two per cent of all men with non-specific urethritis develop

113

Ignore V.D. and it'll get away with murder.

Venereal Disease can be total. Early treatment is essential. It may not only damage your life but your unborn child.

The problems of limiting the spread of venereal diseases are social as well as medical. Education about the effects of venereal diseases—and how they are contracted—can help to persuade those people who have run the risk of infection to seek medical advice.

Reiter's syndrome which can produce arthritis, inflammation of the eyes, skin rash, and sores in the mouth. There may be recurrent bouts of illness, or the condition may smoulder for years. In some cases there may be permanent damage and crippling effects.

In women, non-specific genital infections are far more difficult to diagnose. There may be symptoms of inflammation, but some women are carriers, capable of infecting a sexual partner, without themselves showing symptoms of the disease. In general if a woman's sexual partner develops non-specific urethritis, she is given treatment to reduce the chances of such complications as inflammation of the fallopian tubes.

Although the cause of non-specific genital infection is still a mystery many specialists take the view that a majority of cases are probably due to infection by a virus.

Certainly viruses are responsible for some other forms of sexually transmitted disease. Genital warts are caused by a skin virus like, but distinct from, the virus causing ordinary skin warts. In women particularly, genital warts may be associated with other sexually transmitted diseases. The abnormal discharge caused by any of these diseases provides the moisture essential to the virus growth. Warts may grow externally or internally and it is not unusual to find them also around the anus.

In men, genital warts grow most profusely under the prepuce, or foreskin. They may also appear on the foreskin itself, on the shaft of the penis, just inside the urethra, and around the anus.

These warts are highly infectious.

About half of the sexual partners of people with genital warts develop them within three months. The condition is becoming increasingly common. In England between five and ten per cent of all patients at clinics for venereal diseases have genital warts.

When there are only a few warts, swabbing with a special chemical substance and keeping the area dry and powdered usually produces a cure. Surgical removal may be necessary when the warts are extensive. In some men circumcision may be necessary.

A second viral disease that can be passed on by sexual contact is herpes genitalis, which is caused by a virus belonging to the same family as that which produces 'cold sores' around the mouth, nose, or eyes. The first sign is an itchy red patch on the skin on which a crop of tiny, itchy blisters soon appear. These break down to form tiny shallow ulcers which may resemble early syphilis. Like other forms of herpes there is no satisfactory treatment and the condition tends to recur.

Herpes genitalis is more commonly seen in men. While few women show evidence of infection it is possible that some are carriers of the virus. This carrier state may be long-lasting and there is growing evidence that it may play some part in the onset of cancer of the cervix.

A third, but rarer, virus infection is molluscum contagiosum, which produces tiny blisters, with a central dimple, on the abdominal wall and sometimes on the genitals. The infection can be transmitted just by close body contact, but it most usually follows prolonged body contact during sexual activity. Doctors treat the condition, which is rarely harmful, by opening the blisters and applying phenol.

The commonest cause of an abnormal vaginal discharge is trichomoniasis, a condition caused by infestation with parasites. The trichomoniasis parasite, a one-celled organism only a little bigger

How to tell if you've caught gonorrhoea.

Within 3 to 7 days of infection gonorrhoea will cause a septic discharge, which is usually heavy enough to soil underwear and make urinating painful.

But sometimes this discharge can be slight and watery and only noticeable first thing in the morning.

If these early symptoms are left untreated they'll go on to cause painful swelling of the scrotum (the sack of muscular skin holding the testicles) which could result in permanent sterility.

Women, however, are not so fortunate.

Unless their partner tells them of his own infection, gonorrhoea in women can develop unnoticed. Until it spreads up into the womb.

If you think there's a chance you've caught V.D. please consult your doctor or local hospital. Or contact The Health Education Council, Lynton House, Tavistock Square, London W.C.1. for information.

than a blood cell, is called the trichomonas vaginalis because it is most commonly found in the vagina where it gives rise to vaginitis. The vaginitis may be acute or chronic and gives rise to an abnormal vaginal discharge which is usually yellow and sometimes foul-smelling. Occasionally, the parasite lives in the female urethra and surrounding glands and in some women, when the major symptoms affect the urinary system, the condition may be mistaken for cystitis or inflammation of the bladder.

The diagnosis is readily established by microscope examination of the vaginal

How to catch gonorrhoea.

There's only one way you can catch gonorrhoea.

It's not from lavatory seats or lavatory chains.

It can't be caught just by kissing or touching an infected person.

The only way you can catch gonorrhoea is by having sexual intercourse with someone who's already caught it.

And it's not only prostitutes, and the promiscuous who catch it.

V.D. is now second only to measles as the most widespread infectious disease.

But, unlike measles, V.D. can be very painful and inflict permanent genital damage.

If you think there's a chance you've caught V.D. please consult your doctor or local hospital. Or contact The Health Education Council, Lynton House, Tavistock Square, London W.C.1. for information.

discharge. Where only a few parasites are present, and this method does not reveal them, specimens of the discharge can be sent to a laboratory and the parasites revealed by growth on a suitable medium.

The trichomonas vaginalis can also be found in men, particularly those who have had recent or regular intercourse with a woman suffering from trichomonal vaginitis. A small proportion of these men develop urethritis with discharge from the penis. Most men, however, have no symptoms when they have trichomoniasis, although they are carriers of the parasite.

In the 1950s the treatment of trichomoniasis for both sexes was revolutionized by the discovery of the drug metronidazole. A single course of tablets taken by mouth is enough to cure all cases. Even if the man concerned has no symptoms he should always consult a doctor at the time of his partner's diagnosis. As with other sexually transmitted diseases, tests after treatment are required to ensure that the cure has been complete.

Two other forms of infestation with parasites, scabies, and pediculosis, are also commonly counted among the sexually transmitted diseases although they can also be passed on by close social contact.

Scabies or 'the itch' is caused by a tiny mite. The female mite burrows into the skin and lays eggs. This may affect the finger webs, the fronts of the wrists, the elbows, shoulders, ankles, and, in men, the penis. After an incubation period of three to six weeks itchiness, worse at night when the patient is warm, results.

Scabies is treated by coating the body of the affected person with an emulsion of benzyl benzoate and washing it off a day or two later. Possible contacts are also given the same treatment.

Pediculosis means infestation with lice —small, greyish, blood-sucking insects. Three varieties of lice affect humans— head, body, and pubic lice. The variety that lives in and on the pubic and surrounding hair is shorter, broader, and more crab-like than the other two. Hence the term 'a dose of crabs'. Sexual intercourse is probably the only way the condition is acquired.

The lice, or their eggs or 'nits' which are cemented near the base of the hairs, are large enough to be seen, which makes diagnosis easy. The application of a D.D.T. emulsion, without the necessity of shaving, kills both lice and eggs. As with all sexually acquired conditions it is essential that sexual partners be treated.

A fungus, candida albicans, is another cause of a disease which can be transmitted during sexual intercourse. The fungus produces candidiosis of the vagina, more commonly called vaginal thrush, a white, sometimes curd-like discharge which may be accompanied by vulvar itch which may become more intense when the woman is warm in bed. The fungus is found normally in the hair, on the skin, and in the mouth and bowel. Under favourable conditions, in pregnancy, for example, or after a course of antibiotics, it may undergo rapid growth in the vagina. After sexual intercourse thrush may develop in the sexual partner, causing inflammation and itch under the foreskin. This condition is called balanitis.

Candidiosis can usually be cured by the insertion into the vagina of large tablets containing a fungicide or by the application of a fungicidal cream to external surfaces.

Three other conditions which are transmitted during sexual intercourse have declined in incidence in recent years, even in tropical and sub-tropical areas where they have generally been commonest. To some extent, however, their geographical

spread is wider as a result of the increase in all forms of travel.

They are chancroid, a bacterial infection giving rise to acute painful genital ulceration; lymphogranuloma venereum, a virus disease giving rise to swellings in the groins and internal scars; and granuloma inguinale, which is caused by a bacillus called a Donovan body which gives rise to destructive chronic ulcers of the genitals. With all three diseases antibiotics or sulphonamide drugs effect a cure.

The consequences of infection with a sexually transmitted disease are potentially serious, and the chances of contracting such a disease are rising. In order to control these diseases the provision of adequate facilities for diagnosis, treatment and follow up is necessary. The medical profession and the public must be educated so that those at risk can be warned of the dangers and persuaded to seek treatment. It is also necessary that, if possible, the sexual contacts of infected people be traced so that they may be offered proper treatment.

Individual governments vary in their assessment of the problems raised by sexually transmitted diseases and there is, therefore, a wide range in the steps taken to control them from country to country. There is, however, a growing world-wide awareness that when all methods of control are pursued thoroughly it is to the widespread benefit of individuals, families, and society in general.

In many countries, including Scandinavia, Britain, and the Soviet Union, the most far reaching steps have been taken by establishing nation-wide networks of clinics which deal solely with the diagnosis and treatment of sexually transmitted diseases. In Britain, for example, there are some 230 clinics. Russia, with some 6,000 clinics, was one of the few countries in the world where the incidence of gonorrhoea and syphilis was still falling in 1961.

Attendance at a clinic ensures that not only is diagnosis and treatment easily available, but also that possible complications can be foreseen and all aspects of the disease can be considered.

Countries with no network of clinics may use other methods of attempting to limit the spread of sexually transmitted diseases, for example, by the provision of free medical attention for those suffering from gonorrhoea or syphilis. Ensuring that diagnosis and treatment are effective and carrying out control measures, such as informing potentially infected contacts, is, however, more difficult.

Public education is an essential part of any system for controlling the spread of sexually transmitted diseases. This involves basic sexual education, an explanation of how venereal diseases are spread, a description of the symptoms, and so on. Methods of minimizing the risk of infection by the proper use of condoms and the washing of the genitals before and after intercourse can also be stressed.

Equally important is the need to persuade those people who have risked infection to seek treatment. Of those people who do seek medical advice about sexually transmitted diseases about 25 per cent can

be reassured, after examination, that they are free from infection. Specialists consider this an important part of their preventive work and no one should hesitate to ask for advice

Public education, too, can make clear that diagnosis and treatment are completely confidential, and that the medical staff involved do not pass moral judgements, but are concerned only with giving the most effective treatment possible.

Of all the social methods available for limiting the spread of sexually transmitted diseases, the most direct and effective is the tracing and treating of all the sexual contacts of an infected person.

In an interview the patient is advised of the diagnosis, and is told how the infection has been acquired, and how he or she can help others. In many cases the patient may be embarrassed or ashamed of these sexual encounters, or may feel that his or her marriage is threatened as a result of extra-marital intercourse. However, the doctor or social worker will do everything possible to help the patient. In some cases the sexual contact may have been so casual that tracing is virtually impossible. The more detailed the contact information the more likely is any action taken to be successful.

The patient is sometimes asked to arrange for the man or woman who appears to be the source of infection, and any later contacts that may have been infected, to attend the clinic for examina-tion. For this purpose he will be given contact slips that, as well as giving instructions about obtaining treatment, carry a code that will inform a doctor of the type of infection involved.

In other cases, the doctor or a social worker will write, telephone, or visit the contacts, explain to them that they may have a sexually transmitted disease, and arrange for them to receive medical attention. The people doing this work are highly trained and have great compassion. But they must work quickly to ensure that contacts are reached before they have passed the disease to others or damaging symptoms become apparent.

These voluntary methods of tracing are, however, of limited effectiveness. One survey, in London, showed that only about a quarter of potential contacts were attending clinics for treatment. Some countries, in particular the United States, have pursued more relentless methods.

In 1961, the U.S. Public Health Department established a Task Force whose aim is to eradicate syphilis from the United States. Trained contact tracers visit every doctor twice a year to gather information about patients being treated for syphilis.

Personal interviews with the patients follow, and great pressure is then put on any contacts to attend for examination.

In the most rigorous form of contact tracing, called cluster testing, all those within a social group may be asked to seek medical advice because they are likely to have taken similar risks. In 1962, cluster testing detected 487 syphilitics who might otherwise not have sought treatment—ordinary contact tracing had already discovered 2,047 cases.

However vigorous such methods, the best that can be hoped for is to reduce the incidence of infection, and provide treatment before complications produce disability and give rise to the need for hospital care. Research into new methods of cure, into replacements for penicillin as strains of gonorrhoeal organisms become resistant, and into the causes and treatment of non-specific urethritis, can ensure that treatment is as effective as possible. But the hope for the future, that sexually transmitted diseases can be eradicated as so many other infections have, may depend on the development of immunization techniques. And as yet such research is in its infancy.

The history of venereal diseases

'The French pox', 'Indian measles', 'the Italian disease'—every nation seems to have tried to blame venereal diseases on someone else. What are the real origins of these diseases?

In 1943, as the Allied armies were advancing through Italy hundreds of men lay ill in military hospitals. Out of the battle, using hospital facilities and beds, they were suffering from gonorrhoea, with, in many of the cases, severe complications. The new wonder drug penicillin had just become available. The decision was taken to use it and within three weeks virtually every affected man was back with his military unit. Penicillin proved equally useful in the treatment of syphilis. A simple and effective cure for two of the most frightening venereal diseases had at last been found.

Conquering armies have greatly assisted the spread of venereal diseases, carrying them both from and to their homelands.

The earliest references to a disease that may well have been gonorrhoea probably occur in the Bible. In Leviticus XV God tells Moses and Aaron that a man suffering an issue, interpreted to be a urethral discharge, should be regarded as unclean. Moses recognized that the disease was transmitted by sexual contact. His list of health precautions included the need for washing after sexual intercourse. He also took extreme steps to prevent its spread. Numbers XXXI describes how a victorious Israelite army, returning from war with the Midianites, was kept in quarantine for seven days. Every Midianite woman prisoner who had lain with a man and so might become a source of infection was killed. Despite such drastic measures infections continued among both the high

and the low. In Psalm 38, for instance, King David himself laments that his loins are filled with a loathsome disease.

Hindu mythology also mentions venereal diseases. The god Shiva is described as suffering a disease of the genitals which may have been gonorrhoea. The *Ayurvedas of Susruta*, written in about 400 A.D., specifically described a sexually transmitted disease, detailing how, after intercourse with a woman whose vulva has become the seat of disease, unhealthy humours could attack the penis. The Chinese, too, wrote of diseases passed on by sexual intercourse.

In England the first official recognition of gonorrhoea was a London Act of 1161 which forbade brothel-keepers to house 'women suffering from the perilous infirmity of burning'. The English infirmity of

Gauguin: *Self portrait*/Washington·National Gallery of Art/Snark

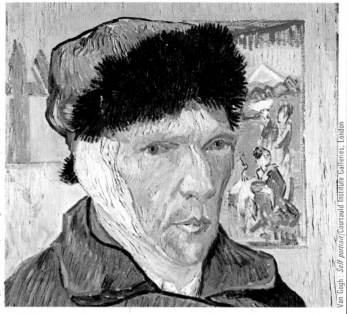

Van Gogh: *Self portrait*/Courtauld Institute Galleries, London

Above *Gauguin and Van Gogh were two great artists who suffered from venereal disease. Gauguin took the disease to Tahiti when he went to live there, and later died in a state of syphilitic madness.*

Below *Louis XIV of France, 'the Sun King', suffered from gonorrhoea. Other great statesmen who are said to have had venereal diseases include Lenin, Napoleon, and Ivan the Terrible.*

burning was in keeping with the French name *la chaude pisse*. The word 'clap' was first coupled with the burning disease in a manuscript by John of Arderne in 1378. although the origins of the term are not known. In 1430, the authorities in London used yet another name when they prohibited brothel-keepers from admitting men with 'the hidden disease'.

Some time after syphilis appeared in Europe at the end of the fifteenth century, the two diseases, syphilis and gonorrhoea, became confused and were thought to be one and the same, a view that persisted until the end of the eighteenth century. Earlier in the eighteenth century, at a time when 'It is hardly one (chance) in ten that a Town Spark of that age has not been clapt', the renowned surgeon John Hunter (1728-93) believed the different symptoms depended on where the 'poison' entered the body. To prove his point, he inoculated himself with pus from an infected man.

The man, however, was suffering from both syphilis and gonorrhoea and the results of the experiment were both misleading and unfortunate. John Hunter was to die from the later effects of the syphilitic infection.

In 1793, Dr. Benjamin Bell finally proved that there were two diseases, clearly distinct in their incubation periods and clinical appearance, by carrying out experiments on his medical students. Philippe Ricord, a Parisian venereologist, confirmed these findings. The organism that caused gonorrhoea, the gonococcus, was identified in 1879, shortly after the introduction of the microscope. Soon it became possible to grow the germ in the laboratory and prove, by injecting it into people, that it was, without doubt, the cause of the trouble.

Not until the mid-1930s did the treatment of gonorrhoea reach a scientific level. For centuries its treatment had been a chancy affair and many tens of thousands suffered from complications. Blindness in

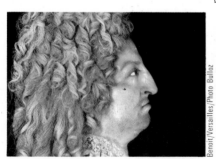

Benoit/Versailles/Photo Bulloz

K. Petrav-Vodkin/Novosti

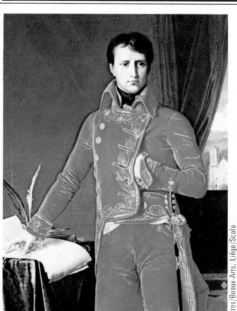

Ingres/Beaux Arts, Liège/Scala

S.C.R./U.S.S.R.-London

Ph. de Champaigne/Versailles/Photo Bulloz

National Portrait Gallery (detail)

CARDINAL WOLSEY

babies and sterility in women were commonplace. Doctors were limited to prescribing local washes, so-called curative vaccines, or weak antiseptics taken by mouth and excreted in the urine. The introduction of the sulphonamide drugs in 1936 brought the first effective cure for gonorrhoea, but its success was short-lived. Resistant strains of the gonococcus appeared and within a decade sulphonamides became of little use. At just this point pencillin revolutionized the treatment of gonorrhoea, although once again, albeit slowly, resistance to this and other antibiotics is developing.

The history of syphilis generally dates from 1495 when an epidemic swept Europe. There are two main theories about how the disease was brought to Europe. One theory is that it was carried from the Americas when Columbus and his men returned from their voyage of discovery in March 1493. The other theory argues that syphilis is

one form of a disease called yaws, which is common in the tropics. In Europe the disease organisms adapted to the conditions of a colder climate. Because the skin on which they had lived was no longer hot and sweaty they had to move to the warm, moist areas of the body, genitals, mouth, and anus. They could no longer be passed on by ordinary social contact, but were transmitted by the prolonged contact of sexual intercourse.

According to the yaws theory, the epidemic which swept Europe could have stemmed from an alteration in the yaws organism brought to Europe by slaves imported from Africa. Alternatively, syphilis could have existed in a mild form for centuries, the organism suddenly developing a new virulence. A third theory is that both yaws and syphilis appeared simultaneously. Yaws died out about 1610, with the spread of education about hygiene, but syphilis has remained.

Above *Among the important figures in the history of the Church are popes and cardinals who suffered from venereal diseases. Two such examples were Cardinals Richelieu and Wolsey who enjoyed enormous worldly power.*

Below *Great writers with venereal diseases include Molière, who died of syphilis, Boswell, who had gonorrhoea, Dostoevsky, and Baudelaire who became insane as the result of syphilis.*

Mignard/Chartres/Photo Bulloz

National Portrait Gallery (detail)

S.C.R./U.S.S.R. London

Deroy/Versailles/Photo Bulloz

Hoping to become immune, John Hunter inoculated himself with pus from a V.D. sufferer—and later died of syphilis.

Whatever the truth, and there is no conclusive evidence of the earlier existence of syphilis in Europe, the Middle East, or the Far East, there is no doubt that the great epidemic spread alarm throughout the European continent.

The first major appearance of syphilis was among the soldiers of both sides during the siege of Naples in 1495. Ruy Diaz de Isla, a Portuguese physician practising in Barcelona, was later to state that the 'Indian measles' for which he had treated some of Columbus's men was the same disease.

The invading army of Charles VIII of France consisted of European mercenaries. The defenders included Spanish soldiers and, possibly, some of the sailors with 'Indian measles'. There was no decisive battle, but the new disease played havoc among both attackers and defenders. Charles abandoned the campaign and paid off his troops who dispersed across Europe, spreading the infection like wildfire. It reached Paris in 1496, London in 1497, and in the same year the authorities of Aberdeen in Scotland passed regulations that clearly recognized that the disease was passed by sexual contact. Within another year, according to records, syphilis had been carried to India, and, by 1505, it had spread to China.

Each country blamed others for the affliction. The French called it 'the Italian disease', the English and the Germans referred to 'the French pox', and the Japanese described it as 'the Portuguese sickness'. The name 'syphilis' arises from a poem written in 1530 by an Italian physician, Girolamo Fracastoro. The hero, Syphilus, offended the god Apollo, and was then struck down by a terrible disease. The symptoms were just those of the infection which was raging throughout Europe.

Tens of thousands of people died in the hundred years or so that the epidemic continued. The new disease was at its most virulent and the symptoms, baffling in their multiplicity, could include widespread rashes, ulcers extending into the mouth, nose, and throat, bone pains, and fever. By the seventeeth century the disease had become less obvious. While it was still a serious infection, early death was unlikely.

At first the only form of treatment was prayer and isolation. St. Denis, patron saint of Paris, was the favoured saint of syphilitics. Later, mercury, which had long been used in all forms of skin disease, was adopted for syphilis. Mercury preparations could be rubbed into the skin, taken by mouth, or the fumes could be inhaled. Unfortunately, the remedy was almost as dangerous as the disease, and patients ran a high risk of mercury poisoning. In the nineteenth century an Irish physician, William Wallace, introduced potassium iodide as a treatment for some late forms of syphilis. This is still occasionally used today.

In 1905 two Germans, Dr. Fritz Shaudinn and Dr. Erich Hoffmann, discovered the organism that causes syphilis, the *Treponema pallidum*, and in 1906 another German, Dr. August von Wassermann, developed a blood test that made diagnosis of syphilis more certain. These discoveries gave impetus to the search for a better method of treatment. By 1912 Dr. Paul Ehrlich, in Germany, had first developed and then improved a new form of arsenic, to be used as a drug, that cured syphilis without killing the sufferer. The arsenical preparations were highly effective, although a course of treatment could last two years or more, and were superseded only by the discovery of penicillin.

Attitudes towards venereal diseases have varied both with knowledge about their effect and with society's feelings about sexual indulgence in general. During the hundred years that syphilis was most virulent it was greatly feared and attempts were made to isolate sufferers. The Puritanism associated with Cromwell's Commonwealth in Britain continued this attitude into the seventeenth century, when venereal diseases were described as loathsome and filthy.

During the eighteenth century, with the Age of Enlightenment, came a greater acceptance of sexual freedom. Casanova himself could remark, 'There is no need for harlots in this fortunate age! So many decent women are as obliging as one could wish.' Not surprisingly, venereal diseases were common and considered lightly. The initial stages of the disease were no longer as severe as they had once been. And doctors had not yet recognized that syphilis could lead to insanity, heart disease, paralysis, and blindness.

The pendulum swung once more during the nineteenth century and venereal diseases again became regarded as sinful and degrading, a dreadful penalty for straying from the path of good behaviour. The law attempted to follow the change in morals. In 1864 the British Government passed the Contagious Diseases Act which euphemistically attempted to protect military personnel from 'venereal disease, including gonorrhoea'. Women suspected of spreading venereal disease could be compelled to submit to medical examination, forced to wear yellow clothes for identification, and were isolated in special hospital wards, which came to be know as canary wards.

Mrs. Josephine Butler, who was born in 1828, formed the Ladies' National Association in 1869. She claimed that this law deprived defenceless and under-privileged women of their rights, and started a campaign that led to its repeal in 1886. By the end of the nineteenth century, the decline in the venereal disease rates among servicemen confirmed that the moral bias against women had been unjustified. Other attempts to control the transmission of venereal diseases through the threat of the law have had equally little success, although they may have reinforced social pressures on individuals to seek treatment.

Venereal diseases have been no respecters of titles, talents, or wealth, and many famous people have been revealed as suffering from syphilis or gonorrhoea. Louis XIV, the Sun King of France, had gonorrhoea. In England, Henry VIII probably suffered from syphilis, and Edward VII had gonorrhoea. Ivan the Terrible and Frederick the Great both contracted venereal diseases. Among writers and musicians James Boswell, the biographer of Samuel Johnson, had gonorrhoea; Guy de Maupassant and Charles Baudelaire became insane as the result of syphilis; Molière and Schumann died from it, and Beethoven's deafness may have resulted from congenital syphilis. Artists, too, have suffered. Gauguin, for instance, spent his last years in a state of syphilitic madness. Such political figures as Napoleon, Lenin, and Woodrow Wilson have been affected, and even Popes and Cardinals have contracted venereal diseases.

Following the discovery of penicillin by Sir Alexander Fleming, and its mass production during the second world war, many people believed that the end of syphilis and gonorrhoea as common diseases was within man's grasp. Indeed, for some years it looked as if this might be true. In the mid-1950s, however, the fall in infection rates in nearly all parts of the world ceased. Incidence levels remained steady for a few years and then began to climb throughout the Western world.

In 1954 the World Health Organization reported that there were 20 million syphilitics in the world. In 1967 the estimate was between 30 and 50 million. In the case of gonorrhoea, 60 million infections were estimated in the early 1960s. By 1970 it was estimated that there were 150 million infections a year. In several European countries gonorrhoea is now recognized as epidemic. In the United States, where there is one of the highest levels of venereal disease in the world, the rate is said to be 800 infections per 100,000 of the population a year. Gonorrhoea is now second only to measles among the reported and notifiable infections.

This serious situation, which exists throughout the world, has arisen for many reasons, but high venereal disease rates are no longer associated with poverty, but rather with prosperity, and not only with war, but with relative peace.

In each of the decades 1930 to 1940 and 1940 to 1950 the world population increased by 225 million people. Between 1950-60 there were 500 million additional births and in the 1960s another 600 million children were born. In many countries, therefore, the number of young and sexually-active people has grown substantially. Many more will soon enter their teens and adulthood. Inevitably, the number of sexual contacts grows. Increased longevity, earlier physical development, and the postponement of the menopause also contribute to the greater incidence of venereal disease.

Technological progress, rapid industrialization, and the resulting crowding of people into renewed and extending urban areas, make a further contribution. Such areas attract the young seeking work or education. They also attract the promiscuous, the prostitute, and the homosexual. Opportunities for casual and promiscuous sex, which lead to increased venereal infections, are provided by such environments.

With increased prosperity, opportunities for travel multiply both within countries and between them. Population movement has many forms. Immigrants, air crews, professional and business people, merchant seamen, and servicemen move about the world in increasing millions year by year. Such short or long absences from home are well recognized as offering opportunities for casual sexual relationships or associations with prostitutes, which all too often carry the hazard of infection, especially for unattached males.

Another factor in the rising venereal rates is the change in people's attitudes towards sexual activity. Modern attitudes towards premarital sex are reflected in the growing number of casual sexual relationships and the increasing frequency of partner change. As in the eighteenth century in Europe there is a demand today in many countries for freedom from existing laws, not least those which concern sexual matters. Pressures exist in many lands for more liberal views regarding homosexuality, abortion, provision of contraception, and divorce. Slowly but surely more homogeneous behaviour patterns cross the old boundaries of customs associated with creed and nationality. These changes have been strengthened and accelerated by the introduction of the contraceptive pill, which frees the woman from the fear of pregnancy. Unlike the condom, however, the pill offers no bar to infection. Increasing rates of venereal disease are a consequence.

The long history of venereal diseases is not yet at an end. The present rise in incidence of sexually transmitted diseases is likely to continue. The future cannot be viewed with optimism. Legal, moral, social, and medical endeavours, even when seriously employed, have shown themselves to be only partially effective as a means of controlling the spread of venereal disease. The hope for the future lies in dealing with these infections in the way that poliomyelitis, diphtheria, and smallpox have been controlled in most of the world. That is by research aimed at the development of immunization or vaccination techniques. R. S. MORTON

121

Advances in sexual research

How varied is human sexual behaviour? What happens during sexual arousal? As the result of sexual research these questions can now be answered—and people can be helped to overcome sexual problems.

Sex, in one way or another, probably interests most people more than any other subject. The impulse for sexual union is a long, complicated process which is intermingled, as Havelock Ellis said, with all the highest and most subtle human emotions and activities.

For hundreds of years, sex has been discussed and written about with little distinction between fantasy and fact. While conjecture and intuition may be accurate enough to disclose the essential nature of such an intimate, subjective experience, objective investigation data have been needed to reveal the physiological processes. This has been needed not only by the layman, whose interest in reading about sex is often prompted by uncertainty about his own sexual adequacy, but also by the doctor, who is often asked for advice from individuals and couples with sexual difficulties and has certainly needed

much accurate information on the subject.

In the past the doctor has, unfortunately, often known as little about sex as his patient. As recently as the 1950s, physiology textbooks studied by medical students included chapters on reproduction and fertilization, but rarely even mentioned the physiology of coitus. The doctor's 'facts' were often learned during adolescence or from such questionable 'medical' literature as marriage manuals—just like everybody else.

Scientific curiosity had led to investigation of every other phase of physiology, but many obstacles prevented research in sex. That may seem strange in today's world where sex sells everything from automobiles to chocolate bars on television screens and billboards. Personal conflicts about sex may have prevented some scientists from studying the subject. Until recently society, too, has played its part in

rejecting any work done on the subject. A scientist requesting funds for sex research risked criticism or censure and might have been suspected of having an abnormal interest in the subject.

Sigmund Freud was, perhaps, the first to break through some of these attitudes towards sexual practices. His work was on the psychological plane, however, not the physiological. He traced infant sexuality through the oral and anal stages to an adult and genital sexual experience. Unfortunately, some of his ideas have become the basis for present-day sex myths. For example, his linking of 'adult' and 'genital' has been interpreted by many people to mean that a person who is capable of enjoying uninhibited, heterosexual intercourse is psychologically more mature than someone who is not capable of being totally uninhibited in a heterosexual experience.

Freud, however, was one of the first physicians to listen to his patients. His talks with them showed the therapeutic value of psychotherapy and led him to develop his theories concerning, among other things, infant sexuality, libido, erogenous zones, and the Oedipus complex. He realized the importance of the early years of a child's development and the relationship between parents and child during those years. His ideas have slowly seeped into the concepts of modern Western society.

The American gynaecologist Dr. Robert L. Dickinson was one of the first to investigate the physiology of sex. In the 1920s he studied the sexual response in women by direct observation, using a glass vaginal dilator and speculum while the woman stimulated herself to orgasm. He did not dare to publish his observations in his day. The pelvic-congestion syndrome, as it is known today, which occurs in women who respond sexually but do not have an orgasm, was recognized and labelled the 'engagement-pelvis syndrome' by Dickinson. His work was the catalyst for the study of sex education.

When Indiana University instituted a course on sex and marriage in 1937 it was taught by Dr. Alfred C. Kinsey, a biologist, who was chosen because he was the pillar of conservatism, a married man with four children. But, being a scientist, Dr. Kinsey decided to research the subject matter of his course and discovered that no valid statistical studies had been done on sexual activity. He set about gathering his own statistics. His work resulted in two publications which are landmarks in the study of sexual behaviour. His books—on sexual behaviour of the male, published in 1948, and of the female, in 1953—became best-sellers.

The first thing that Kinsey concluded from his interviews and questionnaires was that there is a surprising variation of sexual behaviour and attitudes from one socio-economic class to another. He found that petting, for example, is primarily an activity of middle-class or upper-class males who have attended secondary school or university. Lower-class boys pet sometimes, but coitus is generally their goal. Among women, however, this relationship of petting to social class does not exist.

Through his research Kinsey learned about kinds of sexual behaviour of which he had not previously known. He added them to his questionnaire and by 1939 the standard Kinsey interview included questions about six ways in which males and females achieve orgasm: through noctural sex dreams or seminal emissions, masturbation, heterosexual petting, heterosexual intercourse, homosexual intercourse, and contacts with animals of other species.

Probably the most startling conclusion of his study was that orgasm is as much a part of the human female's sexual response

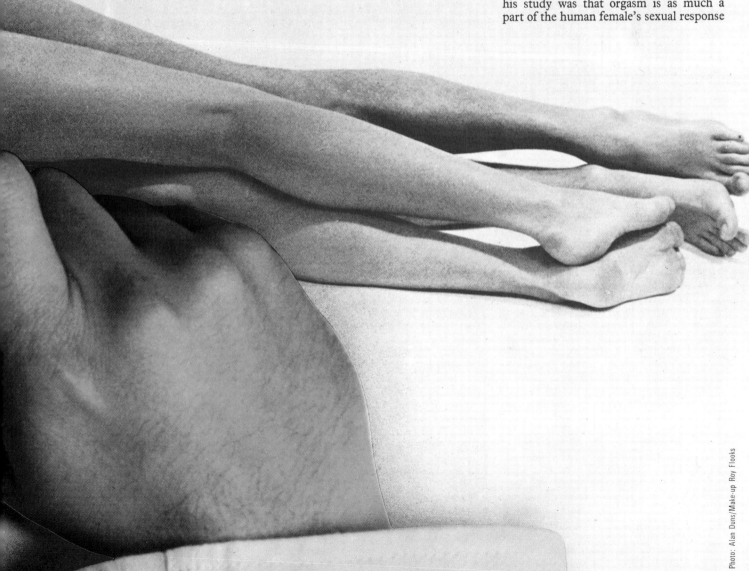

Photo: Alan Duns/Make-up Roy Flooks

as it is for the human male. Previously it had been thought that women always take longer than men to reach orgasm. But Dr. Kinsey found that some women regularly reach orgasm within 15 to 30 seconds after sexual arousal begins.

He found that the average husband experiences 1,523 orgasms before marriage, which is about the same number he will experience during the first 15 to 20 years of marriage. The average wife experiences only 223 premarital orgasms. After marriage most men reach orgasm in almost all episodes of coitus with their wives. The women, in contrast, reach orgasm only about 75 per cent of the time.

Premarital orgasm, whether by masturbation, petting, or coitus, seems to result in greater orgasmic response than in marital coitus. Of the girls who had experienced orgasm before marriage, 45 per cent experienced it in all or almost all marital coitus during the first year of marriage. Of the girls who had not experienced orgasm before marriage, only 25 per cent experienced it always or almost always during the first year of marriage.

Kinsey's research suggested that the probable cause of female frigidity in marriage was the repression of all sexual responsiveness, especially by the prohibition of masturbation, in girls and young women before marriage. This indoctrination, which had never really kept girls chaste anyway, robbed them of the pleasure they might have had and even influenced sexual responsiveness in marriage. A girl's years of conditioning in repressing sexual responsiveness cannot be erased by the marriage ceremony.

Kinsey's one finding which caused an uproar in 1948 was that 37 per cent of males have had or will have had at least one homosexual experience to orgasm at some time between adolescence and old age. Only 28 per cent of the women interviewed reported one or more recollections of homosexual arousal by the age of 45.

Kinsey's aim was not to interpret physiological or psychological response to sexual stimuli. He merely wanted to estab-

lish a baseline of sociological information about sexual attitudes and practices. Many of his critics labelled Dr. Kinsey obscene, but he opened the way to further scientific investigation. 'He hasn't even got love in the index,' one of his critics wrote, not appreciating that first must come the 'what' before research can be done on 'why'.

After Dr. Kinsey's books were published and became best-sellers, the dam which held back plain language about sex broke. Articles appeared in popular magazines, pamphlets, newspapers, and books.

Finally, in the early 1960s, a research team led by Dr. William H. Masters and Mrs. Virginia E. Johnson published the first objective studies on human sexual response. In their work, they asked two questions: *What* physical reactions develop as men and women respond to sexual stimulation? *Why* do they behave as they do?

In their book, *Human Sexual Response*, Masters and Johnson compared male and female reactions to various sexual stimuli.

The first indication of arousal for the male is penile erection and for the female, vaginal lubrication. One important discovery was that erection, vaginal lubrication, and orgasm are all related to what is called the vasocongestive response.

Vasocongestion simply means congestion of the blood vessels in the pelvic region caused by sexual stimulation. Orgasm dissipates this congestion in the man in a quite obvious way. The penis, which is erect because of the congestion of blood, becomes flaccid after orgasm. Masters and Johnson showed that one aspect of a woman's orgasm is detumescence—or a flowing of this extra blood out of the pelvis again. A woman who is repeatedly sexually stimulated, but does not reach orgasm, may develop symptoms and frustrations as a result.

These symptoms may even seem unconnected with sexual tension and may include such feelings as irritability, discomfort, emotional upset, insomnia, backaches, and other common medical and emotional complaints.

Vasocongestion of the pelvic area makes a woman easily aroused sexually during certain periods of pregnancy. In a nursing mother, vasocongestion is the partial cause for the sexual stimulation focused on the breasts. A suckling infant can cause sexual arousal. Some women achieve orgasm by breast manipulation alone. The vaginal response during such an orgasm is identical to clitoral stimulation or coition. The uterus and breasts all take part in the same response.

Masters and Johnson supported some previously held theories with fact and erased many myths. Misunderstandings about the nature of vaginal lubrication, the physiology of orgasm, and the anatomy of the small penis-complex were clarified by their laboratory findings.

The vaginal walls often become lubricated within 10 to 30 seconds from the time sexual stimulation begins. For many years it had been thought that the vaginal lubrication came from glands in the cervix (the mouth of the womb) and Bartholin's glands at the vaginal opening. Masters and Johnson developed techniques for their research work that allowed direct observation of the vagina, including microscopic viewing. They took motion pictures from the first stages of sexual stimulation through orgasm and found that vaginal lubrication exudes through the vaginal mucous membrane that develops. When the woman is effectively stimulated lubrication precedes the massive pelvic vasocongestion to a large extent.

Another myth destroyed by Masters and Johnson was that of the supposed difference between an orgasm achieved by stimulation of the vagina and that resulting from stimulation of the clitoris alone. Physiologically there is no difference. The woman's physiological responses to effective sexual stimulation develop consistently, regardless of the source of psychic or physical sexual stimulation, although the variety of subjective sexual responses among women is, very naturally, infinite.

Masters and Johnson proved, too, that it is nonexistent or extremely rare for vaginas

Life magazine

Above left From 1937 *until his death in* 1956, *Dr. Alfred C. Kinsey, an American scientist, carried out surveys of human sexual activity. His findings revealed the variety of sexual behaviour.* **Above** *During the 1960s, Dr. William H. Masters and Mrs. Virginia E. Johnson investigated the physiological responses of the body to sexual stimulation and, in consequence, formulated a programme of treatment for couples with sexual problems.*

and penises to be incompatible or anatomically inadequate for the sex act. Psychiatrists are consulted by many men who have a 'small penis complex'. A man comes to the psychiatrist complaining that his penis is not large enough to fill a vagina. He tells the doctor he has done his own survey in athletic clubs, locker rooms, or Turkish baths, and he knows that his penis is smaller than average.

Masters and Johnson have completely discredited such a man's conclusions about his sexual adequacy. By measuring the erect penises of 80 men at the moment of greatest sexual excitement, rather than in the flaccid state, they discovered that there is no great difference in the size of erect penises. And, further, they found that penis size has no correlation with the partner's satisfaction. A man who complains of a small penis is actually saying he feels sexually inadequate. Psychiatrists now have scientific proof to back up their own suspicions that the worries of such a man are fantasy.

Women sometimes complain that the vagina is flabby and does not grip the penis. Masters and Johnson say that the vagina is just a potential space which accommodates to the size of the male organ. An artificial plastic penis, the length and diameter of which could be changed, was used in laboratory experiments to show that the first few thrusts of the penis, regardless of size, determine the size of the vagina.

That women have sexual intercourse with varying degrees of arousal, responsiveness, and enjoyment, and with irreg-

ular orgasms, has long been a puzzle. By objectively observing the physiological response of women, Masters and Johnson could eliminate the variety of subjective descriptions about the sensations during orgasm.

In their research, which involved large numbers of women, they found that the total physiological response of breasts, skin, clitoris, and labia always leads to orgasm, regardless of the subjective response or the type of stimulation. An important factor in a woman's achievement of orgasm is the need for continual stimulation until a climax is reached. If her partner stops all movement, perhaps to postpone his own ejaculation, she will need more time to reach a climax.

Masters and Johnson also examined, for the first time, multiple orgasms. They showed that women are capable of multiple orgasms without any break or recovery period between orgasms. Men, generally, need 15 to 30 minutes after an initial orgasm before they are able to achieve erection to continue sexual activity. For many years, however, sex has been considered the male's prerogative. Woman has been seen as the instrument for his pleasure. This research showed that women have as great a capacity for sexual response as men, and that most women are capable of orgasm if they are properly stimulated and the interpersonal relationship is satisfying to them.

One of the strongest criticisms of Masters and Johnson's work is that, because of the subjective nature of sex, facts found in a laboratory by observing human beings copulating or masturbating, while wired from head to foot, cannot be trusted. The researchers say, however, that they have purposely left psychological data out of their studies. The very fact that scientific physiological discoveries were consistent, despite the variety of subjective responses in a large number of experimental subjects, may actually strengthen the validity of their results.

Once Masters and Johnson had established reliable information on the physiol-

ogy of sex, they began to develop therapeutic procedures to treat couples with sexual problems. Both Dr. Masters, a gynaecologist, and Mrs. Johnson, a psychologist, act as co-therapists. They will not treat one person alone since they believe that both partners in a marriage contribute to any resulting sexual dysfunction. This is contrary to attitudes in the past when doctors would treat the impotent man and the woman who could not reach orgasm as separate entities.

Patients are referred by doctors, psychologists, social workers, or theologians, to the St. Louis Reproductive Biology Research Foundation, where Masters and Johnson carry out treatment. They spend two weeks in a hotel as if they were on holiday and must agree to a five-year follow-up study. Relaxation and recreation are adjuncts to therapy and the couple devote the entire two weeks to each other. As well as intensive daily schedules at the foundation they are assigned 'homework' with each other.

All sessions are recorded in order to protect the privacy of the individuals by eliminating the need for an outside person to transcribe and type notes about each session. The couple's first instruction is: no sexual activity until otherwise directed. They are both given thorough physical and laboratory examinations. Then the treatment begins at round-table discussions with both therapists and both partners. At this time, anxieties, prejudices, myths, and misinformation are brought out into the open and discussed. Afterwards they are given their first exercise schedule to follow for themselves in the privacy of their bedroom.

These 'sensate focus' exercises are designed to bring about an appreciation of slow-motion physical contact between the husband and wife. They are told to touch and pet each other everywhere except breasts and genital areas without any demand for sexual performance by either partner.

After four days, breast and genital touching is permitted. Each partner is en-

Paul Fusco/Sense Relaxation/Transworld Features

couraged to direct the other's hands to particularly sensitive areas of the body. Still no coition is allowed. On the fifth day one or both partners is treated for the specific dysfunction which affects him or her. The major disorders which have been successfully treated are premature ejaculation, inability to ejaculate, some types of impotence, orgasmic dysfunction, vaginismus, and painful intercourse.

Masters and Johnson's main goal in developing this therapeutic programme is to train other clinicians who will treat couples at treatment centres throughout the United States.

Indeed, today's more open attitudes towards sex information are already doing away with many causes of sexual dysfunction. Some relationships, for instance, fail because of sexual ignorance. More knowledge of sexual anatomy and sexual techniques prevents such failure. Although knowledge about sex never takes the place of a good emotional adjustment, it is of great importance within a relationship.

Kinsey's work, too, by revealing the sexual habits of thousands of people, has helped many individuals to realize they are not odd or sinful because they behave in a certain way. People who had thought their own desires for certain kinds of sexual stimulation were unusual or perverse finally realized that the majority of men or women had the same feelings.

One of the most valuable results of the research has been dispelling many misconceptions which had been held by doctors. Most doctors have told patients recovering from chronic illness to refrain from sexual intercourse because of the danger of making the physical condition worse. More research must be done on this subject, but many doctors suspect the reverse is probably true.

Recent advances in sex research also question the prohibition of coitus during pregnancy. If a pregnancy is normal there seems to be no reason to avoid sex for six to eight weeks before and after delivery. Some doctors used to tell a pregnant patient to resume petting instead of having full sexual intercourse. Findings that uterine contractions sometimes are stronger during masturbation than during intercourse show what poor advice it was.

Now that the way has been cleared for sex research it is obvious that many other myths will be erased through detailed scientific studies into the physiology of sex and research can be extended into other areas.

Research can be done, for example, on the psychological aspects of coitus. The variety of responses felt subjectively during orgasm are psychological in nature. In Western culture, the main influence on the pleasure of coitus is the love relationship. Now that scientists know the normal physiological responses of sexual intercourse they can begin to investigate how they are affected by individual feelings—such as love.

2

THE ART
OF
LOVING

Alan Duns

The playground of marriage

For a man and a woman love-making can be a beautiful and satisfying experience, but this means they must understand and care for each other's needs. In their love-play, the partners arouse their sexual feelings to the point where they will both derive the greatest enjoyment from intercourse. At the same time, they experience the emotional satisfaction which comes from the expression of their feelings for each other.

Every man knows how to make love to a woman—or thinks he does.

But how many men really understand how to arouse a woman? Surprisingly few.

Doctors concerned with marital relationships find that thousands of men who are convinced that they are 'great lovers', and need no instruction in sexual matters, have wives who are sexually unsatisfied and unhappy. Too often, such marriages fail because the husband does not excite his wife before intercourse by simple techniques of love-play or 'foreplay'.

When Edward married he had had very little sexual experience, and no early sex education. Most of what he knew about sex came from listening to friends. Joan and he were physically attracted to each other and very much in love. Nevertheless, their wedding night was a disaster—as far as Joan was concerned. She was disappointed and unhappy because she had expected intercourse to be a gratifying experience and could not understand why it was not. Edward enjoyed their love-making and was too inexperienced to realize that Joan was unsatisfied.

After a few years of marriage, their sexual relationship settled into a regular pattern. Every Saturday night they had intercourse. But Edward's approaches were nothing more than crude assaults which Joan would pretend she enjoyed, although secretly dreading them. She never reached

129

feel the beginnings of arousal deep within her. By then, however, it was too late. Edward was already asleep.

The next day, Edward would often jokingly refer to the night's sexual encounter, convinced that he had given yet another outstanding performance.

For ten years, Joan endured this, pretending, for the sake of the marriage, that she was satisfied by her husband's love-making. Then she was attracted to another man, a neighbour. His first kisses excited her and one day, alone in the house, they made love. He skilfully aroused her desire so that their love-making was an intense and exciting experience. She felt guilty about the affair, but, when it ended, her married life seemed more futile and unsatisfactory than ever. She confided in her doctor, who agreed to give her husband advice.

Edward was furious. That his wife should seek medical help was, he felt, casting doubt on his 'virility'; and he saw the doctor's suggestion that he learn something of the technique of love-play not only as insulting, but also as an invitation to indulge in 'perversions'. Edward was convinced that his love-making, without any preliminaries whatever, was 'right' and 'natural'. And he also made it clear to the doctor that he possessed a particularly large penis, that this made him 'virile', and that Joan should be grateful for what she was getting, and not want any fancy frills. Because of Edward's attitude their marriage ended in divorce.

T his is not a unique case. A great many women are unhappy and sexually frustrated. Because their partners are selfish, thoughtless, and ignorant many women find sex a life-long disappointment. They hope for a great deal and yet achieve no happiness and little pleasure from sex. They, unfortunately, remain sexually unawakened.

A woman's satisfaction is not a natural result, as some men imagine, of an inborn 'virility' in themselves, but comes from arousing her desire and creating a high pitch of excitement in her body before intercourse begins. Because she is slower to arouse than the man, foreplay is essential if she is to be ready to receive him. This is a period of enjoyment for both lovers because it extends and intensifies the man's own pleasure. In love-play, both the man and the woman explore the body's capacity for sensual enjoyment.

Most people enjoy the flirtation and exuberant fun inherent in love-play. Sexual love treated too seriously becomes an exercise in achieving orgasms and loses an important element of spontaneity.

There are no text-book techniques. A man's enjoyment of his partner's body is for her the greatest stimulation he can give, and her own excitement as they make love will arouse him. Touching, kissing, and caressing increases her desire and gives him great pleasure and gratification. As he learns about her body and what pleases her most, sex becomes an adventure, a developing intimacy.

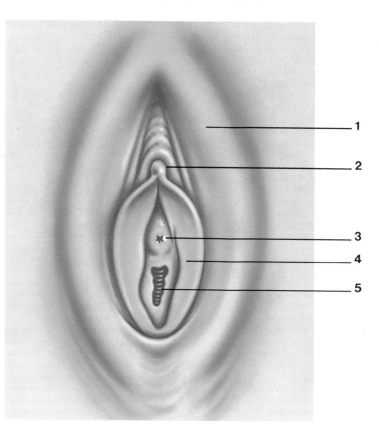

This diagram shows the external sexual organs of a woman: 1 the labia majora or outer lips; 2 the clitoris; 3 the urethral opening; 4 the labia minora or inner lips; 5 the vaginal entrance.

Square One

Love-play is slow seduction. For a man to take a woman for granted, to assume that her favours are readily available, can be disastrous. In bed she likes to be wooed and won every time. And the man must show by the way he approaches her that he is demonstrating his love for her, not claiming a male 'right'.

Some women are easily aroused and want to have intercourse almost immediately and most women occasionally like to be taken quickly and suddenly, with perhaps a hint of roughness. But, in general, a woman responds to gentle kisses and soft caresses of the 'erogenous' zones of her body. These are any areas where she likes to be touched and which lend to sexual arousal. They include the lips, breasts, neck, buttocks, and the vulva itself. A woman usually responds quickly when her breasts and nipples, which are highly sensitive, are fondled and caressed. This can often excite the man, too. He can caress other parts of her body at the same time—the abdomen or thighs, or the clitoris and vulva—and in time will find out what excites his partner most.

The mouth and lips can give great erotic pleasure. A kiss stimulates because it involves all the senses of touch, taste, and smell. Love-play usually begins with kissing, and as the couple become more excited, the kisses become more fervent and erotic. Most couples enjoy deep kissing. where both lips and tongues meet. The penetration of the tongue into the other's

mouth is analogous to the penetration of the penis into the vagina.

A woman enjoys the feel of her partner's mouth on her body. He can kiss the parts of her body where she is most sensitive, nibbling her ear lobes, tenderly sucking her nipples, running his tongue along her neck and shoulders, and even giving gentle and playful bites.

The man can also caress his wife's clitoris and vulva with his mouth—kissing the partner's genitals is a normal and natural part of love-play—and many couples like to lie in a head-to-tail position, so that each can kiss and stimulate the sex organs of the other.

Any activity acceptable and pleasurable to both can become part of love-play. The late Dr. Alfred Kinsey showed statistically that the better a person's education, the more likely he was to use such techniques as mouth-genital contact during love-play.

The more a couple are prepared to experiment with different ways of pleasing and exciting each other in love-play and to try different positions in the act of love-making itself, the more enjoyment and pleasure they will find in their relationship. When a couple are experienced in love-making, stimulation by her partner's hands, lips, or tongue may bring a woman to orgasm even before intercourse begins.

In general, anything that a loving couple both feel like doing as part of love-play is healthy and by no stretch of the imagination can be called unnatural. There are; though, a very small number of people who want their partners to participate in perverse practices involving the use of drugs or cruelty. Such persons are, of course, in need of psychiatric help.

Suspicion of oral love-play and caressing of the genitals, (just as the belief that a man should have intercourse with a woman only face down on top of her), can lead to monotony in love-making and, in some cases, more serious difficulties.

One young man, who had as a child been told repeatedly by his father of the evils of masturbation, was terrified of any contact between the genitals and the hand. In the early days of his marriage, he would not touch his wife's sexual organs, and shied away when she tried to caress his penis before intercourse. Fortunately, she was a spirited and intelligent girl who, after several years, convinced him that what he had regarded as sinful was in fact 'normal, natural—and nice'.

After some minutes of love-play, the couple's hands and lips will find each other's genitals. When the woman is fully aroused her vulva will be moist but before then it could be uncomfortable, or even painful for her partner to try to enter her. Instead he can concentrate on gentle manipulation of the area of the clitoris with his fingertips. When dry, this part is tender, and the man may have to moisten his fingers by licking them. Stimulating the clitoris increases the flow of vaginal secretions in the area of the vulva, and the opening of the vagina widens, preparing itself to accept the penis.

The man can, if he wishes, slip his finger, (usually the middle one with the palm upwards) into the vagina, and move it rapidly back and forth. With practice, this technique can provide immense pleasure for the woman. He can vary the way he uses his hand, sometimes putting in more than one finger, using a different sort of movement, or letting a knuckle press repeatedly on the area of the clitoris as the finger slips gently in and out of the vagina.

Usually, a couple will want to prolong the period of love-play, to explore the possibilities of stimulation. But sometimes they might want to arouse desire quickly, by deep kissing and caressing each other's sexual organs. At this point, when she most desires it and may be approaching an orgasm, the woman will ask the man to enter her, or will move his penis towards her vagina.

Love-play, which leads a woman into intercourse and stimulates her so that she can fully enjoy it, requires skill and concern from the man: he must never take a woman for granted. But ensuring that the woman can respond completely is not a chore. The man who makes his partner happy increases his own sexual pleasure. Love-play can make possible the sexual fulfilment which is one of the cornerstones of a successful relationship.

A great many women regard men as creatures of simple needs, easily able to have sexual intercourse, and easily satisfied.

But love-making may, for a man, be a trivial experience, even though he reaches an orgasm. The success of love-making for either partner cannot be measured in terms of orgasms, but only in terms of the gratification and happiness it brings. The sexual act must satisfy not only physical needs, but complex emotional needs, too. These are very closely inter-related. A man, as much as a woman, needs to feel loved and admired, and appreciated as a man and as a lover. It is a physical reassurance about these things which he wants from love-making.

A woman often places the responsibility on the man for giving pleasure and satisfaction to them both. Apart from giving her body, she takes little responsibility either for pleasing her partner or for satisfying her own needs. Her body may be sufficient to arouse his desire so that he is able to have intercourse with her, but it is not enough to make the experience full and satisfying for him. He needs her active participation, her enthusiasm, and her love.

In many parts of the Western world, man has long been regarded as an animal of almost uncontrollable sexual desires to which the female was forced to submit. Even today, it is assumed by many that a man's desires do not need arousing. Yet every women knows how to attract a man by the way she displays her body and by the way she acts. She knows the ways to suggest the pleasures to be had, to invite, to withdraw, to show desire in her eyes and promise in her movements. But usually she acts seductively only in situations where she is hoping to attract a new partner, or where there is competition from other women. She rarely acts this way with a man with whom she is already familiar, as a way of intensifying his desire and pleasure. Yet men, like women, sometimes enjoy being

seduced. And knowing a man means learning what excites him, whether it is sitting on his knee or removing your clothing in a provocative way.

The first steps of love-making do not always take place at night and in bed. Often, while watching a film together, or having a quiet dinner in a restaurant, or on the way home from a party, the feelings of desire can be expressed, though not always in a physical way. It is possible to reach a state of considerable excitement even before you kiss or touch. Western tradition leads both to expect that it will be the man who initiates love-making, but there is no reason why this should be so. To make the first approach is a very obvious way of showing love and desire.

The foreplay which precedes actual intercourse is an important part of love-making, for during foreplay the man and the woman can communicate the love and the tenderness they feel for each other. And from this comes much of the emotional satisfaction of love-making. At the same time, their mutual caresses lead to a rising sexual excitement which culminates in intercourse.

A man needs to feel that he is a good lover, and to know that he is able to arouse his partner's desire to a high pitch. Although most women enjoy making love, not all of them show it, or respond with sufficient enthusiasm. The more actively a woman responds, the more pleasure she will have, and the more pleasure she will give her lover. This is to say that she must give of herself and respond freely, not that she should pretend. A woman can sometimes be too anxious to please, and simulate more excitement than she feels. This leads the man to enter her before she is fully aroused, and she has pleasure neither from love-play nor from intercourse.

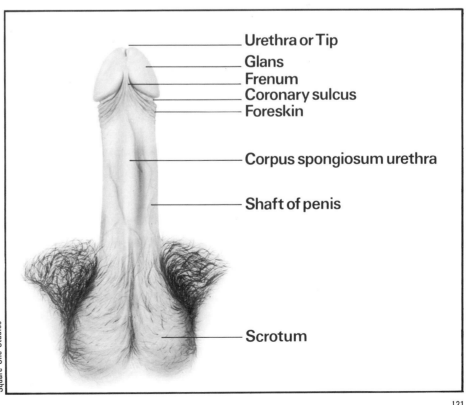

Urethra or Tip
Glans
Frenum
Coronary sulcus
Foreskin

Corpus spongiosum urethra

Shaft of penis

Scrotum

Square One Studios

131

A woman likes to know that her partner enjoys her body, admires the curves of her hips, the fullness of her breasts, the softness of her skin, but she rarely stops to think about the pleasure the look and feel of her lover's body gives her. As an active partner in love-play, the woman can show how she loves and appreciates his body, the way it excites her, and the promise of sexual pleasure it gives. Her awareness of his physical nature grows as she learns how to express what she feels in touch and in words, and she derives more pleasure from their love-making. The man, it is assumed, is sexually aroused by handling the woman's body, and this is equally so for the woman, but not so commonly recognized. The act of touching and caressing someone, is itself stimulating.

Much of the pleasure of love-making comes from giving pleasure to your partner. Everybody likes to be touched, to feel the warmth of another human being. And touch, as the expression of love, is more comforting and reassuring than any words. There is no dividing line between pleasant physical sensations and sexual sensations, and love-play and the sex act satisfy very basic human needs. Above all, it is important to relax, to learn to make love with the body and not with the head, and to lose oneself in the physical pleasures. Being a spectator of one's own performance is the main cause of failures. Many women concentrate on their need for an orgasm and this can prevent them from relaxing and eventually having one. But it also places a strain on the man, who now feels he has something to achieve, something on which his virility depends. And this can prevent any man from enjoying himself to the utmost, and may even prevent erection altogether.

All men are different, and each act of love-making is as individual as a conversation. It is best to regard every man as an unknown and unexplored territory. But there are certain places where most people are sensitive. The lips, the inside of the mouth and the tongue, are some of the most sensitive parts of the body of both men and women, and very important in making love. There is an art and style in kissing itself. Kisses can be deeply erotic; they can be full of excitement and promise. They can be romantic, warm, and tender, or passionately expressive of desire. And the lips and the tongue can be used to caress other parts of the body. Gently nibbling the ear lobes, for example, can excite a man very quickly. He may like to be

stroked or kissed on the neck and shoulders, or the small of his back, or on the buttocks. He may even like to be gently bitten. The navel is usually very sensitive, and so are the insides of the thighs. A man's nipples are not generally as sensitive as a woman's, but many men do like them to be stroked, gently squeezed or pulled, or taken in the mouth. There are, in addition, two very sensitive points on a man's body. One is on the spine, a few inches above the base, and being stroked there gives very exciting sensations. The second is behind the testicles, on the ridge which runs between the anus and the base of the penis. Applying pressure with the fingers at this point can bring about an erection, or strengthen it by compressing blood vessels.

The most sensitive parts of the male body are the testicles and penis, but they are also the most delicate. The testicles, particularly, are easily hurt, particularly by pressure, but gentle handling of them can give a man great pleasure—stroking and tickling, fondling, and caressing with the mouth and tongue.

Some men do not like their penis to be handled, because they find it difficult to control their climax, but others, with more experience and more control, find manual stimulation of the penis gives very intense and pleasurable sensations. The head of the penis, or glans, especially around the tip and the opening, is the most sensitive part. The shaft, too, can be rubbed and manipulated, especially on the upper side. The man may like his partner to kiss the penis, or take it in her mouth, caressing the tip with her tongue, or moving her mouth backwards and forward. Some men like to ejaculate occasionally in a partner's hands or mouth. This can be very exciting for both, and is quite natural.

A man might like his penis to be caressed between the woman's breasts, kneeling astride, placed in her armpit, or stroked with her long hair, or brushed against the moist, outer lips of the vagina. He may want, at times, to take a passive role in love-play, and be made love to by the woman, using any or all of these techniques.

Enjoying love-play also means coping with and indulging each other's sexual fantasies. If a man likes his partner to wear her frilly pants when they begin to make love, or is excited by seeing her in the low-cut, lacy bra that she might think so vulgar, or wants her to take off her black stockings in front of him, or wear them during intercourse he is quite a normal man, and by no means unusual.

Nor are a host of other things people do, or pretend, in the private games of love-play. It is up to each partner to find out what games excite the other. In our culture we are often too shy of adult play. The more frank couples can be about their fantasies, the better.

The man can very quickly reach an orgasm, though it usually takes longer for the woman to reach the same point of arousal. Though sometimes both the man and the woman want to make love quickly, a period of love-play is, usually, essential, if the woman is to enjoy intercourse, and the man's orgasm can be more intense if he is aroused to a high pitch of excitement. It is important that he learns to control his climax. If he does feel the immediate urge to ejaculate, especially while his partner is fondling his penis, she can prevent this happening by what Masters and Johnson (in *Human Sexual Inadequacy*) call the 'squeeze technique'. The woman places her thumb on the inferior (ventral) surface of the head of the penis, and the first and second fingers on the superior surface, one on either side of the coronal ridge (which divides the shaft of the penis from the head). If she squeezes for three or four seconds, keeping the hand still, her partner loses the urge to ejaculate, provided the orgasm is anticipated and the squeeze begun soon enough.

The caresses which one person enjoys, another will find uncomfortable, or even repellent. It is usually obvious enough what someone enjoys by the way he reacts, but at the same time, both partners must feel free to say what they do and do not like. It is part of the pattern of communication on which a good relationship is based. The success of love-making depends, in large part, on each learning to fit the rhythm of the arousal of their body to that of their partner. And this demands a certain open honesty in saying what they feel. Love-making can only be properly enjoyed if there is this frankness between the man and woman, as well as a relaxed attitude, and a determination to shed inhibitions.

Our social lives are so interwoven with conventions, controls, and defences, that it is not always easy to break down the barriers, even with someone we love. But learning to be able to say and do whatever you want, builds a closeness and intimacy, a growing confidence in each other, and a deepening affection. Together with the sharing of physical enjoyment, appreciation, and love, love-play can be the true playground of marriage.

RICHARD SEARLE

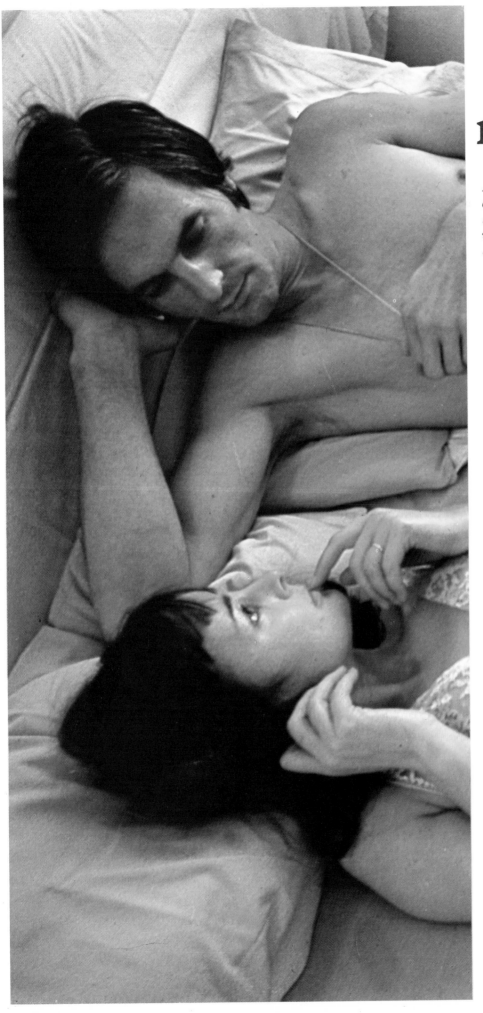

Is orgasm always necessary?

Many women achieve orgasm almost every time they make love, but others do not. Can a woman be sexually satisfied if she does not reach a climax?

When any subject is constantly in the limelight in the communications media, television, radio, newspapers, it is not always easy to remember that what is considered to be news is by definition out of the ordinary. It needs a definite effort to stop oneself from being swept into the assumption that what is discussed is general custom and usage. Changes in sexual climate are not easily assessed and discussion about them is too frequently based on minority trends, often sensationally reported, rather than on what is generally accepted.

Today, for instance, one might think that all women are taking the contraceptive pill as a form of birth control, with total disregard of the possible physical consequences other than pregnancy, and that prior to the development of effective contraceptive methods only the fear of pregnancy stopped women from jumping into bed at every opportunity. With this fear of pregnancy gone—and even that assumption needs to be closely examined—the underlying conclusion is that orgasm for all is the inevitable result of this new freedom. Every girl should have one. If not, why not? It is the new mark of success, the sign of her potency. Without it she is deprived and a failure. But this is a dangerous conclusion.

Throughout history the union of a man and a woman and the problems it creates have been the subject of countless controversies largely involved with morals, superstition, and current customs as well as with the actual relationship. Unfortunately, history was largely written by men and they wrote with a male attitude to women and the pleasure women give to men. Comparatively few women have written from the female point of view on the pleasure men give to women.

Even novelists, whether writing romance, crime, sensational sex shockers, whether including sex in a legal or illicit setting, whether as a serious subject or for titillation, often glamorize sex, and usually see it from the male point of view. There may be marital intercourse or unlicensed seduction, but few women in fiction have

133

ever sat up afterwards and said, 'Well, I can't see what all the fuss is about. That was not very exciting.'

An increasing freedom to discuss sex openly could have the valuable result of more women writing frankly and objectively about sex and the importance of sex in a woman's life and relationships from the woman's point of view.

After all, even the word describing the climax of the sexual act was probably unknown to our grandparents and even today a booklet on various aspects of marriage puts 'climax' in brackets after orgasm in case the word is not understood. Dr. Helena Wright, a founder member of the Family Planning Association, only 25 years ago wrote that interest in the well-being of the clinic patients included asking if all was well with their sexual relationship, but that a blank look was the reaction of the majority of women. Clarified into the direct question, 'Is it enjoyable?' the answer was generally, 'Is it supposed to be?'

The assumption that 'ladies do not move', they just 'do their duty', is not so far back in history as might be thought. The number of women who are relieved when their husbands are no longer sexually active is probably still considerable. The actual situation is not that easy to judge. With today's emphasis on sex one tends to assume that a successful marriage must include sexual satisfaction. But it is not the sort of thing one can easily ask about, even in a fairly permissive society. But it has been estimated that possibly only 60 per cent of women achieve orgasm.

The number of children a couple have is certainly no guide. Man is given a sweet bribe by nature in having to reach a climax in order to ejaculate semen. Whether he procreates or not he has the pleasure. Intercourse without orgasm is not in the male make-up because without erection and orgasm the sexual act cannot occur. For men the climax is a biological necessity.

A woman can have twenty children and never achieve climax. Orgasm was once regarded as a sure sign of having conceived. But it is now known that its lack does not affect a woman's fertility. The children only prove that she has experienced twenty acts of sexual intercourse.

This important difference between male and female biological necessities has a major bearing on the current emphasis on female orgasm. When women are no longer regarded primarily as child-bearers and mothers it is natural to go beyond the function of impregnation to consider the wider implications of the sexual act.

But if society drops, almost in one generation, the attitude that marriage is the price men pay for sex and sex the price women pay for marriage, there must be complications. A woman marrying today faces a greater challenge then ever before. She is not only expected to be well-dressed, a good cook, an efficient house-keeper, to bring up well-mannered, clean children, she also needs to be a passionate, inventive lover, and to prove it by having orgasms. And any woman, seeing the extraordinarily easy way in which a man reaches a climax, can only feel inferior if she cannot do the same. Whose fault is it? Is she inadequate or is he? The possibilities for marital friction are enormous.

A man, brainwashed into believing that he is depriving his wife if he cannot bring her to climax, can suffer premature ejaculation or become impotent out of sheer nervous tension. Or he can work on the problem as though it is an examination he has to pass in order to be a good lover. He cannot afford to fail. The woman, because she has to show her sexual equality, or so that his pleasure will not be spoiled because he feels guilty about her, may simulate orgasm, which is something no man would ever have to do.

Sometimes, when a man believes he has hit the formula that enables his wife to achieve orgasm, he dare not deviate because that way might lie failure. Sexologists report cases where a wife complains that she can predict every move her husband is going to make during the love-play which precedes intercourse. She proves it by relating every action even to the number of strokes on each erotic zone. But after

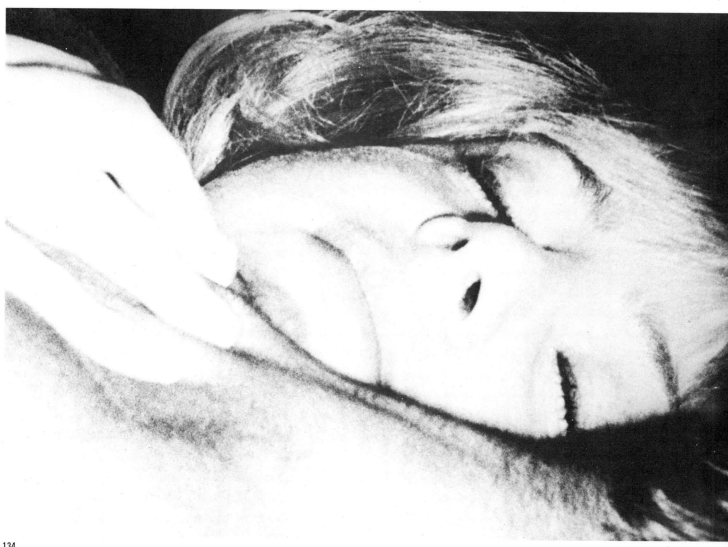

a while she does not reach a climax every time they have intercourse. The boring routine becomes exasperating rather than stimulating and the woman either simulates climax to get it all over or reaches it almost unwillingly, mentally and emotionally irritated. She feels no more satisfied than the woman whose husband speedily satisfies himself and falls snoring at her side. After all, she has experienced sexual relations which were satisfying. She is going to blame her husband for a boring routine which she can only interpret as suspension of interest in her as a person.

It is possible to draw up illustrated charts on the mechanics of sexual technique comparable to the ones explaining the mysteries of the male and female bodies which are used in sex education in schools. The day could come when just such instruction is given in schools. But there is, as the critics of some forms of sex education for children emphasize, more to the subject than just the mechanics.

Love-making is the expression of a unique relationship. The world is left aside and the lovers respond only to each other in the giving and receiving of bodily caresses. But it is far more than the physical contact of two bodies. It should be the expression of affection, tenderness, warmth, concern, understanding, and the mutual need of two people for each other alone. The mental and emotional aspects are quite as important as the physical ones.

Possibly because women are not so easily physically aroused as men, possibly because the tradition of being the chaste as well as the chased sex, is still strong, regardless of the sensationalism of the mass media which might make us think the opposite, in the early part of marriage the man will generally have greater sexual desire and probably greater pleasure than the woman. But as inhibitions fade and greater technical skill is achieved by both partners, the woman's desires can increase and she, too, will have a sexual need, a build-up of tension which will be released only through orgasm.

The experience of orgasm has been variously described as intense pleasure, ecstasy, sheer delight, the ultimate mental and physical experience, and like a sneeze. It is total surrender almost to the point of brief unconsciousness. But it is not such a vital ingredient in a marriage that its achievement signifies total partnership and its absence that the marriage is incomplete.

It is true that the feeling of physical well-being that follows the release of sexual tension casts its glow over marital life, applying an easing balm over situations that normally irritate. Perhaps a greater degree of understanding or tolerance is released but the friction and disunity of a marriage can still go on.

A climax for a woman usually takes longer to reach than a man's and is achieved through a process of dropping inbuilt inhibitions, responding to mental, emotional, and physical attraction and to acquiring sexual techniques. Love-play does not always build up to a tension demanding the

release of orgasm whether through penis, hand, or oral stimulation. And this lack of aroused sexual tension can occur in women who do normally climax and in women who have never experienced orgasm. But that does not mean that orgasm signifies pleasure or its absence the lack of pleasure in sexual relations.

It is known that women's sexual feelings follow a pattern and that this is affected by the menstrual cycle. They are obviously also affected—as men's must be—by the individual's immediate mental and physical health and mood. But there seems to be more even than those elements.

No man, unless he is immature or debased, regards the sexual act as purely an animal function. He, too, is expressing emotional warmth, affection, the need for physical nearness. To a woman his expression of these sentiments is very important. Unfortunately, moods do not always coincide. Without the least indication a man will get into bed and make sexual advances to his wife. Before going to bed they may have been doing something quite mundane such as watching television or even arguing. Certainly no attempt to court her has been made. She is unlikely to leap from checking the children's clothes to high passion without some anticipatory mental preparation.

A woman needs to feel that, apart from physically needing her at that moment, her partner is truly wanting all of her and expressing his love for her as a person. This need is so strong that for many women being tenderly cherished and caressed in a demonstrative physical manner is enough in itself and the loving is more important

Excessive concern about the woman reaching an orgasm may lead to tension and prevent both partners from fully enjoying love-making.

than the climax, whether it occurs or not. Such a woman will enjoy vicariously her man's enjoyment of her, feeling most pleasure in his total surrender which he achieves through her. If he then spoils what should be an atmosphere of relaxation and love by apologies to her and guilty concern over his inadequacies as a lover he is destroying her satisfaction in being a desirable, loved woman who gives her lover pleasure.

This expression of his love for her through physical touch can be vital at certain times in a woman's life, for example when relations are resumed after childbirth and she may feel her once smooth body has lost its freshness, or much later when her body begins to lose its younger charms. Through sexual embraces a man reassures his partner that it is her that he wants, not just a pretty body.

Women vary considerably in their capacity to achieve orgasm or the need to achieve it. To ignore the mood, personality stresses, and needs of the individual partner in a frantic attempt to achieve orgasm as the only acceptable culmination of every sexual encounter can be as destructive as treating women only as the instruments of childbirth. A man should understand and accept that orgasm can be vital to one woman, unimportant to another, and unnecessary to yet another, and that it is the expression of love which is most important of all.

CLAIR WILSON

What is 'normal' sex?

When most people talk of normal sexual behaviour they usually refer to a general standard of acceptability. Concepts of 'normal' and 'abnormal' are invariably subjective and are derived from the consensus of a maximum number of people. Since, however, sex is essentially a private activity and most people are not traditionally or generally frank about what they do in the privacy of their bedrooms, the accepted concept of sexual normalcy is usually wider in practice than in theory. People do, on the whole, what is expected of them because they do not want to be criticized or ostracized.

Psychologists have, for the most part, regarded exclusiveness as the touchstone by which to measure abnormal sexual behaviour. Like society, they consider heterosexual intercourse as the ideal norm and have, therefore, regarded as abnormal those people who reject this basic activity in favour of some substitute. Thus, the compulsive masturbator, the fetishist, or the *voyeur* may be defined as abnormal only when they indulge these tastes to the exclusion of sexual intercourse. On the other hand, a married man who occasionally masturbates while watching his wife undress would not be considered abnormal.

Consequently, normal sex is understood by too many people to centre around sexual intercourse. Most people develop personal standards of normalcy by conditioning. Their parents may have told them, for example, that it is 'not nice' to masturbate. Generally, physical modesty was encouraged and sex education seldom went beyond a simple description of the 'mechanics' of love-making. Thus, too many people assume that sexual intercourse should only occur at night, in bed, usually in the dark, and with a minimal period of foreplay. They believe that it should not happen too often and is completed when orgasm is achieved. They also feel that sexual intercourse should only be performed with the woman supine and the man above her.

The result of such misconceptions is that many people's expectation of sexual behaviour is characterized by an attitude of efficiency, not celebration. Such attitudes leave little room for imagination and exclude a whole gamut of sexual activities which prolong and intensify erotic pleasure. Normal sex is, therefore, still regarded by far too many people as, at worst, the simple gratification of periodic desire and, at best, the means of procreation.

Women, more than men, invariably have a stricter concept of what is normal because they are subjected to greater sexual conditioning. A society which still nominally values virginity and decries the unmarried mother inevitably inhibits the female sex more strictly than it does the male. There is, too, a still active Victorian tradition which accepts to some degree the imperiousness of male desire while clinging to the myth of feminine indifference. Thus, most young men are usually exposed to the possibility of a wider range of sexual activities than young women. The result is that many relationships are marred by conflict on this very point.

In many ways it can be argued that ignorance is better than the sort of 'advice' which Mary received from her mother a few days before her wedding. Mary was told that she should leave the details of sexual intercourse to her husband, but that she should confine this activity to weekends. Otherwise they would both be too tired for work during the week. Her mother supervised the purchase of several nightdresses whose only concession to sexual appeal was that they could be pushed up with a minimum of difficulty. But most damaging of all, Mary's mother hinted darkly at certain unspeakable, masculine desires which Mary was to resist at all costs.

The exact nature of these desires was never disclosed, but they implanted fearsome ideas which made Mary tense and unresponsive to her husband's love-making. The undefined 'perversion' puts a relatively innocent woman on her guard. She cannot distinguish between the acceptable and the abnormal, but constantly suspects that she is, indeed, being wheedled into perfoming the latter.

The physical and emotional problems which such an unreasoned definition of normalcy creates, automatically undermine the trust which two people in love should rely upon in the sexual and social aspects of their relationship. If a woman loves a man, but is taught to regard all men as aggressive violators who will seize every opportunity to 'debauch' her body, she is scarcely going to be relaxed and able to welcome and reciprocate his sexual advances. Such a situation is self-evidently aggravated when a woman has no factual comprehension of what is abnormal.

The conflict between Mary and her husband, Simon, began on the first night of their marriage. He got into bed, nude, demanded that she throw off the 'convenient' night-dress, and refused to turn out the light. Simon was indulging the natural male desire to look at and admire the woman he loved. Mary, on the other hand, felt 'wicked' and was numbed by embarrassment. Furthermore, she soon discovered that the idea of confining intercourse to a specific night was totally unrealistic. Simon wanted intercourse when he felt like it, which was often. To make matters worse, as far as Mary was concerned, he sometimes wanted it in the middle of the afternoon, and in the sitting-room. Because Mary had accepted her mother's view of sexual conduct, for want of any means of proper comparison, it is not surprising that she thought Simon was a 'sex maniac'.

Fortunately, Simon was able to arouse Mary and was able to instil in her a sense of the joy of love-making. Had Simon been less patient and loving, Mary could have resisted him and imposed her mother's extraordinary standards on him. Fortunately, an aroused woman is usually not able to resist. In fact, Mary enjoyed sex and found, by simple experience, that there was nothing wrong in making love in the nude or in daylight. The 'thunderbolt' that she expected to be invoked by their 'wickedness' simply did not materialize. She learned the only practicable definition of normalcy—that which gives pleasure and causes no harm to either partner.

Mary's case is extreme only in the sense that it was concerned with such simple matters. Even after her adjustment to Simon's attitudes to love-making, she still could not be described as an unusually inventive lover. For much of what some people imagine to be normal can impinge upon the truly normal. It is normal for two people to make love when and as often as they wish, but it is relatively abnormal if they set aside one night or one place for the performance of such a spontaneous act. Frequently, the normal desires of a normal man may cause him to be condemned as 'over-sexed'. The slightest variation of technique or position may cause him to be called 'perverted'.

A crucial aspect of this problem lies in the way a concept of what is normal in sexual behaviour is imparted. In most cases only half the story is told. Parents and teachers who lead perfectly normal, but truly imaginative, sex lives confine sexual education to describing the act of sexual intercourse. They leave out details about the variations of the act, of foreplay, and virtually any mention of oral sex. This is done not because they want to prevent young people from enjoying these eminently enjoyable activities, but because they cannot bring themselves to speak of such things.

It is difficult for a woman to tell her daughter of cunnilingus because such intimate information seems to betray the secrets of the marital bed. Most people instinctively hide their sexual abandon from their children. Although it is easier for a father and a son to talk of such things, because there is an accepted tradition of the exchange of sexual information between men, many boys fare little better than girls.

Jim, for example, understood that foreplay was essential to facilitate easy penetration, but he had no idea that this could be a mutual and extended process. He was, therefore, shocked when his wife fondled his genitals and insisted that he prolong

Love-making, rather than conforming to a strict pattern of the 'acceptable and permissible', should be approached with a sense of freedom to experiment.

manual stimulation beyond the strictest point of necessity. He did not understand the concept of pleasure for its own sake. His idea of foreplay was entirely practical and he had to be shown that it can be gratifying in itself.

By far the most common conflict encountered by couples of all ages is an ill-defined feeling that oral sex is perverse. It is not. It may seem so to some people because it is one aspect of sexuality which is seldom referred to openly and because current thinking on this point is still in advance of current practice. There is, too, in some people, a repugnance about the act which severely inhibits them. It has often been said that were the sexual and urinary organs disassociated there would be no hesitation about oral sex. There is an undoubted truth in this claim.

Cunnilingus and fellatio are extremely intimate acts. As such they are valued as signs of generosity. Rightly or wrongly, many people feel, to a certain extent, that someone who is prepared to kiss their genitals must love them very much. This is a healthy attitude, but it should not be forgotten that both acts can be intensely pleasurable to the performer. The essence of sexual harmony is the ability to give and, equally important, to take pleasure. No where is this better demonstrated than in the example of oral sex.

Inhibitions about oral sex are not uncommon. The experience of Malcolm and Jill provides a typical example of the problems encountered and how they may be solved. Malcolm had heard about oral sex from his friends and, as usually happens in such situations, he had understood it to be something secretive and wicked. But the idea excited him and continued to fascinate him. He began to be curious about it. What it would be like to do it to Jill? Since they had never done it, how could they begin? Would she like it or would she think him dirty? Could he, in fact, do it without feeling repugnance?

These ideas lingered in Malcolm's mind and although, for no definable reason, he suspected that it was perverse, he began to realize that there could be little wrong in his doing it with his wife. Tentatively, and intensely excited, he performed cunnilingus. Jill made no comment, but her pleasure was obvious and her love-making afterwards was unusually intense and eager. Malcolm gained confidence with each successive attempt. He found that the performance of the act also excited him and, as far as he was concerned, anything that Jill enjoyed needed no further justification.

Inevitably, he began to imagine what it would be like to be fellated. Having gained confidence from performing cunnilingus he began to discuss oral sex in general

with Jill and eventually asked her to fellate him. She was hesitant, partly out of a sense that it was wrong, and partly because she did not know how. In common with so many women, she was also afraid that Malcolm would ejaculate in her mouth. He promised not to and Jill tried. Like Malcolm, she discovered first the pleasure of pleasing and then, as she became more adept, she took delight in the act itself. From this they progressed to mutual, simultaneous, oral stimulation.

The real lesson to be learned from Malcolm and Jill's experience is that nobody can honestly say what gives them pleasure until they have tried it. Virtually all aspects of sex are pleasurable in proportion to the desire they arouse. Sexual intercourse itself, although universally accepted as normal, is not enjoyable unless both partners desire it and are properly prepared for it. Many women have testified to the entirely unpleasant effects of penetration when they have felt no desire for their partner, or have been insufficiently aroused.

The only sound guide to what is or is not normal, therefore, must be absolutely personal. Of course, all possible sexual activities are not pleasing to all people. Everybody has particular tastes in sex as they have in food and television programmes, but these tastes are formed by experience. No rational person claims that they dislike tomatoes without having tasted them, or claims not to have enjoyed a television programme they did not watch. Sexual tastes can only be formed in a similar way and the only viable definition of normalcy derives from experimentation.

The majority of people have forced upon them, in the course of growing up, preconceived ideas of what is normal. Consciously or unconsciously, they enter sexual relationships with a number of these preconceptions. But even when some of these concepts are justifiable and acceptable they must not be regarded as placing a limit on behaviour. People change continually. The things they like and the things they believe at sixteen are invariably very different from those they like and believe at thirty. They have been changed and modified by experience, by exposure to different viewpoints and various stimuli. Exactly the same open-minded approach should imbue people's attitudes to sexual normalcy. If it does not then they not only limit their potential as human beings, and possibly deprive their partners of the means to develop, but they trap themselves with guilt and fear which can only have an adverse effect upon their personalities and their relationships.

Indeed, such open-mindedness is absolutely essential in sexual matters since nobody has yet discovered a way of conveying the unique pleasure of sex to an-

other person, except by action. Furthermore, people vary tremendously in their appreciation of sexual pleasure. Some people can make love twice in a night with complete ease and satisfaction. Others need lengthy periods between each experience of intercourse if their response is to be properly intense and satisfying. An act which provides ecstasy for one man or one woman might only produce detumescence or coldness in others. The only way to discover what provides ecstasy is to experiment and one can only experiment successfully and confidently if the concept of normalcy is regarded as something personal and constantly evolving.

Many people find this difficult to accept. They are attracted by the implied safety of rigid guidelines, but such an approach stunts proper sexual growth and development. However, as they learn more about the sexual impulse and its enactment, they will have continually to revise their concepts of normalcy.

A hundred years ago oral sex was regarded as a perversion. Today, it is accepted as an essential part of any meaningful sexual relationship. Modern men and women can no longer rely on any firm line of demarcation between the normal and the abnormal. It seems likely that a general criterion of normalcy will come to be based on the concept of harm intended, or the invasion of individual liberties. Western society has already surpassed the idea of a given, rigid concept of normalcy as a viable guide to sexual expectations.

The idea of a definition of sexually normal behaviour as a constantly evolving concept between two individuals is possible only if it is based on proper mutual love and trust. These qualities should help a couple continually to 'progress' sexually.

Marriage, rather than conforming to a strict code of what is accepted and permissible, should provide two individuals with the freedom to discover what is normal for them. This may be radically different from what they expect. The cause may be physical or mental in the sense that the conformation of some women's vaginas makes different positions more comfortable and more conducive to the achievement of orgasm than others, while certain articles of feminine clothing may spark off some deeply arousing masculine fantasy. The causes of sexual tastes are, in marital situations, less important than their responsible formation through expression and continuous experimentation.

A given concept of normalcy laboriously adhered to, for no very clear reason, limits human potential. A proper evolution and acceptance of an individually pleasing normalcy is a process which extends people and enriches their relationships.

MICHAEL BROOKES

Attitudes to oral sex

Sexual practices have always been subject to many different public and private viewpoints. How have attitudes to oral sex varied among different cultures throughout history?

Conclusions about the attitudes of ancient peoples or of other cultures to sexual questions must always be tentative. If we look at the attitudes of our own times we can understand why this must be so, for we can see at once a clash of opinion. Not only do we have an official attitude to sexual matters, embodied in our laws, and a strong opposition constantly trying to modify this attitude, either in favour of greater freedom or greater restriction, but we also have private practice by each individual in response to his own situation and psychology.

Anyone who thinks this ambiguity is a modern phenomenon should study the great sexual debate of classical times on the relative merits of homosexuality and heterosexuality as the highest form of love, and how both were to be realized and regulated. Philosophers, rulers, writers, and visual artists, by their choice and treatment of the subject, kept up a commentary for hundreds of years on the fluctuations in public and private attitudes to this question.

Even with modern statistical methods it is impossible to arrive at cut and dried answers when dealing with sexual attitudes, particularly about oral sex. Kinsey reported that among his sample of American males 54 per cent of the married men admitted to having practised cunnilingus (oral sex with the woman as the passive partner) and 49 per cent of having experienced fellatio (oral sex with the man as the passive partner). Yet, officially, oral sex is illegal in several American states. It is forbidden to the 20 per cent of the population who are Roman Catholics, and many people express disgust at the mere suggestion of it. How much more difficult it is then to arrive at any kind of answer about historical and cultural attitudes to oral sex when we have possibly only a few pots or temple decorations from which to draw conclusions.

Perhaps the most unambiguous testimony we have is from the Chinese and Japanese. In China, from approximately 200 B.C., there were scrolls of erotic pictures created for the instruction of married couples. Many of these include examples of both forms of oral sex, although cunnilingus seems to have been more popular than fellatio. It was a Chinese religious and physiological belief that while the desire of women was inexhaustible, the semen of men was not, and each loss of semen reduced the total individual amount available. Their sexual ideal was, therefore, satisfaction for the woman partner with conservation for the man. In paintings, on ceramics, perfume and snuff bottles, and rice bowls couples are depicted enjoying oral sex. Some of the scrolls themselves also show combinations of three or more people in group sex and simultaneous oral sex.

Like the Chinese, the Japanese, from the seventh century A.D., also had sexual manuals. They were called *shunga*: posture or reclining pictures. There is a charming story illustrating their use. A young man married a girl who was frigid until he bought her a *shunga*. As they studied it in bed together she became more and more erotically excited and allowed him to make love to her. Clearly, the manuals were intended not simply for instruction but for stimulation as well, and in some of the pictures, by a kind of mirror effect, there are couples studying the *shunga* while putting them into practice. In the eighteenth century the introduction of censorship, originally for political reasons, led to their suppression. They were later revived again and continued to illustrate all the postures, including those for oral sex.

Sometimes the manuals told a story. A particularly fine one, called the *Brushwood Fence Scroll*, dating originally from the twelfth century but copied many times, tells of the seduction of a princess. Interestingly, tongue kissing is rarely depicted in the scrolls, since it was considered to be a 'sort of sexual deviation allowed only at the height of passion'. Many African tribes share this aversion and regard white people caught in the act of kissing as 'eating each other's saliva'.

India presents a more complex picture. From the fourth century A.D., a religious revival known as Tantrism permeated Hinduism. The central doctrine was the

Museum fur Volkerkunde, Berlin

identification of the Divine with the erotic, and its sacramental expression was the *maithuna*—a divine coupling in which the human pair were the equivalent of the god and goddess. This is believed to be the origin of the famous erotic temple sculptures which show almost every conceivable, and to Western eyes improbable, variation in sexual position. Among these are several postures of oral sex, which is known as *auparishtaka*. An early Indian medical book mentions a disease caused by wounding the penis with the teeth, providing some evidence that Tantrism was canonizing an already existing practice.

The famous *Kama Sutra*, however, suggests that *auparishtaka* is more suitably performed by a eunuch or a prostitute than a wife. It also mentions homosexual cunnilingus among the women of the harem and mutual heterosexual oral-genital contact, called curiously 'the congress of the crow'. The final comment on the subject is a model of resignation. 'But after all, these things being done secretly, and the mind of man being fickle, how can it be known what any person will do at any particular time and for any particular purpose.' A later work, the *Ananga Ranga* of the fifteenth century, makes no mention of oral sex, but does mention genital kissing by certain 'voluptuaries of Sata-desha'.

Oral intercourse is also reported from the tribal societies of Oceania and appears in Amerindian erotic pottery of the Chimu and Mochica people, which is dated to about 300 B.C. This pottery provides a kind of three-dimensional instruction manual in the different postures possible.

Rather surprisingly, the African continent gives little totally reliable evidence either from Ancient Egypt, the Arab nations, or black Africa, although there is a ritual representation of fellatio in *The Book of the Dead*. A Gandu woman on being asked by a sexologist why she refused cunnilingus answered that the mouth was for eating, the vagina for making love. This seems to reflect a common attitude, springing from the idea of sex only for procreation, and the physical closeness of the genital and excretal areas. Similarly, some African societies are either forbidden, or find it distasteful, to touch the genitals. 'How can you do such a thing and then touch your food?'

Mohammedanism and other Semitic influences may be at work in this attitude. Sir Richard Burton noted in his translation of *The Perfumed Garden*, an Arabic love manual of the Middle Ages, that there was no mention of 'the pleasures which the mouth or the hand of a pretty woman can give, nor the cunnilingus'.

In common with other Semitic religions, including Christianity and Judaism, the emphasis of orthodox Mohammedanism is on reproduction as 'the right true end' of sexual contact. Anything, therefore, which could give sexual pleasure contraceptively

The artifacts of many ancient cultures depicted sexual acts and positions. These two Peruvian water pots, of the Pre-Colombian period, were found in ancient tombs.

was officially frowned upon, although it might, like homosexuality among the Arabs, be extensively practised.

Western Europe has a long and fluctuating history of oral sex. Juvenal, the first-century Roman satirist, makes several references to both fellatio and cunnilingus, suggesting that it was common erotic practice among non-Christian Romans both for homosexuals and heterosexuals. He particularly comments on the Roman beauties being unable to tell head from tail by the end of a banquet.

The advent of Christianity, however, led to an attempted narrowing of erotic behaviour even between married couples. St. Paul's dictum that it was better for a man not to touch a woman coloured the whole of Christian teaching on the subject —even to the invention of a special nightgown with a hole through which a husband could impregnate his wife without their flesh making any other contact.

Not surprisingly, oral sex came under ban along with homosexuality, masturbation, anal intercourse, and prolonged kissing. This did not, on the whole, stop these activities, although it did cause many people to become intermittently guilty about the canonically forbidden forms of sexual activity. The unconscious, too,

continued to harbour the impulse towards oral sex, which emerged sometimes in a religious context. For example, in one painting the seminal words come from God's mouth through a tube leading up under Mary's skirts. And the penalty for swallowing semen to enhance attractiveness was seven years' penance.

From the twelfth century onwards, the Christian Church began to lose its hold over people's erotic lives. Aretino, friend of popes and painters, wrote the first extant Christian version of the sexual handbook as a series of sonnets illustrated by a set of drawings of sexual positions by Giulio Romano. He also wrote a set of dialogues between two women about the lives of nuns, married women, and courtesans which contains references to oral sex. His influence was tremendous. The *Figurae*, as the sonnets were called, circulated throughout Europe in the sixteenth and seventeenth centuries. Subsequently, English poets made several references to them. One of the most successful sustained pieces of erotic verse, *The Rapture* by the Cavalier poet Thomas Carew, mentions Aretino. It is a declaration of the enjoyment of sex.

Then will I visit, with a wandring kisse,
The vale of Lillies, and the Bower of blisse:

Throughout history artists have uninhibitedly portrayed oral sex. **Left** *Gothic sculpture from the church L'Isle Adam.* **Above** *Two nineteenth-century drawings by G. Doré.*

And where the beauteous Region doth
 divide
Into two milkie wayes, my lips shall slide
Down those smooth Allies, wearing as I go
A tract for lovers on the printed snow . . .

Here oral sex is part of pleasurable foreplay.

Not surprisingly, John Cleland's delightful pornographic novel, *Fanny Hill: The Memoirs of A Woman of Pleasure* written about 1750, contains examples of oral intercourse. But by the end of the eighteenth century such descriptions had been relegated, along with almost all mention of physical sex, to the demi-monde, where it was to stay for the next hundred years.

Only in the mid-twentieth century did the Western world begin to emerge from this state. But the shameless delight in love-making that a future Dean of St. Paul's, John Donne, could express in poetry in the reign of James I is still hardly possible. Dylan Thomas came closest to it in his play *Under Milk Wood.* 'I don't care if he is common, I want to gobble him up,' says Gossamer Beynon punning on the term 'gobbling' for oral sex.

Apart from the overall nineteenth-century embargo on explicit sexuality, there are particular reasons for oral sex to be

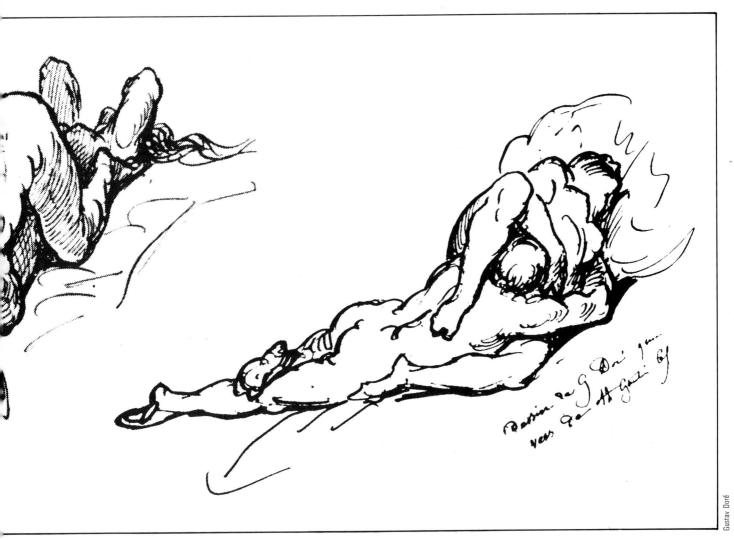

Gustav Doré

considered a taboo subject and practice. There are first the associations made with both eating and excreting, which make it seem unhygienic or quite simply 'dirty'. Then there is the daily observation that animals lick each other's genitals, which makes it seem inhuman behaviour.

This latter attitude ties up with Christian restrictions on the enjoyment of sex which were based on the belief that sex was the indulgence of our animal natures in 'fleshly lusts' and a reminder that animals have no souls. Deep-rooted, psychological prohibitions may be at work in reinforcing this: the forbidden infantile desire to eat one's own excrement, and the unconscious remembrance of the breast also forbidden after weaning. Lovers may find themselves frightened, too, by what seems an infantile regression. As the passive partner in the act, they may be afraid that the other may find them literally distasteful, or be shamed by the position of total submission.

At the same time they may be made uneasy because oral sex obscures the primary sex difference. The mouth is erotic without having a sex. Maleness and femaleness become irrelevant and their traditional identifications with active and passive are easily reversed.

Similarly, there is in many people's minds a strong association of oral sex with homosexuality. This is not surprising, since oral sex has been homosexually practised from the earliest recorded times.

Indeed, the devotee kneeling before the penis of the god or putting out a hand to it is known from Ancient Egyptian and Indian religious art. It is an idea echoed in the Christian symbolism of the communion, where the flesh of Jesus is taken into the communicant's mouth. Conversely, witches were often accused of kissing the devil's anus as the mark of greatest respect.

The Japanese and Chinese include homosexual intercourse among the pictures in their marriage manuals. And since the end of the nineteenth century pictures of women engaged in cunnilingus have multiplied in Western art, partly because these have an erotic effect for many male viewers. At the same time, according to the most recent research done in the United States, oral sex between men is becoming increasingly common.

This association of oral sex with homosexuality helps to underline its ambivalence for many heterosexuals. It makes it 'not quite normal' and, therefore, both frightening and fascinating with an aura of the forbidden. These associations may cause people to question their own sexual orientation or to reject oral sex through an unconscious fear of raising such questions in their own minds.

Traditionally, and in spite of reassurance from modern marriage manuals most of which mention oral sex as a perfectly natural and permissible technique, it is women who are most disturbed by it.

According to Kinsey's figures women show a lower incidence of oral sex experience even within marriage. Some allowance must be made for the continuing residue of women who are not given any proper sex education and who are inculcated with ideas of the general nastiness of an only-to-be-put-up-with attitude to all sexual relations. Something must also be allowed for the attitude that it is still traditionally man's role to initiate, woman's to respond. Women, too, are more likely to be affected by religious taboos. Also, it may be that if a woman is herself feeding a child she may find the unconscious associations with the breast and her own mother too disturbing to allow her to enjoy oral sex.

Although oral sex is no longer a taboo subject, it is still one where nineteenth-century mores retain a certain hold, particularly among older people. Part of its attraction may lie in this. Paul Ableman in his book *The Mouth* considers oral sex as a pleasurable and effective contraceptive in an overpopulated world, and it may be that future generations will hold a much less rigid attitude towards it.

Perhaps the *Kama Sutra* should have the last tolerant word. 'A man should therefore pay regard to the place, to the time, and to the practice which is to be carried out, as also as to whether it is agreeable to his nature and to himself, and then he may or may not practise things according to circumstance.' MAUREEN DUFFY

141

Oral sex in love play

Variation in the sexual side of a couple's relationship means that they constantly discover new aspects of each other. Oral sex is a stimulating—and natural—way for a couple to experiment.

One of the oddities of our world is the way that some verbal taboos still have a powerful hold on society, while others have been brought out into the light of common day. Today it is quite acceptable to ask the man at the next desk what he thinks of extra-marital sex, but ask him how much he earns and you will cause exquisite embarrassment. This odd sense of privacy, of there being subjects that no decent person would ever discuss, extends with particular tenacity to our need to go to the lavatory. Anglo-Saxon races still treat this as a shameful matter and have invented a brilliant range of alternative names to avoid mentioning the actual deeds. The sense of secrecy and furtiveness extends even to architecture. The lavatory is all too often a tiny cupboard where you cannot lift your

skirt without cracking your elbows instead of being included in the rest of the bathroom in the more convenient, but also more frank, manner. As for foreigners, who actually only have one public convenience for the joint use of both sexes—Britons and Americans shy away from these with the sense of horror that our grandparents showed when confronted with a naked piano leg.

This sense of shame over our natural functions, left-over scar tissue from the battle with our parents over toilet training, is probably why people are very reluctant to talk about oral sex, even in today's

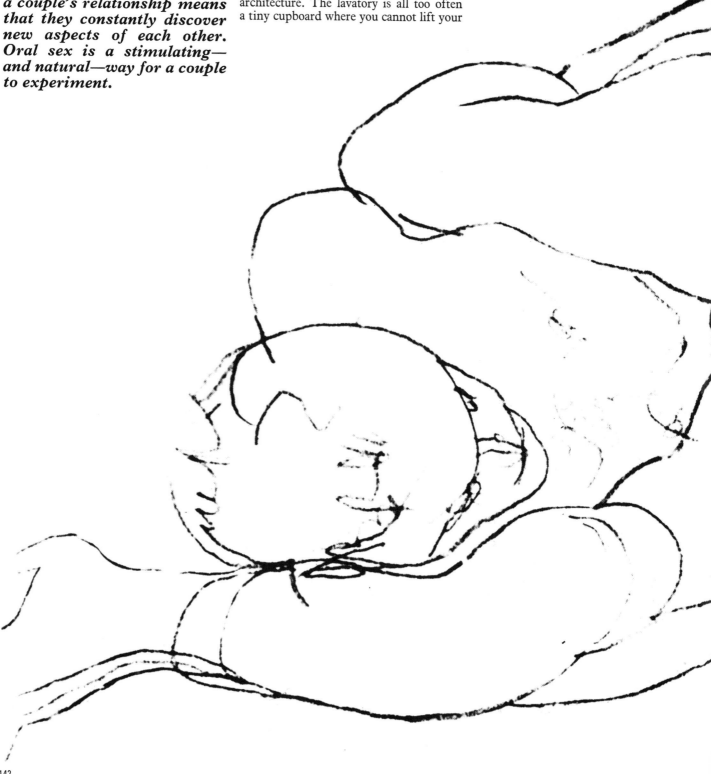

more honest society. To many, the thought of mouth-genital contact is still dirty, offensive, and shaming. A woman may be horrified when a man first suggests it to her or, more often, just acts on impulse without previous introduction. In fact psychiatrists often find people coming to them, men as well as women, because they are seriously disturbed by their partners' requests and want to be reassured that they are not perverted, vicious, or homosexual.

And yet if people can be persuaded to talk about it, it appears that once again this is a case of there being nothing new under the sun. The practice is old, widespread, and harmless. It appears on temple sculptures in India, was practised in Greece and Rome, and was criticized by the medieval Church. It seems odd and sad that it should have been so misunderstood. Yet the misunderstanding, too, has a long history. Vatsayana, writing his treatise on love, the *Kama Sutra*, some time between the first and fourth centuries A.D., quoted the

Schiele: *The Lovers*/Mervyn Levy/*The Artist and The Nude*

143

older authorities as saying that oral sex was 'practised by unchaste and wanton women, female attendants, and serving maids'. But Vatsayana in his sensible way said: 'In all these things connected with love, everybody should act according to the custom of the country and his own inclination.'

There is an old and true saying that there is nothing perverse or obscene where there is love. There is certainly nothing perverse about oral sex considered as a fact of nature. Practically all mammals, as well as fish, lizards, and many birds are in the habit of placing their mouths on some part of the partner's body during pre-coital play or during actual coitus. So the human animal is merely acknowledging his common origin when he engages his mouth in activity during sexual relationships. He can only be said to act unnaturally when he abstains because of the enforced intellectual restraints imposed by his ideas of morality, religion, or hygiene. This restraint has been further enforced in some societies by making oral sex a criminal offence. Kinsey reports that, in those American states where one of the grounds for divorce is 'personal indignities' or 'mental cruelty', the husband's or wife's desire for oral techniques is often used to obtain a divorce.

And yet, despite the attitudes of religion and morality, people in love are more likely to be governed by what pleases them than by what other people say should suit them. Everyone who has ever kissed knows the mouth is immensely responsive in sex, because it is richly supplied with nerve endings. It is equalled in erotic sensitivity only by the genitals. So it is hardly surprising that these two parts of the body, the two that feel the greatest reaction, should frequently come into direct contact. Kinsey found that although people were shy about discussing oral sex, they nonetheless practised it widely. Among those men and women he interviewed, who had a fair amount of sexual experience, nearly half had accepted mouth-genital contacts, and there were very few differences between older generations, born before 1900, and younger ones.

However there is one aspect of oral sex that makes it slightly different from other sexual techniques. It does seem that more men than women enjoy practising it. And although considerable numbers of women do come to adopt it, it is usually at the suggestion of their partner at first. They do not seem to discover it for themselves. The man's urge is much more instinctive. Again, there are many women who enjoy a man making love to them this way—it is, in fact, particularly well-suited to a woman's orgasm—but shrink from the idea of returning the favour. It may have something to do with a fundamental difference between the sexes. Men are able to find stimulation psychologically by letting their imaginations run over erotic pictures, or provocative underwear, or even dreams, while these things leave most women cold. And so a man's imagination would help to rouse him during mouth-genital contact whereas a woman tends to prefer the funda-

mental activity of genital penetration. Yet once the experiment has been made, both sexes continue for pleasure. Freud suggests that some of its delight lies in our submerged memories of the warm, damp pleasure of sucking on our mother's nipples.

However, there are people who are drawn towards oral sex by desire and instinct yet hesitate on hygienic grounds. But this is based on misunderstanding. Actually our whole bodies are covered with millions of minute bacteria which do us no harm, and there are no more upon the penis or vagina than upon the breast or hand—and far fewer than lurk between the teeth in lodged particles of food. You run more risk of infecting your genitals with your germ-ridden mouth than the other way round. But both, of course, are safe provided you keep them scrupulously clean.

The woman faces the additional problem of the man's ejaculation. The amount of liquid that this involves is usually wildly over-estimated simply because a little liquid spilled manages to spread itself over an unbelievable area, making it seem much more than it really is. How much semen the man ejaculates will depend on how long it is since his last orgasm, but a rough guide would be a teaspoonful. And swallowing it will certainly not poison anyone, despite what the old wives' tales say. As well as sperm, semen contains fructose, which is a simple sugar, a number of enzymes, bicarbonates, and phosphates, and high concentrations of vitamin C. It will assuredly do no harm. Nor is there any danger of becoming pregnant through swallowing sperm—it cannot find its way from the digestive system into the womb and is actually safer than normal intercourse if one does not want a baby.

Taste, of course, is another matter. Both the man's and the woman's lubricating fluids have a slight odour but what evidence there is suggests that they have no taste. A lot depends on the state of arousal of the active partner. Although there is a general impression that a person who is erotically aroused is more alert to sensory impressions this is not quite the case. What sensation there is is concentrated deep in the nervous system. Ordinary senses function less well at this time: the pupils of the eye dilate and can see only straight ahead, hearing is diminished and the sense of smell and taste fall away, too. So the person who is deeply roused by performing *fellatio*, oral stimulation of the male genitals, or *cunnilingus*, stimulation of the female, will probably notice no taste, the person who is less stimulated may notice a mild, slightly salty flavour, and some women find that semen stings the back of the throat a little as it is swallowed.

This loss of sensation during the period of maximum sexual arousal and orgasm, which can lead to a few moments of complete unconsciousness after orgasm, also releases psychological blockages in the nervous system which can help a woman to perform fellatio. Just as stutterers are unlikely to stutter when they are very stimulated, so women who tend to gag when anything is placed deep in their mouths will

not do so during fellatio if they are sufficiently aroused, even though it may involve deep penetration of the mouth.

Anyway, what are these techniques that cause all this comment and confusion? They are a special sort of sexual intercourse in which the man tickles the woman's clitoris and labia minora with his tongue (cunnilingus) while she touches his penis with her lips and tongue and takes it into her mouth (fellatio). As in all lip and tongue contact there is licking and sucking as well.

The man approaching the woman usually does so while she is lying on her back, legs bent apart. A woman can fellate a man lying down but he may prefer to stand or sit on the side of the bed with the woman kneeling in front of him. If both want to do it simultaneously, they should lie down, head to tail on their sides facing each other, face curved into the genitals in the position known as 69, because that is the shape the two bodies make.

In cunnilingus the man covers the whole area from the clitoris along the inner vaginal lips to the entrance to the vagina itself, concentrating on the clitoris with lips and tongue. All of this area is extremely sensitive to erotic caresses. In fellatio the woman concentrates on the penis, especially the tip which is particularly sensitive under and around the rim. She takes the penis in her mouth, moving her head up and down and from side to side because the excitement comes from friction. It is important to keep renewing contact with the tip of the penis—sucking it in and out of the mouth gently and flicking it with the tip of the tongue—but even more important is to be guided by what one's partner enjoys.

Oral sex, once discovered, is one of the most practical and useful variations on the old theme of sexual intercourse. By using cunnilingus a man can bring a woman to orgasm quite independently of his own potency. If he finds occasional difficulty in achieving an erection, or has reached and passed his own climax too soon leaving his partner unsatisfied, or is simply suffering from that age-old complaint brewer's droop, after drinking too much, he can still satisfy her this way. And many women find it more exciting than ordinary intercourse, perhaps because so much attention is focussed on the clitoris, perhaps because the warm, wet mouth somehow matches the wave-like physiological state as the rhythm takes over.

It is also a practical alternative for women, who can fellate a man at times such as menstruation and immediately before and after childbirth when it would be uncomfortable or distressing for her to allow him to enter the vagina. This way his sexual tensions can be released in a way that involves both of them. Although both practices can be used as a forerunner to ordinary intercourse, as part of the usual preliminary play before genital intercourse takes place, they also offer complete satisfaction in their own right.

BRENDA JONES

Pleasing a man with small fetishes

The contrast of black nylon against white thigh, or the texture of leather boots against soft skin excites many men. How can a woman indulge such desires to increase the mutual joy of love-making?

Marcia felt reasonably sure that she looked good enough in her new dress to make Peter, her husband, forgive her for having kept him waiting for ten minutes. His grin and whistle of admiration proved her right. Peter put down his pre-party drink and moved across the room to take her in his arms. 'You look marvellous,' he said, 'but there's just one thing. . . .'

Peter knelt down before her, slipped his hands up beneath her skirt and, with one swift movement, pulled her pants down to her ankles.

'What on earth are you doing? Peter, we'll be late for the party!'

'Come on, step out of them,' he replied. Marcia did not understand. 'Stop being 'an idiot,' she answered rather sharply.

'Darling,' Peter pleaded, 'don't you see? I want to know, all evening, while we're surrounded by other people, that under that dress you are quite naked.'

'But why?' wailed Marcia, trying to straighten her clothes.

'It's sexy. It makes me want you. It's something I've always wanted you to do for me.'

'Well, if you think I'm going to a party without my pants on, you've got another think coming.' Part of Marcia still thought that Peter's proposal was a joke, but the tight-lipped expression on his face made her realize that he was in earnest. 'Peter, I couldn't,' she said.

'Why not?' he asked, pouring himself another drink and loosening his tie.

'I don't know. I just wouldn't feel right.'

Peter and Marcia did not go to the party. After a short, heated argument in which Peter accused Marcia of being frigid, to which she retaliated by calling him a pervert, Peter settled down to get drunk, while Marcia spent the evening weeping in the bedroom.

This young couple are deeply in love and happily married. Their quarrel that evening was the result of a fundamental difference between the male and female attitudes to sex. Marcia, in common with the majority of women, enjoyed sex with her husband, but sexual intercourse for her was essentially a way of expressing and sharing her love for him. That love was also demonstrated in hundreds of other domestic and emotional ways. As long as she was making love to Peter, sexual intercourse, as far as Marcia was concerned, needed no embellishments. Peter is equally typical of his sex. He understands and appreciates Marcia's attitude to loving. He is satisfied with the sexual aspect of their marriage. But for him, as for most men, there are many other sources of sexual stimulation which, on occasion, he wants to enjoy.

Neither Peter nor Marcia understood the other's point of view. Women are invariably frightened when their husbands express a desire for some sexual variation, especially if, as in this case, the variation seems to them to have no specific or definable relation to sexual intercourse. In

Marcia's view, to go to a party without her pants on would simply be embarrassing. She would feel self-conscious and inhibited. And when she thought more carefully about it, she began to suspect that Peter was trying to cheapen her in the eyes of others. He seemed to want her to behave like a common tart. This led her to wonder if he had married not her as she really was, but as some preconceived sexual object.

On the other hand, Peter could not understand why Marcia had made such a fuss. At the same time he was angry and hurt because she appeared to be determined not to please him in this way. Like most men in the heat of the moment, he fell back on the old myth of female disinterest in sex. To him she lacked imagination and was frigid. He thought he had married a woman who was only prepared to have sex on her own terms. His long-nurtured dream of spending the evening with his attractive wife in a constant state of sexual anticipation, knowing that only a thin length of fabric covered her nakedness, was shattered. Under the combined influence of alcohol and frustration, he saw himself, quite irrationally, condemned to a life of tepid sexual intercourse, devoid of those exciting little extras which made sex, in his view, so much more pleasurable. Simultaneously, Marcia persuaded herself that she had been insulted, that she had married a man who harboured unspeakable sexual longings.

The fact that the female's sexual response tends to be exclusive, entirely directed to one man, while the male is capable of finding stimulation in all sorts of objects and situations, is to a certain extent aggravated by the social conditioning to which most people are subjected when they are young. There is, still, a marked division between the respectable and the 'easy' girl. Women like Marcia, who are the majority, are brought up to believe that nice girls do not go out without their underwear, or wear high-heeled boots while making love. Men like Peter, who is representative of a masculine majority, are taught to despise 'cheap' girls and to respect women like Marcia. Yet there lingers at the back of men's minds two confused thoughts which explain their reactions to this sort of situation.

Most men retain, despite their conditioning and probable experience, a shred of belief in the idea that the 'easy' girl is more sexually exciting and inventive than the nice girl, although it is always the latter they love and marry. At the same time, despite all their experience to the contrary, there is always a nagging doubt that, after all, women do not like and enjoy sex as much as they do. Therefore, when, out of a quite harmless desire to embellish the accepted sexual relationship with some visual or physical quirk which excites them, they find that their wives will not comply with these small fetishes, they interpret this reluctance as proof that women are sexually cold.

This controversy is all too common. Thus, Barbara felt 'silly and embarrassed' when Martin wanted to make love to her in

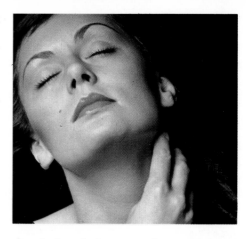

the bath. Andrew nearly precipitated divorce proceedings when he sent away to a mail order firm for a selection of vulgar, lurid 'glamour undies' which he asked his wife to wear in bed. Margaret, on the other hand, found herself collapsing with laughter, and so offended her husband, when she tried to perform a strip-tease act for him in their bedroom. Joan flatly refused to wear a see-through blouse without a bra to please her husband, while Cathy found the idea of wearing black nylon stockings, a suspender belt and high-heeled shoes during sexual intercourse both ludicrous and uncomfortable.

All these women were unable to understand their husbands' desires and, more important, the angry, hurt masculine reaction when they refused. Stung by the apparent sudden attacks on their sexual competence and initiative which their refusals brought down on their heads, these women felt frightened and abused. It is not difficult to understand why.

All of these wives, and thousands of others, had been brought up with a fairly rigid concept of how a decent woman should dress and behave. They had an equally firm view of when, how, and where sexual intercourse should take place. There was no reason for them to believe that their views were in any sense unacceptable since these did not prevent them meeting, being loved, and married by their husbands. Then suddenly, with no warning, after anything from three weeks to three years of marriage, they are calmly asked to behave like common prostitutes, to wear clothes they would never dream of buying for themselves, to make love in strange places and positions. They are asked, in fact, not only to behave contrary to their ingrained instincts, but in the image of those very women they have been taught to despise. Having taken great pains to ensure their respectability, as they see it, they are suddenly asked to appear as sultry strip-tease artists, to dress like vulgar tramps— in short, to reverse their everyday standards and pretend to be that which they have always avoided. Is it any wonder, then, that they feel debased, that they begin to question whether they have married men who have no regard for their true qualities, men who actually like all that they believe to be cheap, common, and vulgar in womankind?

This is the crux of the problem and,

of course, it is quite unfounded. Given the choice, none of these husbands would wish to exchange their wives for a semi-public sex symbol. They would be the first to object if their wives suggested wearing 'glamour undies' for other men. They do care about their wives as they really are and they do appreciate and uphold their concept of respectability and proper behaviour. But, in the privacy of their own bedrooms, they occasionally hanker after something more earthily erotic. The irrational, romantic fascination of the wicked lady in open-crotch panties and 'peek-a-boo' bra still tantalizes them and, sometimes, men seek to make their fantasies come true. They want to pretend, for a few hours, that the erotic ideals of their adolescence are attainable after all.

Women can rarely understand why many men are so excited by the big-breasted, suspender-belted pin-ups in magazines, or why a lady twirling tassels from her nipples is more exciting than a nude body, largely because they lack the same degree of response to visual stimuli. To them, women who conform to a stereotyped masculine fantasy are merely coarse or silly.

But it is invariably the pin-up, or the 'common' girl with the too-tight sweater who first stirs a young adolescent male to sexual arousal. Something of that devastating initial response lingers tantalizingly in the mind, no matter how much the man may subsequently mature. Furthermore, women seldom appreciate that the partially clothed body is more exciting to most men than complete nudity. A partly clothed body has an air of deliberately revealed nakedness which is somehow naughtier and more inviting than natural nudity. That is why so many men are sexually stirred by women's underwear, and why they respond so lustily to the visual contrast of black nylon against white thigh, or the texture of leather boots against soft, feminine skin.

It is, perhaps, this lingering adolescent component in the male reaction to such visual phenomena that most mystifies women. Many of them simply do not see the point of these undressing-up games, or the adoption of stereotyped, unattainable images. For women, sex is about loving and showing that you love. They argue that the female body as nature made it should be sufficient to arouse any husband. They do not appreciate that, admittedly in a limited, physical way, the body *is* more exciting when 'revealed' by a wisp of black lace, or a necklace and a pair of shoes. By the same token, men experience a more conscious awareness of the sexual act if it is performed in an unusual setting or position. It is the same act, but to a great many men it is more exciting when it is varied in this way.

Most women start to indulge in these male whims, after they have been reassured that they are not being deliberately denigrated, from the principle of pleasing their husbands. If it makes him happy, they reason, then why not? This is a good starting point, but it is not sufficient. The compliant wife must realize that it is still

her body that excites her husband even when it is set off by long black stockings, or deliberately revealed by slow and teasing undressing. They are *her* breasts which drive him wild when displayed through a 'glamour bra'. Therefore, if her participation is not to be automatic and mechanical, she must enjoy his admiration of her body, and must learn to revel in her power to arouse him.

Some women have learned this trick, and gained a valuable insight into their husbands' previously mystifying enjoyment, by cunningly turning the tables on their would-be voyeurs, their part-time fetishists. One women agreed to perform a strip-tease routine carefully specified by her husband on condition that he did the same for her. Afterwards, he admitted that he felt foolish and so understood her initial reluctance, while she found his performance very stimulating. Another woman, rationally approaching her husband's desire to have her wear stockings and a suspender belt during sexual intercourse, recalled that she had often felt rather excited by the sight of him in a certain pair of briefs. She agreed to meet his requirements, if he wore the briefs during foreplay. The result was mutually enjoyable.

But most women learn to enjoy indulging

their husbands' whims by sharing in the male's excited response. There is no doubt that these sexual games and adornments do arouse and inspire the men who want them, although it should always be remembered that what raises the beast in one man has absolutely no effect on another. It is seldom a good idea, for a woman to put lipstick on her nipples unless her husband has expressed an erotic interest in body make-up. The reward for any woman's trouble is, invariably, a painstaking and devoted lover.

Most women accept without question that marriage is fundamentally concerned with sharing and adapting to another's needs. Just as she discovers and acts upon her husband's tastes in other things, so she should be prepared to share his sexual desires. But she, and her husband, should be equally aware of any special likings of her own. It may be that she, too, has often dreamed of some situation which she has never experienced, in which case

she should not hesitate to ask it of her husband. The innate masculine curiosity about all things sexual will undoubtedly make him quite willing. For example, a considerable number of women would occasionally like to take the aggressive role in provoking sexual activity. To their surprise, they usually find that husbands, too, like to be seduced.

Men, however, must always remember that these whims and fancies are only games, to be played at intervals. No woman should be expected to dress up or suffer the comparative discomfort of making love on the kitchen floor every night. The sensible man realizes that the special enjoyment he gains from unusual activities and variations is largely dependent upon their infrequency. He should never forget that the essential part of marital sex is harmonious sexual intercourse.

Unfortunately, some women feel that to indulge these whims entails their making some sort of unreasonable sacrifice. This is a dangerous attitude, as well as an unimaginative one. Consistent refusal only aggravates the conflict which frequently results from these proposals when they are first made. The wife who will not comply unwittingly reinforces her husband's belief that she is unfeelingly conformist and, even more importantly, she further feeds his desire for the unusual. In his mind, the whim takes on an exaggerated importance and quite unmerited glamour. It may, in time, become an obsession which some other woman will be only too happy to assuage. The wise wife, therefore, is adaptable, reasonably compliant and, like Marcia, invariably finds that her husband was not being as ridiculous as she thought.

Marcia admits that her quarrel with Peter got so entirely out of proportion that, in desperation, she eventually agreed to go to another party without her underwear. At first she was embarrassed by her own consciousness of being naked. However, Peter's constantly loving attention throughout the evening, the sense she had of his eyes devouring her across the room, the sheer strength of desire he so obviously felt for her, not only made her feel marvellous but excited her as well. By the end of the evening she, like Peter, could not wait to get home and into bed where the promise of the preceding hours was more than fulfilled.

Marcia and Peter finally got the whole subject into perspective when, some weeks later, Marcia insisted that Peter should leave off his underpants as well. His immediate reaction was not dissimilar to Marcia's, but he finally agreed. He, too, felt naked and embarrassed at first, but, gradually, like Marcia, he adjusted to the sensation and their secret knowledge of each other's nudity beneath a conventional exterior kept both in a state of sexual awareness and anticipation during the party. More important, perhaps, it also provided an unspoken bond between them which, though trivial in itself, has certainly helped to deepen their emotional ties as well as stimulating the sexual side of their marriage.   DAVID FLETCHER

The place of imagination in love-making

The natural curiosity of new lovers makes love-making exciting. But habit can dull even the most ardent passion. What new pleasures can imagination bring to love-making and to loving?

Relationships, like everything else, are dulled by habit and custom. No matter how satisfying a relationship, or how deeply the partners love each other, routine and familiarity can cause staleness which, if it is allowed to go unchecked, can quickly turn to sourness.

Courtship is a journey of mutual discovery. There is so much which is unknown about one's partner, so many discoveries to be made. In the early days of marriage both partners will try to learn and understand all they can about each other. But all too often the enquiring spirit of lovers is subdued by domestic cares and routines. This is where imagination enters with its power to transform the mundane into the unusual.

Imagination, in this context, need mean nothing more than not taking your partner for granted, or not allowing yourself to become predictably set in your ways. The proper exercise of imagination provides the element of surprise that enlivens a marriage. It should imbue the whole of a relationship. Unfortunately, the area where imagination is most commonly lacking is the sexual one.

A young, newly-married couple are necessarily not very concerned with the finer points of love-making, or with variations and gimmicks. They are too absorbed in discovering each other sexually and in consummating their relationship. Their eagerness is natural, instinctive, and fulfilling. But so often one hears the cry, 'My husband (or wife) used to be so passionate, so loving, but now sex seems to be just part of the routine.' Sexual orthodoxy is fine for the couple who are virtual strangers and who have to discover each other in bed. But that orthodoxy can quickly turn into predictability without the exercise of imagination.

It is, naturally, impossible to legislate for individual couples in this respect. They must exercise their own imaginations and find their own enlivening alternatives. But many people do not know where to begin. Their longings are often undefined and may even be surprising to themselves when they are revealed.

Obviously, both partners need confidence

in themselves and in each other, and this can be obtained by frank discussions together. For some couples variations of coital positions are sufficient to make their relationship more interesting. These may have the effect not only of making the sexual act more exciting, by adding a much-needed element of unfamiliarity, but also of increasing the physical pleasures of love-making. For example, some women find the achievement of orgasm easier, or its experience more intense, in novel positions. Men often find greater stimulation in positions which allow them to view their partners' bodies more fully than is possible in the classic face to face position.

It is frequently found that novelty in sexual relations is successful in proportion to the degree to which it correlates with existing erotic fantasies. Everyone nurtures some desire or dreams about some act or situation which is peculiarly stimulating. The use of imagination in love-making can either indirectly bring these fantasies into the conscious mind where a person may become aware of them, or it can enable a person to enact some of his fantasies. The important point is that these fantasies should be accepted by both partners without guilt or embarrassment.

Jane discovered a fantasy of her husband Michael's quite by accident. On a shopping trip she impulsively bought two pairs of unisex underpants, one for Michael and one for herself. She thought very little about it except that the briefs were attractive and, significantly, made a change. Their effect on Michael, however, was considerable. As they were preparing for bed that night, he insisted that they should try the pants on. The sight of them both reflected in the mirror, identically dressed, deeply excited him. The sameness of the underwear had, for him, the effect of dramatizing the anatomical differences between male and female, while the mere idea of common underwear for both sexes excited him enormously.

Underwear bears an extraordinary fascination for many men which is often incomprehensible to women. By wearing the favoured underwear, however, many women find that they introduce a new ele-

ment of sexuality into their relationships. In the case of Michael and Jane, their shared interest in the erotic powers of identical underwear, although probably meaningless to others, had the desirable effect of enlivening their sexual relationship. Jane, by making an adventurous purchase, showed an innate willingness not to take her marriage for granted, and, thus, accidentally, touched upon a source of hidden eroticism in her husband.

Some people, on the other hand, deliberately introduce a particular fantasy into the marriage situation. Leonard, like so many men, was attracted by the idea of having sexual relations with a prostitute. Although happily married to Diane, the novelty and passion had disappeared from their sexual relationship through habit and familiarity. Instead of passively accepting this familiarity, however, Leonard persuaded Diane to take part in an elaborate game with him.

One Friday evening he returned home to find Diane transformed from the dutiful wife busily preparing his dinner, to a provocative tart. Heavily made-up and dressed in a transparent negligee, she agreed to have intercourse with Leonard for a suitable fee (actually her housekeeping money). They both were able to enter into the spirit of the game. Diane behaved in a professionally erotic way and treated Leonard as a typical client. Afterwards they shared the joke and found a new closeness and sense of relaxation as they prepared a late meal together. Since that evening the prostitute game has become a regular feature of their relationship and has completely revitalized the sexual aspect of their marriage.

Such a game is an excellent example of the way in which imagination can transform a mundane situation into an exotic adventure. There is, obviously, a world of difference between the casually dressed wife accepting her housekeeping money as a matter of course and the provocative makebelieve whore who earns her money in the bedroom from a demanding client.

Leonard and Diane fully understand the game they are playing and both take pleasure in the pretence. Diane admits that she

Robin Clifford

really imagines herself as a whore and finds a new excitement herself in the experience of intercourse with her husband. For his part, Leonard is able to indulge his fantasy of having sexual possession and power over a hired woman.

Everyone must find his own fantasy, but it is important not to forget that it is only a game. In this way many everyday situations can take on new, erotic meaning without causing harm or damage. Such games, however, are only effective if they are sparingly played. The enactment of a fantasy must be regarded as a means of periodically boosting and varying the usual pattern of the relationship. If overworked fantasies, too, can pall.

Diane, for example, cannot pretend to be a whore every day and be a successful wife as well. If she were to try she would lose not only the attraction this role lends her, but the domestic foundation of her marriage would suffer. Furthermore, unless these games are treated with humour, they can cause pain or humiliation for a person, thereby possibly destroying a relationship.

It is not always possible for two people to wholeheartedly share and enjoy the same fantasy. What is intensely stimulating to one person may be positively ludicrous to another. As in most aspects of marriage, there must be a spirit of co-operation and tolerance between partners if there is to be harmony. All too often fantasies are associated with guilt, which can be destructive and which is almost always unnecessary. A couple who can share their fantasies are much more apt to have a good marriage. Even if the fantasy is not satisfactorily realizable between the couple, openly discussing it usually removes any destructive guilt and can provide stimulation. Many couples have discovered the erotic power of words and by describing and discussing their fantasies have enlivened their sexual lives.

The proper use of imagination can affect the whole fabric of a relationship, not merely the sexual part, and sometimes the two can be achieved simultaneously. Peggy and Donald had reached a stage in their marriage where they felt that their life together had become stale. They were happy, had few worries, but somehow the magic had gone out of their relationship—until Donald used his imagination.

'He rang me up one lunchtime and told me to get dressed and to pack my toothbrush, he would be picking me up in an hour for a trip into the country. Well, of course, I reacted like most other wives and mothers. I couldn't just abandon the kids and take off somewhere in the middle of the day, and I said so. But I'd not counted on Donald's efficiency,' Peggy said.

Donald had spent a busy morning arranging for Peggy's mother to meet the children at school and keep them with her overnight. He had then booked a room at an inn which he and Peggy had once visited and which had particularly charmed her. Peggy was reassured and, although still protesting and worrying, she was ready when Donald arrived to collect her. They drove deep into the country where Donald insisted on parking the car in a deserted spot and making love to Peggy just as they had done before they were married.

'It was ridiculous and marvellous,' she said. 'We behaved like a couple of teenagers again and it was incredibly exciting. When you talk about it, it just sounds mad. But honestly it was fantastic. Then we went to this lovely old inn that I'd admired years before and he'd remembered. He ordered a superb dinner and when we went up to bed he produced the sexiest, most impractical nightdress you've ever seen. We made love again that night—the nightie really inspired Donald—without having to listen for the children. In the morning there was no need to get up at precisely seven o'clock. It was so romantic. I really can't begin to tell you.'

Donald's use of his imagination accomplished much. First, he showed Peggy how much he loved her. Beyond this, he anticipated her problems and solved them for her. He proved his awareness of her tastes by remembering her liking for the inn. He encouraged and enabled her to behave like a carefree young woman again, while, by his gift of a frivolous nightdress, he showed her that she still attracted him sexually. And he accomplished all this while giving her a much-needed and well-deserved break from domestic routine. As a result they not only felt closer to one another, but returned refreshed and able to enjoy their children and domesticity.

The essence of the imaginative partner is an ability to show a proper awareness of the spouse. Many wives and husbands unwittingly, and often inaccurately, create the impression that they are so preoccupied with domestic and job concerns that they never give a moment's thought to their partner. Total absorption in the demands of domesticity and work must be resisted at all costs. Two people who love each other and work to have a successful marriage know a great deal about one another and they should employ this knowledge as a basis for imaginative invention.

All wives will be touched by the occasional surprise present, but so often the edge is taken off the surprise by the very predictability of the gift. Many men seem to be incapable of presenting their wives with anything but flowers, chocolates, or perfume. Acceptable as these are, something totally unexpected and more personal will show a woman not only that her husband has thought about her, but also that he has used his imagination and really tried to please her. Many women will privately admit that they are more flattered by the gift of a blouse in a colour they do not really like, than by the traditional bunch of roses. It at least shows that their husbands have gone to some trouble and effort to surprise them.

Intuition may be a great aid to the person who wants to be imaginative, but also seeks to please in a special way. There are few things more disheartening for married people than to feel that they have to ask for everything that they want, although their demands may be willingly met. The imaginative partner anticipates the other's needs and wishes. He or she does not have to be told what will please or excite the other.

There is little excuse, for example, for a husband not to notice that his wife wants a new dress or pair of shoes. He should be aware of her wardrobe, if only in the selfish sense of wishing to see her wearing something different himself.

Wives, too, should develop the ability to foresee their husbands' needs and desires. The man who wants to try some sexual variation invariably drops hints about it before bluntly proposing it outright. The wife who listens to these veiled hints, anticipates her husband's desires, and sets the scene or institutes the preferred activity will seldom find her marriage palling or her husband unresponsive.

Having to ask for everything creates an impression that the other person is half-hearted or grudging. Usually, they merely seem grudging, and are essentially guilty only of a lack of imagination. Surprise, however, is an element which keeps any relationship alive and makes it enjoyable. A marriage which is totally predictable, which becomes set in a routine mould of clockwork precision, is boring even to contemplate. To be able to predict the future pattern of one's life turns even the most lively person into a dull one. The successful marriage is one which is constantly evolving, constantly changing because both partners seek to please and surprise.

Imagination is basically a natural element in a love relationship and does not really have to be introduced, but, rather, revived. The young man and woman who meet and fall in love spend much time trying to please each other by anticipating needs and wishes. When they marry, both are concerned to discover what gives the other sexual pleasure, what excites, and, what satisfies. Frequently, however, this initial burst of imaginative energy is dissipated. People become lazy and rely upon what they know. Thus, the most erotically stimulating caress, the most delightfully surprising present, through repetition, becomes numbing and familiar. Both partners begin to feel that they have ceased to be of interest to one another. The husband wishes that he had never expressed a liking for steak, or the wife that she had never admitted that her breasts were sensitive. The palate becomes jaded when subjected to the same diet. The body ceases to respond adequately to predictable stimulation.

Variety is essential because so much of everyone's life is necessarily bound up with routine and habit. Even sexual activity is capable of only so many variations. Routine, therefore, must not be translated into a virtue for its own sake. There are areas of life where routine and predictability are essential and admirable. But love is most definitely not one of these. There is always something new to be discovered about the person one loves, always a new way of pleasing and satisfying, provided one uses one's imagination.

MICHAEL BROOKS

Masturbation as a substitute

Although masturbation is now considered to be a normal part of sexuality, many people still believe it to be a sign of immaturity in adults. Yet in some situations masturbation can provide a valuable and mature solution to sexual problems.

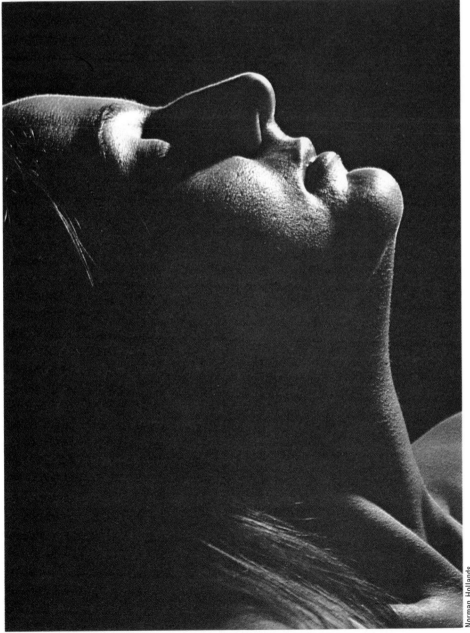

Norman Hollands

In the sex literature of today masturbation is regarded as a harmless activity. There is often, however, an emphasis on its harmlessness in childhood and adolescence —with the implication that masturbation in adults is 'immature'.

Since the Kinsey reports over twenty years ago, it has become obvious that although the peak of masturbation usually occurs in early adolescence, with the practice lessening from the age of 16 onwards, nevertheless a great many people masturbate to some extent throughout their adult lives, usually without either psychological or physiological harm.

In early adolescence masturbation results from a normal exploration of the body's functions and its changing responses. Adult masturbation is often a conscious substitute for interpersonal sex and as such it may be a symptom of withdrawal, consolidating a person's timidity about forming social and sexual relationships. And if such habitual masturbation is accompanied by persistent guilt there is likely to be a progressive decline in the masturbator's capacity for social learning, and in his self-confidence.

But in most instances adult masturbation is a simple activity given little importance by those who practise it. There are many situations in which a person who prefers and has experienced sexual intercourse is prevented in some way or another from having a normal sexual relationship. Masturbation may be needed to relieve sexual tension because of temporary breaks in a relationship through illness, pregnancy, or absence; or perhaps because of a permanent break, with one or both partners living alone; or it may be because of long-term absences, in the army or in prison. Often masturbation is resorted to as a virtuous alternative to being sexually 'unfaithful' to a loved partner or to avoid homosexuality in a single-sex situation.

Occasionally masturbation has been recommended as a deliberate, temporary practice for a 'frigid' married woman, en-

151

couraging her to learn about her body's responses in a relaxed and private way. In fact, a woman who married without any previous sexual experience may well have to work through various adolescent phases of sexual discovery before she is released into an adult ability to enjoy sex. The adolescent girl is often ignorant of the source of the diffuse sexual longings she feels in her body. There may be additional cultural inhibitions which make masturbation in girls less common than in boys. But it is probably primarily due to the fact that her sexual organs are not self-explanatory: an adolescent boy's erecting penis leaves him in no doubt about the source of sexual pleasure and disturbance. A girl needs much more sophisticated knowledge to understand her body. Even if she has some knowledge of the complementary male and female genitals, even if normal exploration of her genitals has taken place, she may not discover the importance of the clitoris for herself.

There is a fairly well-proven correlation between masturbation and education, and to some extent class—the better educated masturbate more. This seems to be because they are more likely to know that masturbation is a normal sexual activity, where the lesser educated are more prone to old wives' (and priests') tales about the hazards of masturbation. The better educated young man is also less likely than the

working-class man to be experiencing sexual release through intercourse—middle-class women are less accessible sexually (although this situation is changing today) and the better educated of both sexes are warier about the risks of conception, and so less likely to indulge in casual relationships.

Class and educational differences may be diminishing however. More enlightened attitudes towards masturbation have coincided with recognition of female orgasm; and women, being better educated than they were, are fulfilling less inhibited sexual and occupational roles than they used to. The rate of masturbation in women is almost certainly increasing. There is a danger that this will increase narcissism in women—a hazard which women already face by virtue of being female in a society with breast-obsessed media and a tendency to treat women as life-long sex objects.

There is much evidence that women achieve orgasm more quickly and more certainly in masturbation than they do in coitus. It seems likely that a growing minority of women will come to regard masturbation as a successful substitute for interpersonal sex. Men, of course, may also prefer the undemanding simplicity of masturbation to the possibility of impotence or other inadequacy (or implied inadequacy) in sexual intercourse. But women have a peculiar difficulty: if they live alone they

feel they lack socially acceptable ways of starting relationships, because of the surviving convention that social and sexual approaches to the opposite sex are made by men towards women and not vice versa.

This convention will probably fade eventually. In the meantime, some women are prompting comparatively new forms of aggressive sexuality. The militant women's liberationist vigorously recommends masturbation as a way of escaping sexual 'degradation' by men. Women of this extremist minority also tend to pervert to their own use the new discoveries that have been made about the physiology of the female orgasm. The American sex researchers William H. Masters and Virginia E. Johnson finally dispelled the myth of the vaginal orgasm in their widely read book *Human Sexual Response* published in 1966. Until then, most people had thought that there were two different types of female orgasm—the clitoral and the maturer vaginal orgasm. Masters and Johnson showed that there was only one type of orgasm which could, however, vary in its intensity triggered off by the stimulation of the clitoris. The extreme woman's liberationists might argue from this that men are not necessary for female satisfaction.

Many prostitutes after a night's work, having been mechanically aroused for some hours, may habitually masturbate and feel

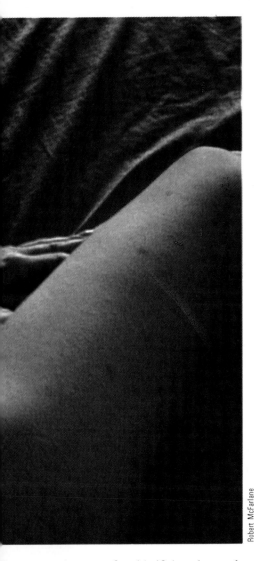

Robert McFarlane

extremely uncomfortable if they do not do so. In fact, any form of sexual activity which regularly stops short of orgasm is potentially harmful, leading to possible mild but chronic congestive conditions as well as psychological disorders. In masturbation it is particularly harmful since the masturbator is probably spending a lot of time in sexual fantasy, before punishing himself for the habit by depriving himself of orgasm.

Countless women, especially in marriage, regularly simulate orgasm in coitus. A few men regularly prevent themselves ejaculating in intercourse—either because they do not trust their partner's contraceptive precautions or because they have religious, medical, or aesthetic objections to the different types of contraception that are available. Such habits are likely to harm relationships, since resentment is bound to be felt at some time: the frustrated partner feeling 'used' or the satisfied partner feeling guilty. If the frustrated partner usually masturbates later, the dissatisfaction is eliminated, but it seems to be placing a relationship unnecessarily at risk. Masturbation can be similarly used or misused where one partner is acknowledged by both to be more highly sexed than the other. This may be so and masturbation may resolve the situation to the satisfaction of both. But such an assumption may simply be a disguise for the fact that they have never

come to sexual terms with each other.

Mutual masturbation solves difficulties for partners where one or both is ill, for instance, or physically handicapped. It is also very common in homosexual relationships, and in premarital relationships where the girl is anxious to remain a virgin or has religious scruples against contraception.

Masturbation can often be potentially harmful, just as coitus can be in certain situations. Dissociating sex from all emotional involvement, for instance, may lead to permanent dissatisfaction, whether the sexual act is solitary or shared—that is, orgasm is obtained, but with little subjective satisfaction. Whether or not this dissatisfaction is a result of social expectations is a matter for conjecture: but it seems a common experience. Men and women are very often conditioned by the way they are brought up into opposing attitudes in this type of situation.

Girls are encouraged to opt for emotion without sex, boys to be biased towards the reverse. Men often continue in adult life to believe in the enviability of a promiscuous, male-dominant sexual life, experimenting with every conceivable variation of sexual experience, accompanied by freedom from emotional commitment of any kind. Recent fashions in portraying sex on the screen and stage and in underground magazines have included masturbation, showing it almost as though it were a politically essential and rather necessary repudiation of prudery and the Establishment. It seems likely that it is rather *less* than this.

Philip Roth's *Portnoy's Complaint* is a famous fictional account of the fierce erotic predicaments of adolescence—which the hero (or victim) carries over helplessly into adult life, endlessly indulging his sexual impulses, endlessly unsatisfied.

Portnoy is, finally, impotent and a psychiatrist's case. He likens his endlessly erect penis to 'some idiot macrocephalic', which is a reminder of the threat previously used against masturbating adolescents: 'You'll go mad.' In fact mentally subnormal people tend to masturbate more frequently and openly: as do some of the mentally ill. And institutionalized life may aggravate the tendency. But it is important to remember that mental illness or mental defectiveness is not the *result* of masturbation.

Anxieties about mental health in connection with masturbation arise from the nature of masturbation fantasies. Sexual fantasies accompany masturbation more often than they do interpersonal sexual acts, but fantasy is common to both forms of sexual activity. It is probably a waste of time for people to worry about the particular type of fantasies they enjoy—whether sadistic, masochistic, homosexual, or narcissistic. Any suggested diagnostic significance is rather negated by the wide disagreement on the matter between various psychologists. Even if, say, a person invariably indulges in homosexual fantasy when he masturbates it may not indicate that he is a homosexual. Even committed homosexuals do not necessarily have homosexual fantasies during sexual activity. In a recent book, *Love Between Women*, Charlotte Wolff explained that many female homosexuals are heterosexual or bisexual in their sexual fantasies. And in 25 cases of voyeur sex dreams that she analysed the dreams were about heterosexual coitus.

There do not seem to be marked differences between fantasy during masturbation and during coitus. Individual experience obviously gives form to the fantasies and most fantasies represent moral and emotional situations which the person would find intolerable in reality. Better educated adults tend, on the whole, to fantasize more abstractly or anonymously—ignoring acquaintances, film stars, and other identifiable people.

Adult masturbation is likely to be obsessional when it habitually involves fetishism or voyeurism. Both seem to be almost entirely male phenomena, although much research still needs to be carried out on this point. The fetishist tends to become attached to particular items, often of clothing, which have some special significance—such as underclothing.

The typical fetishist is usually a withdrawn, depressed man suffering from considerable feelings of sexual guilt. But a mild degree of fetishism is a common part of masculine experience and, even in masturbation, does not necessarily add to the feelings of guilt or shame which tend to be the most destructive element of sexual behaviour.

If adult masturbation releases you from preoccupation with sex, rather than increasing it; if it eases interpersonal relationships (social or sexual, casual or stable), rather than making them more difficult, then it is only sensible to practise it.

If, however, living in a non-sexual situation, you do not feel the need for sexual relief, you should not let current thinking bully you into feeling anxious about your lack of sexual appetite: you can be alone and well and living in Western society and still not need regular sexual outlets.

Views on masturbation have changed drastically since the last century when it was thought to be the source of spiritual damnation and mental and physical ill-health. But there is a danger that the pendulum will swing too far the other way.

Masturbation as a substitute for sexual intercourse should be seen in its proper perspective. The solitary pursuit of sexual pleasure will never be able to match the shared enjoyment of sexual intercourse within a mature relationship. Some people who have not yet found this kind of satisfaction or who are separated from their partner do not feel the need to masturbate, nor should they be stampeded into a belief that they will suffer emotionally and physically if they do not want to. For others masturbation affords a welcome and harmless relief from sexual tension. Seen in its proper context masturbation is no more and no less than a normal and natural addition to human sexuality.

JANE ALEXANDER

Masturbation in love-making

A couple must know and like their own bodies if their love-making is to be successful and relaxed. Only personal experience and experiment can teach them this.

Lovers are in danger of becoming the most paradoxical of beings, comparable to those motorcyclists who race around and around an indoor track in order to get ahead.

No doubt love-making has been complicated by the new habit of writing about it, talking about it, and seeing films about it, for all of these clinical dissections have blunted the mystique of the sexual act. In an odd contradictory way, by encouraging freedom, they have made sex less spontaneous. Thus, the lover who is supposed to be in the velvet throes of life's most ardent and natural experience is at the same time a lonely investigator of what has become our most heavily-documented activity. Where before he thought only of love or lust and she of love or security, now before and after the sexual act, and even during it, they both are very likely

wondering if their techniques are impressive, if their partner is receiving a fair share of bliss, if that actress they saw in a recent Swedish film could possibly have been double-jointed.

'It's so consoling,' a young man told me after seeing his first blue film, 'to know one is doing it properly.'

Propriety would once have been thought a very odd bedfellow, but now we know from sex manuals that there is a 'proper' way to make love and another way, a Saturday night ritual, which if not 'improper' is certainly a deadly bore. We know because they tell us so, and you are going to be reminded once again: in love-making anything goes. But many people who *think* Liberated Sex do not actually *feel* Liberated Sex and, ultimately, the only 'decent' love-making is done with feeling.

To be totally relaxed with a sexual partner, and thus capable of that warm, true feeling which liberates the act of love from lurid textbooks, the lover must be totally relaxed with his or her own body. The woman who has reservations about caressing her partner's sex organs, or about oral-genital contact, must have reservations and shames about her own body. If she is curious about her body she will be curious about his. If she is not offended by hers she will not be offended by his, for the fact is that as well as expressing an attitude towards the particular body next to ours in bed, we also express our attitude towards bodies in general and the way they function. The man who likes himself and his partner will want more than the splendid impact of coitus. He will want to be indulged, to indulge her, to

stroke, caress, be stroked and caressed, to lick, to taste, to be tasted. Sex, after all, unless done strictly for procreation, is a very self-indulgent activity and our society on the whole disapproves of self-indulgence.

Within this area of sexual activity masturbation is the most self-indulgent expression of lust and thus the one that has traditionally inspired the greatest guilt. Mutual masturbation, the manipulations and caresses of love-play between a couple, also inspires guilt among many people who cannot really feel, although their sex manuals tell them, that it is a perfectly acceptable form of foreplay and, for that matter, a very pleasant form of play. The guilt experienced is part of our complex reaction to any sexual act which cannot produce babies and thus must show us how very self-indulgent sex can be.

Men and women have a great potential for physical pleasure. And that is a rare fact in an area full of mists and paradoxes. Indeed, this potential for physical pleasure is so avid that its power suggests that to deny or

Monty Coles

155

be denied pleasure is the only "improper" thing that can ever happen in bed. Mutual masturbation, if it gives pleasure, is good and according to every study of sexual activity, it does give pleasure. Although it is generally seen as part of intercourse, a sort of curtain-raiser, mutual masturbation, or 'petting' to orgasm, often becomes an aim in itself. There are no moral judgements to be made about any sexual activity. Those who indulge in mutual masturbation to orgasm presumably do so by mutual agreement and because they want to.

However, some young people fearful of pregnancy or simply of the loss of their virginity frequently 'pet' to a climax. It is impossible to say that this activity does them any harm. Some sexologists suggest that if it is done habitually, it arrests the woman at clitoral orgasm and condemns the man to premature ejaculation. But, as often happens, the conditions for this to occur were there already and may even have accounted for the reason that mutual masturbation was selected by the couple instead of premarital intercourse. If the young people are without guilt and, above all, without fear in the first place it is unlikely they would continue 'petting' to a climax without having full intercourse sooner or later and enjoying it.

Technical virgins who have teased, touched, and even spent whole nights 'petting' without full intercourse, have a problem to begin with. Either guilt or a paralysing fear of failure prevents them from surrendering those extra centimetres and committing themselves to the act of love. If technical virginity extends into adulthood, when people should be able to make moral and responsible decisions for themselves, it may be indicative of emotional problems. People who habitually and irrationally agree to 'everything but' sexually are quite simply agreeing to everything but the ultimate physical contact. We can do what we will with our sex organs, but a loving mind and heart cannot honestly do 'everything but'. If, however, there is a religious or moral stricture which, perversely, appears to allow the young people to 'pet', but will not allow them intercourse, then they are very fortunate if they have found the courage to take pleasure in each other through mutual masturbation, since it is the only method permitted to them outside of marriage. After marriage such a young couple, having received sanction for it, will probably progress to a full, loving, and exciting act of love.

The most dangerous time for sexual relationships is after marriage when excitement is tamed by routine and the sexual act displays its resemblance to the sneeze —to which, some say, orgasm is distantly related. It is not marital duty to keep sex fresh and exciting, for that suggests that sex is always for the other fellow's pleasure, but it certainly makes sense that for the sake of both partners the bed must represent something more than another piece of furniture to be dusted.

Wives frequently have problems in adding a bit of spice to their sex lives. Such an absurd price is put on female virginity especially that many women still think the mere act of losing it makes them sexually sophisticated. This is just not true. The sexually-sophisticated human being is the one who not only gives pleasure, but also receives pleasure. Currently, there are many writers, some of them light-minded and others serious, who say that by practising masturbation a woman can literally teach herself, and sometimes her partner too, how to have extreme pleasure. Orgasm, these writers suggest, can be a learned response to love-making and in pursuit of this response vibrators, imagination, even the aid of a lover, should be enlisted.

Mutual masturbation as the prelude to the sexual act can stimulate more response in a woman than she ever expected she could feel and more gratification in the man. Even if she has achieved a mild orgasm before actual coitus she may find herself relaxed and ready to experience yet another orgasm during coitus. The man, for his part, can enjoy a languorous sensuality through pre-coital stimulation by his partner which he only imagined before. Another interesting point mentioned by one married woman, who enjoys mutual

masturbation with her husband, is that during this foreplay they are free to give gentle instructions and they have thus revealed to each other more of their personal sexuality than unadorned coitus ever allowed for.

Furthermore, there are occasions during marriage when full sexual intercourse is not feasible: during the menstrual period for some, during certain months of pregnancy, or when either partner is very tired. At these times, when the spirit is willing to make love but the body would rather not, mutual masturbation to the orgasm of one or both partners is a charming outlet and can be a generous, loving gesture on the part of the incapacitated partner towards the other. Among women who are capable of achieving orgasm only by direct stimulation of the clitoris, the fortunate ones in their reasonable search for pleasure have learned that masturbation and mutual masturbation is their greatest source of satisfaction. Maybe someday these women, or women like them, will be helped to experience orgasm through other means of stimulation, maybe not. But whatever happens, as long as pleasure is a wholesome animal product of sexual contact, they are fortunate to have found a means to achieve it.

Many of those people who resist mutual masturbation do so out of a fear of homosexuality, since caresses are enjoyed by homosexuals and are the source of orgasm.

When we are prevented by fear from certain sexual activities, it is not the activity which we must examine, but the fear. Where there is a prohibitive fear of enjoying a so-called homosexual caress, there is obviously a fear of being a homosexual. Such a fear is one which the individual must face alone or with professional help if he is to extend his sex life. If, however, he derives satisfaction from heterosexual activity, except that of mutual masturbation which repels him, and his partner is also satisfied, his fear of homosexuality hopefully can remain the sleeping dog of his subconscious. Of course, there is a chance that the dog will rise, snarling, one day but that is a risk that must be run.

For those others who are not actually fearful of being homosexual, but find the idea of a caress without thrust, of mutual masturbation, distasteful because of its homosexual connotation it would be as well to remember that homosexuals are our fellow creatures who create their unions, too, with love and hope. That because they enjoy a particular caress it must be theirs exclusively makes no more sense than to say only Italians should eat spaghetti.

'All my husband and I ever do,' one woman told me, 'is mutually masturbate. It is an infallible method of contraception and we enjoy it heartily.' This couple, as amazing as it must seem, have been married happily for twelve years. They masturbate mutually, and with some very elaborate props, by common agreement. Whatever path of fantasy, or trauma, or bitter experience each of them followed, it led them both to the same place where, fortunately, each found the other waiting and where they were able to create their own sort of sexual contentment. Analysts could have had a field day with them, their most 'liberal' friends are scandalized. No doubt there is some deep, problematical resistance to sexual intercourse in both of them. Yet by their unity and their even-tempered love for each other, they embody the truth that in bed, between consenting human beings, nothing is ever wrong except just possibly failing to try something that might bring them closer and give them mutual joy.

For the sexually well-adjusted and uninhibited, patterns do not form too rigidly inside their sexual unions. They are curious, they investigate, they change. One woman, for example, told how she and her husband enjoyed mutual masturbation almost exclusively, as if they had invented it, for about six months. Then, one day, they tried something else, an unusual position, simply because they wanted to.

'Now,' she said, 'sometimes I'll say to him, "let's do what we did last summer" and sometimes we will, sometimes we'll do something else. Sometimes we'll just go to sleep. You can't make rules, can you?'

LOUISE SHORT

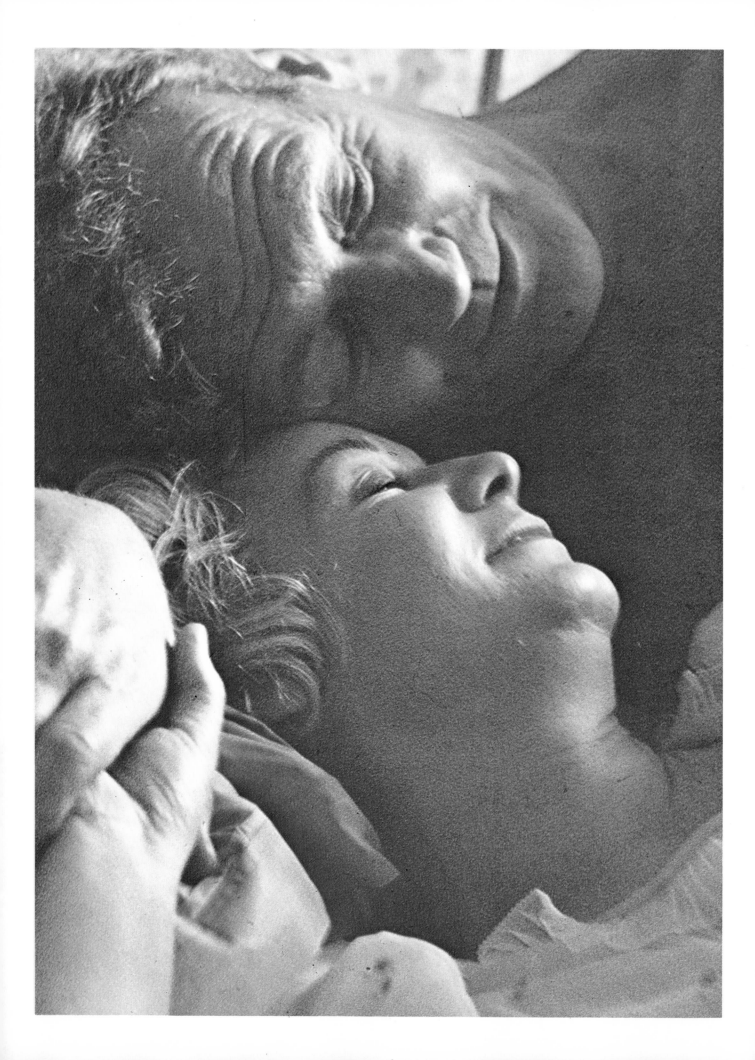

Sex
after
menopause

New techniques and deeper emotional understanding can make sex in middle age more enjoyable for both partners. A sexual relationship should not end with the menopause.

Many women associate the loss of fertility caused by the menopause with a loss of sexual desire and their own attractiveness. While it would be a mistake to minimize the importance of this inevitable loss of fertility to women, any attempts to perpetuate the myth of post-menopause asexuality would be equally wrong and infinitely more damaging.

Because the female libido is closely intermingled with the physical process of procreation and the emotional fulfillment of the maternal instinct, it is not difficult to understand why some women equate the cessation of fertility with the loss of desire. Frequently, this attitude is strengthened by the physical disturbances which some women experience during the menopause. There is, often, a short period when menopausal women do not desire sexual intercourse, and even feel a repugnance towards it which they themselves are unable fully to understand or explain. This may be caused by the physical side-effects of the change of life, or it may be entirely induced by psychological fears and tensions. Certainly, in some cases, the mental traumas of the menopause aggravate physical symptoms.

There are many misconceptions about sex after menopause. Most women do not realize that men do not associate desire with fertility. A woman may not be desirable to her husband after the menopause, but that has nothing to do with the biological changes taking place in her body. It is either a result of previous marital difficulties, or it may be directly attributable to her failure to make herself desirable. If a woman experiences a repugnance to sexual intercourse during the menopause, she must remind herself that this is temporary. It will, in all probability, be prolonged in direct proportion to the extent of her concern about it and will only become permanent if she allows it to do so.

The real antidote to the psychological difficulties of the menopause is to think about the future and the unique opportunities it creates. Too many women instinctively regard the menopause as the end of a vital part of their life and as a diminution of themselves as women. But menopause should be considered the beginning of a new phase in their own life and in a marital relationship which has survived the vicissitudes and tests of time. In many ways the menopause is the last and most severe of these tests, but, even while it is occurring, it provides an opportunity for a reinforcement and extension of the emotional bonds between two people.

Women should share with their husbands the problems and difficulties they experience during the menopause. The majority of men have an innate and dependable sympathy with 'female troubles' and will welcome the opportunity to reassure their wives, while being themselves reassured that their wives do not reject them as individuals.

This was the approach used by Helen who, at 49, is as happily married and sexually active as she has ever been. She and her husband, Colin, had always had an excellent sexual relationship. Then, although she still loved Colin and wanted to please him, Helen found herself increasingly preoccupied by what was happening to her body during the menopause and conceived a positive repulsion at the mere thought of intercourse.

'I had never refused Colin's advances, and I felt awful when I pushed him away. But my body refused to respond and I couldn't face the thought of going through with something I suddenly didn't enjoy.'

Because Colin had always found Helen a loving and responsive partner he was not prepared simply to accept her rejection. Instead, he encouraged her to talk of her feelings about the menopause and, by assuring her that he could wait until she was again able to reciprocate his desires,

Does a man get too old for sex?

Many people think that the older a man gets the less virile he is. What really happens to his sexuality as he ages? Must a man be prepared for a steady decline into impotence?

The belief that men automatically lose their sexual abilities as they grow older is a myth. The truth is that sex, like almost everything else, becomes less urgent with age. The myth, however, is compounded by widespread ignorance and misinterpretation of the inevitable physiological changes which occur in the male body in middle age.

A man's attitude to and expectation of his sexual performance is fixed in youth—when desire is strong, reaction is speedy, and performance intense. As a result a man takes this natural physical response for granted. When, as he approaches late middle age, his sexual-response patterns change, he immediately mistakes this for evidence of failure. Often real failure is then induced by pessimism and anxiety.

It is essential that the older man should understand these natural changes and be able to adapt his attitude to sexual activity, for they do not signify the end of an active sex life. Aging is a process of slowing down and this, in essence, is what happens to a man's sexual responses.

Of course, physiological changes differ from person to person. There are no rules which determine what will happen to a man's sexuality and at what age. There are many physical and psychological factors which affect each individual differently. Thus it is difficult to say when the changes will occur, and whether a particular man will show all the signs of sexual aging.

Probably the first sign of a change in his sexuality that a man notices will be that it takes him longer to achieve a full erection. A young man usually becomes erect in a matter of seconds, and often without any direct physical stimulation. Mere contact with a female body, kissing, or even mental anticipation of intercourse are sufficient to produce erection.

The older man often panics when these accepted stimuli do not produce the desired and habitual effect. It is as though there were a gap between mental and physical reactions, between desire and erection. If he panics, becomes tense, or unduly concerned, he may either try to will an erection or abandon any further effort to achieve one. Both these reactions can be disastrous. For to try to will an erection increases anxiety about sexual performance, brings it into sharp focus, and inhibits the response even further. A man in this situation must accept that full erection will take minutes, possibly many minutes, and will require consistent and direct stimulation.

A woman must learn to adjust to her husband's slower response rhythm. Accustomed to his easy arousal, she may not realize the need for more direct stimulation. His response will be greatly helped by caressing his penis and other erogenous zones, and fellatio, of course, is also effective. Penetration, however, can be affected without the man achieving full erection, and the first coital movements will almost certainly complete arousal.

The other major change which a man may notice as he becomes older is that the testicles do not retract as an accompaniment to erection as strongly as in youth. Sometimes this may not occur at all. Fortunately, few men are concerned about this, since, from a practical point of view, it is a side-effect of sexual arousal that in no way affects performance.

In addition, the older man takes much longer to achieve orgasm and ejaculation than the young man. But fear of incompetence too often turns this potential advantage into an obstruction. Some men feel that failure to reach orgasm swiftly indicates a form of impotence, and the resulting anxiety not only delays ejaculation further, but may cause premature loss of erection.

Thus, a negative attitude can destroy the beneficial effects of one of the greatest advantages of age. The slowing-down of sexual response effectively only means that a man can enjoy the unique sensations of intercourse for a much longer period of time. The prolongation of intercourse is also highly enjoyable for the woman. Since women are slower to reach orgasm, the longer intercourse lasts the greater are their chances of complete satisfaction.

The speed and urgency of the young man's sexual response frequently leaves a woman dissatisfied, and without orgasm. But the older man has the staying power necessary to make him a more satisfying lover—provided he understands and welcomes the lengthening of the pre-orgasmic phase and adapts his love-making to it.

The young man passes through another brief phase before orgasm in which, for a few seconds, he is aware of the inevitability of ejaculation. He can feel the approach of the climax and is powerless to stop it. The older man is often disconcerted to note a change in this respect. As men age, the contractions of the prostate gland become weaker, producing varying effects. In some cases, the phase of inevitability will be much shorter. In others it will be longer, or it may cease to be perceived altogether. Each of these possible alternatives can affect a man's entire attitude to his sexual abilities.

In cases where this phase of orgasmic inevitability is speeded up, the man will still know that his orgasm is approaching and will only be surprised that it follows so quickly. When the phase is prolonged, however, there is a danger that he will again fear failure, assuming that he can only approach orgasm and that the final moment of ejaculation will elude him by some mysterious means. This is not true, but anxiety can postpone ejaculation and cause the very failure that he feared.

The complete absence of an intense approach phase affects most men less dramatically. Although they may regret the loss of those few seconds of intense, tingling pleasure, the unannounced occurrence of orgasm will not give them time to worry.

None of these changes should cause alarm, for they most definitely do not affect sexual performance. The much greater period of time required to reach orgasm assures the partner's pleasure, and the need to be warned as orgasm approaches becomes unimportant.

When he ejaculates, an older man will notice a few changes which may worry him. The urethral contractions, which accompany and cause ejaculation will be less intense. The semen will, therefore, be ejected a shorter distance and will, in any case, be smaller in quantity. However, this will in no way detract from the intensity of the pleasurable sensations. The experience will be as enjoyable as ever, although the mechanism will be less dramatic.

Finally, an older man may be concerned when his penis becomes immediately flaccid after ejaculation. Having been accustomed to a gradual process of detumescence he wrongly regards the quite natural speeding up of this phenomenon as yet another sign of sexual incompetence.

Of course, as a man becomes older he will probably discover that he has a much longer period of sexual disinterest after intercourse than he did when he was young. But men vary greatly in this respect whatever their age. When young, some men are susceptible to restimulation and become erect again within minutes of orgasm, but others require anything up to twenty-four hours before they are again completely ready. The older man may well need twenty-four hours and possibly longer, but this should only be regarded as a problem if physical response fails to keep up with desire. Basically, if an older man really wants frequent intercourse his body will probably respond to proper and lengthy stimulation, and he should try to discover and accept his natural rhythm in this respect. Few men, provided they are properly confident about their abilities, will find a longer gap between bouts of sexual activity a problem.

The most common cause of the loss of sexual ability in the older man is mental negativism and fear, rather than physical deterioration. The changes in male sexual response often occur at a time when a man is generally depressed about growing older. Middle age is a difficult time, a transitional phase when the ambitions of youth are not quite dead, but the reality of achievement is increasingly obvious. Children are usually grown up and leading lives of their own. A man often becomes intensely aware that he is not quite as energetic as he was,

and he may fear that he is no longer attractive to women.

Most men feel that sexual ability is the vital panacea left to them during this generally depressing time, but some imagine that this ability will soon fail them as well. Even if they accept that they are sexually adequate in middle age, they are nevertheless concerned about how much longer their luck will hold. Sexual performance, which has always been a source of masculine pride, the realization of manhood in physical terms, becomes even more important, and many men aggravate their unfounded fears by placing too much importance on continued sexual ability. Consequently, as they begin to notice the physical changes in their sexual reactions, they pessimistically feel that these are evidence that their fears are becoming reality. By worrying, by searching for signs of failure and incompetence, men can actually bring them about.

Medical opinion is unanimous that, provided a man is generally healthy and has a positive mental attitude, he can continue to lead an active sexual life at least until he is eighty and possibly beyond. By far the most effective way of ensuring that he continues to be sexually active is never to stop. The research work of William Masters and Virginia Johnson has shown that those men who regularly have sexual intercourse are less likely to have sexual problems in old age than those who, because of marital difficulties or illness, go for long periods with no sexual activity.

But a man should prepare himself for the inevitable sexual changes that will occur, and so avoid being taken by surprise when they first manifest themselves. He must not yearn for the urgency and imperiousness of youth. The man who regards prolonged sexual intercourse as a chore probably never really enjoyed sex at all. The opportunity to relish and savour pleasurable responses while being completely confident of the ability to satisfy one's partner is a boon, not a drawback. The change is essentially one of rhythm— not a loss or failure. In fact, the older man should trust in sex as a continuing source of pleasure and comfort. It will not fail him if he does not misinterpret his body.

A woman can do more than anyone to reassure a man about his sexual performance as well as about all aspects of ad-

Many famous men have demonstrated that age need not involve a loss of sexual interest. **Right** *The musician Pablo Casals, film comedian Charlie Chaplin, and painter Pablo Picasso are just a few who, at an advanced age, have married young women.*

vancing age. She should encourage her husband to make himself attractive and tell him that he is. She should show that she desires him and, above all, adjust her own attitudes and role to complement the physiological changes he undergoes.

Most women, when they are young, trust entirely in the instantaneous response of their husbands. Many of them deliberately avoid protracted direct stimulation for reasonable fear of precipitating ejaculation. But as a man becomes older he needs and welcomes this stimulation and there is no better way for a woman to demonstrate that she desires her partner than by actively arousing him. Most women enjoy taking a more active role in the love-play which precedes intercourse and, of course, they ensure their own satisfaction as well as their partners' sexual happiness.

There is the attitude in Western society that age is synonymous with failure, that the body's slowing-down processes makes a man incapable. The accent is on youth. Speed and energy are displayed as the most desirable traits. This view overlooks the many artists, writers, politicians, and businessmen who have achieved their greatest success in middle and old age. That men are equally capable of having a great deal of effective 'sex appeal' although they are over 50 years old is exemplified by men like Yves Montand, Cary Grant, and John Wayne. Pablo Picasso alone gives the lie to the popular myth that life stops rather than begins at forty.

Not every man is a Picasso, of course. But every man, if he takes care of himself physically, and if he has the right mental attitude, can lead an active, useful, and enjoyable life right into old age.

The modification of sexual desire and response are by no means signs of decay and incompetence. They are a natural readjustment to the continually varying rhythms of life, and have the potential for a new phase of sexual activity which should be welcomed and enjoyed. If a man does not continue to lead an active sexual life as he grows older it is because of incipient defeatism and failure to adjust to these changes.
                                    DAVID FLETCHER

Robert Capa/Magnum

How to satisfy your partner

Sexual intercourse can bestow greater gratification and pleasure if a couple learn to unleash their imaginations to express their desire and to openly communicate their love.

Owen Wood

Biologically, in the interest of the survival of the human race, there is good reason why a man and a woman should unite sexually. But this does not completely explain the urge a man and a woman have to make love. For most people, though the physical sensations are similar, masturbation is by no means the same experience as sexual intercourse. The uniting of their bodies has, for a man and a woman, a special emotional significance and is capable of satisfying not only their physical needs, but many other complex and interrelated human needs.

As sexual excitement mounts with the caresses of love-play, both the man and the woman become aware of their need for union—the man's urgent desire to enter the woman and relieve the overwhelming tensions that he feels, and the woman's growing desire for the man's penis to enter her. As he caresses her genitals and feels for the entrance to her vagina, the man should know when she is ready. As she becomes excited, secretions flow from the walls of the vagina, and when she is sufficiently aroused, her genitals will be wet and the clitoris and outer lips swollen.

There are times when a man urgently wants to make love, but generally he should not try to insert his penis unless he knows that the woman is highly aroused. There are a few women who, however excited, never respond with sufficient secretions, and then surgical jelly can be used as a lubricant, to make penetration easier. But the usual explanation if the woman's vagina is dry is either that she is in no mood for love-making, or that she has not been sufficiently stimulated during love-play. It means that the man should look for new ways to excite her, or prolong foreplay.

The woman, when she feels highly aroused and ready for intercourse itself, will say so, or suggest it by the way she moves, by holding her partner closely and, as she caresses his penis with her hands, guiding it towards her vagina. If the man can control himself and hold back for a minute or two before he enters her, the woman's excitement and desire will build to a high point and the pleasure and relief as he enters her can be very intense. Usually one or the other should use their hands to guide the penis into the vagina. People who have an aversion to touching the genitals with their hands have many problems. A man can be easily disturbed at not being able to find the entrance to the vagina, and so lose his erection.

Both partners should go on stimulating each other with kisses and caresses, as they did during foreplay, but, depending on the position they are in, some caresses are easier than others.

If the woman is lying under the man, she should have her legs well bent so that the man's penis can enter her vagina easily, and thrust as deeply as they wish. Sometimes she feels more pleasure if she places a cushion under her buttocks or the lower part of her back. It is important that both be comfortable. Many a man has forgotten, in the excitement of love-making, that he is heavy and he is lying on top of his partner without supporting himself, or he does not realize that he is forcing her into a cramped position in which she can barely move, or is severely restricted.

The man should enter the woman slowly and gently. A few quick and forceful thrusts are usually all that a man needs to bring him to a climax. If the woman is already highly aroused, her lover's excitement and approaching orgasm and the physical stimulation may be enough to make her reach an orgasm at much the same time. The quickly squandered passion may be what pleases them both. More often, the woman takes longer to reach a climax, and can only properly enjoy their

love-making if the man delays his orgasm. Most men, by learning to control their ejaculation, find they derive much more pleasure from prolonged intercourse, and their partners, certainly, are a great deal more likely to be fully satisfied.

People have always tried to find ways to increase the pleasures they experience in the few seconds of orgasm, or to make intercourse last longer. But no magic, herbal preparation, aphrodisiac, or drug has yet been found to work. It is possible to prolong intercourse, but the control needed will only develop with practice.

The sort of movements the man makes with his penis in the vagina, depend entirely on what the man and woman find they enjoy most on a particular occasion, and they will probably vary their movements according to the sensations they are feeling. At first, gentle thrusts, shallow and tender,

167

or deep and slow, probably give the woman most pleasure—while allowing the man to control his climax. But as they both approach orgasm, thrusting usually becomes quicker and more forceful. The woman can respond by moving rhythmically with him and her enjoyment usually depends on the co-ordination of their movements. She can move her pelvis to meet his thrust and withdraw as he withdraws, or make more circular movements. The couple usually learn with practice, by doing what feels natural to them and what gives the most pleasurable sensations.

The woman can help her lover to control his climax by not moving too much and by allowing him to rest when he feels he is becoming too excited. Sometimes the woman likes to be the more active partner, and by taking a position on top of the man she can move freely. Some men find it easier to control their climax in this position.

Desirable or not, it is often impossible for the man and the woman to reach a climax together. It is best for the man to try to control himself until his partner has an orgasm. This usually excites him so that he achieves orgasm shortly after she does. She can, in any case, continue moving and stimulating her lover, and may even have another orgasm. If he reaches a climax first and she is highly aroused, her lover's excitement and more vigorous action, and the awareness of his semen inside her, may be enough for her to have an orgasm.

But the man's erection quickly subsides after ejaculation, and his penis becomes very sensitive so that friction with the vagina is uncomfortable. Some men can maintain their erection long enough if their partner is on the verge of orgasm, but usually any movement or effort interferes with their relaxation and enjoyment. Sometimes the man can bring his partner to a climax afterwards by manual stimulation of the clitoris, if she feels that is what she wants. On the other hand, a woman's desire subsides slowly, and the man may be able to make love to her again after some time, when she is still sexually aroused and can quickly reach an orgasm. He is likely to be less excited the second time, and so he will be able to contain his orgasm for a longer time.

Neither should worry excessively about their partner's having an orgasm, as this may lessen their own enjoyment. The man, particularly, should not feel obligated to give the woman an orgasm each time they make love. For a woman, there are many other important factors which contribute to her gratification. The pleasure she gives her partner may be, for her, very important, and she may also like to feel that at times he is so excited by her that he cannot control himself sufficiently to wait until she has an orgasm.

Both the man's pleasure and the woman's —and her ability to have an orgasm— depend on many things, but largely on their being able to relax and lose their inhibitions. The excitement and sexual tension they feel is a product of both physical and psychological stimulation which comes from their own enthusiasm for love-making and anticipation of sexual pleasure.

The difference between a good lover and a bad one is likely to depend not on technique but on the erotic atmosphere he or she is able to create. Most important is that each treats the other as physically desirable and exciting.

Psychological stimulation perhaps plays a larger part for the woman, since the physical stimulation she receives from the contact of the vagina and the penis is less than for the man. Physically she is most excited by the stimulation of the clitoris, with which little contact is made by the penis thrusting in the vagina. The clitoris is stimulated indirectly by the violent movements of the parts around it. If the woman is highly aroused before the penis enters the vagina, the stimulation, both physical and psychological, she derives is usually enough to bring her to orgasm. But to help her achieve orgasm more quickly her lover can caress her breasts, or, if it is possible, continue stimulating the clitoris with his hands. The woman herself can do this if she knows she has difficulty in reaching a climax. There is no reason why she should not.

The importance of psychological stimulation is clear in that it is possible for the woman to reach an orgasm while the penis is inside her, but not moving, if her thoughts are centred on the penis and the emotional aspects of the experience. A technique known as Karezza, makes use of this to increase the pleasure of intercourse. The man, by not moving his penis in the vagina, or by moving it very little, and reducing the tactile sensations, can prevent himself from having an orgasm. It is a technique which has been used to prolong intercourse, but some people have used it as a means of contraception in which case the man never ejaculates but allows his erection gradually to subside. Doctors and psychiatrists have reported harmful effects if this technique is used continuously over a long period of time. Its proponents, however, claim that great heights of spiritual delight can be reached.

People behave in different ways after making love. Many men want to sleep immediately afterwards, and so do some women; but some people feel the need to talk and others want to get up— they feel full of energy and ready to do anything. Some like just to lie quietly in each other's arms. When partners have different needs it is important that neither is made to feel ignored or unwanted. Women, particularly, are often very conscious of a romantic mood after intercourse which a wrong word or action can destroy and cause them to feel disappointed and unhappy. With a little care and empathy this can be avoided, and both can relax happily.

It is important to talk to one's partner about what one feels about making love, making it known what one likes and does not like, and discussing doubts and fears.

It is often very difficult to discuss these intimate things with one's partner, but if one is persistently worried by something and, from embarrassment, says nothing about it, it can haunt one's sexual life and become unreasonably important.

It can be disappointing if one partner does not instinctively know what pleases the other; what one feels is natural may not excite both partners. But this can be rectified: communicating about sex can build an intimacy which is the basis of a strong and loving relationship. It takes frankness and sympathy, as well as time and practice, to develop a sensitive awareness of each other's body, and to be able naturally to adjust to each other and to make love-making satisfying for both.

Love-making is not always the elevating or even enjoyable experience people expect it to be. Sometimes it is good, and sometimes it is a disappointment. It is better, in general, not to be too serious about it, or expect too much. People are sensitive sexually and the wrong mood, the wrong place, or simply things like tiredness or too much alcohol, can ruin everything. But if a couple can laugh together, nothing is lost. There is always another time, and it is an important part of a close relationship that they see and love each other when they are not at their best—as they wish to be seen by the rest of the world.

Should the man lose his erection when he is supposed to be most excited, as long as both can treat it lightly there will be no problem the next time. If it is regarded as highly significant, it can make him doubt his powers as a lover and, because he will be worried the next time he makes love, the same thing might happen again.

If one partner cannot, or does not want to, make love, it should not be treated as a personal insult, for the explanation is usually simple. People are very vulnerable sexually, and we are usually all too instinctively aware of this. Sexual failure and disappointments can be used to hurt; the effects can reach further than intended, and can easily undermine a relationship.

What is important to the satisfaction of both the man and the woman is not a successful sexual performance each time, with both having an orgasm, but the warmly expressed physical attraction for each other, a sureness of love and appreciation and of the continuing desire to make love. It can be one of the few constant things in a person's life, a security which he or she needs to cope with the world.

Love-making can be many things— violent, sad, beautiful, passionate and it can form the strongest and most enduring bond between a man and a woman. At its best, it reflects and expresses the emotional and spiritual union they feel. But no explanation of why sexual union with another person is so profoundly satisfying and necessary to a human being, can be complete. It remains one of the most mystical experiences of human life.
RICHARD SEARLE

Positions
for
loving

Love-making can be slow or quick, gentle or rough. Just as there is a wide range in the emotions a couple experience, there is diversity in the ways they can express them sexually. For love-making involves far more than genital stimulation. It includes a regard for the other person, enjoyment for the other's body, and concern for mutual pleasure. Part of that pleasure comes from variety in the sexual act.

For most couples, enjoyment is the main factor in their love-making—although the release of sexual tension provides the drive to sexual intercourse—and in seeking fulfilment they want to experiment and look for new ways of showing their love.

Just how a couple makes love depends on their mood. Sometimes they will want to be close, to kiss, and murmur endearments. The man may want to protect and envelop the woman. On other occasions, he will wish to dominate, to be able to caress her freely; while sometimes the woman will take the initiative. Their positions in intercourse can respond to and mirror these moods—if they use their imaginations. For successful love-making is a matter of imagination.

Here are 11 basic positions for sexual intercourse. Some positions ensure more effective stimulation of the genitals, which can help a woman achieve orgasm; others make mutual caresses easier; some are suitable when the women is pregnant or her partner too heavy for her easily to bear his weight; and some may help couples who wish to make conception as certain as possible.

I

1. Face-to-face, with the woman on her back, her knees slightly drawn up, and the man lying above her, is the basic position of sexual intercourse. The couple can kiss easily, murmur to each other and respond to each other's facial expressions, while their bodies are closely in contact. If he bears his weight on his elbows he will be able to kiss and nibble the erogenous zones of the lips and face, breasts and nipples. The woman is completely supported, she can caress her partner as she wishes and, at the climax of intercourse, can allow her muscles to tense in the spasm of orgasm. The man's pelvis is free and he can, therefore, control his movements and thrust deeply. From this position, the woman can draw her legs up to clasp them about her partner's hips. This increases the angle of her pelvis, and the penis penetrates deeper into the vagina, increasing sensation for both—and favouring conception.

John Seymour

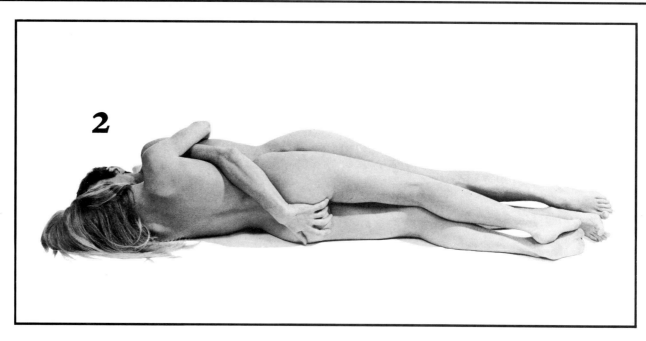

2

2. By lying on their sides a couple have the advantages of the basic position—faces close together, bodies touching along their length—in addition to others. The woman bears none of her partner's weight. The man can move without strain on his back. With one hand, too, he can stroke his partner's body. A couple may use this as an intermediate position; they can lie together for long periods, hardly moving, and so, by reducing excitation, prolong intercourse. As the climax approaches they can shift to another position for the intense body movements of orgasm.

3. By rolling from the basic face-to-face position through the side-by-side attitude, a couple can reach the reverse position in which the woman lies above the man. This may be useful if the man is tired, for he is fully supported while his hands are free to stimulate the woman. However, there is a drawback: although the woman can respond strongly, the man's pelvic thrusts are limited, awkward, and difficult to synchronize with the woman's movements. As in the previous attitudes, the woman can clasp the penis firmly within her vagina by keeping her legs tightly together. The increased pressure from the inner thighs stimulates penis and clitoris more effectively and, by pressing her legs firmly together, the woman can keep the penis within her vagina after the man has ejaculated, which slows the rate at which his erection subsides and so can lengthen intercourse.

3

Love-making need never become routine. Embraces that express love and empathy produce their own vitality and freshness of approach. Sexual intercourse does not have to be limited to the bedroom after a couple have retired for the night, but can take place whenever a couple's sexuality is mutually aroused, and their privacy is guaranteed. Indeed, making love in different surroundings and at unaccustomed times can itself provide stimulation and excitement. So, too, can making love in different ways, and in different positions.

4. Sometimes a couple will want to have intercourse quickly. Some partners enjoy the novelty of making love standing up, or with the woman leaning against a wall, when they are both highly aroused.

5. When the man wants to dominate, by kneeling and moving his partner's body into position, he can use his strength to spur and aid her agility. In this, and other positions in which penis and vagina are unaligned, elastic pressure from the penis produces highly effective clitoral stimulation.

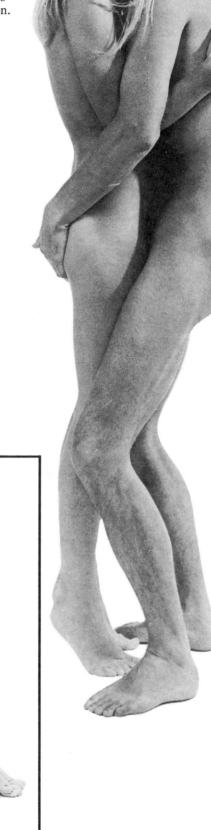

4

5

6. Cushions placed on the floor, or a bed that is at the right height for the man to stand or kneel beside it, allow stimulation of the genitals that a couple might otherwise achieve only by gymnastic exertion. By drawing her legs up and apart, the woman exposes her vulva and ensures full penetration of the penis without putting strain on her back muscles. Because her vagina is horizontal, the penis is forced downwards producing pressure against the clitoral area. This causes great mutual friction and increases erotic pleasure. In this position, each partner can touch and look at the other's body. The man can easily lean forward to kiss and caress the woman, and she can caress him.

7. The sedentary position is one of the gentlest. Because the man bears his partner's weight against his thighs, he can take special care as his penis slides into the vagina and easily control the depth of penetration. When the woman is pregnant, or her sexual organs otherwise delicate, he need make only superficial contact—at other times penetration can be complete. In either case, the penis presses strongly against the clitoris, ensuring maximum sexual excitement. And if, with deeper penetration, the man firmly clasps his partner's hips or thighs with his hands, each can move freely while maintaining the mutual rhythm of intercourse that leads both to climax.

6

7

II

10. From a position with the woman astride the man, a couple can move to a semi-sedentary attitude easily. This keeps many of the advantages of the astride position—the penis penetrates deeply, the woman can control her own movements and thus her progress to orgasm, each can enjoy looking at the other—and frees the man's pelvis to thrust and set the rhythm of intercourse.

11. In one other main attitude for love-making, the man approaches the woman from the back. In this position, the penis and vagina are not naturally aligned and there is little clitoral stimulation. But if the man kneels upright, the tip of the penis presses against the back wall of the vagina, which pushes the lower surface of the penis against the clitoris and produces intense friction and excitement for both man and woman. The man, too, can easily use his hands to stroke his partner's breasts and nipples, and to stimulate her clitoris and so help bring her to orgasm.

This, too, is a suitable position for love-making during pregnancy because the woman bears no weight and her uterus sinks into the body cavity away from the thrust of the penis. A variation of this posture, with both partners lying on their sides, is especially appropriate during pregnancy or when either is convalescent.

IO

Positions
for the adventurous

Excitement is a keynote in sexual relations. Here, for the adventurous, are positions for sexual intercourse that can introduce a new excitement into love-making.

Every act of love is a variation on a simple theme, the sexual union of a man and a woman. For every couple, and for each encounter, the experience is subtly different, a new intermingling of emotions, mental arousal, and physical stimulation.

Love-making for many couples follows familiar patterns and, happily, satisfies both partners. For others full enjoyment of sexual intercourse includes the imaginative use of physical agility, a celebration of the role the body plays in the expression of love. The excitement of varied approaches and the stimulation of using

their bodies to the utmost are, for them, part of the thrill of making love.

Unconventional positions can heighten that ecstasy. They are neither an essential part of the art of love, nor a guarantee of sexual happiness, but rather a contribution to a total experience. Dexterity and imagination combine to extend the sexual repertoire.

Adventurous couples may want to use these positions as starting points to develop their own love-making variations. But everyone can benefit from the underlying concept. Sexual intercourse should always

involve adventure, for adventure is an attitude of mind, not a plethora of physical skills.

1. The position a couple chooses for love-making can reflect their mood and express a range of emotions. Clinging tightly together restricts movement and reduces genital stimulation, but the sense of close union can greatly enhance erotic pleasure.

This position can be reached from one in which the woman is above the man. She brings her legs forward to take her weight, thus allowing him to sit up.

I

Michel de St. Oven

179

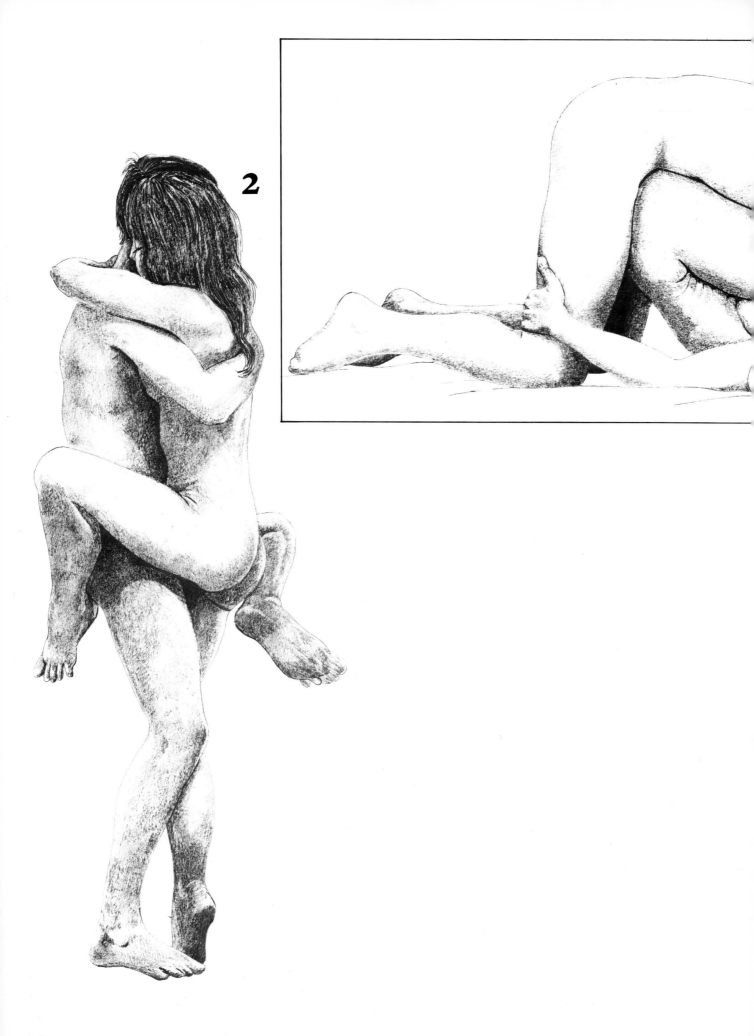

2

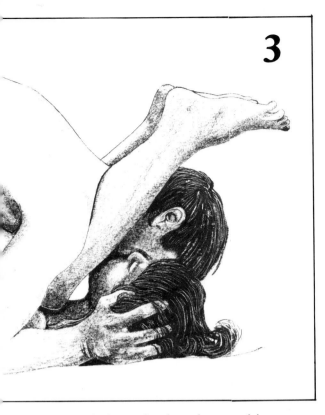

3

4

2. A couple who enjoy sexual intercourse while standing may gain further stimulation by adopting a variation of the exotic Lotus pose made famous by Indian sculpture and literature. Standing together, the man supports the woman while she raises her leg so that he can insert his penis into her vagina. Both can then place one leg around the other's hips.

3. From the face-to-face position a supple woman can bring her legs above her partner's shoulders. This position, which brings the couple into close and exciting contact, restricts the woman's movements, but it effectively exposes her vulva, and gives her partner freedom to control his pelvic thrusts.

4. For a couple attuned to each other's movements, and with a sense of balance, this position is easy to reach from a standing, sitting, or lying position. Once reached it causes little strain because the woman's weight is resting on her partner's hips and legs, the strongest part of his body.

5. Although penetration of the penis into the vagina is shallow, this position leads to maximum sexual excitement for both the man and the woman because his penis presses firmly against her clitoral area.

Both partners bear their own weight and, so long as they are kneeling on a soft surface, they can prolong love-making without tiring. They can also move easily from this close, exciting contact to a position in which each can admire, and be stimulated by, the sight of the other's body.

3

THE
PSYCHOLOGY
OF LOVE

struct the past and to envisage the future colours his every action·because it makes it possible for him to foresee the consequences of a present action and to reproach or congratulate himself for what he has done in the past. Through the exercise of imagination a man is aware of how his behaviour may affect his fellow men, and his own image among them. The tiger has, apparently, no means of sympathizing with the sensations of his prey, nor does the male dog trouble himself about his sexual technique and whether or not he is giving his bitch satisfaction. There is nothing that humans do which they do not invest with meaning. Especially in activities involving relationships with others, each sees a reflection of what he is, of what he would like to be, and of his image in the eyes of others. Above all, this is true of the sexual relationship.

What do we expect, then, when we engage in sexual activity? It may seem to be the 'natural' expression of an overwhelming love for another. In the extraordinary condition of being 'in love' there is generally a longing for fusion, for closeness of mind and of body, for complete identification. 'Nellie, I *am* Heathcliffe!' says Catherine, the dying, passionate heroine of *Wuthering Heights*, expressing her total involvement with her lover. And in the sexual act lovers can reach an illusion of unity—illusion because their bodies, though joined, are not one, and their sensations remain their own.

Perhaps what is valuable is not the fantasy of fusion, but the fact that it is a situation, rare in life, in which each of the protagonists gives and takes at the same time. There need be no question of unselfishness and this itself increases the love. To be able to give pleasure to a beloved person and, at the same time, to receive it can seem like a miracle.

Sexual activity is also one of the very few areas in some societies, in which it is possible to express feelings physically. And it is hardly surprising that this activity in which people can experience physical and emotional union and release should acquire more meaning than it might otherwise carry. Sex is seen by some as the great, the only liberator.

For many people there may be only one possible sexual partner, only one person they trust enough, love enough, and find sufficiently attractive to break down their inhibitions and to allow them to enjoy sex. But most people are not—in the strictly sexual sense—monogamous creatures. They may be loyal and loving, and they may prefer to keep one marriage partner as long as they live; but this does not mean that they might not or do not appreciate sexual relations with more than one person.

Many people enjoy sexual relationships with several partners and these affairs are not always the outcome of great involvement or of passionate feeling, but may express a delight in the other person's body, usually combined with emotions of liking and respect. Now that efficient contraception exists, the traditional attitude that women, unlike men, cannot lightly undertake sexual affairs may also be changing. For such people, sexual intercourse means friendship, not love.

But the need for a sexual relationship does not always depend on love or friendship. It can arise from a desperate need for reassurance, or as an escape from loneliness. It can come from curiosity or competitiveness, or from a wish to demonstrate one's own sexual powers (a form of narcissism) or from the desire to conquer or to be conquered.

Sexual intercourse may be the manifestation of the need to avoid the isolation of the human spirit, to escape from the prison of a separate existence. In exploring another's body we may hope to see something of the soul.

In their sexual relationship two people can create a private world in which they can act out their feelings and relieve the tensions of their every day lives. They may take different roles at different times, depending on their feelings. Some people, at times, want to act out aggressive feelings in the way they make love. These are feelings which everybody has, but which may have no acceptable outlet in other relationships. It is not unusual to want, in sexual play, to be treated like a baby, cossetted, cuddled, and protected, as an escape from the responsibilities and difficulties of the day.

People often take roles in their sexual activities which are far different from those they play in the outside world, acting out needs and desires which they normally suppress or which may be subconscious. At times, the best-behaved housewife wants to play the wicked seductress, the mistress, or the prostitute. A very successful man, with a great deal of power and influence over other people may act a submissive role in his relations with a woman. He may want her to be active and aggressive. The mild and unassertive man, who allows himself to be trampled on by other people, may need, in his sexual life, to conquer and to dominate. A woman, competing on equal terms with men in her work, and presenting a hard and capable image to the world, can often play a sweet, dependent and pliable role in her sexual relations with her husband.

Obviously sexual behaviour is more than just the search for pleasure and relief from sexual tension—as Freud propounded in his early works. If it were not, the relief from masturbation, the bringing of oneself to the point of sexual climax, would be as effective as sexual intercourse. And here lies one of the answers to the question: what is the meaning of making love?

For every one of us is a social animal. We need other people. We need them not only to perform for us the tasks we can't do ourselves, to make up the whole complicated structure of our society, but in a more personal and more intimate way. We discover the use of our mouths, our hands, and our feet and fix our physical boundaries in our mothers' arms. We discover what we think by talking and listening to our friends. Later we need our lovers to prove to us not only that we are sexually mature and potent, but also that this aspect of ourselves is acceptable, that our currency, so to speak, is valid. Solitary sexual activity might provide all the sensation, but it cannot satisfy the need for—what shall we call it? It is not merely a need for approval, nor for comparison; it is also the need to share. This need can be seen even in the extreme case of sex criminals who, driven by their terrible inner conflicts to assault strangers, still desperately long to be welcomed by their victims and, even while they are inflicting pain, desire to give pleasure.

Making love, then, is essentially a matter of communication and, just as with words, some people are better at expressing themselves in this way than in others. The manner in which a person uses this language of the body depends on innumerable factors—his upbringing, his personality, his education, his background, the people he meets, the society in which he lives. It seems natural to want to stroke a dog, to hold a baby, to laugh, or to cry; the sexual impulse is as much a part of our spontaneous reactions as these, and as natural a way of conveying what we feel.

It may for him always be a serious language, to be used only to express deep and lasting feeling; it may be a language in which he tells others, lightly and amusingly, that he finds them attractive or likeable. He may be able to vary this method of expression, and to make love briefly, lightheartedly with a friend, and agonizingly, comfortingly, or ecstatically with his lover.

Our feelings—love, liking, sexual desire, affection, sympathy, tenderness—are not, static and fixed. They are dynamic, they change, they fluctuate. Social and personal considerations may determine when or where we make love; but the impulse to communicate in this way through our bodies is always there.

CATHERINE STORR

The psychology of the female

Gentle, protective, tender-hearted, and devoted—but somehow less intelligent and less forceful than men. How realistic is this common ideal of female psychology?

Thousands of words have been written about female and male psychology. But scientific sounding jargon can often lead us to forget that the modern science of psychology is, at best, only an attempt to explain observed behaviour, and at worst an attempt to corroborate age-old prejudices and assumptions about human nature. There is no such thing as total objectivity, even in science, and the nature of man and woman seems to be a subject where people are less likely to question traditional theories than almost any other.

The very first assumption made about the nature of men and women is that they are essentially different from one another. Because men and women are physically different and fulfil different functions in the reproductive process, it is automatically assumed that male and female minds also work in different ways, and that men and women have entirely different personality structures. Because men and women do behave differently, in fulfilling different social roles, for instance, it is taken as proof, when actually these patterns can be explained in purely social terms. People may behave in a certain way merely to conform to common beliefs. For example, a person who is upset may say, 'I am a man, therefore I will not cry.'

Most assumptions about women have been made by men since, traditionally, Western society has been male-dominated. As a result, woman is in most respects considered inferior—in strength, intelligence, and moral worth. Men have also tended to view a woman in terms of the very limited social roles they assigned to her. If a woman was not allowed to become a priest in the Church it was because she was more likely to be corrupted by the Devil. If a woman was not allowed education it was because she had no higher intellect. If a woman could learn reading and writing, but not physics, chemistry, or medicine, it was because she had no capacity for abstract thinking. If a woman was to spend her life in the service of others, nursing children, husband, and aged parents, it was because she was more tender-hearted. If a woman was to spend her life as a sexual object it was because love was all she cared about.

The Victorians propounded the theory

Many men believe that giving birth and bringing up children is a true expression of the female personality. But is it?

that women did not like sex. This theory has persisted in a dual standard of sexual conduct. More recently the male view of female sexuality has changed with a changing morality and a more accurate understanding of sexual behaviour. A woman is now supposed to be insatiable, capable of multiple orgasms.

One theory is that since women can bear children they must also want them, even if they are not consciously aware of any such desire. This is usually referred to as the 'maternal instinct', and the woman

who is not overcome with tender emotion on first holding her new baby in her arms, or who is provoked into outbursts of rage and resentment against her children, is made to feel guilty and unnatural. And, indeed, a psychologist, having assumed that women must want children, will go on to say that women who do not conform to this pattern are sick in some way, are denying their essential nature, or are trying to ape men.

A corollary of the theory of 'maternal instinct' is the assumption that since

Above From an early age little girls learn to be feminine. They are taught to be charming and compliant. *Below* They are also encouraged to imitate their mothers' skills—sewing, washing, cooking, and housekeeping—and to become conventional women.

childbearing and child rearing confined women to the home (although in fact it need not do so) women really *prefer* domesticity. They are passive, docile creatures who like to stay at home and care for others, whether children or aged relatives. When some kind of employment is available, a 'normal' woman is still expected to put her home first, for this is considered her 'natural' place. We are told that women do not like taking responsibility. As a result they are usually prevented from reaching the higher ranks of management. They are said to like caring for others, and are, therefore, expected to accept low salaries for nursing and teaching.

Unfortunately, this view of the female psychology tends to be self-fulfilling. If one questions the traditional assumptions on male and female psychology one tends to get the answer, 'Just look around you.' But this is to ignore the powerful social pressures which force people to conform to certain patterns of behaviour. They may think they are acting freely, from personal choice, but this is not so.

The way individuals behave, the things they like and dislike, the kind of conduct they consider right or reprehensible, is the result of a long process of conditioning which begins at birth. And since parents and elders, the people most influential in the conditioning process, were themselves conditioned from birth, it is not surprising that behaviour is often explained in vague terms of 'human nature' rather than social conservatism. But, in fact, even the most basic human functions, like walking and talking, are learned rather than instinctive or innate. Even sexual behaviour is learned.

From birth children are labelled according to sex. As a result their whole sense of identity when they become self-aware is tied in with the concept of being male or female, which from then helps to determine the way they behave. If a person were asked to describe himself or herself, he or she would almost certainly start with 'I am a man', or 'I am a woman'.

A toddler knows it is a boy or girl, even if it knows nothing about genital differences. By the time a child is four years old it will conform to sex-role patterns, long before the hormonal changes connected with puberty begin. A child will also conform to the wrong sex identity so long as this remains unquestioned.

From birth children are dressed in different clothes, treated differently, given different toys to play with. Little Tommy expects to grow up to be like Daddy, or like the cowboy on television. Little Susy expects to grow up to be like Mummy. She practises by bathing her doll, or washing up her miniature tea set. Little Tommy is encouraged to be aggressive. He is given toy guns and boxing gloves, told to 'stick up for himself', and is scolded if he cries because this is 'sissy'. Little Susy is told not to play rough games because she might spoil her pretty clothes. If she cries she will be picked up and petted. She is liable to be reprimanded for acts of aggression. Later on, in most families, she will get more parental approval for looking sexually attractive than for getting good examination results. She will be told that it is her job to help with the housework, while Tommy goes out to play.

If mother falls sick or dies the girl is expected to give up her ambitions for education and career and take over the functions of housekeeper and nurse. When family funds are limited they are used to further the boy's career, regardless of ambition or ability. In addition, the boy is expected to be competitive. He is constantly reminded that he must become a breadwinner and that his success at this depends largely on academic achievement.

The girl, on the other hand, has no motivation to learn, let alone to excel. In fact, cleverness in a girl is often considered an embarrassment. It is said that 'Men do not like clever women.' Her family assumes that her career will be through marriage, and so a compliant personality, domestic skills, and an attractive appearance are the prime requirements. A career training is seen as insurance in case she 'fails' to get a husband.

In addition, there are the social pressures which tend to drive women back to a traditional position as housewife and mother. There is discrimination in higher education and employment, lack of child-care facilities, and punitive attitudes towards abortion. There are strong enough reasons for 'feminine' behaviour and attitudes, without recourse to any theory of innate female psychology.

However, the image of domesticated woman, tender wife and mother, is by no

Umberto Moggioli: *The Artist's House*/Museum of Modern Art, Venice/Scala

Moro/Rome

Library of Congress

Idealized popular conceptions of the nature of women often emphasize one aspect of her dual sexual role. She is seen as the robust and joyous bearer of children, or as a temptress—the beguiling seducer of men.

means universal. In Western society it has been largely confined to the middle classes. Working-class women were forced to become 'unnatural', farming out their babies, or going to backstreet abortionists, since it was necessary that they work. Anthropologists have found very different arrangements in other societies, where sometimes it is the men who look after the young children. In the modern Western world many young people reject traditional sex roles, the men take as much interest in the care of their young children as the women do. The satisfactions, and drawbacks, of caring for young children can be experienced by both parents.

In recent years there have been attempts to test people for their masculine and feminine traits. To do this psychologists first construct an MF (Masculine-Feminine) scale, with what are considered masculine characteristics at one end and feminine characteristics at the other. The most obvious weakness of this kind of test is that the psychologist first has to decide what these sexual characteristics are, so that he is really only testing his pre-conceived assumptions. One surprising result, which will not surprise anyone who has thought about social conditioning, was that men of unusual ability tended to swing to the F end of the scale, while women of outstanding ability tended to swing over to the M end of the scale. In other words, social conditioning makes most people repress large areas of their

potential in order to conform to their sex role and image.

Some psychologists try to explain this apparent anomaly by a theory of bisexuality —that every man is part woman, and every woman is part man, but this is only a way of trying to make the original thesis, that personality characteristics are linked to sex, workable, and explain the many people who do not conform to the image.

Thus a woman who takes command easily is thought to be masculine. At one time any woman who wrote a book was suspected of being a man in disguise. Since no woman was considered capable of logical or intelligent thought, any correct conclusion on her part was put down to 'feminine intuition'.

But the invention of effective birth control is bringing about a radical change in the old sex roles. Women have, in the past, apparently accepted the role assigned to them largely because they had little real choice. Conforming to the image, being what society demanded, was one way of making the best of a bad job. The alternative was usually to be a social outcast or labelled a neurotic. Now that sexuality and procreation are no longer inevitably linked, women will fall less easily into the traditional pattern of marriage and homemaking. For the first time women have a genuine choice, biology has ceased to be destiny.

The rapid spread of the women's liberation movement is indication enough that, given the choice, women do not necessarily want to be wives and mothers, they are not naturally passive, are, in fact, just as capable of aggression as men. Freud confessed himself to have puzzled all his life as to what women really wanted, but today

young women are beginning to make it clear that they want the same as men.

The social pressures which forced women to conform to a set pattern of behaviour are also changing. Serious over-population is beginning to require that social approval withdraws from the woman who produces many children. Instead of being thought patriotic her behaviour is more liable to be thought anti-social. The growing numbers of professional and working women also provide a serious challenge to the woman who is simply a wife and mother. At one time a woman who earned her own living was simply somebody too unattractive to find a male breadwinner, now a housewife is made to feel inadequate by the challenge of the professional woman, particularly since men have begun to find an attraction in clever women after all.

Birth control has changed sexual morality. In the last century the married woman felt fairly safe from sexual competition. Now any woman is a potential rival. Less and less can she rely on sexual favours to provide her with a lifelong meal ticket.

Man is an evolutionary animal. Many people, reacting adversely to social change, tend to shout 'unnatural', forgetting that their own social norms are just as much so. If it is unnatural for a woman to control procreation by taking the contraceptive pill, it is also unnatural for her to have sexual intercourse when she is not 'on heat', or wear clothes, or walk on two legs. We are what we are because of our environment. Once men and women are treated alike they may find out what male and female characteristics are. But it is doubtful whether, a thousand years hence, people will even concern themselves with the problem.

EVA FIGES

189

Frigidity

The term frigidity wrongly suggests a cold and unloving nature. But why is a woman frigid, and how can her sexual problems be solved?

We are supposedly living in the 'permissive society'. Both a cause and effect of this society, we are told, has been a radical change in our attitudes to sex. This is regarded as especially true for women. Undoubtedly women's attitudes to their sexual experience and society's attitudes towards women have changed. Indeed it is not only accepted that a woman may expect to enjoy her sexual relationships, it is almost demanded of her that she should. We are so proud of the greater freedom we enjoy compared with our Victorian ancestors, that we are inclined to forget that not all our attitudes are as radical as we imagine.

Of course, today's sexual morals are very different from those of Victorian England. However, in much earlier times it was not uncommon for women to take lovers before, during, and after marriage. It was not considered a disgrace, rather the contrary, for a woman to offer herself to a knight whose valour made him worthy of the reward. What evidence we have of pre-Christian Europe indicates that virginity was not the prized possession it was later to become. It is possible that in those days there was a far greater degree of sexual freedom than is the case today.

The spread of Christianity influenced every aspect of life in Europe, and especially attitudes towards sex. Monogamous marriage was the ideal. In theory, the monogamous family and the moral upbringing of children was considered of such prime importance that for its sake other needs should be sacrificed. This, of course, applied particularly to women. Sex was confused with sin. Sexual love was lust. Even the proximity of the sexual organs to the organs of excretion demonstrated the connection between sex and defilement. The ideal woman was chaste and virginal, and her prized virginity was to be sacrificed only on the altar of monogamous marriage. A woman's sexuality and pleasure in the sexual act was denied and even men were inhibited in their sexual attitudes. For both men and women sex was associated with guilt.

Ideally, even in marriage sexual intercourse was to be performed solely for the purpose of procreation and, even within marriage, moralists laid down strict procedures, mainly prohibitions, concerning the manner in which intercourse should take place. Even today, in certain American States married couples could in theory be convicted as criminals for indulging certain positions during coitus and for forms of caresses, such as the mouth-genital contact, which most clinicians would regard as falling well within the scope of normal behaviour.

It would not be overstating the case to say that the Victorian feminine ideal was 'frigidity'. But one should also bear in mind that, perhaps even more than today, publicly expressed attitudes were vastly different from people's actual behaviour. The proof of this hypocrisy could easily be discerned in the flourishing trade of prostitution. It is impossible to estimate the number of prostitutes who plied their trade in late Victorian London, but certainly in proportion to the population they far exceeded the number today. The prostitute was the guardian of the 'chaste' woman's morality and people willingly accepted this double standard. Great changes in attitude, related to a rising urban middle class, transformed sexual morality in the nineteenth century. The middle-class ideal was respectability and a respectable lady did not have sexual feelings—she was as legless as a mermaid. To understand the problem of frigidity, it is necessary to relate it to what was a growing tradition of repression. However modern we think we are, we are still affected by the weight of this repression; sexual pleasure is still often related to feelings of guilt. The very rebellion in attitudes which is now taking place, the stridency of the claims of the young that they are free, points

perhaps to a lack of real conviction in their freedom.

Frigidity is a term that has been used to describe a range of sexual unresponsiveness from a complete inhibition of all feelings of sexuality, no matter what stimulation occurs, and embracing the notion of repugnance towards any form of sexual contact, to the capacity for sexual arousal but failure to achieve orgasm, to yet a further category of failure to achieve orgasm in coitus, only reaching it via clitoral stimulation. For example, some women are very easily aroused and enjoy making love up to the point of penetration when all feeling is lost, or during coitus feeling may be present but accompanied by a sense of dissatisfaction. There is a wide range of physical response to encompass under the term 'frigidity'.

Frigidity has also taken on moral overtones as an attitude of coldness, rejection, and even sadism towards one's partner. While some of these feelings may well accompany difficulties experienced by women in sexual response, they are not necessarily part and parcel of inhibitions of sexual feelings. The term inhibition is, in fact, a more accurate one than frigidity, for inhibition it is that prevents certain women attaining sexual pleasure. And the growing body of information we have about female sexuality strongly reinforces the view that unresponsiveness to sexual stimulation in females, the idea of total permanent frigidity, is not accurate. It is an inhibition capable of release and alteration under certain circumstances. There is virtually no evidence to support the view that a percentage of

females is totally incapable of response.

However, we do have evidence to suggest that a very high proportion of women have problems of sexual adjustment and experience a great deal of anguish in their sexual relationships. After the Victorian era of repression, the first real breakthrough in understanding sexuality in general, and female sexuality in particular, came through the work of Sigmund Freud. Although a lot of people have criticized certain details of his views upon female sexual response and frigidity, some of his basic findings from psychoanalytic investigation and treatment are pertinent.

Perhaps the most important aspect is that the inhibitions from which the adult female may suffer are derived from her infantile fantasies and experience. Freud described a series of developmental periods through which all infants pass, in which the attachments the child forms to its parents are charged with erotic feelings and in which certain areas of the body are the focal points at different times in this relationship. We are all, as infants, prey to the most wide and diffuse fantasies of a sexual nature, many of which are considered perverse if expressed in adult life. We 'grow out' of our perverse satisfactions, but they are potentially present in each and every one of us. This 'growing out of' implies that we are being civilized in the process and that civilization is achieved at the cost of repression. The ideal is, of course, the balance —to be neither as repressed as our Victorian forbears, nor so disinhibited that 'anything goes'. The latter panics us as much as the former. But it is clear that the process of growing up, of becoming civilized, carries with it the potentiality for acquiring guilt and, with the guilt, repression and inhibition of feeling.

Our Victorian tradition handed down to us a conviction that masturbation was a sin that would drive one crazy or make one ill at the very least. The removal of the clitoris was a common practice in many primitive tribes. It was not so common in European civilizations, but there are documented case histories in the early part of this century where clitoridectomy was carried out to prevent female infants from masturbating. And, as astonishing as such attitudes may be to some of us, there are still quite a high proportion of people who regard female masturbation in infancy or adolescence or adult life as perverse and calculated to bring disturbance of one sort or another. Thus, through their own anxieties and lack of knowledge, adults inflict guilt on the young with important consequences upon the child's subsequent sexual development.

A fair proportion of psychoanalysts consider that a woman who does not achieve orgasm through coitus has a problem which falls within the compass of frigidity. The woman who achieves orgasm through direct clitoral stimulation but is anaesthetic vaginally is considered to have a problem in her general identity of herself as a woman. She is inclined to be masculine in attitude (this by no means implies she either acts or feels like a man, or is homosexual) but she is considered to resent male domination and to achieve a certain unconscious satisfaction that it is not the male penis that provides her pleasure. It is thought that she had a great envy of boys and men who had penises and that in her childhood she never overcame this envy and its corollary, a sense of feeling that she was inferior, degraded somehow as she did not possess this valued object. So in later life, because of her envy, she has an investment in pretending that her own clitoris is a penis and in failing to achieve satisfaction through penetration.

This attitude and reaction to sexuality is contrasted with the totally frigid woman, who suffers the complete inhibition of all sexual response, and is anaesthetic in every respect. Such a sexual difficulty is regarded as occurring in certain personalities—those of an hysterical type. It may quite suddenly disappear in the context of a change in the person's life or love-making experiences, or it may require special treatment. In all events, while it may sound a more serious disturbance of sexual behaviour, analysts consider it far easier to treat total sexual inhibition than a partial one, and so the prognosis for such a disorder is considered to be good.

Whether the sexual difficulty is total or partial or only occurs under certain circumstances, it is reasonable to infer that its origins do lie in childhood fears and experiences. These may include a very repressive childhood in which masturbation was forbidden and any sexual behaviour and expression criticized, to lack of warmth of love in the home, or institution life, or more complex difficulites where the infant has failed to resolve the feelings of attachment of an infantile sexual nature towards its parents.

While Freud and his followers have provided us with a great deal of knowledge about female sexuality and about frigidity, there really was very little known about female sexuality up to the time of Alfred Kinsey. His was really the first large-scale study of human sexual behaviour which involved an investigation into the attitudes and described the sexual behaviour of ordinary men and women, a large sample of Americans of different occupations and interests. Kinsey produced the first objective evidence of the extent of sexual difficulties experienced by ordinary men and women and their contribution towards marital disharmony and divorce. Freud was so much associated with people who were ill with neurotic disorders and, as his theories of neurosis had sexuality as their origin, he might well have thought that a lot of people not suffering from actual neurosis were neurotic because of their sexual problems. While there had been a number of studies carried out on female sexual response and orgasm, it was Kinsey who really helped clarify certain facts. Among these was the fact that while sexual difficulties of one sort or another are very common indeed in people with actual neurosis, they also commonly occur within the general population.

He showed, interestingly, that orgasm was reached increasingly as the years progressed; strongly suggesting that experience and psychological reconditioning in the marital setting did improve the female's capacity to respond to the point of orgasm. He also had data to suggest that it was not always, as marriage manuals so often suggested, lack of extended and varied technique in foreplay that interfered with female orgasm. On the contrary such techniques may even interfere with the attainment of orgasm. This finding has been corroborated by the work of Masters and Johnson, who after Kinsey have carried out an investigation into the physiology of human sexual response. While we are concerned here with psychology, physiology is inextricably bound up with psychology, and the knowledge we have gained from Masters and Johnson's study is invaluable in understanding the psychology of female sexuality. Masters and Johnson have stressed the irritability of the clitoris and that for some women, or indeed any woman under certain circumstances in the sexual-response cycle, direct manipulation of the clitoris may retard or prevent orgasm and act as an irritant rather than a stimulant.

The other findings of Masters and Johnson which is of considerable importance in the psychology of female sexuality is that the clitoris is indeed the signal box as it were for a woman's sexual stimulation. It is all seated there and, while feelings may radiate through the whole pelvic area and include the vagina, the clitoris remains the

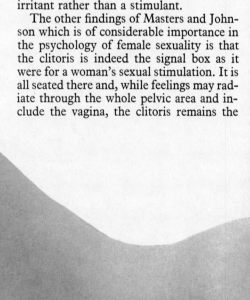

central point. The orgasmic peak in coitus includes a very marked clitoral reaction. This finding is very important in reconsidering the stress laid by Freud on the importance of the transition from the clitoris to the vagina as an indication of mature and full sexual development. While anaesthesia vaginally is an indication of some inhibition, if the clitoris is the central site of stimulation for the female, then Freud's ideas must be re-evaluated. Masters and Johnson also point out that in any coital activity some indirect clitoral stimulation occurs and physiologically vaginal and clitoral orgasm are identical.

The implications of this are that women who feel that the clitoris is the centre force of their own sexual response are not necessarily less 'mature' than women who regard the vagina as the strongest site of sexual response.

However, there is a difference between feeling the clitoris as the central pivot of sexual excitement within the context of coitus contrasting with feeling that only manual stimulation of the clitoris is satisfactory and vaginal penetration is experienced as unpleasant. If the latter is the case, there is some inhibition psychologically which interferes with response.

What is it that many women fear about sex and that interferes with their pleasure? The fears are many and predominantly unconscious. There are women who consciously fear pregnancy and so withold themselves, keeping a watchful eye, wilfully. There are conscious fears of dirt—the sexual and eliminatory process being so interwoven that this is intensified. Moral strictures that 'it is dirty' make women feel afraid to express their feelings. Some women fear that penetration will be painful and hold their bodies so tense that this is what they experience. Some women fear that if they show the extent of their response their partner may disapprove and think them disgusting. Indeed, Kinsey stressed that within certain groups he investigated in America the man was disturbed by the woman's sexual excitement.

There is the other side of the fear of being hurt, which is the fear of hurting. Fear of her own aggression and antagonism, but on an unconscious level, may interfere with a woman's response. In intercourse one does let go, one has to go out of control, as it were, to experience orgasm. If one links being 'out of control' with being out of control of one's aggressive impulses, then fears of really injuring one's partner do act as an inhibition of response.

For certain personalities, being in control is of such vital importance to the integrity of their personality, that they can never allow themselves to relax and fully enjoy their sexuality. A person with a markedly obsessional personality who has to control, and who is afraid of dirt and contamination, is likely to have problems in sexual relationships. The personalities that split themselves off and retreat into their own inner world may fear being engulfed by the other, literally eaten up, in coitus.

For some women frigidity is a symptom of a general neurotic disorder, be it hysterical, obsessional, or a schizoid personality organization. Such women may experience some sexual arousal and pleasure but not orgasm, or may experience it initially, or with certain people, and then subsequently retreat further and further into a shell of unresponsiveness so that they are quite split off from their sexual feelings. They do generally require psychotherapy, and even in apparently longstanding cases it is possible to give women a great deal of help and, in many cases, to help them reach full sexual enjoyment. There is of course a percentage of women whose defences are so entrenched that they do not even wish to experience sexual pleasure consciously. Kinsey laments that they are the ones who are so often in the forefront of the outcry against sexual enjoyment and freedom, who set themselves up as the moral watchdogs of their time, and voice the fear that without repression in the form of stern legislation we are heading for destruction. They seldom seek help or consider themselves in need of it, but do, in fact, live in fear of their own impulses.

But there are a large number of normal women who experience sexual difficulties at some point in their relationships. They are not fundamentally neurotic and do not require extensive treatment, but may well benefit from greater understanding of what is happening to them both in their relationships and in general information about sex. Ignorance is often a cause of minor sexual difficulties and a feeling of lack of sexual enjoyment which a woman may interpret as 'frigidity'. The ignorance may be her own, or her partner's. She may be shy, rather than afraid of showing her sexual response, or she may be afraid to tell her partner what arouses her most and what irritates her about his love-making. If he doesn't know, he cannot always instinctively please her. She may go through a temporary cycle of reduced sexuality, sometimes following the birth of her baby, and then develop a fear that she has become frigid. And fear breeds fear and tension, and triggers off old unconscious attitudes, turning a temporary inhibition into something more enduring.

Some women do have stronger sexual impulses than others—a combination of physiological as well as psychological factors. For a woman who has not got a particularly strong sexual drive, reading and hearing about 'woman's rights' and particularly the right, almost obligation, to have sex and orgasm, creates an inhibition and fear in itself. There are women for whom it is natural to have what may be termed 'mini' orgasms—a series of heightenings of sexual pleasure in coitus or love-making—rather than an overwhelming climax. If they do not understand this about themselves and do not know that this is within the normal range of experience of a lot of women, they may feel they are lacking in some way and become completely cut off from sexual feeling through doubts about their adequacy.

While it should be every woman's right to enjoy and experience full sexual pleasure if she wishes to, it seems such a pity that in revolt against our Victorian fathers we now almost make orgasm obligatory as an ideal of the 'permissive' age and imply by this banner of sexual freedom that those who do not or cannot are somehow inferior. There is such a wide variety of attitudes and responses in human beings—for some an asexual existence may not be their choice, but nevertheless does not exempt them from many of life's pleasures—and one should not replace one anxiety with another.

It should be possible for those women who do feel dissatisfied and lacking in fulfilment sexually, to be able to do something about it. And the greater permissiveness in the times in which we live does make this possible. There are Family Planning Clinics where advice on sexual difficulties and not simply contraception is now available to the married and unmarried. There are more specialized clinics for those with problems that are more deep-seated. Providing a woman wishes to have greater sexual enjoyment and is prepared to face herself, and her fears, it is no longer necessary to be resigned to an existence in which she labels herself 'frigid' and miserably leaves it at that. While 'cure' may not be possible for all, exploring inner feelings and attitudes can at least help in a woman's adjustment. BERENICE KRIKLER

John Garrett.

193

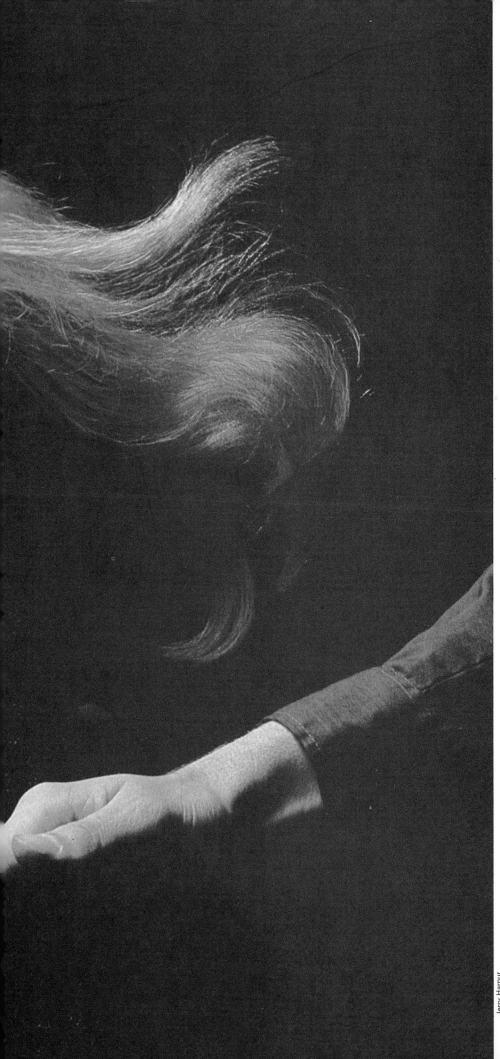

Are women masochists?

Masochism as a characteristic peculiar to the female sex is probably a myth. But what of the many women who consider themselves to be victims? Are they masochists?

Before considering whether women are, as some psychiatrists claim, intrinsically masochistic, and what forms of female behaviour can appropriately be described as 'masochistic', it is necessary to consider briefly the history of the concept of masochism.

The word 'masochism' is of comparatively recent origin, having been coined in the 1880s by the German sexologist Krafft-Ebing, who used it to describe a sexual perversion occurring in man. The perversion so named being that of men who require to have pain inflicted upon them before they can become sexually excited. Krafft-Ebing named this perversion after the Austrian novelist Count Leopold von Sacher-Masoch, whose novel *Venus in Furs: The Confessions of a Super-sensualist* describes a man whose delight it is to be beaten by the glamorous, red-headed, fur-wrapped, whip-cracking Wanda. Krafft-Ebing assumed, probably incorrectly, (*Ve-*

Some women need to see themselves as 'sufferers' and get satisfaction from feeling hard-done-by. A woman may even provoke her partner into actually hitting her. She then feels justified in her conviction that she is ill-treated, and the man is forced into the position of being a brute and owing her an apology.

Jerry Harpur

195

nus in Furs can be read as an allegory about the evils which arise if either sex is allowed to dominate the other) that this novel was autobiographical. He, therefore, used the author's name to describe the sexual perversion of enjoying pain and suffering. At the same time he named the opposite perversion, that of enjoying the infliction of pain, after the eighteenth-century French writer the Marquis de Sade, whose writings contain numerous accounts of this perversion. Krafft-Ebing, then, described the two perversions as a complementary pair, one involving the infliction of pain, the other involving the desire for pain, and named both after aristocratic practitioners and advocates of these perversions. The Marquis de Sade, being long dead, was not in a position to object, but von Sacher-Masoch is said to have deeply resented Krafft-Ebing's appropriation of the family name for such a purpose.

The next phase in the history of the word was Freud's adoption of the terms masochism and sadism to describe not only specific perversions of sexual behaviour, but also general psychological attitudes. He used 'masochism' to describe all forms of submissiveness and passivity and 'sadism' to describe all forms of cruelty, bullying, and even aggressiveness, regardless of whether the submissive, passive 'masochist' or the cruel, aggressive 'sadist' had any *conscious* sexual feelings while being passive or aggressive. He did, however, believe and imply that such sexual feelings were *unconsciously* present.

Having extended the meanings of these two words thus far, Freud further complicated and, some would say, confused matters in three more ways.

First, he maintained that masochism and sadism were intimately connected. Until 1922 he regarded sadism as an innate, instinctual tendency which under certain circumstances underwent reversal into masochism. After 1922 he held that masochism was an innate, instinctual tendency —a manifestation of the death instinct— which under certain circumstances became transformed into sadism.

Secondly, he maintained that many neurotics are simultaneously sadistic and masochistic in their relation to themselves; that they derive sadistic gratification from forcing themselves to do things that they do not want to do and from stopping themselves from doing things that they do want to do—and at the same time derive masochistic gratification from submitting to such injunctions and prohibitions. Looked at in this way much religiosity and scrupulousness, many tendencies to self-abnegation, and much apparent dedication to duty can be interpreted as subtle forms of self-torture, in which the individual is simultaneously torturer and victim and derives a double income of satisfaction from playing these roles.

Thirdly, Freud postulated that there was an inherent connection between mascu-

linity, activity, and sadism, on the one hand, and femininity, passivity, and masochism on the other. According to this view men are innately active, aggressive, self-assertive, and their sexuality inevitably contains a streak of sadism, while women are innately passive and submissive, and their sexuality inevitably contains a streak of masochism. In retrospect this view of the innate differences between men and women seems untenable—or rather only tenable by verbal sleight of hand, by, for instance, interpreting all submissive behaviour in men as being due to their unconscious femininity, and all active, assertive behaviour in women as an expression of their unconscious wish to be male. According to Freud all women suffered from 'penis-envy'.

Freud's view that men are innately active and sadistic and women are innately passive and masochistic was challenged almost immediately by many of Freud's own disciples, and particularly by the first generation of women analysts, and, indeed, was belied by Freud personally inasmuch as he encouraged many of his female patients and pupils—and one of his daughters—to become active and ambitious professional women. But the idea that women are innately passive and masochistic and that all active tendencies in women are neurotic, still forms part of the popular conception of psychoanalysis. This very theory is largely responsible for the hostility frequently shown towards psychoanalysis today, particularly in the United States, by the Women's Liberation Movement. For instance, Betty Friedan in her book *The Feminine Mystique* holds Freud and the psychoanalysts largely responsible for the idea that a woman's proper place is in the home and that she should devote herself exclusively to the care of her husband and children.

Starting then as a word to describe a masculine perversion and transformed by Freud into one for describing a submissive tendency which he believed to be an essential aspect of feminine character, the word 'masochism' has now passed into general circulation denoting the concept that it is possible for human beings to derive pleasure from pain. The Concise Oxford Dictionary defines it as a 'form of (esp. sexual) perversion in which a sufferer derives pleasure from pain or humiliation'. Furthermore, it is generally accepted that this perverse, paradoxical, and indeed mysterious phenomenon is exemplified more commonly by women than by men. And, as always happens when technical terms pass into general usage, it is often used glibly by people who have no idea of its full implications, who fail to appreciate how extraordinary it is to assert that there exist people whose behaviour runs counter to the basic principle that human beings— and indeed all living creatures—pursue pleasure and avoid pain.

Personally, I suspect that the idea that there is an instinct which compels some

people to derive pleasure from pain is a myth, and that sexual masochists deceive themselves when they claim to do so. Certainly, men who claim to enjoy being whipped take good care to avoid being seriously injured or even bruised in the process. It would also appear that the phenomena which led Freud to assert that women are masochistic are capable of alternative explanations, without reference to any innate, instinctual need to suffer.

The first point to be made about the so-called masochism of women is that their sexual and reproductive processes give them a greater familiarity with pain than do men's. Most, although not all, women experience at least some degree of pain in connection with menstruation, defloration, and childbirth. Diseases of the female genital organs are much more common than those of the male—there is no medical speciality of andrology corresponding to gynaecology—and it is probably easier for clumsy men to hurt women in the sexual act than it is for clumsy women to hurt men. Added to all of these physical facts, there exists a mass of folklore, superstition, and old wives' tales, which is passed on from one generation of neurotic and malicious women to their daughters, insinuating that it is woman's destiny to suffer and that, to modify slightly a Victorian folk ballad, 'It's the men wot gets the pleasure and women wot gets the pain. Ain't it all a bleeding shame?' Many girls are brought up in an atmosphere in which their mothers constantly complain about the treatment they receive from their husbands. Such women constantly point out to their daughters that all men are lazy and only out for their own good. The girl is brought up to believe that she must accept a man's bidding and that all her life will be a misery because of this.

Given these physiological facts and the superstructure of anxiety and superstition derived from them, it is hardly surprising that many women incorporate the idea of themselves as sufferers and victims into their self-images and construct theories to persuade themselves that they acquire virtue, nobility, and the right to special deference from men by reason of their capacity to endure suffering. Neither is it surprising that they learn the art of using suffering as a gambit to make their menfolk feel guilty and, therefore, more amenable to control. What I am suggesting here is that much so-called masochism in women is a manipulative technique for controlling and demoralizing men, used by women who secretly envy them and resent their apparent freedom from sexual pain and their greater opportunities to pursue careers.

Since the majority of women marry and raise children, such masochistic techniques are mostly employed within the home and on the family. Skilled masochistic women are adepts at making their husbands feel that they are clumsy, brutish, and over-demanding in bed, at producing headaches and backaches to justify their refusal to have sexual relations or, more effectively, at demonstrating how noble and self-sacrificing they are being when they do accede to demands for sex. They generally attempt to convey the impression that running a home and looking after children are burdensome chores which leave them exhausted at the end of the day and, therefore, entitled to infinite sympathy and consideration from their husbands when they return from work. A woman of this type ignores the fact that her husband's work provides the income by which she and her children are supported. She is incapable of considering the possibility that her husband may have had as difficult a time at work as she has had at home and may have been as harassed by his boss or clients as she claims to have been by her children.

Such women, if they are wise in their neurosis, marry either brutes or suckers. If they marry a man who is in fact brutish, selfish, and a bad provider, then their complaints are indeed justified. They really do suffer. Their masochistic stance appears to be a natural response to the realities of their situation and they can honestly present themselves to the world as victims of circumstance. But why, a detached observer may ask, did they marry such a man in the first place? Selfishness and brutishness are not, after all, traits difficult to recognize.

If, on the other hand, such a woman marries a sucker, her conception of herself as a sufferer will be accepted without question by her husband. He will admire her for the courage with which she endures pain, illness, and fatigue. He will help about the house and with the children even when he himself is feeling exhausted. He will be grateful for small kindnesses which a less gullible man would accept as his due. Marriages between masochists and suckers are often, in their ghastly fashion, extremely successful. The wife is admired for her endurance, instead of being criticized for her moaning incompetence, while the husband feels compensated for the frustrations he endures by the conviction that he is deeply needed.

There are, however, two hazards attached to such marriages. The husband always looks tired and drawn, and this may evoke maternal sympathy in another woman who may then embark on a rescue operation. Or the worm may turn spontaneously, in which case the wife will one day find herself suddenly confronted with an extremely angry husband who is deeply resentful of the years he has spent being conned.

Masochistic women of the kind I have been describing also engage in complicated ploys with the medical profession. Their sufferings entitle them, or so they believe and their doctors all too often concur, to special therapeutic attention and sympathy, and being ill often becomes a part of their way of life. In mild cases this leads to comparatively harmless though time-wasting relationships in which the woman makes

visiting her family doctor or the local hospital's out-patient department a regular feature of her life, while he (it almost always is a male doctor) prescribes treatments which mysteriously never quite succeed in relieving her of her aches and pains. In more serious cases, however, she may manipulate the doctors into performing surgery on her and embark on the dangerous career of being a chronic surgical case, losing organ after organ in a vain search for—is it health or the penetration which her anti-sexual upbringing has prevented her from ever consciously desiring? According to an ancient oral tradition among surgeons, any woman with more than three abdominal scars should be regarded as a neurotic unless proved to the contrary.

Another aspect of women's lives which is often discussed in terms of feminine masochism stems from the fact that a number of biological and social factors conspire to make it inevitable that women have frequent experiences of subordinating their will to that of others and, if they have children, of caring for others instead of pursuing their own interests. It is, however, by no means obvious why subordinating one's will to another's should necessarily be painful—indeed *voluntary* surrender of one's will to another can be quite enjoyable—nor why caring for others should necessarily be self-sacrificial. It will obviously depend on whether one is fond and proud of those for whom one cares.

Nor, of course, are men immune to such experiences, although in Western society they tend to occur more frequently in their work than in their personal lives. Men who are not self-employed or in positions of authority often have to subordinate their will to that of their employer or superior at work, while members of the therapeutic professions (and to a lesser extent of all the learned professions) spend their lives responding to the needs of their patients and clients. Yet no one would argue that all doctors are masochists—although some undoubtedly are—or deny that they can get great satisfaction from the exercise of their professional skills and from personal contact with their patients. Similarly with women, the fact that the social and material circumstances of their lives are determined more by their husbands' occupations than by any other factor, and that while their children are young they spend much of their time caring for them, is not necessarily a source of pain and humiliation. It all depends on whether they love their husbands and are fond of their children. However, these two aspects of women's lives can be, and, indeed, often are used by masochistic, grievance-collecting women to rationalize their discontent and to maintain their conception of themselves as hard-done-by sufferers.

Finally, and in order to avoid misunderstandings, I must make two last points. First, in view of the fact that my description of masochistic women must inevitably have conjured up an unpleasant picture, I must state explicitly that such women are right in regarding themselves as victims, though not, as they imagine, of their present circumstances. Ultimately, they are pathetic not vicious, but they mislocate the source of their troubles. If they have to blame anyone for their inability to enjoy life and their adoption of a pain-orientated attitude to it, they should blame their parents and their upbringing, not their husbands and their children.

Secondly, masochistic tendencies are far from being the only or even the most common cause of the discontent with marriage expressed by so many women today. Numerous other psychological and social factors also contribute to this feeling—including poverty, poor housing, the repercussions within marriage of the husband's occupational frustrations, the separation of men's working and home environments which leaves so many women isolated and lonely during their husbands' working day, and, last, but not least, the existence of stereotyped assumptions about the roles to be played by wives and husbands, which all too often allow no scope for either to grow and develop within marriage and thereby remain interesting and lovable people.   CHARLES RYCROFT

Jerry Harpur

The psychology of the male

What is a man? Physiologically the answer may seem obvious, but psychologically there is no easy definition. Must a man be aggressive, strong, and courageous? Must he dominate and take responsibility? Or can he be timid, passive, and dependent? Is he born masculine or does he have to learn to be a male? Just what, in fact, makes a male a man?

Most of us are interested in discovering what characteristics go towards creating a concept of ourselves as a person, towards establishing our own particular identity. We like to know how clever, how good, how kind, or how strong we are. Of all these qualities the one that is most central to our idea of ourselves is our sex-role identity.

Physiologically, male characteristics are governed by genetic and hormonal factors. The male sperm carries the genetic information that determines whether the growing foetus will be male or female. When the reproductive cells from the father and mother come together at fertilization the chromosomes, which bear the genetic information, form into 23 pairs, one of each pair coming from the male, one from the female. One of these pairs, the sex chromosomes, controls the sex of the developing embryo. In the male this pair consists of two different chromosomes, one called an X chromosome, the other a Y. The female has two X chromosomes while the male carries one pair that is XY.

These sex chromosomes instruct the growing organism in terms of masculine or feminine growth characteristics. But the success of their instructions depends upon such other conditions during growth as the important influence of the hormones circulating in the blood.

In just the same way as the physiological determinants of masculinity are a combination of genetic instructions from the chromosomes interacting with and affected by the growth environment, particularly the hormones, so psychologically what makes a man is an interaction between his physiological characteristics and the cultural-social environment within which he grows and matures.

Physiologically, if the hereditary mechanism goes wrong because, for example, the Y chromosome is abnormal, the baby may have malformed genitals. Hormonal disturbances are more common. The sex glands secrete hormones in the human foetus well before birth. Until puberty boys and girls produce both male and female hormones, in small and fairly equal quantities.

Early in adolescence production of the male hormone secreted from the boy's testicles and the female hormone secreted by the girl's ovaries increases greatly. The endocrine system which produces hormones does not relate exclusively to sexual development, but governs a wide range of bodily development and activity. In certain hormonal disturbances growth can be af-

fected by a failure in one set of hormones. As the hormones tend to act in unison, this may not only cause dwarfism but indirectly fail to stimulate the ovaries or testes so preventing the physical changes of puberty occurring. The affected female fails to menstruate and the male remains sexually infantile, with a tiny, impotent penis.

While sexual growth and maturity is dependent upon hormonal functioning, in the more highly-evolved species sexual impulses are less strikingly related to hormonal change. Rats mate only when the female rat is in oestrus, that is at the time of ovulation. When the female rat is infertile the male is not attracted and the female is not receptive. In humans, with the greater development of the brain, the central nervous system gains far greater influence, and mating is no longer so dependent upon hormonal factors.

Just as all forms of behaviour are more flexible and less stereotyped in humans than in animals, so do sexual behaviour, attitudes, and identity come to be more under the sway and influence of the mind rather than the body.

What makes a male with a correct genetic coding of XY chromosomes and a normally active and developed hormonal balance think and feel like a man depends as much upon the influences on his mind of the particular culture in which he is reared as upon the fluctuating conditions of his physiological make-up. Mind and body interact to produce behaviour. The central nervous system influences the hormones as well as the hormones influencing the central nervous system.

The growing boy learns his sexual role identity at an early age. One of the first distinctions he makes is that both he and his father have characteristics that his mother does not. By watching he learns that there are differences in the way girls and women look as compared with boys and men, in the things they do, in the clothes they wear, in their voices. He achieves a conceptual awareness of distinct physical differences between the sexes by the age of two, if not earlier. And rapidly, in the wake of this awareness, he learns that opinions, feelings, motives, and behaviour are also different and one set becomes attributed by him to one sex as opposed to the other.

What does it mean to be masculine? The only definition is that within a given culture a person holds what are considered to be male values and follows male behaviour norms of that society. Within Westernized

culture, for example, and many other cultures, too, aggression in the widest meaning of the term is more permissible and, indeed, encouraged in males as compared with females. Males are expected to be strong, physically and mentally, to have courage, a sense of adventure, to master technological skills, to be capable of high levels of abstract thinking. Dependency, passivity, and conformity are traditionally part of the female sex role standard. Dominance, independence, self-control, and power are traditionally part of the male sex role standard.

Even within different areas of the same society different characteristics will be given greater weight. Where intellectual prowess is considered the most discriminating feature the clever boy who is not necessarily so skilful athletically, but who is mechanically adept and mentally quick, will be considered masculine by his group. Where the premium is placed upon physical prowess and the tough athletic skills such a boy will be rated as not highly masculine. So even within the same society and culture there are wide differences of opinion as to what essentially characterizes maleness.

Because all these ideas and attitudes are transmitted to children very early in life, it is extremely difficult to have any concept of 'male' that is unrelated to the prevalent attitude in a particular society. Within Western society there is at present a re-evaluation of the concepts of male and female roles and attitudes. Women's Liberation movements challenge many of the assumptions about what is acceptable differentiation in roles between men and women. Even before this direct challenge questioning of the rigid distinctions between male and female attitudes and behaviour had begun. Before education and technological skills had become as widely available to women as they are at present, the traditional role the man saw for himself was as the breadwinner of a family. He was expected to have to compete, to have to master some skill, to have to provide for a family, although in his youth he was allowed to be 'wild' within limits, to be adventurous, somewhat reckless, and to enjoy the full exercise of his bodily strengths and their challenge.

The male role in society must take into account the female role. Until very recent times the different prescribed roles of male and female can be understood as part of a system of organization for ensuring the continuity of society. It is ob-

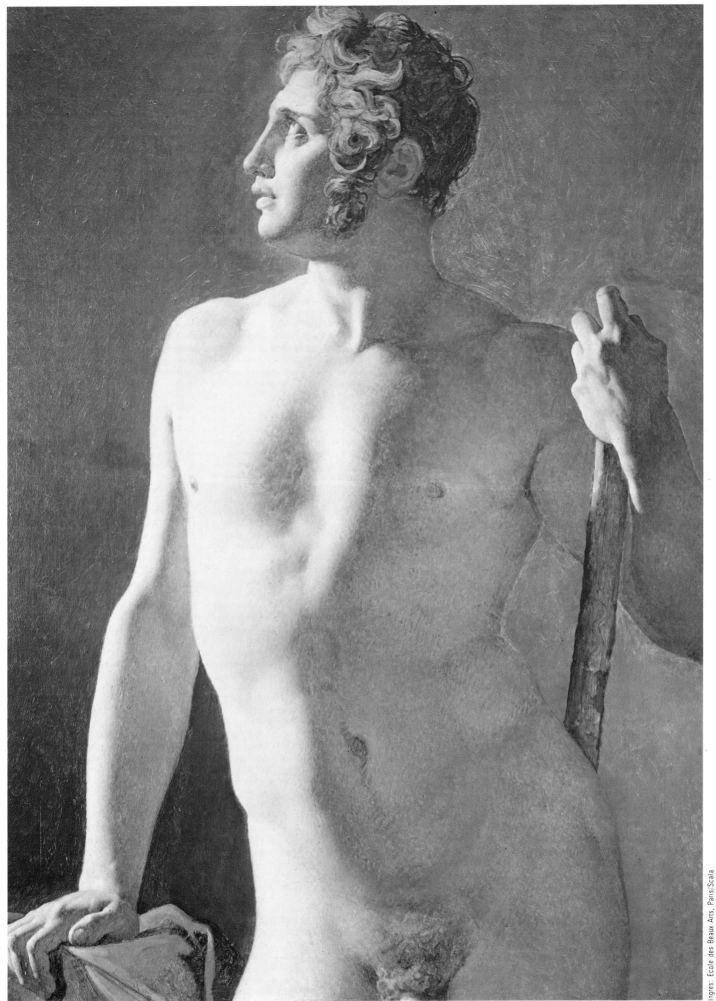

vious that women bear children. It is also obvious that for the child to survive it needs care and, therefore, some social order is necessary that will. allow for this care. The family unit was no accident but an effective guarantee of the survival of the children and therefore the society.

In different times and places male and female roles have varied. But the care of the young has universally been a social extension of the female's biological role and the protection of the family the social extension of the male's biological role. The question of to what extent these differences are biological and basic and to what extent cultural would never have been asked before the Industrial Revolution. It can be asked now because of the changes that have been wrought by technology. A man no longer hunts for the family dinner but works in an office or factory. Many women do not devote their whole lives to the family but also labour in offices and factories. The availability of contraceptive devices, emphasizing the pleasurable rather than the procreative aspects of sex, has further weakened the division between the sexes. For these reasons, many people would now claim that the cause of differentiation in sex roles is sociological.

However, all societies have evolved different roles for male and female. It seems rational to assume that biological differences do condition individual psychology and so cultural roles, and possible to accept this without falling back into old attitudes of sexual dominance and exploitation. To deny a sexual role identity may be as dangerous as to over-emphasize it.

There is no absolute male or female. Every male has some female characteristics and every female some male characteristics. The balance varies. Here psycho-social factors affect each person's development. The small boy begins life with an intense relationship with his mother, and identifies and absorbs certain characteristics from her before he begins to identify with his father. In his development he passes through the Oedipal stage in which his passion for his mother and rivalry with his father reach a peak of great intensity. The success with which he achieves a resolution of the conflicts that arise at this stage (around the age of four to six years) plays a considerable part in his future sexual role identification. In resolving the conflicts of the Oedipal phase, identification with the father is a major factor.

The next hurdle that faces the boy is school and the patterns that influence him here. In any school playground clear patterns of play are discernible—boys and girls may play together, but by and large they are in groups of their own sex. The boys' play is usually rougher and more active, and they are likely to chase and tease the girls. To be tough is a highly-prized role. To be naughty in class and self-assertive is considered an admirable objective.

In adolescence a yet greater turmoil arrives. Hormonal functions change, secondary sexual characteristics develop accompanied by strong sexual arousal. Coping with his emotional and physical changes at the same time as he is trying to learn academic skills creates enormous turbulence. The role an adolescent boy seeks to play is strongly influenced by his peer group and less by identification with adults, and often the role expected by parents and teachers conflicts with that expected by his friends.

A boy with an academically-minded father, who has identified with him and accepted his father as an ideal, may find himself in a group that despises such standards and for a while he may totally renounce his home influences, become unruly, neglect his studies, and engage in total rebellion against all the things he seemed previously quite willing to accept. If his identification with his father is strong, his basic home relationships stable, and previous school-teacher experiences reasonably good, he is likely in later adolescence to return to his father's standards and views. If his hostility to his father is too overwhelming he may remain very much a rebel without a cause.

Should this rebellion proceed over an extended period it may affect his job future, too. He may always resent authority, be unable to settle in any work and his own concept of what it is to be manly remains at a level of being male in revolt. At its extremes such a man is often unsure about his identity as a man and feels forced into an aggressive rebellion he does not fully experience as a part of his basic self.

The boy at the opposite pole, the boy who can never rebel at all, who totally conforms to the patterns of an adult society and who completely rejects his peer influences, beside finding himself the odd one out, can in his isolation feel inadequate and doubtful about his masculinity.

He always does what he is told, is fearful of assuming responsibility, wants to be told what to do, and in his relationships with women often takes the passive role.

The aggressive boy, when he is a grown man, may demand complete dominance over his women and resent any signs of independence, while the passive man wishes to be dominated by his mate. This may reflect itself in the sexual as well as in more general relationships, although there are many shades between. The over-aggressive rebellious male, for example, while dominating his mate in most areas may enjoy himself sexually if he is passive and she the active one. The passive male may fear an active female as much as he longs for her and perform better with a more passive woman.

All men and women pass through a homosexual phase in their development. The security they feel about their sex-role identity determines how much they can accept the homosexual component in their own make-up and live comfortably with it. The man who is able to accept that he is a creature of many parts, who is drawn to members of both sexes, although aroused sexually only by women, who can live with parts of himself that in his society may be rated as feminine, can feel secure in his basic sex-role identity.

Many occupations, in fact, allow men to exercise certain characteristics that are regarded as feminine. For example, jobs such as those of a doctor or a male nurse allow feelings of care for others to be expressed in a socially-accepted way, at the same time as they give expression to the technological skills more commonly associated with masculine ideals.

To live comfortably as a man, one's ideal of what a man is should approximate to one's idea of oneself. If a man absorbs a concept of what an ideal man is which deviates markedly from his ideas of what he is, he will automatically attempt to adjust either or both concepts. The more widely these ideas differ the greater his conflict, and the more likely he is to have problems about his own identity.

Each man must assess the particular ideas regarding masculinity and femininity prevalent in his society; and decide for himself which make sense and which are simply stereotypes, having no real reference to the complex features that combine to form a masculine personality.

BERENICE KRIKLER

Premature ejaculation: causes and treatment

If a man's sexual reactions are too quick to satisfy his partner, the relationship may suffer. Premature ejaculation often has psychological as well as physical causes, but it can be treated successfully.

Almost every man has experienced times when he has made love and, while meaning to give pleasure and satisfaction to the woman and to himself, has been so excited that he has reached his climax too quickly. For a man's body functions in such a way that he is capable of being very quickly aroused, and of experiencing orgasm within seconds rather than minutes. But because he wishes to prolong his own pleasure, and give his partner the opportunity to become aroused and enjoy their love-making, he learns to control his reflexes. Only sometimes—perhaps it is the first time he is making love with a particular partner and he is specially anxious to please her—does his sexual tension build up too quickly.

Unfortunately there are some men who, for one reason or another, never learn to control themselves sufficiently. Their disability, called premature ejaculation, is the cause of much personal distress and marital unhappiness.

It is impossible to estimate how many men suffer from premature ejaculation because some at least may even be ignorant that their partners are not receiving the same physical release as they are themselves. And wives who have been brought up to expect sex to be distasteful and unpleasant may welcome their husband's disability—it relieves them of what they feel is a duty rather than a pleasure. Where a couple do seek professional help, it is usually the wife who makes the first move. After all, it is she who suffers.

Some people would regard an ejaculation of semen as premature only when it occurred before the penis had entered the vagina. On the other hand, one man complained to his doctor that he suffered from premature ejaculation because he could not retain his erection for longer than ten minutes after intromission preceded by a long period of love-play.

The sex act is, ideally, a communication in which both the man and the woman play equally active though complementary parts, and reach climaxes within a space of time short enough for both of them to enjoy it together. If the male partner cannot restrain his ejaculation for long enough to enable his partner to reach her climax, then the ejaculation could be regarded as premature. This happens sometimes with any couple, but it becomes a problem if it happens almost every time they make love. This condition often affects men whose attitudes towards sexual intercourse are learned from early experiences which make the main aim of sexual acts the relief of male tensions, and the woman merely an object of achieving this end. These experiences might be with prostitutes, masturbation when the person is ashamed and frightened that he might be discovered, petting to the point of orgasm, or hurried intercourse where there is little privacy. Any of these are quite likely to be within a young man's experience. The common factor is the strongly felt need to achieve orgasm quickly which stems from a fear of being caught, or from some other circumstance which arouses an attitude of vigilance or a sense of urgency. The interval of time between the first stirrings of desire and the ejaculation is filled not with the pleasures of physical communication between a man and a woman but with suspense, anxiety, and impatience. The man attempts to reduce this period, and the more completely he succeeds the more certainly this conditioning will over-sensitize him and produce premature ejaculation when he wants to experience true sexual communication with a woman.

John's is a typical case. He was brought up in a strictly religious home. Sex was never mentioned, and he learned about it only from jokes and boastings of his school friends. He began to masturbate; it had to be done secretly and as quickly as possible, usually in the privacy of the bathroom, so that his parents would not be suspicious. His shame and fear only intensified his preoccupation with sex. The idea became firmly established in his mind that sex was something to be hidden, something dirty and shameful, and, of course, he believed that it was wicked to enjoy sexual intercourse with a woman outside marriage. When John married, at 24, the marriage was sexually disastrous. His only sexual experience had been of masturbating to relieve his sexual tensions, and the fear of being discovered had always made it necessary for him to reach an orgasm as soon as possible. These years of self-conditioning had made it inevitable that he would ejaculate within a couple of minutes of being aroused. The tension produced by the couple's continuing sexual difficulties meant that in other ways too the marriage was not a success. John and his wife are now in their early forties, and go on living together only because their religious convictions forbid them to separate.

Maria and Andrew, too, show a common pattern in their relationship. They met during their first year at university. After a few months they were eager to get married but they agreed that it would be unwise to do so while they were studying. They spent a lot of time together and made love when they had the opportunity.

Maria was a Roman Catholic. Though not devout, she refused to use any contraceptive device, and as neither she nor Andrew was ever quite sure about the 'safe periods', Andrew always had to withdraw before reaching a climax. Maria consented to this way of making love to please him, although she realized that it meant allowing herself little satisfaction.

It was three years before they got married. They both wanted children, so Maria was now freed from the fear of pregnancy. She expected their love-making to be as complete and satisfying for her as it was for her husband. But Andrew had become used to being quickly aroused to the point of orgasm and withdrawing when he began to feel orgasm approaching. He could maintain his erection for only a few seconds after entering the vagina. His orgasm occurred long before Maria had been fully aroused and gave her no time to respond to him, to experience the accumulation of erotic sensations that culminate in an orgasm. At first Maria was understanding and sympathetic, but their sexual life did not improve. She eventually began complaining for, naturally, she felt frustrated and resentful. She told Andrew that he was selfish, that he was only using her, and did not really care about her at all. But the more she protested, the more precipitate and uncontrollable Andrew's emission reflexes became. If they had not sought professional help, this pattern might have persisted.

Such a long term problem does not result from just one or two 'failures' in intercourse. A couple need not be anxious if the man suffers from premature ejaculation during their first experiences of sexual intercourse together. He is likely to be overexcited and anxious to acquit himself well, and may well be embarrassed about the exposure of his own body to a woman.

If then he ejaculates prematurely and his erection subsides, he feels ashamed and humiliated in his partner's eyes as well as in his own. A simple remedy that is usually effective when this happens is for both partners to remain still for long enough to allow the effects of over-stimulation to subside, and then start again, but this time

more slowly and tentatively. An alternative is to relax, let orgasm occur, rest for half an hour or so and resume love-play as soon as the penis is erect and firm enough to be inserted into the vagina. Most couples counteract the over-excitement of sexual novelty in one of these ways without instruction, guided by common sense, and usually the results are mutually satisfactory. If the condition persists, the cause may include both physiological and psychological factors and so must the treatment.

Possible physiological and psychological factors combine in various ways to play a part in premature ejaculation. The human body is sensitive and reacts to changes of many different kinds going on in the world about it—changes of atmospheric pressure, changes in the colour and intensity of light, temperature changes. The effect of these changes is not the same upon everybody. One man shivers at the slightest hint of frost in the air: his neighbour goes for a swim every morning and enjoys it even when the temperature is well below zero.

Equally, there are very marked differences in people's sensitivity and modes of response to the many kinds of stimulation that can arouse sexual desire. Seeing, hearing, touching, smelling, and all other forms of physical communication play their parts, but sometimes one or another will become disproportionately provocative. For example, a glimpse of a woman's bare nipple will greatly excite one man but will leave another unmoved. Some people are just more sensitive than others to certain forms of stimulation.

When someone suffers from premature ejaculation, his medical history is likely to show that he also suffered during his formative years from some physical condition indicative of hyper-excitability of the central nervous system, probably bed-wetting, and for this he may have been punished or ridiculed. Inevitably, the more frightened of his inability to control his bladder the boy became the more certainly his anxiety would spread as puberty approached. To the fear of enuresis would be added fear of nocturnal emissions and, in due course, of premature ejaculation.

Hyper-sensitivity of the central nervous system may greatly lengthen the time a child requires to learn how to control his desire to release urine and, later on, the impulse to ejaculate; but he *can* learn and usually does. The emission reflexes get out of hand only when the physical over-sensitivity is reinforced by an emotionally charged situation.

The emotionally charged situation need not have any direct sexual significance. Anything that arouses fear, surprise, aggression, or some other unexpected and intense kind of feeling can precipitate an unwanted emission if the physiological predisposition is there.

Clinical observations made independently in Britain and in America have compiled an 'Identikit' picture of the kind of man most likely to suffer from premature ejaculation.

His outstanding characteristic is his sense of personal isolation which may find expression in timidity or aggressive self-assertion. It reflects his conviction that other people are not to be trusted very far, because their acceptance or rejection of himself depends entirely on his ability to live up to their expectations.

When his sexual curiosity first awakened, he had to try to satisfy it secretly, for his observations had convinced him that adults regarded it as a shameful thing. At school, in his early teens, he probably went in for some furtive sexual experiments with other boys. Later, there would be hasty and fumbling sessions of 'heavy petting' with girls picked up in coffee bars or discotheques; and then, probably in young manhood, a stable love relationship in which, for the first time, the symptoms of premature ejaculation would cause alarm.

The climate of thought in industrialized, Western societies make it likely that, as he grows, the boy should become steadily more individualistic and competitive in his dealings with other people, and more egocentric in his attitude to sexuality. The influences that encourage secretiveness, fear, and shame make him impatient to attain orgasm. He sees his wife or girl friend not as an equal partner, sharing with him the most intimate of human communications, but merely as the animated instrument of his sexual gratification. He takes it for granted that she will be satisfied when he reaches orgasm and, when she is not, the tears, protestations, and other signs of her disappointment and frustration bewilder him. They are often the first intimations a young man receives that he is an inept and clumsy lover. When they are due not to his indifference but to his ignorance, they may arouse intense anxiety from which premature ejaculation will probably develop.

Social stress, too, can cause difficulties. There can be few practising psychiatrists who have not been consulted by very anxious young men who, after marrying, have found that they have lost their sexual capacity. Hitherto, as they explain, they have had no difficulty at all in completing the sex act to their satisfaction. They were free from self-consciousness because they regarded the girls they went to bed with as their social or intellectual inferiors. But now things are different. They find it difficult to see as sexual partners girls of the kind they could marry.

The treatment of premature ejaculation will depend on the outcome of diagnosis. If physical examination clearly indicates that nervous hyper-sensitivity of the urethra, for example, is the main source of trouble, sedative medicines and desensitizing creams locally applied may be of great help. It is obvious, though, that no amount of medication will do any good for a man whose ejaculatory prematurity has psychological causes. In all such situations psychological help is required, and everything will depend on how quickly it is sought. Husbands and wives who go on suffering sexual frustration for months or years rather than risk the embarrassment of seeking professional help are inviting marital disaster.

Perhaps the most promising treatment for premature ejaculation is the practical sexual re-education that is being used in the American clinic of Masters and Johnson, the researchers into human sexuality, and which they describe in *Human Sexual Inadequacy*. Most couples with this problem try the 'don't touch' way of making love, in which the woman does not touch the man's genitals although he caresses her until she becomes highly aroused. The man then hurriedly tries to enter her. But invariably the stimulation this involves causes him to ejaculate almost immediately. In the method that Masters and Johnson recommend, the woman is told to stimulate the genitals of her partner so that he develops an erection. The immediate impulse to ejaculate is counteracted by her applying pressure to the tip of the penis for a few seconds. She places her thumb on the frenulum on the underside of the penis, and her first and second fingers on either side of the coronal ridge on the upper side. This pressure diminishes the urge to ejaculate. A few seconds later after relaxing the pressure, she can continue caressing the penis. The squeeze technique can be repeated several times so that it is possible for the couple to experience 15 to 20 minutes of active love-play. The man gradually regains ejaculatory control, and the woman loses her anxiety about his sexual inadequacy.

The next stage is for the couple to attempt intromission of the penis into the vagina, with the woman in the superior position. After she has brought the man to a full erection and employed the squeeze technique several times, she then mounts him, but remains motionless and undemanding. When the man feels he is about to ejaculate he tells her. She raises herself and applies the squeeze technique again. With practice the penis can be contained for 15 minutes or more, and this gives the woman the opportunity to enjoy the new experience and to think and feel sexually. And this gives her a strong motivation towards orgasmic release. Practice in this technique can provide the basis for an increasing improvement in ejaculatory control. Masters and Johnson claim success in almost all of their cases. As with every case of premature ejaculation, the success of their method requires the active co-operation of both sexual partners, not only in their willingness to learn how to approach each other sexually and control their responses, but also in their common acceptance of responsibility for the happy consummation of their relationship on the personal as well as the functional level.

PETER FLETCHER

The truth about impotence

Nearly every man, at some time in his life, experiences impotence. What causes it and how can it be successfully treated?

Everybody tries to play doctor or psychiatrist to himself at some time or another. If his diagnosis is correct, self-help is often the most beneficial and satisfactory kind of help. But this does not always happen. A false diagnosis can have serious consequences when the problem is psychological. One field in which much misery can be caused when proper advice is not sought involves the condition known as functional impotence.

Impotence is the inability of a man to play his part in the act of sexual intercourse and consummate it in orgasm. 'Organic impotence' occurs as a result of physical injury or disease; but this is rare. The vast majority of cases of impotence (about 90 per cent) are not 'organic' but 'functional'; that is to say, the condition is psychological. Something in a man's mind is preventing his body from responding in the normal way to his desires. This 'something' may be a feeling of guilt, anxiety, shame, or an acquired distaste for the sexual act. It may be an emotional disturbance of some other kind, completely unrelated to sexual activity, or a repressed memory of a traumatic childhood experience. The condition is produced by a state of mind, and is not a symptom of physical illness.

Functional impotence is one of man's commonest psychogenic disorders. It can cause great misery both to those afflicted by it and their families, mainly because social ignorance and prudish reticence have infected with fear much of our thinking about sexual behaviour.

Any healthy and normally virile man may, for example, temporarily lose all desire for sexual intercourse because he is struggling with difficult professional problems, is committed for a time to long hours of work, or is preoccupied with some other personal vicissitude, like grief, that depletes his energies. If he and his wife have been sexually well-informed and enjoy each other's confidence, they will know that the remedy for this condition is a period of abstinence, and they will accept it gracefully together. There is nothing neurotic about this. But if this wife implicitly believes, as many women do, that a man can produce an erection and engage in sexual intercourse at will, or the husband has learned by experience that any sign of his reluctance to make love will arouse her suspicion that he is losing interest in her, then the stage is set for the development of an emotional disorder of which the outstanding symptom in the husband will probably be functional impotence.

The reason why this happens can best be understood by recalling an elementary fact about animal behaviour. The positions animals must assume for love-making, and the intensity of their interest in each other while doing so, make them most vulnerable to attacks by their natural enemies at a time when they are least able to withstand them. The higher animals, including man, are therefore endowed with a built-in incompatibility between fear and sexual desire—a safety device that has great survival value. Creatures that indulge their sexual appetites when in danger run a risk that could well be fatal.

This biological fact of life can be related to the situation of the husband we are discussing. At the end of the day all he wants is to drop into bed and have a good night's rest. But he knows his wife expects him to make love, and will be hurt or affronted if he does not. So he tries and fails. At first, his wife accepts his explanation that he is tired, but when the failure is repeated on two or three occasions her resentment and suspicion begin to show. This increases his anxiety and arouses his fear. This fear makes the husband unresponsive to sexual stimulation and incapable of achieving erection. His earlier 'I don't want to' now becomes 'I can't', and the harder he tries to work up excitement the more adamantly his sexual organs refuse to be aroused by love-play with his wife, by masturbation, or by any other device he may employ to produce and retain his erection. He finally concludes that he has become impotent. The fear that this condition is organic—probably, he thinks, a retribution for youthful sexual escapades—is added to the original anxiety. This, of course, exacerbates the victim's condition. In fact, his impotence is functional, a sexual symptom of a non-sexual neurosis. But he rarely thinks of this explanation, and seldom believes his doctor or psychiatrist when they present it to him.

Some years ago a psychologist was consulted by a young professional man who had recently got married. On the first night of the honeymoon his desire for his wife was replaced by a strong aversion, a few minutes after he had begun to make love to her. He could not account for this feeling and would not, for obvious reasons, admit

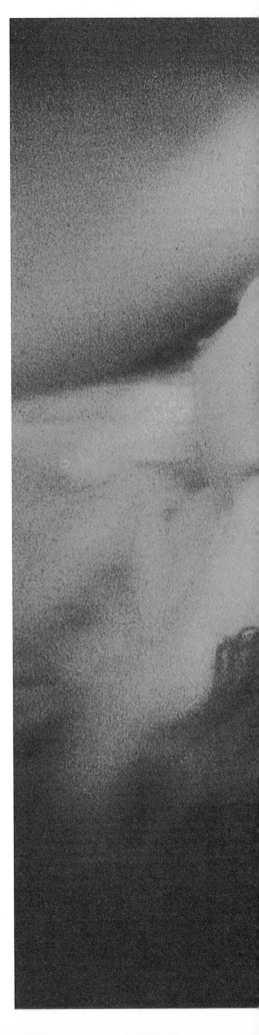

it to his wife. He explained away his incapacity by saying that the strain of the wedding ceremony and subsequent journey had exhausted him. Six months later the marriage was still unconsummated and both partners were on the edge of despair.

During one of the consultations, the young man suddenly remembered an experience in early boyhood. At the age of six he was sleeping in a cot in his parents' bedroom when, one night, he was awakened by an unfamiliar noise. He opened his eyes and saw his mother urinating into a chamber pot. She was crouched over it facing him. He had a clear frontal view of her genitals and pubic hair. The spectacle shocked and disgusted him, and he felt very guilty at having inadvertently seen a forbidden thing. He later forgot the traumatic experience, but it had made its mark.

On his wedding night, the sight of his wife's pubic hair had resurrected the intense feelings of revulsion associated with this incident, but not the visual memory that could have accounted for them. His wife was persuaded to remove her pubic hair, the husband recovered his potency, and their love-making became normal and fully satisfying.

Hidden fears, the result of suggestions implanted in early life and uncritically accepted, are far commoner causes of neurosis than overt anxieties. Few children are fortunate in their early learning about sex. The Western social climate is still infested with taboos, superstitions, and misunderstandings that, very early in life, colour children's views. They pick up from their elders, as well as from contemporaries, the idea that sex is something shameful, sinful, forbidden. When, with the approach of puberty, the signs of this mysterious force become clear to them, they are fascinated and frightened. They discuss it eagerly among themselves, yet feel guilty because they are curious about it.

Even in the 'permissive society', many young people embark upon the adventure of marriage ill-informed or misinformed about sex, and unprepared emotionally to deal with the psychological tensions through which their hidden fears, shames, and guilt feelings rise to expression. These may remain latent for years, but they become convenient pegs on which to hang explanations when a man becomes impotent for no apparent reason.

For example, a husband in his forties is seized by an infatuation for a girl on the staff of the firm he works for. The tension of conflicting loyalties makes him impotent with his wife and his girl friend as well. How does he account for his disability? By recalling that when he was twelve he read a book about sex that frightened him by telling him that boys who masturbated became impotent when they reached adulthood. The real issue is evaded with the aid of an explanation that fails to explain.

A nagging wife undermines her husband's confidence and arouses smouldering resentment. Making love to her becomes first distasteful, and then impossible. He thinks his inadequacy accounts for her dissatisfaction. Why can't he satisfy her? Because, he thinks, his penis is too small. The other boys at school told him so. Again the real issue is evaded by rationalization.

Like the victims of other forms of neurosis, men suffering from functional impotence are adept at finding explanations that do not explain. This is because the neurosis itself is a psychological device used to conceal from the sufferer, even more than from his friends, the real emotional problems he is wrestling with. This is the reason why any man troubled by impotence should seek professional advice about it at the earliest opportunity. His own doctor will almost certainly be able to ascertain that his impotence is functional, and knowing this alone will be a great relief.

It is asking for trouble to try to treat functional impotence oneself. One might as well expect to be able to see one's own face, 'warts and all', without the aid of a mirror. Nevertheless, many men do expect miracles of this kind to happen, and often they are encouraged to do so by their wives. Married couples will go on enduring unnecessary sexual frustration for years, rather than suffer the embarrassment of disclosing their difficulties to a doctor.

The sexual reticence and secretiveness of the woman is often the decisive factor in such situations, as indeed it may be in producing the impotence itself. In a recently published book, by Dr. L. P. D. Tunnadine, about the educational work of the Family Planning Association in England, there are a surprising number of cases described in which the husbands' impotence has been completely cured, although they have not even seen a doctor. But their wives' attitude to sex has been changed with the help of the Association's trained women physicians.

Although the symptoms of functional impotence appear only in the man, the condition itself is the direct or indirect outcome of something that happens *between* a man and a woman. Sexual intercourse is a form of communication closely analogous to speech. People engaged in conversation will often reveal unwittingly, by their tone of voice, what is in their hearts, while the words they use convey only what is in their minds. A similar process happens in sexual intercourse. The outcome of the encounter, its long-term effect upon their relationship, depends much more on what they mean than on what they say. When a man and a woman make love joyously and spontaneously every movement and gesture is eloquent. Neither partner is afraid of the other, nor wants to subdue or humiliate the other. The tempo of discourse rises and falls as it does in good conversation, and reciprocity is its essence.

The similarity between verbal and sexual communication is so close that the psychological conditions under which functional impotence occurs are almost identical with those that render a person, endowed with the power of speech, incapable of using it. There are various occasions when people find themselves at a loss for words—a moment of sudden shock, surprise, or grief, or a situation where fear of self-commitment or self-betrayal has held them silent. What one feels in such circumstances has the precise quality of the emotional state that produces functional impotence.

Even stammering has its sexual counterpart. A young solicitor, eight months married, had been unable to consummate the union. He explained that circumstances had so far made it impossible for him to find suitable occasions for intercourse. He felt it would be inconsiderate to make advances to his wife in the evening when she was tired. Morning was unsuitable because the household routine would be upset. He described a number of circumstances under which he felt a woman would not welcome intercourse, and others under which 'well bred' people would not do that sort of thing. By the time he had reached the end of his recital it was clear that only a mathematician with a slide-rule could have made the calculations required to ascertain when, for him, intercourse might properly occur.

Needless to say, this young man's explanations concealed a deeply rooted fear of sexual incompetence derived from boyhood experiences and a habit of procrastination, by which he rationalized his unwillingness to make clear-cut decisions and take responsibility for them. His vocal stammering provided the first clue to his sexual stammering.

The question is often asked, 'Why is the fear of impotence so terrible for a man?' A woman who is sexually frigid or unresponsive does not usually suffer serious emotional disturbance because of it.

But, as pyschiatrists have pointed out, a woman can engage in sexual intercourse without revealing that she is disinclined for it or uninterested in her partner. A man is physiologically incapable of this kind of dissimulation. He cannot produce an erection at will. Any reluctance, distaste, or preoccupation that diminishes his desire diminishes or extinguishes his ability to play his part in the sexual act, and reveals his disability to the woman. She at once becomes suspicious, reproachful, or inquisitorial. A man is sexually very vulnerable and easily humiliated in these circumstances. Knowing this, he dreads impotence itself less than the powerful threat to the stability and security of his relationship with the other sex that is implicit in it.

Functional impotence is not an illness. It is an end result of a man's inability to cope with the anxieties and fears of his life within, and outside, marriage. It is a manifestation of incomplete social adaptation, in turn the result of inadequate personal education. It is surprising how many young people reach adult years blissfully ignorant of the language of emotion, and unaware of the conditions under which men and women can establish both personal and reciprocal relationships. As with all the common neuroses, the greatest danger lies in ignorance.

PETER FLETCHER

Nudity

Complicated social rules dictate what parts of our bodies we cover. Why should a South American Indian need no clothes, but an Arab woman have to cover herself from head to foot?

Most people in the West assume that the primitive inhabitants of the world are 'naked savages'. Anthropologists, however, who have lived among them have found that these pre-industrialized people are not ruthless savages, and they have begun to consider the customs and ideas involved in their supposed nakedness.

To the eye of the average Westerner, the Tupari peoples of Brazil are 'naked'. The men, for example, cover only their penises, leaving even their scrotums exposed. But when the Tupari discovered that Europeans bathed in the nude, even if segregated by sex, they likened them to tapirs and monkeys. It seems that the Tupari do not remove their penis sheaths while bathing and assume that to do so is indecent. Yet most of us would consider a Brazilian Tupari naked.

Obviously, nudity is not simply a matter of not having any clothes on. Ken-

neth Clark, the British art expert and historian, in his book *The Nude*, makes a distinction between being nude and being naked. For him, while the term naked suggests embarrassment and shame, the term nudity has an 'educated' edge to it and carries no uncomfortable overtones. Most people would agree that there is a difference between being undressed in front of the family doctor and performing a strip-tease in Soho.

The respectable art world, those who practise 'naturism', and intellectuals have long assumed the respectability of the nude human form. Long before the liberalization of censorship laws in some Western countries, the display of the nude form in art galleries, in magazines, such as *National Geographic*, and in medical publications, has been legally acceptable. Indeed, the Sistine Chapel of the Vatican in Rome is covered with Michaelangelo's

paintings of nude figures. How shocked many primitive peoples, such as the Tupari, would be to see Adam's exposed penis!

Very recently, various groups in the West have begun to reverse Kenneth Clark's distinction between nudity and nakedness. Hippies, members of certain types of encounter groups, and some of those who have taken to living in communes have rejected the idea that to be nude is more respectable than to be naked. For them, there are no parts of the human body of which to be ashamed and, therefore, no need to 'clothe' oneself in the respectability of nudity.

Morally speaking, there is no need to choose sides in this issue. Everyone can agree that the nude is not stark naked. And if the nude is not naked then it must be 'clothed'. In fact we usually find this to be the case, provided we accept a broad enough definition of 'clothing' to

Nudity in the cinema and theatre is becoming increasingly acceptable in most Western countries. Theatre Today, a company of young American actors from Los Angeles, use nudity and sex on the stage to mount an attack on hypocrisy and to shock and disturb their audience.

include flowing hair, flowers, drapes, and fig leaves.

Much of the clothing worn both in the West and in primitive societies serves to accentuate rather than hide sexual attributes. The incredible gourd penis sheaths worn by the men of many New Guinea tribes are a case in point. Gourd, bamboo, shell, large nuts, and, recently, even such things as toothpaste containers are worn over the penis. Obviously a gourd, several feet in length, is not meant to hide anything. Such clothing is intended for purposes of display, and is not very different from the Western custom of women wearing brassieres to support the breasts, thus ensuring that this feminine attribute attracts proper notice.

The point must be made that clothing is often an important part of nudity and of sexual enticement in general. Any professional stripper would understand why the men of the Admiralty Islands—who are normally naked—wear shells to cover themselves when dancing. Clothing is generally designed to allure, and it follows that much of Western and non-Western sexuality is based on hiding things rather than revealing them. Today, sociologists question whether excessive liberalism in censorship will destroy the fragile foundations of traditional sexual seduction. Indeed, the catch phrase of the 'new morality' theologians is not that 'God is dead', but rather that 'sex is dead'.

For many of the women of the Middle East to be without a veil in public is to be naked. Algerian women suffered great shame during their country's war with France when French soldiers forced them to remove their veils so they could search for hidden ammunition. What constitutes a society's minimal definition of clothing, or, rather, of not being naked, varies greatly around the world.

This great variety of acceptable body covering does not always correspond to climatic conditions. Eskimos, in their traditional society, were apparently quite lax about exposing themselves inside their igloos even though several families shared connecting igloos. Inhabitants of Tierra del Fuego, at the very southern tip of South America, where the climate is famous for its extreme cold temperatures, astounded Charles Darwin by their skimpy attire.

This is not to suggest that people never clothe themselves for practical protection against the climate, the vegetation, and the animal life. However, an ecological determinism fails to account for all types of clothing. The necktie, for example, offers little or no protection from the elements and yet how naked some men would feel without it, even in Hong Kong or Istanbul. Whether it is hot or cold, dry or raining, does not seem to make much difference to proper etiquette. In Paris, New York, and London, one can see girls in maxi-dresses in the summer, and girls in mini-dresses in the winter.

Although certain aspects of the clothing of a particular society will reflect the environmental conditions, the definition

*Right Sexual display in public is frowned on in every society, although it may be a miniskirt that causes outrage, or just the sight of an ankle. But **below right** nudity is acceptable in art, although the painting may have an erotic appeal. **Far right** The stripper, too, may excite her audience with her naked or semi-naked body, but she is almost as inaccessible as the woman in the painting.*

of acceptable concealment of the genitals is quite a different matter. The Nuer, a tribe in the African Sudan, always went naked until the twentieth century, when white influence made them decide to wear trousers. Yet the climate has, of course, remained the same.

More and more, with the increasing Westernization of the world, are primitive and peasant peoples adopting trousers, shirts, ties, and shoes as a standard of acceptable dress. In Tanzania, for example, the government has decreed that members of the Masai tribe, who traditionally wore animal skins and blankets, were to be considered naked and not allowed into the main cities until they changed their dress. In their attempt to eliminate the image of 'Naked Africa', the Tanzanians failed to keep up with the times. When a group of Tanzanian girls appeared in mini-skirts on a Tanzanian street in 1968, a riot broke out which resulted in a government ban against mini-skirts.

Perhaps the greatest world-wide change in attitudes towards nudity has come about as a result of the activity of Western missionaries. In most areas of missionary activity there eventually arose a great wave of feelings of shame and embarrassment. The Adam and Eve story became popular with the natives and a change developed in the attitudes concerning what constitutes the proper covering of the body.

However, the primitive people with whom the missionaries came in contact had, in all cases, possessed their own concept of the difference between decency and indecency prior to the arrival of the missionaries. Often the missionaries themselves were found to be behaving indecently by the natives. Missionary doctors, for example, frequently caused offence by insisting that their patients undress in order to be examined.

Most Westerners who have worked with primitive people have failed to appreciate that there is frequently a great fluctuation in what is acceptable dress, depending upon the particular social situation. An anthropologist might say that the people of the Nuer tribe traditionally went about naked. This would, however, overlook a very important situational distinction, namely that a Nuer man must cover his genitals if he is in the presence of his wife's relatives.

Most societies recognize that there are times when it is acceptable to be naked for practical reasons. This is another kind of situational variation which ought to be considered. The Trobriand Islanders wear pubic leaves and they feel naked in most situations if their genitals are exposed. But when fishing or diving, they find that

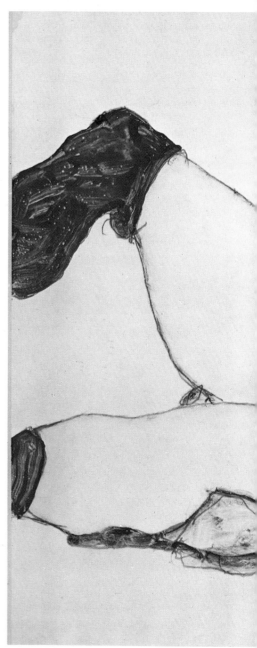

209

Picturepoint

Rex Features

Picturepoint

*Social customs in the West allow nudity or near-nudity in certain circumstances: **left** in small children at play; **centre left** in the carefully secluded setting of a nudist colony; **bottom left** on the beach, although complete nudity is frowned upon, people tend to wear very little clothing, and the topless bikini is becoming popular in some resorts.*

their pubic leaves are impractical and they unashamedly remove them. It would certainly not surprise most people to see a Pacific Island native diving naked into the sea. But what would surprise them is to see that when he is finished he carefully replaces his pubic leaf, and that he is subject to public condemnation if he fails to do so.

The traditional British and American custom of bathing in the nude only in groups of the same sex hardly represents a universal norm. Many Scandinavians take sauna baths together in family groups while, on the other hand, some North African people do not approve of members of the same sex bathing together in the nude. There is, of course, the hippie alternative: Save water; bathe with a friend. We can conclude, therefore, that even what constitutes the 'practical' justifications of nudity (or should we say nakedness?) vary from country to country and from society to society. A Danish exchange student studying at an American school was reprimanded for his criticisms of American customs. The principal suggested that, 'When in Rome, you should behave like the Romans.' The Danish boy replied by asking the principal whether, if he were bathing in Denmark, he would disrobe on the beach as did his Danish family.

But what of nudist colonies? Why is it that in many countries which are fraught with great battles of censorship in the arts, there exist colonies of people playing volleyball completely naked? Respectability exists for the nudist in much the same way that the nudes in the National Gallery are exempt from the censor. Whether this is justified or not, it is worth noting that nudist groups have had to work very long and hard for their place in the sun. Often naturists, who fought very hard to prove their seriousness, are liable to condemn hippie groups which they say are only masquerading as nudists.

A more frank approach to 'nudity' would make things easier for the censor who would not have to sort out the problem of what is and what is not art. But the censor would still be left with the more straightforward problem of what distinguishes being clothed from being naked. First, however, the question might be asked why there need to be censors at all. A simple, but not especially helpful, answer to this is that censorship exists in all societies and all societies restrict in some ways the behaviour of their members. While there are societies which accept nakedness in most situations, these same societies may be highly restrictive in other ways. They may, for example, require their members to speak to certain relatives in a special respectful language. For everyone,

Different societies have different views on nudity. **Right** *African children playing cricket do not think it strange to wear only cricket caps.* **Centre right** *Many Moroccan women would be very ashamed to be seen outside the home without a veil.* **Bottom right** *Luo tribesmen from Kenya wear only loin-cloths but paint their bodies.*

codes of dress and behaviour are restrictive on certain special occasions such as religious festivals. If nothing else, the proper feathers must be worn. The Nuer were traditionally naked to Western eyes and yet their society was quite insistent on the need for each individual to cover himself with a light coating of wild cat's fur. Even now that the Nuer have adopted Western trousers, they still accept the necessity of a covering of cat's fur.

To point out that all societies perform censoring and restrictive functions is, however, hardly a step towards resolving the problem of nudity and censorship in modern Western societies. A start to unravelling the problem comes from noting that Western countries are each composed of a multiplicity of societies, each of which face censorship problems which may be very different from those of other cultures within the same country. What is acceptable dress for a young secretary in a suburb of London may be seen as a shocking display of nakedness by her Indian or Pakistani neighbour. In America, similar problems exist for American Indians as well as for all of the various immigrant populations.

A first step towards a possible solution is to realize that nudity is defined differently for different people. In Western societies and in the cities and markets of developing countries, there is the complication that individuals do not exist in separate isolated tribes but must function in a heterogeneous mixture of customs. Mixing together in public places, they must strive to adopt an attitude of respect for others' concepts of nudity, be they more liberal or more conservative than their own. Ironically, perhaps, some primitive peoples face the same problem. The Seka people of New Guinea believe that it is proper for a man to wear a sheath on his penis when in public. Their neighbours, on the Humboldt Bay, wear nothing at all and yet are given a prestigious welcome when they visit to trade.

There probably never will be a valid cross-cultural definition of nudity. Even the seemingly obvious definition of 'not having anything on' breaks down on considering a Nuer man who would feel naked without a covering of cat's fur and the scars on his forehead which he received at his initiation to manhood. Naturists debate whether the use of make-up detracts from the naked condition. Going a step further, it has been suggested that pubic hair detracts from total nakedness. Undoubtedly, to be nude is not to be completely naked, but just how naked does one need to be to be truly naked?

TED RICHARD POLHEMUS

Radio Times Hulton

Camera Press

Picturepoint

The psychology of orgasm

Many sex manuals today imply that orgasm is nothing more than a reaction to a physical stimulus. Here, a distinguished psychiatrist questions this rather clinical point of view.

Orgasm is the climax of the sexual act, that moment at which tension is followed by release, excitement is replaced by relaxation, and—in technical terms—tumescence gives way to detumescence. In the male it is accompanied by ejaculation, and in the female by spasmodic contractions of pelvic and vaginal muscles. Although there is controversy about the precise physical processes involved in female orgasm, the physiology of orgasm is a straightforward matter in comparison with its psychology, about which there remains, and will always remain, something mysterious and indescribable.

A case could, indeed, be made out for maintaining that orgasm is, by its nature, an experience too great for words because of the change in the quality of consciousness that occurs during it. Freud maintained that we are unconscious during orgasm, and although most people disagree with him on this, there is certainly such a loss of self-consciousness during orgasm that no one is ever, while having one, in the detached frame of mind necessary for an acute and accurate psychological analysis of his experience. However, most attempts to describe orgasm retrospectively are in terms of words such as release, ecstasy, joy, and bliss, and include references to the melting away of self-consciousness and to feelings of merging with the partner to the act.

It is noteworthy that religious mystics resort to sexual, orgasmic metaphors to describe their experiences of religious ecstasy and that, contrariwise, lovers sometimes use religious terms, such as adoration and worship, to describe their sexual experiences and their feelings about the beloved one.

In addition to the difficulties involved in describing an experience which is characterized by diminution of self-consciousness, there is also the further difficulty involved in describing and explaining pleasure—and orgasm is probably the most acute pleasure of which human beings are capable. The problem here is that although the pleasure appears to be a

213

physiological phenomenon and to be the result of physical stimulation—and although, we are inclined, too, to think of pleasure as being the opposite of pain—all the evidence is in favour of the view that pleasure is basically a psychological phenomenon, dependent on the subject's state of mind and his attitude towards the physical stimulation. Anyone knows that it hurts to have a pin stuck into our skin and that this will be so regardless of our feelings about the person wielding the pin, but that being touched, stroked, and caressed is only pleasurable if we are fond of the person who is touching us. Furthermore, it will only be erotically exciting if we find that person attractive. In other words, the pleasure of orgasm seems to depend not so much on the physical stimulation that occurs in the preceding love-making as on our psychological feelings about our partner and on our being in the right sort of mood to welcome erotic excitement.

Of course, orgasm does not occur only during sexual intercourse. It can also occur as the climax of masturbation, spontaneously during sleep, and even occasionally—particularly in teenagers—involuntarily and unexpectedly while awake. However, even in these circumstances, the orgasm is not a purely physical phenomenon. Masturbation is almost invariably accompanied by vivid sexual day-dreaming, spontaneous orgasms during sleep are regularly accompanied by erotic dreams, while involuntary, unexpected orgasms which occur when a person is awake typically occur while reading sexually stimulating literature, watching erotic scenes in films, and so on.

This all goes to show that orgasm is a psychosomatic phenomenon, which only happens if the imagination as well as the body is engaged in the experience—the imaginative, psychological contribution being provided by day-dreaming in masturbation, by night-dreams in spontaneous orgasms occurring during sleep, and by our feelings about our partner in orgasms which take place during sexual intercourse.

The nature of the imaginative activity is, however, extremely variable, since it depends on the temperament and personality of those taking part, on their mood, and on the degree of physiological tension which is impelling them to seek orgasm. At one extreme the accompanying fantasies of a crude, unimaginative person who is at a high level of physiological tension may consist solely of images of sexual organs without any reference to the personality of the real or imagined partner; at the other extreme, a romantic woman may, as the French writer, Henri Stendhal mentions in his book *De l'Amour*, be so psychologically immersed in her sense of union with the beloved that she is entirely oblivious

of what her body is doing, and incapable of saying afterwards whether she has had an orgasm or not.

Most of this applies to the orgasms of both men and women but, in fact, male and female orgasms differ profoundly from each other, both physically and psychologically. Much marital disharmony and, indeed, general misunderstanding between the sexes stems from the failure to appreciate this fact—and from the related fact that, in Western culture at least, many people have great difficulty in imagining what it would be like to be a member of the other sex, and therefore lack any intuitive understanding of the physical and emotional needs of their partners.

The most striking difference between the sexes in respect of orgasm is that male orgasm is a necessary part of the procreative act, whereas female orgasm is not. Unless the male is capable of sustaining erection, penetrating, and having an orgasm, the sexual act cannot occur and conception cannot follow. Male orgasm is, therefore, a biological necessity, whereas female orgasm is a biological luxury, since copulation and conception can occur without it. All that is *necessary*—as opposed to desirable—is that the woman should respond sufficiently to love-making to allow penetration, so that male orgasm can occur within the vagina.

This difference between the sexes leads to some varied consequences. On the one hand, it may lead to the idea, which was commonly held among the Victorian middle classes, that women do not have sexual feelings or needs, and that, therefore, the sexual act was a marital duty of the wife's, in which she engaged solely for her husband's sake—doing so willingly if she was fond of him and resentfully if she was not. This attitude, incidentally, is far from being dead today and is exemplified by those women who count themselves lucky that their husbands do not 'bother' them very often.

On the other hand, the reverse state of affairs can result. It can be assumed that every woman 'ought' to have an orgasm whenever her husband does, and if—as often happens—she in fact does not, then marital trouble is liable to ensue. Either the wife accuses her husband of being selfish and technically incompetent, or the husband accuses his wife of being frigid—or alternatively, and more nobly, each spouse blames himself for their joint failure to achieve their ideal of simultaneous mutual orgasm. An American psychoanalyst, Leslie Farber, has written an ironically amusing account, entitled *I'm sorry, Darling*, of the knots many advanced American middle-class couples tie themselves into in their self-conscious and often

self-defeating pursuit of female orgasm.

The truth of the matter seems to be that women vary enormously in their natural capacity and aptitude to experience orgasm. Some do so easily and frequently; others do so only rarely, or only under very special psychological and physical conditions. There are, for instance, women who only experience orgasm if they believe that the intercourse is likely to lead to pregnancy, while there are others who only do so if they are confident that it will not. Yet other women go through life without ever having an orgasm. According to some estimates, as many as 40 per cent of all women belong to this last group.

It should not, however, be thought that women who rarely or never have an orgasm are necessarily frigid or that they do not enjoy sexual intercourse. Frigidity and 'lack of orgasmic capacity' are not the same thing, despite being frequently confused. Frigidity is total failure to respond to sexual stimulation and renders penetration either impossible or painful for both partners. 'Lack of orgasmic capacity' is failure to achieve orgasm despite enjoying the preliminaries of making love and despite welcoming penetration. Women who lack orgasmic capacity indeed frequently enjoy the sexual act very much, appreciating the sense of intimacy involved, taking vicarious pleasure in their partner's orgasm, and enjoying being enjoyed.

There is, however, an unfortunate group of women who feel themselves approaching an orgasm but do not in fact quite make it. As one such woman put it, they feel as though the gates of paradise had been suddenly slammed in their faces. They experience considerable distress and post-coital tension; either they or their husbands are in need of either sexual counselling or psychotherapy.

Nor are women who lack orgasmic capacity necessarily as neurotic as are men who suffer from the apparently parallel complaint of impotence. There are probably two reasons for this disparity between the sexes. First, in Western culture at least, male self-confidence is closely linked with the sense of achievement, whereas female self-confidence is linked with the sense of being appreciated. This difference in the basis for self-evaluation applies in the sexual field as much as elsewhere. And secondly, women often develop a predominantly maternal character which leads them to set higher store on giving pleasure than on receiving it. It does not occur to women of this kind to pursue or insist on their own orgasmic pleasure, and many of them would, misguidedly, think themselves egocentric if they did.

It is, incidentally, of considerable interest and importance that men and women seem to differ markedly in their attitude

towards one another's orgasmic capacity or lack of it. Even women who do not themselves enjoy sex feel contemptuous of men who are impotent—an attitude which can lead to a vicious circle in certain marriages. The wife's lack of interest in sex demoralizes the man. He becomes impotent and then his wife becomes contemptuous of him for being so, thereby further demoralizing him. On the other hand, men vary enormously in their attitude towards female orgasm. Some men feel deeply mortified and inadequate if their wife does not have an orgasm, a reaction which some wives deal with by simulating orgasm. Other men seem to be indifferent or oblivious to their wife's orgasm or lack of it, while yet others feel threatened by women with orgasmic capacity. This last is undoubtedly a neurotic reaction, deriving from the man's fantasies of woman as a devourer and castrator.

There exist currently two incompatible explanations as to why orgasmic capacity is less common in women than in men. The first, which derives from psychoanalysis, attributes the lack of orgasmic capacity in women to a psychological inhibition. According to this theory, anatomy makes it possible for girls, but not for boys, to remain unaware of their genital equipment and its sensual possibilities, while educational pressures make them regard it as a taboo area which must not be explored. As a result fewer women than men discover their orgasmic capacity during childhood and adolescent masturbation.

In addition, the sexual act is all too readily, again for anatomical reasons, initially conceived by girls as a dangerous attack, in which an enormous penis is thrust into a vagina too small to receive it. As a result the capacity to respond fully during the sexual act may be inhibited by 'penetration-anxiety', by the dread of being damaged or destroyed by the penis. According to this inhibition theory orgasmic incapacity in women is always, in principle, a symptom of a deeper fear which should be treatable by psychotherapy.

The second theory, which derives from the study of anthropology, asserts that female orgasmic capacity, on the contrary, is not a general, inborn potentiality but a special aptitude, somewhat analogous to musical ability, which some women have and others lack, and which some societies value and cultivate and others ignore. Proponents of this theory point out that female orgasm fulfils no known biological function, occurs in no animal other than man, and that incapacity for it seems to be compatible with normal mental health.

They also assert that there are several cultures in which not even verbal recognition is given to the possibility of female orgasm, but in which, nonetheless, women are considered to enjoy sexual intercourse as much if not more than men. According to this aptitude theory, orgasmic incapacity in women is only a symptom if it is accompanied by a general lack of enjoyment of sexual intercourse, and the demand that all women should have orgasms, which is current in most 'advanced' circles today, is not only doomed to non-fulfilment but may also be demoralizing for both non-orgasmic women and their partners. Such couples, may, indeed, need to be liberated from what has been called 'the tyranny of the female orgasm'.

It is generally and probably correctly assumed that psychological factors enter more into women's sexual responsiveness than into men's, but it is difficult to know to what extent this is due to biological or to social factors. In Western society women are markedly less interested in dirty jokes, pornographic literature, and filthy pictures than men, and it is rare for a woman to assess a man's attractiveness solely in terms of his vital statistics. It is, however, difficult to know whether one should seek to explain this difference between men and women in terms of women's greater inhibitions about physical sex or men's apparently greater tendency to sexual perversion. It is, however, possible to list a number of reasons which probably contribute to the greater psychologization of sex in women than in men.

First, women are in general smaller and physically weaker than men. This, combined with the fact that for girls the initial, childhood conception of sexual intercourse is often an alarming one and that the conventional position for it puts the woman physically at the mercy of the man, means that women have a greater need than men to trust their partner and to assure themselves that the man's vigour will be tempered by gentleness and affection. However, too much cannot be made of this point, since many men are frightened of women and require assurances that the woman they sleep with is not a bitch or a harpy, while the claim of many other men that they could be potent with any physically attractive woman is often an idle boast.

Secondly, for obvious reasons, women have a greater, built-in awareness than men of the connection between sexual intercourse and pregnancy. As a result they appreciate that any man they have intercourse with is one by whom they might very well have a child, a consideration which is likely to influence their choice of sexual partners, and to make them attracted by men whose children they would be proud to bear. But this reason for women assessing men in terms of their potential role of father to their children would cease to apply if absolute faith in the reliability of contraceptives ever became general.

Thirdly, women's self-confidence tends, in Western society at least, to be based on their sense of being admired and appreciated. As a result, women are only likely to relax and feel sufficiently at ease to enjoy sexual relations if the man gives her evidence that, in addition to desiring her physically, he also loves her and appreciates her value as a person. One of the commonest complaints made by wives against their husbands is that he takes her for granted, that he uses her as a convenience and omits to court her before having sexual relations. These complaints—and the similar ones often levelled by husbands at their wives that, for example, she will always insist on doing the washing up just when he feels like making love—show, yet again, that many sexual difficulties and misunderstandings seem to arise from the fact that in the West too many people grow up and marry without acquiring any conception of what it feels like to be a member of the other sex, to appreciate their hopes, desires, and fears, and are therefore unwittingly tactless and unimaginative in their intimate relations with their spouses.

Fourthly, if it is indeed true that about 40 per cent of women rarely, if ever, have an orgasm, the motivation for having sexual relations for many women cannot be, as it may be for men, the conscious wish to relieve physical tension and must therefore be solely for the sake of its psychological value as an affirmation of love, and as an opportunity for intimacy and closeness.

It cannot be over-emphasized that there is something paradoxical about orgasm and the role it plays in human affairs. On the one hand, it is a physical phenomenon, an instinctual need or appetite, which almost all men and most women crave, and which can be satisfied egocentrically, either solitarily by masturbation or by exploitation of a willing or reluctant object. On the other hand, it is the psychological experience which can lead to the greatest feeling of loss of self-consciousness and union with each other, of which mankind is capable. It is indeed *the* psychosomatic (mind and body) experience, combining in one event the most intense physical pleasure with the most spiritual sense of ecstasy, and the most lively sense of being oneself with that of transcending oneself. When, as too often happens, it is artificially divided into its physical and psychological components, it forms the central theme of, on the one hand, dirty jokes and, on the other, of much of the greatest romantic poetry and mystical literature of the world.

CHARLES RYCROFT

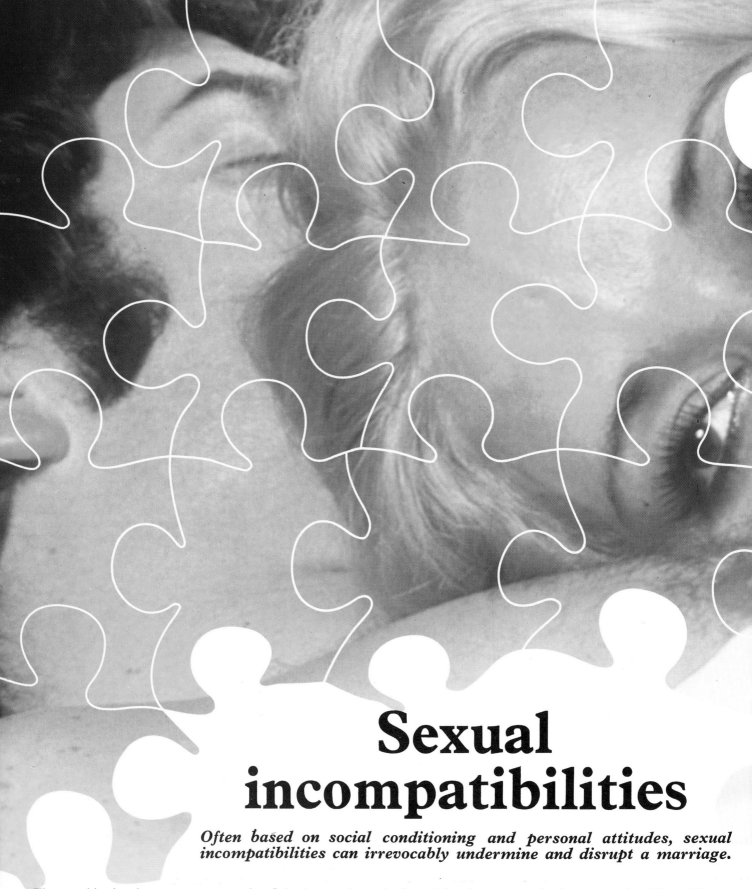

Sexual incompatibilities

Often based on social conditioning and personal attitudes, sexual incompatibilities can irrevocably undermine and disrupt a marriage.

The sexual instinct is so strong, so natural, that very few unmarried people realize that a good sexual relationship is seldom automatically achieved.

In the immediacy of love-making our physical responses burst upon us with an urgency which we cannot totally control. The urge to make love is rightly regarded as a pleasant and natural instinct. This desire crystallizes when we fall in love. We may

feel nervous about the first night, about the physical side of the honeymoon, but really that is the least of our problems. Or so we think. Most people enter into marriage in a state of intense sexual expectation and they rely upon their love for the partner and their instinctive sexual urge to carry them through.

This may not be sufficient. Of course, a lot of the barely concealed disappointments

over the honeymoon breakfast table may be essentially unimportant. The first time two people make love is unlikely to be a complete success. Lovers need time to get to know each other physically, as well as emotionally and mentally. The first time a couple have sexual intercourse is nearly always beset by tensions, fears, and a sense of emotional strain, all of which can affect sexual performance. As the couple

learn to relax, the failures and disappointments should vanish.

But if familiarity and growing mutual relaxation do not eradicate the difficulties then obviously more drastic measures are required if the sexual aspect of the relationship is to be satisfactory.

Sex provides a good basis for marriage as a whole. It is the fullest expression of two people's love for each other and so it is important as a means of reassurance. Many petty quarrels have been resolved in bed but, equally, many minor irritations have taken root there and have been exaggerated by subsequent sexual frustration. Intercourse, on a simple physical level, provides a couple with an important release from sexual tension which builds up quite naturally. If this necessary release is not attained other areas of life can be adversely affected and strained.

After only six months of marriage Tony thought that he had made a terrible mistake. The attractive girl he loved and married now seemed to be a bad-tempered virago. 'Everything I say is wrong,' he complained. 'It's getting so that I have to watch every word. It's like living with a volcano. The tiniest thing can produce an hysterical explosion.' As a result of being

217

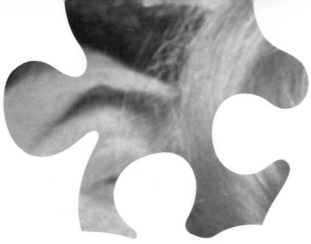

constantly under attack, Tony became increasingly edgy himself. Goaded by Anne's inexplicable bursts of temper, he retaliated. Minor disagreements were transformed into major arguments which left an undissipated residue of tension between them.

To Tony, Anne was desirable even when she was sulky and tear-stained. After one particularly fierce, but pointless, quarrel, he pressed himself against her in bed. Anne pushed him roughly away. Tony persisted.

'I don't want to,' she said.

'Why not darling? I love you. I want you,' Tony said.

'You always do,' she said bitterly.

'Of course. That's one of the reasons I married you,' Tony admitted.

'Well, that's fine for you, isn't it? But what about my feelings?' Tony defended himself. 'I don't force myself on you. You've always been perfectly willing.'

'Yes,' said Anne, 'but that was in the days when I still thought there might be something in it for me. I'm sick and tired of being your sexual convenience. You think all you have to do is throw yourself on top of me, exert yourself for five minutes, and everything in the bedroom will be lovely. Well, it's not.'

Tony and Anne were the victims of the most common sexual incompatibility of all —an incompatibility which is virtually endemic in any heterosexual relationship. Tony, like many men, had simply assumed that the female sexual response was identical with that of men. He was aroused in seconds and satisfied in minutes. He was quite right to attribute this urgency to the effect Anne had on him. But he was wrong to think that his enthusiastic, instantaneous response would be sufficient to satisfy her.

Men reach a peak of sexual readiness very quickly. In Tony's case, watching Anne undress, and her proximity in bed, were sufficient to produce complete sexual arousal. Women, however, respond to a much slower, more gradual sexual rhythm. Their approach to orgasm is a constant building of tension, produced by foreplay and a sense of emotional engagement. This tension is then dissipated in explosive orgasm. Tony had never bothered with any but the most perfunctory foreplay and was, again in common with many men, largely ignorant of the full importance of the clitoris. Consequently, Anne had never experienced orgasm.

When, at last, Anne became sufficiently angry to explain what was wrong, the problem was easily solved. Tony quickly discovered the wonder of patiently awakening her body. Penetration them became the climax of an extended act of love, not the hurried release of one-sided desire, suffered by a tense and indifferent woman.

Equating male urgency with the gentler, more diffuse (but not less intense) response of women is something which every couple has to achieve. But it cannot be left to chance or instinct. A conscious effort and a constant alertness to each partner's natural rhythm is required if sexual harmony is to become a reality.

Other incompatibilities are less common. One highly-sexed young husband thought that marriage would enable him to control his seemingly insatiable desire. Instead he found that increased opportunity only fed that desire and that his wife was becoming exhausted. 'He would wake up in the middle of the night and start making love to me, with the result that I was exhausted and short-tempered the next morning.' He required little sleep. She, on the other hand, needed a good eight hours' solid sleep. But since she had no complaints about the frequency of her husband's desire, only his timing, the problem was solved.

'I rest for a couple of hours in the afternoon,' she said, 'and I've introduced us to early nights. We go to bed early and usually make love twice. Then we both get a good night's sleep.'

Obviously, there must be a willingness on both sides to accommodate the other partner's needs. An energetic, lively person married to a slower, more lethargically metabolated individual invariably finds that compromise on both sides provides the necessary adjustment. If this is undertaken in a spirit of willingness, incompatibility diminishes. Conflict only arises when the husband is made to feel like an insatiable monster or the wife like a frigid block of stone.

Often the most distressing sexual incompatibilities arise out of conditioning and education, exacerbated as are so many sexual conflicts by the different attitudes of men and women. Margaret, in tears, left her husband, Paul, and sought the advice of a marriage guidance counsellor. Margaret found Paul's bedroom gymnastics extremely inhibiting. As a result she became tense and self-conscious and so failed to gain

proper satisfaction from what were to Paul, intensely stimulating variations.

Sobbing, she said, 'He's always making me get on top of him, or wants me to be on my hands and knees while he enters me from behind. And he always keeps the light on.'

Margaret, an only daughter, born when her parents were approaching middle-age, had been brought up to believe that sex was something furtive and largely unmentionable. This rigid attitude had been tempered to some extent by her reading and information picked up from other girls. She was passionate by nature, which had caused her to be attracted to Paul in the first place. He was virile, inventive, and demanding. All this aroused Margaret, but his frankness, his open enjoyment of variations ran counter to Margaret's unresolved guilt feelings about sex. Paul's approach had shocked her and shock had numbed her natural responses.

Paul was contrite when he came to meet the marriage counsellor. His background and experience were very different from Margaret's. She had always been willing and responsive so that when he introduced variations into their love-making it had not occurred to him that she would be anything but enthusiastic. He loved Margaret and was genuinely sorry that he had made her unhappy. He also acknowledged that he had been carried away by his own enthusiasm. Margaret would have been more responsive had she been introduced to these variations gradually. Now Margaret's fears have been resolved because of Paul's patience and understanding. He has proved that he loves her and that sexual inventiveness is merely something he enjoys as an

occasional extra stimulus and not as an end in itself.

Because they are protected and even taught to live up to a rigid but false ideal of female sexual behaviour, many women encounter very real difficulties when they marry and find that their husbands have a more flexible and openly passionate approach to sex. Some women feel that it is sufficient that they be passively willing, but not all men are content always to be the aggressive, dominating partner. Some men complain that their wives are selfish, that they will not touch their genitals, or stimulate them manually. But these women are not selfish. Many were brought up to believe that it is 'not nice' to show that they enjoy their husband's bodies. But men, too, need to know that they are desirable. There is nothing more daunting for a man than to feel that he must work for every moment of pleasure.

The most dramatic example of this sort of incompatibility often involves oral sex. Attitudes to oral love-making are still confused and surrounded with misunderstandings.

The first time Andrew kissed Carole's genitals she was frightened and disgusted. 'All my pleasure vanished. I honestly thought, and I know it sounds silly, that only prostitutes allowed a man to do that. It seemed to me filthy and embarrassing. I couldn't think why he wanted to do such a thing and when, afterwards, he tried to kiss me, I turned away. I couldn't bear him near me.'

Unfortunately, many women do not understand that the performance of cunnilingus can afford a man great pleasure. The genital kiss is a genuine and unique expression of love. It is also intensely pleasurable. Carole's physical response was neutralized by her mental and emotional resistance to an act which she thought was perverse and immoral. Furthermore, this erroneous belief was so ingrained that she could not believe Andrew when he said that he enjoyed it. Andrew knew perfectly well that Carole's experience of sexual pleasure increased his own excitement. Carole saw this, to her, incomprehensible preference as a trick to persuade her to perform fellatio.

'I thought he was trying to put me under an obligation and I felt sick at the thought of taking his penis in my mouth.' But Andrew persisted. He never suggested that Carole should 'return the compliment'. He pointed out that there was nothing unhygienic in the practice of cunnilingus and he continued to prove that it pleased him. As Carole learned to relax the mental barrier was gradually broken down. Her mental reservations were overcome by the sheer physical delight Andrew gave her.

After a time she began to experience orgasm through cunnilingus. 'On one particular night, I'd had quite a lot to drink, and he was making oral love to me and it was marvellous. I reached out and grasped his penis and suddenly it seemed the most natural thing in the world to fellate him. I really wanted to. Nothing else would do.'

It took a year of patient, loving reassurance on Andrew's part to break down Carole's resistance. She has now found confidence, a sense of liberation in her love-making, despite her earlier belief that Andrew's fondness for oral sex made them truly incompatible. It was, like so many incompatibilities, a temporary thing and one which was resolved in the best possible way—by loving patience and the will to please.

Perhaps too much has been made of sexual incompatibilities and not enough of how to deal with them. The root of the trouble is that people are not encouraged to think objectively and constructively about the sexual side of marriage. They rely too much on instinct. This is aggravated by the tendency of men to take a superficial and mixed view of women as sexual creatures, while most women are not encouraged to think of men as physical lovers. All too often, therefore, couples bring a mixture of ignorance and bravado to the marital bed.

Every individual has to get to know his partner's body. The best way to approach this is to remember that men and women are very different sexually as well as physically. The achievement of sexual harmony automatically implies the resolution of incompatibilities. Harmony is composed of two related but essentially different elements. While it is true that we cannot control or entirely change our arousal rhythm, or sleep cycle, we can modify them, and compromise so that we do not detract from our partner's needs. There is a pattern of behaviour which allows two individuals to fit together and achieve harmony. Finding it is not a difficult task, although it can seem so because too many people still take sex for granted. Women, in particular, are too quick to assume that they are to blame and that future effort is pointless if the very first act of intercourse is not perfect.

Compatible lovers must always question themselves and each other. As one becomes more and more familiar with a partner's body and responses, so one learns from experience what pleases and when. Unfortunately, many people, and especially men, are too easily satisfied by the simple achievement of orgasm. They assume that their partner's satisfaction follows automatically from their own, and often they do not realize how far from real satisfaction is their own experience. Sexual incompatibilities are overcome by asking one's partner about preferences, by informing oneself, by learning to relax, and by working to make each act of love-making a protracted and truly pleasurable experience.

Occasionally, of course, incompatibilities cannot be solved so simply. Sexual frustration, particularly in women, is not always recognized for what it is, and nothing breeds resentment so quickly. The dissatisfied woman all too easily falls back on old wives' tales. She accepts sex as a barren chore which she must perform to keep her husband happy. Men, too, are not free from blame in this respect. The slightest sign of reluctance on a woman's part is too readily interpreted as lack of attraction or even as evidence of frigidity.

Many people do not recognize incompatibilities soon enough. They are not sure what they should expect from sexual intercourse and will repress their vague feelings that it should be something more than they are in fact experiencing. Such people often cannot bring themselves to talk to their partners about their frustrations and doubts. Many women feel, with some justification, that the slightest criticism of a husband's technique will be disproportionately damaging.

In these cases it is advisable to talk to someone else, someone with experience of the kind of problems involved but who can be objective about the whole situation. The family doctor can usually help. Marriage guidance counsellors always will. The mere fact of consulting a third party shows a willingness to improve the situation and the wish to do so is not selfish. Sexual intercourse can never be good for only one person and it is only marvellous when it is properly shared and mutually satisfying.

Tact is certainly required in the resolution of common incompatibilities, but one should not be too subtle or oblique. If love exists between two people it follows that there is the will to please. The over-eager husband or reluctant wife should not be harshly criticized for personal failure, but gently shown how to be a better lover, a more compatible partner. This protects the individual ego and stresses the essential note of selflessness which makes sex a matter of mutual, spontaneous giving. DAVID FLETCHER

Masturbation- the realities

Western society has been burdened since the nineteenth century with a heritage of fear, self-recrimination, and guilt about masturbation. Priests preached against it; physicians pontificated on its horrifying results. Yet today, doctors and sexologists alike are totally agreed that masturbation is a normal part of growing up and a natural—indeed healthy—way of relieving tension when sexual intercourse is not possible. Yet still the public is not able to believe this. Why?

At least nine out of every ten men and six out of every ten women masturbate regularly at some time in their lives, according to the figures published in 1948 and 1953 by Dr. Alfred C. Kinsey in his reports on human sexual behaviour. This was the first scientific inquiry of its kind, and the extent of its disclosures—particularly about masturbation—startled physicians and laymen alike. Yet in spite of a more enlightened attitude towards the subject since Kinsey released his figures, and although the vast majority of the population has masturbated at some time, many people still regard masturbation with a certain degree of guilt.

Although people no longer consider masturbation to be the sinful perversion that our grandparents did, and while it is now recognized by doctors that it has no physical ill-effects, it is still difficult for some people to accept as a natural and normal phase in a person's sexual development. These fears may persist into adult life—not always on a conscious level —and the psychological effects of such anxieties can impair normal sexual relations.

The common and terrifying myths surrounding masturbation can easily be disproved medically. And Kinsey's statistics make nonsense of the fear of many that they would become social outcasts if it ever became known that they masturbated. But even the most liberal-minded person can feel self-disgust at masturbating. It seems that the reasons for such illogical guilt are historical rather than personal.

The religious and social attitude in Western societies, until quite recently, was that 'self-abuse' or 'Onanism' was loathesome and sinful. Like the female orgasm, it was discussed only in smutty

whispers. It was something little boys did at boarding school and, as a result, they grew warts, became impotent, went blind, or even mad. These myths, stemming almost entirely from the anti-masturbation mania of the nineteenth century, became so ingrained in the social thought that they have proved extremely difficult to eliminate. Grandparents passed them on to parents who pass them on to children who, although they do not really accept them, recognize parental disapproval and so are liable to the guilt.

Public figures like Henry Varley had an enormous influence on the Victorian social attitude towards masturbation and so, to a certain extent, on our own. In 1883, Varley delivered a lecture to a rapt audience of 3,000 men in which he dealt with the 'terrible and destructive sin of Onanism or self-abuse—a practice as common as it is hateful and injurious'. He pointed out the dire effects that he claimed were visible in thousands of unhappy masturbators: a low stature, contracted chest, weak lungs, liability to a sore throat, to mention just a few. There is a tendency, he said, 'to cold, indigestion, depression, drowsiness, and idleness which are results distinctly traceable to this deadly practice'.

He added, 'The chief cause of disease, decay, and death among our young men is traced to this baneful habit.'

The lecture was an astounding success and was repeated by special request. It appeared in book form and a much praised, carefully revised second edition was immensely popular. His talks were designed to horrify—and horrify they did. It is little wonder that their repercussions had long-term effects. His speeches did not put an end to the populace's masturbatory activities, but they certainly had a tremendous effect on the public's emotional attitude towards masturbation.

Varley's theories are laughable today and are easily quashed by medical fact, but it is hard to shrug off the deep-rooted impression that masturbation is wrong and the vague suspicion that it may be harmful.

Even men more balanced than Varley, respected members of the medical profession, became infected by the hysterical fears of their generation about masturbation. They attributed physical symptoms to it and prescribed cold showers and lots of exercise in the open air as a cure.

Today, however, doctors agree that masturbation as a physical act, is harmless. And they even tend to think that it can exert a positive influence on the development of a person's sexuality.

Masturbation is a physiological transitional phase in the adolescent and, later, a by-product of the healthy sexual impulse which can act as a safety valve when sexual intercourse is prevented for any reason. Far from being regarded as unhealthy and unnatural, masturbation is now generally considered to be a normal, healthy part of sexual maturation.

Some sexologists believe that masturbation can play a positive role in successful love-making. If a woman experiments with masturbation, she will learn exactly which parts of her body are the most sensitive, and will be able to guide her partner in the all important love-play which precedes sexual intercourse.

An interesting sidelight on the advantages of masturbation was discovered by the sexologists Masters and Johnson in their research into intercourse during menstruation. A significant proportion of the women they questioned said that they found that orgasm experienced shortly after menstruation had started, considerably lessened menstrual cramps and backache.

Moïse Kisling: *Solitude* (fragment) Collection Jean Kisling/A.D.A.G.P.

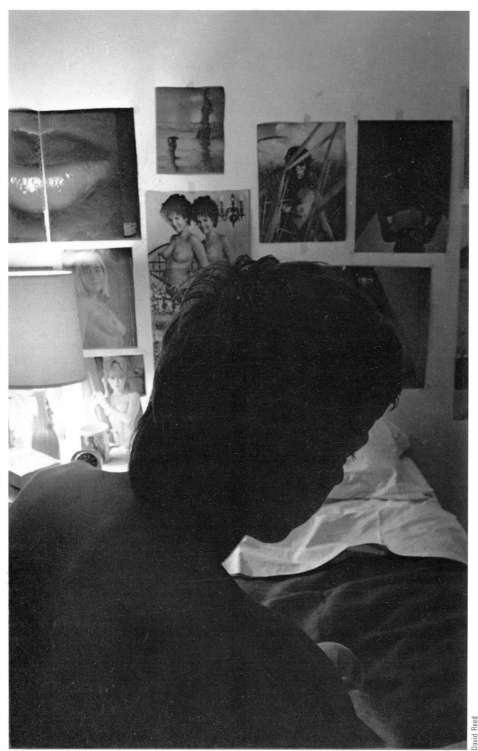
David Reed

When looked at sensibly, masturbation is far from harmful and can be beneficial.

One of the arguments used by the anti-masturbation school was the religious objection to masturbation or Onanism which the Bible called 'the abomination of the Lord'. Modern opinion says that Onan, who was condemned for spilling his seed on the floor, was not masturbating but practising *coitus interruptus*.

Such explanations are easy to accept when they are discussed logically but, unfortunately, it is not always our conscious attitudes that determine our emotions. We are all influenced by the hidden anxieties of our unconscious minds and there is little doubt that many people suffer guilt complexes because of masturbation. The reasons can still be traced to social conditioning.

Masturbation normally begins in childhood with a natural curiosity about the sexual organs. Children are particularly susceptible to parental reaction and an ignorant parent, misguidedly insisting that sexual exploration is wrong and sinful, can very easily lay the foundation for sexual difficulties later in the child's life.

Although fewer parents today are concerned with the old myths surrounding masturbation, many fear that their son's masturbation may lead in adulthood to a rejection of women or to homosexuality. Fearing the reaction of society to such an outcome—obscure though it may be—they try to frighten the child, risking disastrous results. Family attitudes play a huge part in determining our sexual and emotional adjustment. Much of a child's guilt about masturbation can be blamed on ignorant parental guidance. But the parent's dilemma is a common one. What is over-indulgence? When can masturbation become excessive? The answer will obviously vary with each individual. To find the answer to this question, it is obviously vital to examine the 'normal' pattern.

If a young child does not discover masturbation for himself in accidental exploration, he will almost certainly be introduced to it by more sexually advanced friends. The initial discovery usually takes place at a very early age, but, as the child develops interests in books, sports and other activities, the phase passes until his sexual interest is reawakened at puberty.

Experience of masturbation

proportion of people who have masturbated—from a sample population of men and women, single and married, in the United States

age in years

adjusted percentage of total male population	age	percentage of female sample
2.0	10	13.0
82.2	15	28.0
92.1	20	41.0
93.4	25	51.0
91.5	30	56.0
90.2	35	61.0
88.3	40	62.0

Diagram

There is little doubt that masturbation is going to be more frequent if the child as a teenager is bored, lonely, or feels unloved. Masturbation is pleasurable, free, and requires no effort. And it can create an illusion of love, where self-love has to be sought as a substitute for parental love. As he grows older and is able to enjoy a normal sexual relationship, and the opportunities for sexual intercourse become more frequent, there will be less need for masturbation.

Fantasizing while masturbating often accentuates underlying guilt feelings, although fantasies themselves are a perfectly normal part of any sexual activity. Few people masturbate as a mechanical procedure. In most cases, erotic thoughts stimulate sexual pleasure—the face of an unattainable film star or even a girl friend or boy friend—these are quite natural uses of the imagination. However, totally unrealistic fantasies, perhaps expressing hostility towards women, are symptoms of underlying problems.

The extent to which masturbation is pleasurable depends very much on the extent of the guilt associated with it, but the physical release of sexual tension is the same as if intercourse had taken place, although the climax may not be as intense.

Before contraception became sophisticated and accessible to the majority of the population, masturbation was, for many, a necessary alternative to intercourse. And there are instances when continual masturbation in adulthood is perfectly normal—in prisons, the army, or when intercourse in marriage is impossible. But it is when masturbation is preferred to normal intercourse in adulthood, that it may be called abnormal. When it becomes the exclusive form of sexual expression even though there are other alternatives, it may be called excessive.

Within the normal pattern, masturbation has no harmful effects at all. Most people, no matter how frequently they may have masturbated before, grow out of the phase in their late teenage years or when they marry. But many people still continue to go to their doctors complaining of physical repercussions—such as lassitude, premature ejaculation, and impotence. These symptoms may be physical manifestations of the psychological difficulties resulting from guilt about masturbation, but are never a direct result of it.

One of the most common myths about masturbation is that lassitude is caused by loss of the 'vital fluid'. Not surprisingly, Henry Varley had quite a lot to say about this. On the value of the 'vital fluid', he wrote: 'It imparts muscular strength to the body, it gives strength to the hair, depth of tone and masculine power to the voice, manliness and dignity to the countenance and walk, energy, ardour, noble, daring and endurance to the mind, Hence, the loss of it cannot fail to produce extreme debility, disorder, wretchedness both to body and mind.' All of which is, of course, absolute nonsense.

The body does not contain a fixed amount of semen, this 'vital fluid'. The 300 million sperm that are released in each emission are continuously being produced in the testes. When there is no opportunity for intercourse, there may be a spontaneous emission if they are not released by masturbation. The production of sperm, however, slows down to a certain extent if regular intercourse does not take place.

The lassitude that can follow masturbation is one result of the depressive guilt an individual may feel—and unfortunately often does—as a result of it. Such self-recrimination will naturally entail the expenditure of enormous nervous energy.

Because the basic reason for masturbating is to produce a quick orgasm, many people fear that it can lead to premature ejaculation and an inability to sustain an erection in intercourse. In such cases, the problem is the man's attitude towards women, and his need to adjust emotionally.

The psychological effects of subconscious guilt derived from masturbating in youth can occasionally appear in middle age, when the long-expected punishment for childhood sins arrives in the form of impotence. However, individuals who grow out of the masturbatory phase in the normal way, even though they may have felt guilty about it at the time, rarely suffer any mental or physical ill-effects afterwards.

A more realistic example of how masturbation can have harmful repercussions is the case of a boy whose parents were divorced. He lived with his mother, who tried to turn him into a husband substitute. He was educated to hate all other women by her insistence that all girls are out 'for what they can get' and he should keep away from them. As he grew older though, he developed a normal, healthy sexual desire for women which, because of his upbringing, he had to repress. To express his desire he masturbated, and his masturbation thus became an expression of his hostility towards women. Ultimately he was unable to have normal intercourse.

But this extreme case is an exception. Generally speaking, if there is an unpleasant reaction, it is the feeling of self-disgust and guilt immediately after the act of masturbation. Such self-recrimination is unnecessary. Masturbation should be viewed as a natural part of sexual development. For adults, where normal sexual relationships are impossible, it should be looked upon as a safety valve which relieves sexual tension.

If guilt is felt at one's own masturbatory activities, it is important to recognize the reasons, and so overcome the stress the guilt causes. It is only when masturbation is preferred to sexual intercourse that medical help should be sought.

The way a parent views a child's masturbation can be of the utmost importance in the child's development. It should be treated as a normal phase which passes as sexual maturation progresses. Most doctors recommend that it should not be ignored, that it is discussed with the child. It should be mentioned casually and treated without complications, so that the child is not made to feel guilty about it. He should be made to feel that he is maturing in the way his parents did—as everyone does.

That the guilty Western attitude to masturbation arises from social and historical reasons and has no basis whatsoever in medical fact, becomes evident when Western society is compared to other cultures. In certain West Indian communities, for example, masturbation is totally accepted as a normal part of life. And although the West Indians have problems in other areas, studies have shown that excessive guilt and self-recrimination as the result of masturbation are certainly not among them. They have been fortunate in escaping the Henry Varleys of this world. BARBARA TONER

Frequency of masturbation
average weekly frequency of active cases related to age and marital status—from a sample population of men and women in the United States

married	single	age group	single	married
	2.36	below 16	1.4	
0.43	1.66	16-20	1.0	1.1
0.45	1.37	21-25	0.9	0.6
0.42	1.22	26-30	0.9	0.6
0.36	1.02	31-35	0.9	0.5
0.35	1.20	36-40	0.9	0.6
0.34	1.01	41-45	1.0	0.6
0.30	1.15	46-50	1.0	0.5
0.38		51-55	1.0	0.4
0.22		56-60		0.2

Sexual inhibitions

When modern man asks psychological experts to help him 'get rid of his inhibitions', he usually thinks foremost of any inhibitions that may impede his proper sexual enjoyment.

The layman's priorities in this respect tally remarkably with those of Freud, who, when he wrote *Inhibitions, Symptoms and Anxiety* in 1926, placed disturbances of sexual function at the head of his list of the effects of inhibition on man's normal life. However, Freud went on to list other 'instinctual' activities, such as eating, walking, and even work, as subject to the same sort of restriction.

Where the layman does not follow Freud is in Freud's concept of sexuality, or unconscious ideas associated with early sensual experiences of the young child, as affecting all sorts of pleasurable activities that are not, in the usual adult sense of the word, sexual.

The link between inhibitions, symptoms, and anxiety derives from the effects of anxiety, usually unconscious, that arise when some function, such as sexuality or aggressiveness, would normally be put into action. Either the function is stopped or restricted (inhibition), or it is altered into some unusual type of behaviour or feeling (symptom). And there may or may not be an awareness of anxiety at the same time as the inhibited or symptomatic behaviour appears.

The anxiety which underlies or accompanies both types of reaction is a warning that the individual, if he yields to his natural urge to perform a pleasurable activity, will be liable to some danger. So he had best put on the brakes and inhibit his impulse, or disguise it into the shape of a symptom.

Human behaviour is constantly affected by inhibitions. At an early age children are conditioned to ideas of decorum and modesty. Because of this, as they mature, people are prevented from behaving in ways that others might find objectionable. Eating habits, manners of speech, and the way people meet and become acquainted are all affected by inhibitions.

A clear demonstration of how strong these social inhibitions are can be found in attitudes to nudity. In industrial societies most people are inhibited about nudity because nakedness has specifically sexual overtones for them. To see, out of intimate context, a man's penis, or a woman's breasts, buttocks, or genitals, is considered shocking and, often, titillating.

John Garrett

Anxiety about nakedness is strong and results in people wearing unnecessary clothing to cover themselves. And it may cause considerable pain and embarrassment if nakedness is accidentally encountered. The taboo on nudity also leads to some people's attraction to strip shows and 'girlie' pictures. Even between a husband and wife nakedness can cause embarrassment, and some couples always undress and have sexual intercourse in the dark, and thus avoid seeing each other's bodies. This same modesty sometimes makes people even ashamed to look at their own bodies, or to examine their own sexual organs.

Attitudes to modesty change swiftly, however. Until recently a woman who covered her body discreetly and did not flaunt her sexuality was considered decorous and modest, and, therefore, admirable. Today such a girl might be considered prudish and sexually inhibited in her behaviour with the opposite sex. The more permissive societies of the West now accept nudity on the stage and the young tend to be less inhibited about their own nakedness and that of other's. They may enjoy mixed nude bathing and not be afraid to see each other unclothed in other, non-sexual, circumstances. Certainly, Western society has moved a long way from the obsessive prudery of the Victorians, whose sexual inhibitions were exceptional even when compared with earlier periods of history.

In the relationship between a man and a woman it is probable that sexual inhibitions cause more unhappiness and suffering than any other type of interpersonal conflict, and excessive modesty may be merely a symptom of far more serious sexual problems.

A common form of sexual inhibition in men is impotence. This may vary from complete aversion to the sexual act, to an inability to obtain an erection by the normal preliminaries to love-making. In other cases a man may be unable to sustain an erection sufficiently long to produce satisfaction for his partner, or even to achieve orgasm himself. One common form of partial impotence is termed premature ejaculation, the man having his ejaculation either before or shortly after he has effected penetration of the vagina. This probably leaves the woman stimulated but unsatisfied, and both partners may feel humiliated and tense.

Impotence is by no means unusual when an inexperienced man is making his first

225

Top *Despite the rigid views of the Church on chastity and modesty, the crowded living conditions of Medieval Europe made privacy a luxury that few could afford. Mixed bathing was practical and not considered shocking or immodest. The puritanical obsession of the Victorians with covering their bodies, **centre,** even when bathing in the sea, now seems ridiculous. Modern society has, to some extent, overcome such inhibitions, and today people wear suitably brief clothing on public beaches **below**. But even this covering would not be necessary were sexual inhibitions still not strong.*

attempts at intercourse, or in the stressful circumstances of an illicit affair, or where there is the possibility of being disturbed during love-making. It can also occur in any well-sexed, normal man when he is emotionally upset, unduly fatigued, or otherwise disturbed for various reasons.

Occasional impotence is nothing to worry about and an understanding partner will disregard it. But where there is an inhibition that does not yield to practice or more favourable circumstances, the matter should be taken more seriously. Not only does habitual impotence deny a man and his partner proper mutual enjoyment of their sexual life, it strikes at the roots of the man's self-esteem and may incur the contempt or grudging pity of the woman, unless she is exceptionally understanding.

Men who suffer from habitual impotence, or who derive little or no pleasure from the occasions when they do manage to perform the male role successfully, may suffer a conflict about their male sexuality derived from very early life.

Often, they have been reared in an unusually close, emotional relationship with their mother, or with sisters, or other female relatives. As their early childish experiences of attraction to the opposite sex have been closely tied with persons forbidden by the barriers against incest, such men may grow up to feel that all intimate physical contact with a woman is taboo. Very often, too, the boy kept too close to his mother may turn to other boys with unusual fervour during his adolescence. The normal phase of homosexual attraction to other boys, ranging from hero-worship to frank homosexual acts, may then prove so attractive that the youngster cannot outgrow it when he emerges from adolescence.

Peter suffered from almost total impotence from his early 20s, when he first began to attempt to have sexual affairs with girls. He was the youngest in his family. He had been a handsome child and his mother had made more fuss of him than of his brothers. At school he was a 'pretty boy', subject to more than the usual amount of homosexual attention from fellow-pupils, and he had enjoyed taking a passive role with other boys. But at university Peter felt afraid of openly joining other homosexuals and began to try to establish himself as a normal young man, with normal interests in girls and sport. He was still good-looking and he had a number of girl friends. But as soon as an affair began to get 'serious', Peter would panic. He either picked a quarrel with the girl to end the affair or, if he had got so far as to take her to bed, became impotent.

This pattern was repeated for some years until Peter fell in love with a girl who showed more than average devotion and determination in helping him resolve his immature difficulties. With the aid of psychiatric treatment and his girl friend's loyalty, Peter was at last enabled to overcome his sexual inhibition and enjoy a normal married life.

Many men are impotent with one woman, or one type of woman, and not with others. In such instances, it is often found that a man has a mental split between feelings of tenderness and love, and those of physical desire. If he respects and loves a woman, a man like this may see her as being above a base, physical relationship, and so, if he tries to approach her sexually, he fails in the attempt. He may be able to feel sexual lust only for a woman whom he considers earthy, sensual, and somehow socially or morally inferior to him.

Other men may be impotent because, in their early development, their aggressive instincts have become 'bad' and thought to be dangerous. This fear is such that aggressive instincts must be inhibited whenever they might be directed towards anybody whom the man loves or respects. Because male sexuality needs some measure of aggression to be successful, such men may easily become impotent with any woman whom they love, and who is not herself prepared to take the initiative and thus show some aggression herself.

Some inhibitions are created very early in life. A young child of either sex is naturally attracted to the parent of the opposite sex, and feels the parent of the same sex to be a rival for the affections of the beloved one. Thus, a small boy often declares that, when he grows up, he is going to marry Mummy. At the same time, in normal circumstances, the boy at this age (about four years old) is usually a great admirer of his father, and his wish to oust his hero from the mother's affections leads to what Freud called the Oedipus conflict.

Freud suggested that the myth of Oedipus, who murdered his father and married his mother, had arisen because it so dramatically conveys the central conflict in the psychosexual development of the human child. Its theme is recognizable in works like *Hamlet*, *Macbeth*, *Don Giovanni*, *Faust*, and *Tristram and Isolde*, in all of which defiance of an older, more powerful man—or a king, or God himself—is fatally involved in a young hero's quest for his ideal love (mother, queen, angelic being).

The inhibition brought about in a man's personality by an unresolved Oedipus complex may lead him, subconsciously, to seek out only women who are not available to him—other men's wives, or those much older than himself, or hopeless invalids.

George, a middle-aged bachelor, lived with his widowed mother. He was unable to break away from his dependence on her, although he told himself and everyone else that it was she who would be devastated if he were to marry. However, he had daydreams of meeting a suitable wife one day, picturing her as a widow with a ready-made family. In this way, unconsciously, George hoped to win possession of his mother without having actually to compete with his long-dead father in having sexual relations with her and giving her children.

In women, the most common result of sexual inhibitions is some form of frigidity. As with male impotence, this may be of varied severity. It may amount merely to the woman feeling uninterested in the male sex, or showing indifference or coldness towards men whom most other women would find attractive or exciting. Such a woman may be intriguing and attractive to the more adventurous type of man just because she 'plays hard to get'. And she may enjoy the somewhat spiteful triumph of leading him on and then refusing him when he has had to make an overt play for her. She will choose, ideally, to make this rejection in company, where she can feel safe and have the added pleasure that others may witness the man's chagrin.

If she sees a man regularly, the frigid woman may be capricious and unenthusiastic for preliminary endearments such as kissing and embraces. She may seem unduly attached to her home and her parents, and may make numerous pretexts for delaying any decisive step such as getting engaged or fixing a day for the marriage. Usually, she will strenuously deny her boy friend any chance to try out their sexual adjustment prior to the actual wedding. Only on the honeymoon will her true reluctance for the physical side of married life become apparent. Even if she submits to her bridegroom's embraces, she may remain unmoved and express herself as bored, disgusted, or outraged. Severe inhibitions can make such a woman tense, so that all her muscles contract, especially those of her thighs and around her sexual organs, thus making actual intercourse difficult or impossible. With tenderness and consideration these fears may gradually be overcome, and the woman may begin to allow and finally to share in the pleasure of her sexual life with her husband. But in some cases, a wife remains a virgin, even after months or years of marriage. In these cases, unless the couple seek help, the marriage may be annulled, or continue until the husband either leaves, or acquiesces in a platonic relationship that makes no sexual demands upon the woman.

Very often the sexually inhibited woman is unduly attached to her father, or to a brother, uncle, or other male relative. This leads her unconsciously to feel an unseen incest barrier coming down across the pathway to any sexual feeling towards the opposite sex. Here again, as in the case of George, she may make all manner of excuses to herself for not letting herself fall in love with eligible males. And she will often form a chronic, hopeless attachment to some obviously unsuitable, quite unobtainable man. But she may be capable of passionate, sexual love with an unsuitable partner. In this way she allows herself some fulfilment, while she also punishes herself for her unconscious wish to rival her mother, and prevents herself from forming a satisfactory, and adult, partnership.

The sexually inhibited woman often experiences particularly painful menstrual periods from the onset of puberty, and she is likely to take all the burdens of femininity as extremely onerous. Thus she may have prolonged morning sickness during pregnancy, is more apt to complications during pregancy and childbirth, and is sometimes more emotionally upset by its stress than other woman are.

Much feminine inhibition in sexual life stems from being reared by mothers who themselves did not enjoy, or wish to admit to enjoying, their own sexual life. If a little girl often hears how much her mother suffered in giving her birth, and vague stories of how beastly men are to women, it may well reinforce her natural wish to worship her own father as a being superior to all the other horrible men of whom her mother has forewarned her. This may be charming in a small girl but quite disastrous for her later chances of happiness.

Being reared in a family where the father and mother show that they love one another, and also love their children, is the best preventive measure for minimizing human inhibitions. A young child's innate drives, such as curiosity (often first shown as sexual curiosity) and self-assertion, must be allowed expression, as well as the natural pleasure shown in his or her own body. If sexual curiosity is discouraged or punished, the child's wish to learn all he can about the world may suffer lasting damage, and his later capacity for learning and work may be inhibited.

The person whose aggressive drives have been severely inhibited may become outwardly exceptionally gentle and compliant, but he may, in fact, be capable of extreme cruelty rationalized as 'a matter of principle' or a 'political issue'. Sexually inhibited people are liable to become moralistic and intolerant towards other people's more liberal behaviour. As Oscar Wilde remarked, 'To the pure, all things are impure.'

Despite the sophisticated unshockability that many inhibited people can assume as the outer layer of their social façade, at their heart's core they remain frightened children, fearful of transgressing mythical taboos, and in desperate need of help. But, unfortunately, since their fears derive from very early years, and from experiences or fantasies hidden in the depths of the unconscious mind, they are not easily removed. Alcohol has long been known as an aid to relaxing inhibitions, but its effect is only temporary and it often provokes unwanted side effects, as do other social drugs. Those who are severely inhibited will need more lasting help, either from a loving and sympathetic partner or from a doctor or psychotherapist, before their fears can be successfully overcome.

F. R. C. CASSON

Love and laughter

Two people quarrel, they stare at each other in stony silence. Then, slowly, they begin to smile and the smile turns into a burst of laughter. The wound has been healed. Laughter, one of the most intriguing aspects of human behaviour, continually affects our lives.

It is a disturbing paradox that often we know least about those aspects of life which are most important to us, and most about those aspects which are trivial. Laughter is a topic which is of great importance in our daily lives and relationships, yet about which we can say little with certainty. Essentially, laughter is a human phenomenon, although one which recent research indicates we also share with some of the other primates.

A mother waits eagerly for her child's first smile, the smile that means 'I am happy, I know I am happy, and I love you'. But even the emotions lying behind a baby's smile are complex. Indeed, the reasons why we laugh and the things that make us laugh are so complex that to unravel them is extremely difficult. In this respect laughter and the emotions associated with it are not unlike sleep. We know that sleep is essential to both mental and physical health. We probably spend as much as one-third of our lives asleep, yet understanding this phenomenon is still one of the most difficult tasks facing the psychologist and physiologist.

One of the clues to understanding laughter is, in fact, associated with sleep. The sleeper dreams. Sigmund Freud in trying to understand the mechanisms of wit compared them to the mechanisms of the dream. He demonstrated that when a dream was analysed, that is explained, it was seen to be a distorted form of the dreamer's thoughts. Wit, one of the sources of laughter, shares this quality of distortion. Furthermore, one element of the successful joke, particularly where double meanings are concerned, is that it should take us by surprise. Laughter stems from the recognition of the hidden meaning. Where this meaning is outrageous, we have, so to speak, to disguise it in order to get away with it. Dreams, too, disguise and contain hidden meanings for our minds to assimilate. Jokes, however, present a further complication. As soon as we explain a joke it ceases to be funny. It depends for its effect upon its immediacy. If we really understand why we are laughing, then what we are laughing at ceases to be funny.

One particular type of joke depends on the distortion of normal emotions for its effect. This is the sick joke, the joke in which fun is poked at human afflictions. Here, it is easier to see why we laugh. It is considered normal, right, and decent not to make fun of injuries or abnormalities. Our laughter in this instance is indicative of our unconscious aggression. It is largely a release from normal constraints and inhibitions.

Release then is the crucial word. Laughter, like crying, represents a discharge of emotional energy—a discharge which seems to be most necessary. The origins of laughter go far back into infancy. From an early age children get pleasure from playing with words, from making nonsense. This appears to be a fundamental source of human pleasure. Perhaps one factor in such behaviour is that it gives us a sense of power. In making fun of the world, we somehow dominate it. The pleasure we get from some of the most bizarre comedians—the Marx Brothers, Chaplin, Laurel and Hardy—is that they behave crazily, against all the rules of logic, and yet triumph over their surroundings.

At this stage one should distinguish among some different types of laughter. But one should bear in mind that any classification is arbitrary, and that each type may at times overlap with the others. The first type is the crudest, the laughter brought about by physical contact. When we are tickled, we laugh. The laughter is an expression of pleasure—the release of physical pleasure. The tickler derives his physical pleasure through his power to evoke a physical response.

This source of fun is often thought of as merely childish, but it can play a part in the relationship of lovers. Marriage and sex manuals with their frequently overserious and pontificating attitudes about sexual relationships sometimes neglect the childlike enjoyment of another person's body which can be an important expression of love. Giggling and tickling represent a sexualization of the entire body, not just the genital areas, and when indulged in unself-consciously is a way in which a lover can cement his physical feelings for his partner with affection.

The second type of laughter to note is essentially cruel and destructive, the laughter of the practical joke. Basically, the practical joke consists of both taking the victim by surprise and of causing him discomfort. It is easy to see that here aggression is at the root. Indeed, the prevalence of practical jokes alone seems to substantiate Freud's belief in aggressive instincts. One of the major functions of the practical joke seems to be to reassure the joker. In it, the joker symbolically puts his fear into the other person while simultaneously ridding himself of his aggressive feelings towards the person.

Practical jokes are sometimes used by people in close relationships to reassure each other. The variants of the game of 'peek-a-boo' illustrate this. The child pretends to hide, the mother to look. He then reappears suddenly, announcing he has not gone after all—he still loves his mother and she loves him. Unfortunately, with adult lovers practical jokes can destroy their love. What may start as a joke can end with the victim feeling a real sense of injury and hating the joker. It is also not uncommon for a practical joker, unconsciously, to seek a victim as his partner, and to establish a sado-masochistic relationship.

One should add here that in a wider context the practical joke may be seen as a means of ritualizing aggression, and thus of preventing it from taking more dangerous forms.

Many primitive societies practise a type of ritual destruction of property which anthropologists have referred to

Laughter between lovers can express a wealth of shared experiences. The things which amuse people can reveal much about their personalities.

as a 'joking relationship'. The essence of this relationship is that one member of a tribe is allowed, perhaps even expected on certain specific occasions, to damage the property of someone in the tribe who stands in a special relationship to him. The victim does not do what he might normally do in such an event, in other words, attack the perpetrator, but rather accepts the damage as a joke. There may be in particular tribes a whole network of 'joking relationships', aggressors and victims. What seems to happen here is that by finding a ritual means of expressing aggression, the aggression itself is formally limited and is used to cement tribal bonds, rather than to destroy them.

The third type of laughter is related to what may be called wit. This involves many complex techniques. Even Freud's discussion of it, while enlightening, is somehow unsatisfactory. He likened the techniques of wit to the dream as has been noted. Essentially, for Freud, the dream is disguised and distorted so that thoughts can appear which would otherwise be censored. In a sense this is also true of the joke. But there is an important difference. For a joke to be a joke it must be shared. The response of the other, his laughter, reassures the joker. One of the purposes of the joke, therefore, is to gain such reassurance, such acceptance.

But jokes have another significance as well. They can be like black magic. In that art the practitioner may attempt to hurt someone by making an effigy and pricking it with pins. In effect this is what we are doing sometimes when we try to evoke the laughter of others. For example, the schoolboy who hates his schoolmaster can take his revenge in the playground by imitating him, caricaturing him. He overcomes the fear he feels by ridicule. Reducing the person feared in his own eyes and in the eyes of others, makes the feared person, in fantasy at least, a more manageable figure.

This is a very important clue to the use that laughter serves in the relationships between people and in one's attitude to life in general. The things we fear in life, be they people, ideas about people, or ideas in an abstract sense, always have the habit of increasing in size and of assuming alarming proportions. One of our aims is often to 'keep things in perspective'. Jokes and laughter frequently serve to alter our perspective in such a way that we feel we can be in control of a situation. Fear renders us helpless, laughter acts to size down the feared object or to increase it ludicrously, beyond all possibility of actuality. By such a means we feel we are the masters and not the helpless victims of a feared person or a sense of menace. We are often told at times of crises throughout childhood not to take life so seriously, and particularly during adolescence, when we tend to suffer from a certain sense of despair, from a growing awareness of the difficulties that there are in life. It may not feel very helpful, if trapped in an adolescent or adult crisis, to be told not to take the crisis or

yourself so seriously. In fact, if people can find some humour in their predicament, it will help to reduce fear and allow them to feel some measure of personal control over the circumstances.

Being able to laugh at oneself and at a crisis in a relationship with a person one loves, particularly if one can share the amusement, can greatly heal the rift that the argument or crisis has produced. This is true if the relationship is between mother and child, lovers, or friends. If the laughter is not used as a way of reducing the other person in an argument, but is a shared experience of 'look at me as well as you', it can have enormous healing powers. One knows that when people are asked to rate the qualities they consider most important in a prospective spouse or lover, they will frequently give 'a sense of humour' a high priority. What they usually mean is that the other person finds the same jokes or situations amusing. While this can be an additional bond, a shared experience, it is not the same as being able, in a relationship, to use humour and laughter to reduce one's own self to size for the sake of one's partner, and to take the fear out of a potentially explosive situation by laughing together at themselves.

People who genuinely have the capacity to see their own behaviour and tantrums as potentially funny at times and who can laugh at themselves, not only privately but in the context of a relationship, are often the sort of people who do not feel themselves to be desperately vulnerable. On the whole they are more stable because they do not feel so threatened by fear of the judgement of other people or of their own judgements.

The different sorts of things people find funny can be indicative of certain fundamental attitudes. For example, in Western society 'dirty jokes' have had a sustained popularity over a long period of time. People who never find a 'dirty joke' funny are often extremely inhibited people, who are likely in their sexual relationships to be strained and over sensitive. People who only find 'dirty jokes' funny also express sexual anxieties, although in their case laughter is used as an attempt to master that anxiety. Also, sometimes, such laughter is a means of expressing permitted sexual excitement which is shared with others.

Some people like to tell jokes, but they seldom laugh themselves, either at their own jokes or at the jokes of other people. Laughing is seen as a loss of control over oneself, and such people fear that they might lose face or appear to be vulnerable by expressing strong sexual impulses, or angry impulses. A person with this kind of perspective never laughs, but gets satisfaction from seeing others laugh. He uses his wit as a way of making other people appear helpless (as he basically feels himself to be) and he uses it as a way of exciting the other person. The pleasure he receives is vicarious. He dare not laugh, but by making the other person laugh he can identify with the other and feel some

excitement without the risk of losing self-control. Such a person has great difficulties not only in expressing laughter, but also in expressing love.

Laughter can also serve as a very direct release for anxiety. Most people have experienced the situation in a theatre or cinema, when, at a particularly tense moment in the production, someone in the audience emits a laugh—loud, inappropriate, and deliberate. The person uttering it cannot bear the tension and anxiety and laughs to reduce this discomfort. In effect he is saying—'It isn't real, it's only a play or movie'—and the effect on the remainder of the audience is to reduce their tension. He will earn the gratitude of some but not all of the audience. For some of the audience, with tension reduced, certain of the pleasure is gone.

People who are shy often laugh not because something is funny, but because it helps them to camouflage their embarrassment. They appear to laugh easily, readily, and often inappropriately. Their embarrassment may be the consequence of unspoken impulses, of which the shy person is often unaware. Thus the young girl whom the boy tries to flirt with, unable to answer his banter with quick words of her own, giggles at everything he says. If he is not attempting to be funny, her giggle is more likely to put him off.

In a sense, the reverence for sex which religion has tried to instill in people in an attempt to encourage a seriousness and a stability in relationships, has allowed the fun element of sex to remain largely disregarded. The way in which so many of the underground magazines poke fun at sex and the postures of intercourse is an exaggerated rebellion against the over-reverence, and a plea in favour of a more lighthearted attitude.

But for most people laughter in love-making can increase bonds of affection and enhance a relationship. It can, of course, be used destructively if it is inappropriate. No one at the point of orgasm is likely to be enchanted by his or her partner having a belly laugh. But in the course of love-making and the intimate familiar exchanges between lovers, laughter has a place.

People who smile readily tend to please other people and tend to have the opportunity to make relationships with others more readily. A warm smile encourages the other person in any relationship, be it deep or superficial, to trust the other person and to lower his own defences. Most people who are warm and loving have the capacity, too, to laugh readily.

The baby's first smile is the first clear sign to the mother that there is a relationship between them. In the lifetime which follows, despite the anger at times, resentments, doubts, rejections, if one can afterwards laugh at the postures one has taken in one's defensive attitudes, and can learn from childhood to regard oneself and others with humour, life can be a great deal easier and relationships infinitely less hurtful than would otherwise be the case.

BERENICE KRIKLER

Group sex

Today, a growing number of married couples are participating in group sex—a recent phenomenon more commonly known as wife-swapping. Why are some men and women drawn to this form of extra-marital sex? What are its dangers and benefits?

To what extent does the phenomenon of group sex exist? What are its causes?

Recent extensive research by sociologists has found that group sex is not only widespread but has almost become a subculture, with its own jargon, advertising magazines, and ritualized code of behaviour. The reasons for this particular form of marital 'promiscuity' seem to stem from both personal problems within marriage relationships and the changing sexual climate of Western society. However, the practice is still considered by many to be a more sordid by-product of the permissive society —a Roman orgy without the banquetry. This concept has often been engendered and fostered by the sensational sections of the press who depict group sex, and the people who participate in it, as 'sick' or 'deviant'. But to call it such is certainly a simplified misnomer.

Most sociologists and anthropologists believe that monogamy is not a necessary condition for human beings, but one which has been imposed by society. Certainly the compact nuclear family, consisting of man, woman, and children, is more easily governed than a communal anarchist structure. But there still exists a number of cultures in which wife-lending is accepted as a normal social custom. Indeed, a society's attitude to sexual freedom is more often dictated by practical considerations than by moralistic ones. Thus among the Eskimos, whose isolated igloos can be separated by hundreds of miles of unbroken ice and snow, the offer of one's wife to the visiting hunter is a common act of hospitality, appreciated by all parties.

The Judaeo-Christian ethic has enforced a certain sexual prudery in the Western world which many now feel is redundant because it no longer serves the needs of society. In pre-industrial society, when a man's work was from sun to sun and a woman's work was never done, the

Mate-swapping, under the guise of worship to the god Bacchus, was rife in pre-Christian times. Although forbidden by Greek and Roman laws the practice was widespread and characterized by wild dancing, excessive wine drinking, and wanton orgiastic rites. This form of religious orgy is portrayed in the painting The Wedding of Thetis and Peleus, *by the sixteenth-century Flemish painter, Joachim Wiewael.*

Wiewael: *Wedding of Peleus and Thetis*/Musee de Nancy/photo Giraudon

sheer toil of subsistence, to say nothing of outright fatigue, was relieved by the social aspects of religion which in turn influenced attitudes towards sex. The lack of communication and opportunity afforded by this society constrained fidelity in all but the most determined of adventurers. In addition, life expectancy in those days was shorter and limited the scope of sexual experimentation. This atmosphere culminated in the Victorian age—the backlash of which is still being experienced today.

The emancipation of women has afforded another significant change in the modern world. From chattels and second-class citizens women have come to be accepted as persons in their own right, having attained the right to vote, to work on equal terms with men, and to take a responsible place in society. There is a general acceptance that their sexual life involves more than their being a mere vehicle for man's satisfaction. The development of safe and simple contraceptives has aided this change.

This factor, combined with the breakdown of traditional values which followed the two world wars, necessitated an alteration in attitudes. Frustration and ennui created stresses in the marriage situation which were unprecedented. When Alfred C. Kinsey did his famous study of marriage in the 1950s he found that one half of American males and one quarter of females had had extra-marital affairs. These figures are doubtless higher today. Kinsey's study did not, however, take cognizance of the deleterious effect these lapses had on the fabric of marriage, given

the possessive and jealous feelings which they outraged. If the family which plays together stays together these sexual excursions, clandestine and possibly sordid, might easily destroy what might have been an otherwise viable marriage.

Group sex among married couples, which sometimes includes homosexual participation, is generally supposed to have started in the United States. The picture of bored suburban couples holding raffles of each other's car keys has become a cliché. It is true that all over the United States there are clubs, agencies, and other aids to enable would-be 'swingers' to meet each other. Indeed, large-scale parties are frequently organized in motels for this purpose. One organization issues car stickers to members for easy identification. A public bar, The Swing in Los Angeles, regularly projects coloured slides of couples prepared to participate in exchanges.

Couples in Britain and many European countries have not been slow to follow the lead. A London publication called *The Adult Advertiser* lists people interested in swinging. In Scandinavia, particularly in Sweden and Denmark, which have recently been in the vanguard of permissive sexual behaviour, group sex has become almost respectable. There are clubs for this explicit purpose and some sexual clinics, which operate in all major cities, recommend a broadening of sexual experience to be beneficial and therapeutic.

Dr. James L. Grold, a professor of psychiatry at the University of Southern California, has interviewed a number of

Group sex is not necessarily a leap from decadent Roman times to the modern permissive society. The whole pantheon of medieval European nobility is filled with titles and lands gained by the submission of wives to successive monarchs. These revels were often furtive and secretive and were seldom conducted at palace banquets because of the prevailing sexual prudery induced by the doctrine and moral law of Christianity.

people involved in group sex. He has uncovered attitudes which would, on the face of it, seem rather strange. One is the complete absence of jealousy. Swingers often describe themselves as having been very jealous before they became involved in group sex. Many consider swapping a cure. Another interesting point is that it is usually the husband who initiates the experiment, but frequently it is the wife who encourages them to continue.

Dr. Grold says, 'Although the external form of group sexual activities varies considerably, certain basic ground rules are discernible. "We don't cheat on one another," says one swinger. "We always come to the party and go home together." There is no pressure to perform.' Another of the tenets of the new movement is an emphatic disavowal of any emotional involvement. Many couples feel that participation brings them closer together. On their return to their own homes they discuss the events of the evening much as others do after returning from any party.

The reasons which impel couples to take to swinging are as varied as the people themselves. There are, naturally enough, those who enter into the experiment from frank physical desire, finding it impossible to obtain complete satisfaction within their own marital relationship. The resultant frustration leads to tensions which cause disruptive elements in their marriage, quarrels, and threats of separation. They claim that giving free rein to sexual expression lessens the stresses in the home, bringing them closer together than they

had been before their extra-marital indulgence.

There is little doubt that sheer boredom is another motivating factor for a large number of swinging couples. Dishwashers, frozen foods, and patent cleaners have taken the drudgery out of the home and left a vacuum of time on the housewife's hands. In the same way shorter working hours have increased the husband's leisure. Golf, television, and do-it-yourself projects can fill the gap somewhat, but they, too, tend to pall, while the diversion they afford is largely vicarious in any event. Entering into such basic relations with other couples, the participants claim, strengthens the bond of friendship and broadens the horizon of all concerned.

For women swinging seems to reaffirm, in the most positive fashion, their attractiveness and desirability for the opposite sex—swinging parties being based on a code of selection. After several years of marriage, no matter how happy, it would be strange if a woman did not feel that she no longer had the strong physical appeal for her husband that she had during courtship and when they were first married. Few couples are able to sustain over the years the intense desire which characterized the early days of their relationship. But if the husband can see clear evidence that his wife is an object of desire to other men his interest in her will frequently be stimulated or reawakened.

Many couples enter into group sex as a means of learning new techniques in lovemaking. In the case of two people who

The Regency era of early nineteenth-century England was noted for its slack morals often amounting to open promiscuity as depicted in this engraving. It was soon superceded by the prim prudery of the succeeding Victorians, who considered sexual love to be inherently sinful and equated genitalia with something sordid, hampering infidelity in all but the more determined of adventurers who risked social stigma.

marry without previous or with little sexual experience, it is often found that one or the other is left unsatisfied. Increased awareness of possible variations in foreplay and of positions for sexual intercourse may strengthen the bonds of the marriage.

Dr. Gilbert D. Bartell, an American anthropologist, recently completed a three-year study of the motivations and behaviour of swingers. He discovered that, underlying practical reasons, the basic causes of group sex are directly related to the moral expectations of most Western countries. In his book *Group Sex* he explains that Western society is essentially dualistic, with men, at least overtly, considered the dominant partners in marital and premarital relationships. Although this dominance is challenged by female liberation movements, he found that women were still being strongly influenced by men's ideas in the sexual realm. Women's magazines and some sexologists give instructions on how to develop female sexual talents in order fully to satisfy their mates. Increasing *female* pleasure often seems of secondary importance, reflecting the fact that female sexuality is less physically than socially orientated. Conversely, men's magazines emphasize male fantasy images as a compelling selling point. In most of the couples interviewed during his study, Dr. Bartell also found that the decision to participate in group sex had been instigated by the husband and later agreed to by his wife. From this he conjectured that middle-class males involved themselves and their partners in group sex essentially to act out their sexual fantasies. For the female it fulfilled a social-romantic need and gave ego reinforcement. Group sex afforded the opportunity to do this without breaking up the marriage.

What happens at a swinging party? These parties usually take three basic forms: open or closed foursomes; open or closed larger parties; and three-way parties with an additional man or woman, almost invariably single. Closed swinging means that a number of couples exchange partners and retire to separate bedrooms, returning to the party after an agreed time. Open swinging for a foursome entails sexual activity in the same room and usually in the same bed, in pairs or as a group; for larger parties it means group intercourse on the sheet-covered floor of the largest room in the house. Many swingers have a definite preference for either open or closed swinging while some combine the two. Swingers usually indulge in most variations of sexual activity, including fellatio and cunnilingus, but the majority strictly exclude 'kinky' sado-masochism.

American researchers have discovered a particularly intriguing aspect of swinging. While two women would not 'pair off', many of them engaged in homosexual activities. The incidence of this was found to be highest during open foursome parties: when they had satisfied their respective men, the women would indulge in petting and mutual cunnilingus. This seems to be accepted among swingers and some male swingers have admitted to researchers that they enjoy watching this activity and find it exciting. The incidence of male homosexuality was virtually non-existent. Three-way parties, involving a fellow married swinger or single person, usually a man, were found by researchers to be popular among the majority of swingers.

What kind of people participate in group sex? What are their attitudes and social status? Dr. Bartell's study, conducted around Chicago, Illinois, found that the median age for swingers was usually from 25 to 35 but he also encountered younger and much older couples. Many of these were middle-class suburbanites whose professions ranged from teaching, medicine, and law to executives, salesmen, engineers, and chemists. Unprofessional people were usually rejected in the swinging scene and there was no evidence to suggest that they had formed their own coterie. There was no religious bias. Eighty-seven per cent of the couples interviewed by Dr. Bartell had children whom many felt should know all about sex at an early age. A small minority went to the opposite extreme and thought that their family required careful guidance and strictness in sexual matters. In short, Dr. Bartell found that most of the swingers were very average people.

What are the benefits and dangers of group sex for the people involved? American sociologists believe that this enlarged sexual field can instigate a renewal of interest between the partners and give them a better relationship both socially and sexually. Their new openness about sex often extends into other areas of the marriage and can forge a stronger bond. Women shed the sexual inhibitions acquired in their upbringing. Because a couple could observe the behaviour of others they could discuss and explore this knowledge.

Dr. Bartell feels that the inability of one of the partners, especially the man, to live up to their own sexual self-delusions constitutes a potential danger. For any man the impossibility of living up to his own fantasies may cause profound anxiety which can deeply hurt his ego. The woman, according to Dr. Bartell, is also in danger of ego puncture. She may intensively compare both her physical appearance and sexual performance with that of other women. She may be hurt if she does not attract a reasonable number of males or achieve her own sexual standards. If one or the other partner is better and more popular it could introduce a damaging jealousy into the marriage.

Inhibitions and taboos often regulate the unchanging structure of societies but clearly in the West much is changing rapidly. Group sex may loom large and frightening to those accustomed to a more traditional, sheltered existence. They may feel that this is a logical extension of the permissive society which has allowed divorce, abortion, and overt homosexuality. In today's society sex is more accessible and readily talked about. The institution of marriage in this context is perhaps not breaking down as some believe, but undergoing a transition to fit it to the new needs of society. Group sex may be part of this transition.

RAMSAY WILLIAMS

Why infidelity?

Love is founded on trust, and in marriage a couple promise to remain faithful to one another. Why are some people driven to break this pledge?

In every society men and women form special intersexual relationships. For purposes of breeding, sexual satisfaction, and companionship, there are strong reasons why they choose to share their lives, for a period at least. In the modern world this need has come to have an institutionalized form, in the bond known as marriage.

Marriage involves a pledge of mutual fidelity until death, and most couples expect this from one another. It is, of course, a convention and not an integral part of man's psychological make-up. The sexual drive will not be directed towards one person alone by the mere fact that we marry them. Others do remain sexually interesting after marriage in accordance with man's sexual psychology, no matter how hard a person may try to repress this.

One of the primary causes for the convention of sexual fidelity could be the traditional desire of men to have their own offspring inherit their property, thus preserving the identity of the family group. This would explain why the infidelity of women has been viewed with so much greater severity than that of men. For a woman's infidelity could lead to childbirth within the family unit, and to the introduction of new kinship ties.

Whatever its origins, the promise of fidelity is, in theory, rigidly adhered to, and society has a history of punitive measures to be taken against the 'adulterous' woman, while the man's infidelity is traditionally considered to be immoral, at least. The rising divorce rate could be attributed in part to the failure of many couples to maintain their promise.

Several social factors contribute to this decline in the rigid permanence of marriage. Prostitution, the traditional means open to a man to obtain sexual relief outside his marriage, has declined. As a result a man who wants a brief extra-marital sexual encounter, will probably seek an affair, thus endangering his marriage because of the greater likelihood of psychological involvement with a lover than with a prostitute. In addition, the fear of unwanted pregnancy, which in the past could deter sex outside marriage, can now be eliminated by more efficient forms of contraception. Again, venereal disease no longer causes the fears that it did in the past, as methods of treatment are now far more effective. All these points show a changing attitude towards marital fidelity, which needs a new basis as its negative, or fear-inspired, reasons become less valid.

Opponents of marriage as an institution point to the obvious dissatisfaction and unhappiness of many pairs, and claim that marriage has little to do with people's real needs. But the fact remains that almost everybody does want to share his life with someone else, and even those who attack marriage usually choose to live in sexual union with a particular person. What is more, they may well expect many of the obligations legalized in marriage, including the promise of fidelity.

In fact, whatever theories are discussed, however vociferous the attack on marriage, most people *do* believe in fidelity inside the permanent relationship, and are deeply wounded when their partner is unfaithful. Further, even the unfaithful spouse will believe in the value of fidelity, and will almost invariably experience some degree of guilt over his unfaithful conduct. For the pledge of fidelity has come to represent and symbolize the importance of a relationship to the partners, and to break it is to accept that all is not well in the marriage.

A marriage partnership, or any long-lasting relationship, *must* begin with some sort of declaration of trust or faith in the other person. Two people consciously agree not to hurt each other, and to assume the responsibility of caring for one another and contributing to their interpersonal happiness. Together they determine to seek some form of mutual self-fulfilment. They must develop this through work and co-operation to ensure that their love remains a growing and vital force. When one partner turns away from his mate, and secretly takes another partner, this vital co-operation is broken. The trust upon which the relationship was founded is in danger of collapse by the mere fact that deceit has damaged their communication.

Of course, faith or fidelity can be broken in other ways besides extra-marital sex. In other words sexual infidelity is not the only form of unfaithfulness in marriage—a husband and wife can be unfaithful to each other in a number of significant ways by refusing to share their responsibilities. A husband can violate the ideal of marriage by permitting his wife to carry the burden of caring for the children while he plays golf or goes out drinking with his friends without inconvenience. A wife is virtually being unfaithful to her husband when she spends thoughtlessly on luxuries while he struggles to earn enough money to provide for his family's needs. More seriously, married couples can be breaking their trust when they maliciously reveal unfavourable facts about their partner to other people, or when they become antagonistic to each other in social groups. The husband who cannot, or will not, communicate with his wife about matters which concern him deeply, but discusses them with other people, betrays his trust towards his mate.

Sexual infidelity seldom occurs suddenly, as the result of a temptation which comes quickly and is immediately accepted. Usually the married person sees the dangers, and debates with himself whether or not to permit the situation to develop. It is this hesitation which allows the stimulus to grow stronger, the sexual attraction to increase. Sexual infidelity is, in fact, usually a symptom of a deeper personal dissatisfaction. It is not the direct cause of marital breakdown, but the result.

Often infidelity actually conceals the real personal problems of a marriage, or causes those problems to become worse. This is usually the situation when a 'perfect marriage' suddenly disintegrates. The partners in this case probably lacked the courage to admit that something was seriously wrong with their marriage relationship, and consequently failed to do anything about it. Once the real problem was uncovered, divorce seemed to be the only solution. This can happen when there is a breakdown in communication, when one partner fears the other's reactions, or feels embarrassed, or is merely ashamed to ask for help. Neither partner will risk saying, 'I'm unhappy. I feel frustrated. I have feelings you don't even know about.'

Instead of seeking an honest personal confrontation, both partners choose to accept the dishonesty implicit in infidelity. Usually one partner accepts it actively, the other passively. Both become distressed by thoughts of divorce or separation, and this leads to the acting out of elaborate pretences. Either may seek sexual satisfaction outside of the marriage. In just one way they may try to be rational—in trying to keep the physical security of home and comfort. But eventually one partner will probably take the first step towards divorce unless a more satisfying foundation for a life together is established.

People who argue that 'what a person does not know cannot hurt him' simply misunderstand human nature. For people have other ways than speech of receiving information from those close to them. In the intimate surroundings of the home even the most subtle indications of unease may be felt in a vague and uncomprehending way. For instance, when a husband fails to tell his wife about the problems he feels within their relationship, she will almost certainly notice the moments of silence and moodiness when he is pre-occupied with his secret. This behaviour will gradually alienate the couple emotionally, narrowing still further the areas within which they can communicate, and creating a greater distance between them.

Several considerations contribute to infidelity, but basically the causes are to be found in the dissatisfaction of one or other partner with some aspect of the relationship. This may lie in the individual, or in the functioning of the partnership.

One factor that may lead to infidelity is that one partner has a lack of self-regard in relation to his mate. The spouse, not feeling a sense of personal value or love from his partner, seeks to prove that he is lovable by engaging in extra-marital affairs. In other words, the extra-marital experience is actually the expression of an emotional need, and of hostility towards the partner for failing to make him *feel* loved. Often these feelings are not conscious, and, therefore, the partners do not even begin to find solutions to them. If the problem is not identified it cannot be resolved, and further problems may be created and the possibility of a permanent breakdown introduced.

Alternatively, the partner who turns away from his spouse may be seeking to confirm or prove his sexual adequacy, as he lacks evidence of this within the marriage. As when the object of his infidelity is to seek the love he feels he lacks, these difficulties may be real or only imagined. Seeking reassurance outside the marriage is not the best course of action, for it only superimposes further problems on those that already exist. It would help to tell one's partner that one feels a lack of love, or that one's sexual satisfaction leaves much to be desired—for in either case, knowledge of the problem may enable the couple to take a constructive course of action to improve the situation. Whatever the outcome, an expression of honesty in the face of difficulty is an expression of trust—the foundation of love.

Infidelity may be motivated by dissatisfaction with a marriage failing to realize what was originally expected of it. A couple may be deeply in love, and marry—the honeymoon the culmination of their romantic dreams. But if they did not allow for the fact that life together would be very different, involving practical difficulties such as boring housework, and each other's irritability, it could easily turn sour.

When the romance fades from a relationship that is founded on little else, either partner may decide to seek it elsewhere.

The frustrations of living in the real world become too tedious, and the attractions of fantasy too inviting. In fact, our tendency to 'dream' increases as we become more dissatisfied—and it is only a short step between dreaming of 'love as it was before we were married' and taking the opportunity to renew it when it arises.

In the same way, one partner may feel a need for adventure in life; rather than trying to regain something that he feels he has lost, this person is seeking something he never had. But here again, there is probably some frustration in the personality that encourages a person to take risks with his spouse's happiness in the name of 'adventure'.

Infidelity can be the result of hostility towards the partner. Deep, unconscious resentments may encourage one to want to cause pain—although this will be conscious only in the most extreme cases. This type of infidelity also, is demonstrative of other, less obvious, problems within the relationship.

The breaking up of a marriage is clearly not always the answer to the problem of infidelity. The situation must be examined in greater depth. For, as long as the underlying causes are not uncovered, these people often find themselves in similar quandaries later. The reasons are simple—that they have failed to resolve the personal, inner conflicts which masked the original breach of communication.

It is not just the faithful partner who is likely to be hurt by a rashly entered extra-marital affair, for sex outside of an important relationship can be destructive to the self. Deceiving one's partner has emotional ill-effects but self-deceit is more serious. It can inflict both pain and confusion. We normally seek pleasure and withdraw from pain, and dishonesty is often an attempt to avoid punishment or pain. It seems natural to want to tell the truth in trusting situations, and to be dishonest in situations which have the element of danger or punishment. If we lie to someone whom we trust and whom we love we find ourselves in a psychological dilemma. Whatever we do under these conditions, we must eventually lose.

For example, when the unfaithful partner, say a husband, comes home to his wife he usually wants to restore his sense of emotional closeness with her after he has had intercourse with another woman, but he knows he cannot tell her about his sexual behaviour, so he is dishonest and lies to her. This verbal behaviour has a reciprocal effect—instead of bringing him closer to his wife, it leaves him feeling further away from her. The harder he tries the greater becomes the emotional distance between the two of them.

Understanding *why* infidelity occurs is the starting point for a realistic appraisal of a failing marriage relationship. To accuse, blame, or condemn such behaviour only causes antagonistic feelings and emotions. Such reactions often lead to further alienation between the two married partners, and may lead to more infidelity. It becomes a vicious circle.

In the first place, if a husband accuses his wife of infidelity without sufficient evidence, it is possible that he is merely projecting his own guilt feelings on to his wife in order to relieve his own disturbed conscience. If the husband is at fault, a wife can react constructively by asking herself what she really wants. She may desire a divorce, or may want to save her marriage. If saving the marriage is her objective, appropriate steps can be taken. To make her husband feel guilty, or to refuse sexual relations will not help.

Often wives assume that their husbands' extra-marital sexual behaviour is solely based on sex, but this is usually a mistake. Further, a wife may seek help from relatives and friends, but this is not effective either. It is also unhelpful if she assumes that her husband's behaviour is entirely his fault. If she is to take positive measures, a wife must reappraise her marriage relationship, and attempt to find out if there are needs which are not being satisfied within the marriage.

It is rare that a marriage cannot be saved. It is up to the people involved to decide whether they want to try to stay together, to establish a new basis for their relationship. Infidelity, in some cases, can provide the shock that will convince the couple of the need to reconsider the state of their marriage. Before the appearance of extra-marital sex, there were two very unhappy people, neither knowing what caused the difficulty. Afterwards, there may be two people who are determined to do something about their problems.

If their solution must be divorce, this will most probably be better than a miserable life together, based on nothing more than adherence to the outward forms of marriage. Infidelity can bring clarity to a confused situation.

Infidelity can be beneficial in other ways. If some form of mental or physical handicap is present in one partner which prevents sexual intercourse, an extra-marital experience may contribute to marital stability. But an indiscriminate extra-marital sexual experience, undertaken as an adventure by either partner, will not contribute towards emotional satisfaction. The choice must finally be left to the individuals concerned.

Morality is dependent on social norms and ethics. On this basis, adultery or extra-marital sex is considered to be morally wrong simply because it is socially unaccepted. Since our social needs are changing, some sociologists believe that in our modern society the traditional rigid attitudes towards extra-marital sex are inadequate. Therefore, infidelity must be considered in this new framework.

In fact, many experts are seriously questioning the validity of fidelity in marriage. Some are convinced that infidelity often serves as a safety valve which releases pressures and unwanted emotions which otherwise could disrupt a relationship. The logical analysis goes further. A husband who is having a sexual relationship with another woman can actually feel that sex and love are two different things. Although unfaithful, he loves his wife, and values his marriage. As he sees it, his responsibility is to protect his family from any knowledge of his infidelity. He meets his responsibilities in marriage, and his wife may even gain by his having sexual intercourse with another woman, if he returns to her a more loving and a more relaxed man.

Another modified pattern of marriage could be one where neither partner expects sexual fidelity. Such an arrangement or agreement would involve no dishonesty, because neither partner would deceive the other. Each mutually agrees to remain an individual in his own right. Neither possesses the other. Each can then have the opportunity of a physical sexual relationship with another person, if so desired, without causing ill effects in the deep permanent relationship the couple share. Prior agreement is required and no partner has the right to change it without the expressed consent of the other person. It must be a mutual, lateral decision.

There are people who accept this kind of relationship, claiming that they can live closer together by allowing total sexual freedom. They would point to relationships which have maintained a deep and lasting love despite the fact that both partners have had numerous lovers. But it is difficult to find evidence of such arrangements providing couples with the same emotional satisfaction that the more conventional pair-bond has. At any event, it is up to each individual couple to decide its own attitude towards extra-marital sex and it is up to individuals to decide how seriously they are to consider infidelity when it occurs.

EDWARD HERNANDEZ

The appeal of pornography

To the addict pornography promises all and threatens nothing. In his dreams he can inhabit a world in which every fantasy is fulfilled, in which any limitation can easily be forgotten.

What motivates people to read or look at pornographic material, and what are their reactions to it?

Curiosity is invariably the primary motive. This explains why young people are so often drawn to pornography. At one and the same time pornography confirms and extends their rather vague knowledge of what occurs when two people have sexual relations and arouses them physically. They will probably masturbate, either while looking at the material, or later when mentally recalling the images or accounts they have seen.

The majority of people, however, quickly move on to establish sexual relationships. Their excitement and satisfaction comes wholly from a proper sexual relationship with another human being. They have no need for pornography, little desire for it, and will certainly not exert themselves to obtain it. This does not mean, of course, that they never read a pornographic novel again. If the material comes easily to hand, their interest in sex will probably prompt them to read it and it may provide a certain amount of excitement and enjoyment. This, however, will

be perhaps no more significant than the rather more readily accepted occasional visit to a strip-club.

But pornography does exert a powerful fascination on some people who seek out sources and pay high prices for it. A passion for pornography may be not unlike that for stamp or coin collecting and may even involve the devotee in considerable

Curiosity might prompt anybody to look at pornography. But for some the purchase of each new book becomes a compulsion, a mirage promising the perfect sexual experience.

legal risks. Obviously, if people are prepared to spend a lot of money and to take risks to obtain pornographic material it must provide them with some reward or pleasure which is irreplaceable or perhaps even essential. But just as it is extremely difficult for one who regards a stamp as something stuck on a letter to comprehend the philatelist's involvement, so the obsessive attraction of pornography remains a mystery to most people.

Two crucial points, however, define the motives and rewards of those who habitually enjoy pornography. The first is dependence, the acceptance of the written word or pictorial image as a source of sexual arousal and gratification.

Arousal and gratification are normally provided by another human being for whom the individual concerned feels love and affection. But for some people pornography acts as a substitute for the human relationship, either out of necessity or from personal preference. Whatever the specific reason in a given case, the common factor must be a failure to form the usual human relationships.

The most common reasons for this are fear of others, in one form or another, and fixation at an essentially adolescent, masturbatory stage of sexual development. Some people are afraid to form sexual relationships. They fear rejection, inadequacy, and responsibility. Other people literally do not reach maturity in their attitudes towards sexual involvement. They may not even reach the stage of being afraid of forming a sexual relationship, but are content with solitary practices. In a sense they are self-sufficient, but they frequently require the stimulus of pornography which feeds their masturbatory fantasies.

The second point concerns the interaction between pornography and sexual fantasy. There is a considerably greater demand for the depiction of the sexually bizarre than for those practices which are, in the narrowest sense, accepted as normal. (This fact, of course, disturbs many people and is probably one of the major causes of any outcry against pornography.) Similarly, virtually all recent surveys of prostitutes have revealed a growing demand for the unusual rather than for straightforward sexual intercourse. Both the prostitute and the pornographer have traditionally provided the exceptional and this is, in all probability, the true secret of their success.

Pornography is almost always concerned with reflecting and embodying the common fantasies of its readers. Many Victorian pornographic books, illustrations, and photographs were concerned with flagellation, not sexual intercourse. In the days when a woman's clothing entirely covered her body there was a boom in books about glove and shoe fetishism. In the days of the mini-skirt and the bikini this may seem laughable, but laughter should not conceal the fact that pornography is essentially and deliberately commercial in intent and must provide, if it is to be successful, that which the reader desires. There is no more certain and revealing guide to the sexual

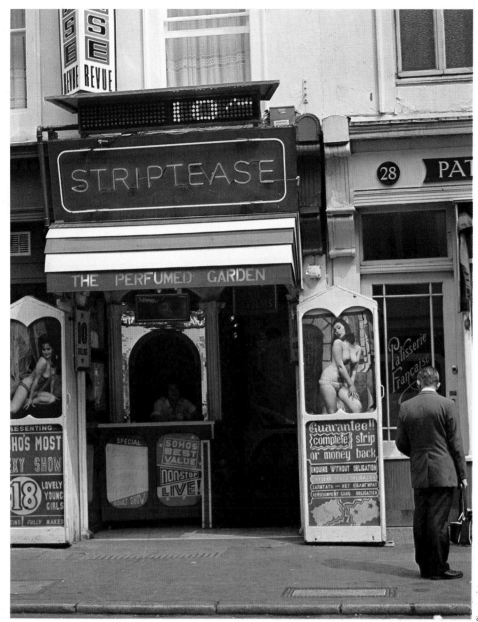

Picturepoint

Strip-tease, like pornography, stimulates fantasies and seems to offer the chance of sexual fulfilment without the hazards of complete involvement with another person.

preoccupations of an age or race than the pornography it consumes.

Pornography must attract those whose sexual preoccupations and desires go beyond, or do not reach, the idea of sexual intercourse. The fetishist, the flagellant, the man who is excited by naked girls tied up with rope, or women clothed in tight rubber suits, is virtually forced to turn to pornography to 'realize' his sexual dream just because few women are likely to pander to his special desires.

Sexually abnormal people, then, are almost certain to be dependent upon pornography solely because it is the only available means of gratification. Many would undoubtedly prefer to share their preoccupations with a live woman, but how could they meet such an accommodating creature, how would they explain their unusual wishes?

But one does not have to be sexually abnormal, exclusively concerned with ob-

jects and poses, to have fantasies. The concept of what is unusual is dependent upon a great many factors beyond the individual's control. Different societies and ages, different classes and even families, instil into individuals widely diverging concepts of the sexually forbidden. Oral sex, for example, is widely accepted today as a permissible sexual variation, not an unspeakable perversion. Yet in Denmark, where pornography is openly on sale, great stress is placed on fellatio and cunnilingus in films, pictures, and written pornography. This undoubtedly reflects a widespread concern with these activities, and such concerns invariably indicate a lack of actual practice.

Thus a great many people are attracted to pornography as an expression and confirmation of their fantasies. The man whose wife will not agree to oral sex, but who himself thinks a great deal about it, who fantasizes, in fact, about the delights thereof, will probably be drawn to accounts or depictions of these practices. With the aid of such material he can mentally experience what is physically denied him.

In other cases people cannot bring

239

themselves to admit their fantasies, their secret desires. They fear ridicule by their partner, or that they will be regarded as 'unnatural'. They are certain that their partner will not agree to take part in these sexual games, or they know that they are incapable of ever realizing them. Indeed, the essence of sexual fantasy is that it should be unrealizable. The little evidence that exists of people's attempts to put their wilder dreams into practice inevitably indicates disappointment and disillusionment. The imagination can envisage situations which range from the ludicrous to the mundane. What makes them exciting and fascinating is their difference, their tantalizing unattainability.

Pornography can bring these dreams a little closer, lend the impossible a semblance of reality. It provides a proxy enjoyment of the fantasy. The imagination is reinforced by a written description or a photographic representation. In one's head anything is possible, because one can omit the likely hindrances, select one's role, and guarantee success—while in real life other people, with their own needs and desires, are intrusive.

Pornography always lacks the human element. Women in pornographic novels never get pregnant, never pause to swallow a contraceptive pill, and never refuse any masculine demand. Men are never impotent, never tired. Pornography depicts a dream world in which the masculine sexual ideal is made manifest. The reader, or the viewer, enters into this world in a purely escapist way. The threat of punishment, whether it be by ridicule or legal action, is entirely omitted from pornography. For a moment, that vague question 'I wonder what it would be like to . . . ?' appears to

the reader, or the viewer, to be answered.

Sex, as with all important aspects of life, is something which is never entirely explored, understood, and exhausted. A person always feels the need to go a little further, to experiment, and discover, but because he cannot, or dares not, he has to invent a means of providing himself with the illusion that he can attain the unattainable. The means, in this case, is pornography.

Crucial to the enjoyment of pornography is identification with the characters or models. Similarly, it is identification which makes some people react against it. Many people, especially women, who accidentally come across pornography are disgusted. Their disgust is the result of fear: fear of being exposed to the merciless gaze of the camera, of being used for other people's sexual ends, or of being revealed as sexually enthusiastic individuals. None of these fears need be founded on fact. However, when faced with pornography many people immediately put themselves in the place of the characters or models and so experience a mental awareness of denigration, loss of privacy, or exposure. This does not always mean that they are not excited by what they see or read, but that their excitement is so bound up with guilt and fear that they reject the material entirely because it threatens them. Such people will not only avoid contact with pornography, but will probably be concerned with banning it altogether.

People's reactions to pornography are undeniably influenced by many external factors and conditioning processes. In most Western societies at least, the very

fact that pornography is officially forbidden makes it attractive to certain people. That which is prohibited is always glamorous to some. That this may be a sign of social immaturity does not invalidate the strength of the attraction.

Because the individual's sexual fantasies and their embodiment in pornography have an air of naughtiness, or wicked daring, this strengthens their appeal. Such ideas are also influential in the behaviour of practising sexual deviants, which has caused some people to regard an interest in pornography as a deviation in itself. Although society's restrictive attitude to sexuality is more truly responsible for the appeal of defiance through sexual deviance, the *frisson* of wickedness associated with the enjoyment of pornography is certainly integral to the enjoyment of many consumers.

Obviously, a deep involvement with pornography as an accepted source of sexual stimulation must have an effect on any relationship the individual may have. (The exception, of course, is the man who turns to pornography for the sexual pleasure he cannot find elsewhere.) The person who enjoys a sexual relationship yet augments it, as it were, with a proxy indulgence through pornography in practices or situations which are generally regarded as unacceptable, walks a dangerous line.

It is largely a question of the degree of dependence. Some people can understand their desire for the unusual and regard it with a degree of objectivity. For them, the odd foray into the bizarre world of pornography is satisfying in itself and acts as a valuable release of sexual tension. Such people respect the reluctance of their partners, or are able to settle for

Left In London, **above** *New York, and virtually every other city in the world, pornography is a thriving business. For in every society there are some people who never become mature enough to gain full sexual satisfaction from a relationship with another person, or whose sexual fantasies and desires outstrip both their own capabilities and the willingness of others to participate.*

something less than their peculiar idea of perfection. Pornography, in that sense, does not impinge significantly on their lives or their relationships. It is merely a safety-valve from which they take heart, through which they escape frustration. Such people are not dependent upon pornography, but it would be foolhardy to pretend that they do not risk becoming so.

This does not mean that pornography is addictive in itself. Dependence is directly proportionate to the degree of individual frustration experienced. For example, the man who dreams of sharing his bed with two women, but knows that his wife will never agree to such an arrangement, may develop in one of two directions.

If he enjoys an otherwise satisfying relationship with his wife and she is enthusiastic and willing in bed, he will probably see his fantasy for what it is— a tantalizing pipe-dream which can be occasionally satisfied by reading about or looking at pictures of a three-sided situation.

But if that same man is put under direct pressure, if his wife is a rather cold woman who regards intercourse as a duty to be strictly rationed, the sexual frustration resulting from his actual situation will

increase the desire for the fantasy. If this fantasy is continually fed by pornography, it is possible that he will develop a dependence upon it. Apart from bringing the exaggerated glamour of his dreams closer, it will also provide an easy way out. In such a hypothetical situation, a man may prefer the masturbatory fantasy to the constant struggle with, and tepid response of, his real-life partner.

Pornography, then, is something which must be handled with care. It should be regarded as a symptom, rather than as the disease itself. The emotionally-balanced, intelligent person can recognize pornography for what it is without danger, for he will know that it can never be a satisfactory substitute for a shared emotional and sexual relationship. Such people obviously do not have important gaps in their sexual lives. They are free, therefore, to regard pornography as a form of escapism which they may or may not enjoy. It will not dominate their lives, nor will it threaten their equilibrium which is why they neither seek it out, nor campaign against it. For others less fortunate it provides more than escapism, perhaps even the semblance of a way of life.

Some people, whose sex lives are non-existent, may need no more than to see a photograph of a naked woman—even definitions of pornography are relative and personal. For the majority of people, however, pornography means the flagrant depiction of the sexual act and, especially, of perversions. Yet even these may be no more alarming than a photograph of a girl in a rubber dress and six-inch high heels. The sexual excitement which such material brings may, at best, encourage a lover to excel himself with his partner or, at worst,

provide the impetus for solitary gratification.

But as well as this sexual curiosity human beings have sexual longings which, in some cases, are, for social or personal reasons, unrealizable without risk. Pornography provides a compromise by giving an impression or confirmation of the existence and possible satisfaction of the desires without that risk. Pornography may enable some people to release aspects of their psycho-sexual persona which the practical requirements of social living render taboo and impractical.

Pornography can, consequently, be alarming, both to certain individuals and as a general concept, because it gives expression to human sexual concerns which have been repressed and condemned by a circumscribed view of sexual morality. Pornography exposes that which society tends to deny and repress.

Pornography does not present something new nor can it convert where no prior interest exists. Its success depends upon meeting an existing demand. The pornographer's talent lies in recognizing the demand for a certain type of material, in realizing that some people need pornography to fill a hollow at the very centre of their lives, and that others possess dreams which can be safely fulfilled by such material.

The crime of pornography is not that it feeds the unfortunate, or the sexually imaginative, but that it is able to exploit them financially and morally denigrate them. Pornography begins with people, and it is their entirely human but officially denied motives that enable it to flourish.

DULAN BARBER

241

Fantasies

No one can have everything they want, and one way of making up for the lack is to day-dream. But our fantasies can mean a great deal more than this. What is their role in our lives?

From an early age all human beings are capable of seeing in their mind's eye. They can conjure up objects that are not actually present, and imagine themselves doing things that they are not. Psychiatrists and psychologists call this capacity of the human mind 'fantasizing' and its products 'fantasies'. Writers and artists call it 'imagination', while orginary language possesses a wealth of terms to describe different forms of this mental activity—such as day-dreams, pipe-dreams, reveries, fancies, and whimsies. Psychiatrists and, particularly, psychoanalysts also assume that there are *unconscious* fantasies at work in the mind and that night-dreams are a manifestation of their activity. They are also held to influence the normal person's waking behaviour in unexpected ways.

Many people realize that fantasies often contain a wish-fulfilling element—that when we have day-dreams we imagine ourselves doing things that we would *like* to do. Furthermore, when we are unable to satisfy some wish by real action, we are liable to attempt to satisfy it by fantasizing its gratification. In this way, explorers who are short of food are liable to have both day-dreams and night-dreams of attending banquets. Those who are failing to achieve worldly success are liable to have fantasies in which their ambitions are fulfilled. The sexually deprived are likely to have erotic fantasies, sometimes culminating in orgasm.

However, not all fantasies are wish-fulfilling. Some night-dreams are nightmares and extremely alarming, and some conscious, daytime fantasies concern events the day-dreamer would certainly dread actually happening. Typically, these unpleasant fantasies consist of vivid imaginings of being punished, tortured, or humiliated, of being abandoned or orphaned, or of losing all that one values. Such fantasies are inexplicable on common-sense grounds and can only be explained by recourse to psychopathology, which will often trace them to the day-dreamer's unconscious sense of guilt.

For instance, a fantasy of being punished or tortured is explained by postulating that the day-dreamer has other, usually unconscious, fantasies, for which he believes that he deserves to be punished. Much of the clinical work of psychotherapists consists of tracing the origins of such unpleasant, *masochistic* fantasies in the patient's sense of guilt for having, usually in his childhood, entertained aggressive and murderous wishes against those whom he believed he ought to love.

We may also imagine ourselves doing physical violence to persons whom we, in fact, would not wish to injure. Such *sadistic* fantasies are wish-fulfilling in the sense that they express anger which, justifiably or unjustifiably, we are actually feeling, but they are not wish-fulfilling—for we would be horrified if they were realized.

Although most people on occasion have fantasies of this kind, they only constitute a serious problem to persons who suffer persistently from strongly ambivalent feelings; in other words, from the compulsive tendency to hate those whom they also love, and to love those whom they hate.

This tendency, which is seen most clearly in the illness known to psychiatrists as *obsessional neurosis*, originates typically in childhood—especially in circumstances in which deprivation or oppression have led to the hatred of parents, brothers, and sisters, side by side with love and respect.

Although most sadistic and masochistic fantasies are experienced by the person who has them as alien, involuntary phenomena of which he would happily be rid, in a minority of people they do become acceptable. In such cases they form the basis of the sexual perversions sadism and masochism, in which the individual takes pleasure in the realization of his wishes to hurt or to be hurt, to humiliate or be humiliated. Such behaviour belongs to the pathology rather than to the psychology of love, but it should be mentioned that one of the reasons for lack of spontaneity in love-making may be the need to repress or suppress such tendencies. The individual holds himself back for fear of releasing sadistic or masochistic impulses and thereby either injuring his partner or debasing himself. Since both sadistic and masochistic fantasies may be totally unconscious, the individual who is inhibited in this way may be totally unaware of his motive for such restraint.

The fact that many fantasies are wish-fulfilling has given rise to the mistaken idea that they act as a compensation, and that people only have fantasies in order to counteract feelings of frustration and disappointment. However, fantasies also have an anticipatory or prospective function, since they enable us to rehearse imaginatively activities that we intend to carry out in the future. For instance, ambitious fantasies may be a response to worldly disappointments and humiliations, but they may also be the way in which we look forward into the future and decide in what direction we intend to direct our energies. A young person's career decision may be based not only on a rational assessment of the practical pros and cons of becoming a doctor, a writer, or a lawyer, but also on fantasies in which he discovers that one profession seems to suit or excite him most. Such fantasies will be more or less realistic, depending on how much knowledge the young person has about the various pro-

fessions which occur to him. But they will also be influenced by a number of highly subjective, personal factors.

One special form of anticipatory fantasy is displayed by artists or writers, who have the ability to construct imaginary worlds which transcend the private quality of ordinary day-dreams and acquire a universal character which makes them enjoyable to others. In the same way, scientists or inventors can provide novel solutions for scientific or technical problems.

The distinction between anticipatory, reality-orientated, and wish-fulfilling compensatory fantasies is particularly important, and yet often difficult to make in the case of sexual fantasies. There are basically three reasons for this difficulty.

First, in our society at least, most people do not have sexual intercourse for several years after reaching puberty. As a result their bodies engender sexual wishes and fantasies which they are unable to realize except in masturbation. Adolescent sexual fantasies are therefore both wish-fulfilling and anticipatory; they both relieve the physical tensions of the present by wish-fulfilment, and they rehearse the sexual relationships which the individual anticipates having in the future. The same dual function is also performed by the masturbation fantasies of mature, experienced adults who are separated from their partners or who are between marriages or affairs.

Secondly, the sexual instinct is unique in being at least partially satisfiable in the absence of its appropriate object. If we are hungry, we will want a meal and may, indeed, imagine vividly the food we would like to eat, but our hunger will not be appeased. The longing for food may be controlled for a while but it cannot be repressed or wish-fulfilled by fantasy, and, if we do not eventually have something to eat, we will die. With sex, however, things are quite different. It is possible, though usually at the cost of developing neurotic symptoms or a rigid, over-controlled character, for people to repress their sexual needs entirely. It is also possible to canalize sexual energies into non-sexual activities, though this process is not as easy as some traditional educationalists make out. Lastly, it is possible to satisfy at least the physical components of the sexual instinct solitarily by masturbation, which can in a few cases have complicated and undesirable effects.

For instance, for some people masturbation fantasies may lose their anticipatory quality completely, in which case masturbation will become the preferred or only possible form of sexual activity. This could lead to the sexual anomaly of *narcissism*, in which the individual is in love with his own body. In other people, masturbation fantasies may become stereotypes so that, although they still regard masturbation as a substitute for the 'real thing', their sexual aim in life is to discover someone who is identical with the fantasy-figure which their imagination has constructed. Such people encounter severe difficulties in adapting to the actual nature and needs of their partner when they abandon masturbation in favour of a sexual relationship with a real, live person.

Such difficulties are compounded by the fact that masturbation fantasies are often constructed before the individual has had sexual contact with the opposite sex. As a result they are likely to contain elements which derive from childhood experience and conceptions of the sexual act. In other words, masturbation fantasies tend to revolve round an imaginary figure derived from the individual's conception of his mother or sister—or in the case of a woman, of her father or brother—and may include details which derive from speculations about what his parents did together. The fact that masturbation fantasies often contain an 'infantile' core is made use of by psychoanalysts in their search for the origins of their patients' neurotic symptoms and inhibitions.

It might be thought that men and women would resent being treated as substitutes for the ideal object in their partner's masturbation fantasy, but in fact this is not always so. This is partly because there can be something flattering about being cast as the only star in the firmament created by the other's imagination, and partly because of the desire to please. One partner may be led to accommodate his or her responses to the preconceived pattern of sexual behaviour already established in the other's fantasies. According to Freud, hysterical women are educable into their husband's perversions, but this tendency seems to derive not only from the desire to please but also from the need to appease a partner who is feared as much as he is loved. The discovery by one partner that he or she has not been loved for his or her actual qualities, but only for his willingness to act as a screen on to which the other could project an ideal fantasy figure, is a common cause of marital breakdown.

In addition, human adults are capable of both self-deception and of deceiving others. As a result they can persuade both themselves and others that they are feeling things that in fact they are not. For instance, a young man eager for sexual experience may succeed in persuading himself that he is in love with a girl whom he believes to be accessible—and in persuading her, too. If this happens, both partners in the relationship will develop fantasies and expectations which will bear little relation to the actual course of events. When the man has satisfied his craving for experience, both he and the girl may be appalled to discover his total indifference to her as a person. Similarly, but more simply, successful seducers of either sex have the ability to pretend to be having fantasies of a higher, more intense, and more imaginative order than they in fact are, and by doing so to evoke fantasies and expectations in the other which they do not intend to fulfil.

Sexual deceit of this kind can be explained if one assumes that there are two kinds of sexual fantasy, one of which is genuine and sincere, and another which is false, insincere, and 'made up'. This distinction is well recognized by writers, artists, and critics, who distinguish between works of art that are 'truly imaginative' and those that are 'merely fanciful', between those that are true expressions of the artist's personality and those that are 'contrived' products consciously constructed with an eye to fashion and the market. Rather similarly, sexual fantasies may be either true expressions of the individual's sexual needs and nature, or they may be contrived products designed either to enhance the self-image or impress the partner.

The unconscious deceptions and self-deceptions which are made possible by fantasy occur, it seems, very frequently. They are present, for instance, in the state of 'being in love with love', when couples build up a joint romantic fantasy which the facts of life are unable to sustain, and also in various 'collusive' relationships in which each partner falls in love with the fantastic self-image of the other and offers himself as the other's ideal fantasy object. Such relationships can last a surprisingly long time, though the eventual disenchantment is liable to be correspondingly catastrophic. The history of such relationships has been tersely summarized in the saying: 'They lived happily together for years, and then they met.'

Of course, conscious, deliberate deceptions occur too. It is quite possible for a person to make love with one partner while imagining that he, or she, is making love with someone else. A few people can only make love to their marriage partners if *they* pretend to be someone else. In such instances, the fantasies going on in one or both partners' minds may be very different from the actual physical activities they are engaged in.

There are various reasons for such emotional contortions. Sometimes they arise from one partner's dread of being possessed, which compels him to conjure up a second imaginary image, so that he gives himself only partially to his real partner. Sometimes it is a technique for reconciling a disappointing reality with romantic aspirations. This solution of a not uncommon dilemma is hinted at in the story of the man who was asked whether he preferred to sleep with a woman or dream of sleeping with one. The answer was, 'Dream of sleeping with one,' and the reason, 'You meet a better class of woman that way.'

Paradoxically, sexual deceptions cease to be deceitful if they are openly admitted and accepted by both parties, since they then become playful; though couples capable of such honesty with one another are unlikely to want to play such games.

CHARLES RYCROFT

Homosexuals— who are they?

Homosexuals have traditionally been marked by society. But generalizations are misleading. Can we really identify the homosexual, or is he just another face in the crowd? The most tolerant attitude towards the homosexual is one of pity. Does he need pity, or can he, in fact, find personal happiness?

Who are the homosexuals? The question itself assumes a clearly identifiable group; a sexual minority who are strange, sick, odd, 'queers'; people who are easily perceived as being unlike the great, wholesome majority of the 'normals'.

But is this true? Many of the popular notions of what homosexuals are like are merely stereotypes. And they are stereotypes which, by their very existence, condition the thinking not only of the majority, who react hostilely or amusedly or pityingly to them, but also that of the homosexual men and women who identify with them, or feel that they should do so. Indeed, such people's personalities can be fundamentally distorted and warped by the strain of adopting either a hypocritically hetero-

sexual life-style or an exaggeratedly 'camp' homosexual one—neither of which expresses their true feelings. The need for 'gay liberation' is a reaction against such a false and unnecessary choice.

The most widely-held image of the homosexual is probably that of an effeminate man or a tomboyish woman. In *The Boys in the Band* or *The Killing of Sister George* one can recall the swishy, limp-wristed males and the butch, aggressive females who were depicted more readily than the normal-seeming characters who were also affected by an emotional pull towards their own sex. The entertainment media do not merely fixate the vulgar stereotypes as being always good for a laugh. Worse still, they make them into caricatures which too many people equate with reality. These characters may be good box-office draws, but they are often far removed from reality.

Homosexuality has been variously regarded, in different countries and ages, as a crime, a sin, a disease, and a way of life. In fact, homosexuality is most probably a universal component of human nature that is latent in all of us, but conscious in only a minority who, because they are as varied and different from one another as it is possible to be in every other respect, react to their situation in very different ways. For they have a 'problem' which springs not so much from their propensity as from society's attitudes towards it.

Homosexuality is an attraction to one's own sex, which may be combined with a degree of heterosexual attraction, but which is quite often a man's or a woman's sole orientation; and which frequently finds expression in overt physical sexual acts between people of the same sex.

To a society which, despite the much-vaunted 'sexual revolution', remains basically antisexual and repressive, and in which many people still believe that any sexual relationship outside marriage is wrong and even that sex itself is 'dirty', homosexual behaviour often appears shocking and unacceptable.

In England, before 1967, every physical sexual act between two men had been treated as a serious crime. The reforming Sexual Offences Act of that year legalized the private homosexual relationships of two consenting male adults over 21 years old. In the United States, the law still varies, but as yet only two states do not consider the private acts of homosexuality a crime; the rest make some or all homosexual acts a criminal offence, even when carried out by consenting adults in private. In most Western European countries, while there are laws prohibiting soliciting and the seduction of minors, homosexual acts in private are usually allowed. The age of consent varies from country to country.

Women were never so severely penalized

by law for lesbian behaviour, but they nevertheless also suffer—in some ways possibly more than men—from a lack of public awareness and understanding of their situation.

Is homosexuality 'unnatural'? Is it a wilful vice, or a perversion? Is it a disease-like deviation of a healthy normal sexual instinct? Or is it simply one among many possible variations of the basic sexual drive which all human beings carry within themselves?

Until just over 20 years ago, most people—including nearly all the 'experts'—would certainly have answered 'yes' to the third if not also to both the first two questions. Since Dr. Alfred Kinsey's studies of human sexual behaviour in the male and the female appeared, it has become increasingly apparent that the view of homosexuality as being simply part of a spectrum in which innate bisexuality is more truly 'normal' than either exclusively heterosexual or homosexual responses may be nearer the truth.

The concept of bisexuality as an authentic orientation, rather than an unresolved ambivalence, has of course been hotly contested by the theorists of sexuality. Freud's followers elevated heterosexuality to a pedestal of exclusive adultness and maturity—a notion which Freud himself would not necessarily have agreed with. Like Kinsey, although from a psychological standpoint rather than the biological one, Freud postulated a bisexual response as innate in the unconditioned human being. His description of the infant as being, sexually speaking, a 'polymorphous pervert' expresses this truth, though in a way scarcely appealing to sentimental baby-worshippers.

If these two great pioneers are correct, important theoretical consequences follow. For the lack of either a heterosexual or a homosexual response is, in this case, the result of repression or inhibition; and its absence, rather than its presence, is 'pathological'. Exclusive homosexuals are therefore no more 'sick' than exclusive heterosexuals are; and bisexuals may be 'better adjusted' than either. Meaningful treatment would consist of removing the psychological and social blockages to absent forms of sexual expression—not the endeavour to remove desires or behaviour already present. According to one psychoanalyst, Dr. L. S. Kubie, if one type of sexual ex-

pression is adopted to the exclusion of any other, it often indicates the influence of an underlying neurosis. No form of sexual activity should be regarded as inherently 'normal' or 'abnormal'.

Yet not everything is for the best in the best of all possible worlds. We, in fact, have to live in a world where, humanly speaking, many exclusive homosexuals—and exclusive heterosexuals, too—will remain as they are throughout their lives. Even though our individual patterns of sexual response are not innately instinctive but learned, the conditioning process is usually completed with the attainment of puberty at the latest, and is extremely difficult, if not impossible, to reverse (despite the claims of 'behaviour therapists').

Kinsey's figures—which have been strongly criticized, but have never been effectively refuted, and indeed, his statistical methods were careful and sound—imply not only that one out of every 25 males between the ages of 16 and 60 are exclusively homosexual throughout their lives, but that one out of every 13 is exclusively homosexual for a period of at least three years during adult life. Also, one man out of every six has as much of the homosexual as the heterosexual in his history throughout such a period. The figures for women are somewhat lower but of a similar order.

Homosexuality, then, is a much more widespread phenomenon than most people are accustomed to think. In Britain, for instance, to say that at least five million men and women are personally conscious of homosexuality as at least an element in their sexual makeup is probably quite a conservative estimate: it is, in other words, a considerably greater social problem, in terms of numbers, than that of race.

'Homosexuals' may be anybody—and could conceivably be everybody. In the light of this realization, the stereotypes dissolve and fall away; the complexity of the subject becomes more apparent and the essential ordinariness of the group we are considering is made clear.

It is probable that there are twice as many homosexuals in Britain as coloured people. What people should try to realize is the ordinariness and commonplaceness of homosexuality. Every time we walk down the street we will probably pass homosex-

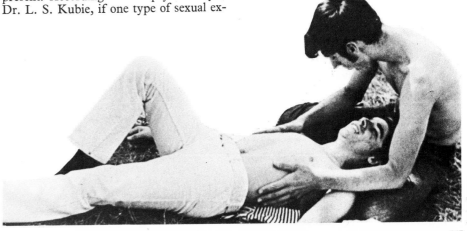

uals without knowing it. Among everybody's circle of friends there are homosexuals, and most people will have at least one relative who is homosexual.

The homosexual (or bisexual) may be any age, of either sex, from any class or occupational section of the population, and living anywhere. More will tend to concentrate in big cities because of the greater opportunities to make contact there with others like themselves. Certain occupations —the stage, catering, and hairdressing reputedly high among them—may attract more than their quota of homosexuals; but there are also numerous homosexual lawyers, engineers, bus drivers, factory workers, and policemen who are less noticeable because they exist and must survive in a less accepting atmosphere, which makes it more necessary for them to conceal their emotional attitudes.

Unlike a coloured person or a member of a religious or racial minority, homosexuals can 'pass', merging themselves unnoticeably in the majority of their heterosexually-orientated fellows. In one sense this possibility for concealment has proved a valuable protection against victimization: in another sense it is a great weakness, because the extent and commonplace nature of homosexual people and homosexual behaviour remains unknown to the public. The late Gilbert Harding is said to have observed that if all homosexual and bisexual people turned blue overnight, there would be so many indigo-tinged individuals, including some very famous ones, in all strata of society from the highest to the lowest, that their common 'problem' would largely resolve itself.

The real question, then, is not so much 'Who are the homosexuals?' as 'How do they identify and adapt themselves?' How do they come to terms with their situation in a largely hostile, indifferent, and uncomprehending society, and cope with the practical problems of living as reasonably well-adjusted and integrated human beings?

When a particular form of sexual expression is prohibited by law—or at least reviled and misunderstood by most people —it affects not only the sex act itself, but all the human relationships and personal consequences which flow from it. Everyone involved feels self-conscious and vulnerable. If marriage was illegal, any close emotional ties between a man and a woman would become the subject of suspicion, needing to be camouflaged with furtive, deceptive casualness. Cohabitation which leads to social ostracism, and sometimes criminal persecution, with the risk of probable dismissal if it became known to employers, can scarcely be conducted with carefree happiness. All affectionate instincts and desires to find and live with a permanent partner—or even to have a more casual, light-hearted affair—become frustrated and thwarted by society's condemnation.

Homosexuals are sometimes condemned for their fickleness, promiscuity, and poor relationships. Living under such circumstances, it is a wonder that most of them achieve any enduring relationships at all. For those who do, the emotional and psychological cost in self-doubt, insecurity, and the complete lack of any supportive social framework is enormous. Indeed, if homosexuality is in any way a mental health problem, this is largely because of the incalculable amount of unnecessary suffering caused by 'man's inhumanity to man', the social cost of which is great.

So it is not really surprising that there is a wide range of different and indeed contrasting ways in which homosexuals relate to themselves, to other homosexuals and to the world in general. Attitudes vary from the repressed 'closet queen', whose only public identification with his own homosexuality may take the self-destructive and ultimately anti-social form of extreme hostility to 'queers', to the rarer, but increasingly manifest, aggressively militant 'gay liberation' approach which tells oneself, other homosexuals, and the world at large that 'Gay is Good'.

A far commoner, but surely still radically unsatisfactory, attitude is that of more or less unwilling acceptance of one's condition coupled with a guilt complex about it which effectively prevents the formation of stable and happily fulfilling relationships.

Paul was 22, and had homosexual relations with other men since he left school. At the same time, although he was never particularly attracted to women, he had tried, without much success, to have relationships with several girls. Instinctively, he preferred men to women, yet he could never bring himself to accept the fact that he was homosexual. His 'affairs' had never lasted more than a few weeks since he would always suffer feelings of guilt after having sexual relations and could not build up an affectionate relationship with another man. He would torture himself with recriminations, and struggle desperately to find an attraction in the opposite sex. But every time he would finish up with another short-lived boy friend.

Paul's problem was that he could not come to terms with his own condition. He could not accept that he was a homosexual. All his close friends were heterosexual, having fulfilling relationships with members of the opposite sex. He saw himself alienated from this group because he was not attracted to women as they were. He felt that if any of them knew, they would make fun of him and despise him, even if they did not drop him altogether.

Consequently he was reduced to conducting secretive affairs with other men, which sometimes lasted only a single night, hating them and himself for it afterwards, and never being able to satisfy his real emotional needs and desires or to find happiness. The self-dislike exhibited by so many male homosexuals who more or less compulsively seek one-night stands and do not care to acknowledge acquaintance with their bed partners of a month ago is pathetic, if understandable.

What all homosexuals share is a need to come to terms with the burden which the rest of society imposes on them—the handicap of belonging to a minority for which not merely is there no social acceptance but which is positively looked down upon and discriminated against, for example by landlords and employers. Whatever our sexual orientation, and whether or not the theory of universal innate bisexuality is correct, we all share a common humanity: this being so, the homosexual's dilemma is in present circumstances much more fundamentally one of civil rights than it is one of 'sickness' or of 'crime'.

It is, consequently, meaningless to depict or dwell upon a gallery of 'homosexual types'. Nevertheless, there is in every society a homosexual subculture which is conditioned by and responds to (or reacts against) majority attitudes and values. Self-conscious rejection of conventional standards of morality and virtue characterizes some homosexuals who by force of circumstances (and perhaps also from inclination) regard promiscuity and 'unfaithfulness' less seriously than most heterosexuals do. But many homosexuals also possess a greater honesty and integrity towards other people and a franker enjoyment of the pleasures of sex than many heterosexuals achieve.

One of the myths that needs dispelling is the popular notion that *all* homosexuals are *always* miserable, lonely, unfulfilled individuals. On the contrary, a great many (though not all) homosexuals achieve an ultimate balance and stability in their lives which enables them to enjoy successful professional careers and a high degree of personal happiness. Especially if they are men, homosexuals may well be more promiscuous than their heterosexual counterparts; but they will frequently have one or more long-lasting if not lifelong relationship of deep and sustained emotional intensity.

John and Simon have lived together for 15 years. Both have made a success of their careers. John is an insurance broker, Simon a photographer. They each experienced strong family disapproval at the beginning of their relationship and, in fact, had been forced to leave their parents' home town. In new surroundings they were able to establish a different social life, in which they were accepted by both heterosexual and homosexual friends, and in which they could find mutual happiness. Their home is a warm and friendly one, where they enjoy entertaining and welcoming people, just as a heterosexual married couple would do.

It is, indeed, surprising not that there are so few such relationships between homosexuals, but that there are so many. Their nature and atmosphere obviously differs from that of a happy heterosexual marriage, for in a single-sex relationship, whether between males or between females, the relative balance of masculinity and femininity is, of course, not the same as in heterosexuality. But the extent of rapport between mutually compatible homosexual partners of long standing compares favourably with that in many marriages that are looked upon by the world as successful.

Those homosexuals who attain such relationships, at any rate for some time, are most probably outnumbered by those who do not; and adverse criticisms of the average quality of homosexual values and relationships can quite easily be sustained; but why?

Two men or two women living together in a joint household are conspicuously 'odd ones out'. For women, the effects of social incomprehension, or even of positive hostility, may not be as destructive as for men —who are still the targets of more generalized hostility and discrimination if their homosexuality is known or suspected. But for both male and female partners, living together has its hazards except in the largest, most anonymous of cities. Consequently, a great many homosexuals never 'take the plunge' of endeavouring to live with or build a life for another. Instead they remain essentially solitary, promiscuous, with only fleeting, short-lived emotional involvements.

Law reform in England has provided the needful legal foundation for free expression of the homosexual's point of view on which progress towards understanding, accept-

ance, and ultimate social integration may be built. The 1967 Act was a stepping-stone to self-emancipation which is still almost entirely yet to be accomplished. It is a two-fold task, reaching both inward (to the homosexual minority itself) and outward (to the heterosexual public). In the initial phases, at any rate, the inward-looking aspects will be the most important, because of the urgent and primary need to raise the morale of so many homosexual people and to help them build a more wholesomely integrated view of their homosexuality in relation to all the rest of life. In this endeavour both social welfare agencies, like the Albany Trust in London, the Samaritans, whose work is world-wide, the

Tangent Group in California, and self-help groups like the Gay Liberation Front, have their distinctive parts to play.

Once a concerted effort of this nature has begun to bear fruit, a much more widespread campaign of public education will become possible. Its aim must be to make everyone aware that the 'problem' of homosexuality—and the popular stereotypes of homosexuals—are the product of ignorant assumptions fostered by a culture which has unhealthily exaggerated feelings of shame and guilt at *all* forms of sexual expression, whether so-called 'normal' or 'abnormal', far above the natural pleasure which we should all be capable of feeling through sexual fulfilment.

A. E. G. WRIGHT

Below The average person will pass a homosexual in the street every day without realizing it. Few homosexuals conform to the traditional image given them by society. How many people would you recognize as homosexuals in this group without being told?

The mystery of personality

Professor H. J. Eysenck, of the London Institute of Psychiatry, discusses the hereditary factors in personality.

Professor Eysenck gives examples of introverts and extroverts in fiction. Introverts are shown here in rectangular boxes, extroverts in circles. They are, from top to bottom: Gulliver, the hero of Jonathan Swift's satire Gulliver's Travels; *Punch, the traditional puppet character, ugly, hunch-backed, and hook nosed, but much loved by millions of children; Sherlock Holmes, the hero of Sir Arthur Conan Doyle's detective stories, who solves crimes with logic rather than with action; Sir John Falstaff, the fat, fun-loving, and witty old knight, the friend of Prince Hal in Shakespeare's* Henry IV; *Don Quixote, the hero of the book by the sixteenth-century Spanish writer Miguel Cervantes, an idealist and a thinker who, on his long travels, is constantly defeated and disillusioned by reality.*

People have always wondered about the remarkable differences in behaviour which are so characteristic of human beings. One man is cowardly, another brave; one woman is flighty, another is steadfast; one child studies diligently, another plays truant. The Don Juan or Casanova behaves in a manner quite different from the happily married man or the misogynist. A shy person cannot understand the social expertise of the salesman, or the compulsive talker the motives of a silent recluse.

The notion of 'personality' refers to all these individual differences which distinguish one person's conduct and behaviour from that of another. In particular it refers to the more firmly rooted, long-continued types of behaviour which often cause us to attribute a particular trait to a person—traits like bravery, or sociability, or persistence, or amorousness. Such traits, of course, do not explain anything. To say a person is sociable because he has a trait of sociability is as senseless as explaining the power of hypnotic drugs to put one to sleep in terms of their *vis dormitiva*, in other words, their power to put one to sleep. Traits are useful only in description and in causing us to look for an explanation. By themselves they explain nothing.

The concept of personality traits is as old as language; that of personality types is much younger. The ancient Greeks who gave us so much in art and science, also contributed this theory. It is often attributed to Hippocrates, but was fully worked out by the Greek physician Galen, who lived in the second century A.D. His four temperaments, or personality types—the choleric, the phlegmatic, the sanguine, and the melancholic—have become universally accepted, and the terms are still widely used. The choleric personality type is touchy, restless, excitable, aggressive, changeable, impulsive, and optimistic. The phlegmatic type is controlled, careful, passive, even-tempered, and reliable. This realization that certain traits tend to be found together was an important contribution. It is still basic to our conception of

250

personality types such as extroversion and introversion.

Another point about Galen's types, however, was less realistic and has given rise to much criticism of the very concept of personality types. He thought that a person belonged to one or other of these types, so that humanity could be adequately characterized by suitable diagnosis into four categories. This is so clearly absurd that many people have reacted quite strongly against any such theory as type.

A more modern approach began when it was noticed that cholerics and sanguinics had something in common that set them off from phlegmatics and melancholics. The traits characterizing the former two types showed them to be extroverted, while the latter two types were introverted. These terms were popularized by the Swiss pyschoanalyst, C. G. Jung, and they are widely used today. The psychological meaning of these terms is not very far removed from the popular meaning. The extrovert is a sociable, impulsive, talkative, outgoing, optimistic, emotionally responsive, lively, easygoing, changeable, and carefree sort of person under most circumstances. The introvert is quiet, passive, reserved, thoughtful, unsociable, sober, pessimistic, controlled, reliable, and introspective. Not all extroverts are alike, of course; neither are all introverts. Within each group there are bright and dull people, neurotic and stable ones. Extroversion-introversion is only one typology among many.

A few examples of literary and historical introverts and extroverts illustrate the wide range of personalities which are accommodated within each category. But they show that there is, nevertheless, something in common to all those people within a given group. Here then are some introverts: Hamlet, Sherlock Holmes, Robespierre, Spinoza, Cassius, John Stuart Mill, Newton, Sir Stafford Cripps, Cato the Elder, Don Quixote, Kant, and Gulliver. Some extroverts might be Mr. Pickwick, Bulldog Drummond, Boswell, Mr. Punch, Caliban, James Bond, Dumas, Donald Duck, Pepys, Churchill, Cicero, Falstaff, and Toad of Toad Hall.

Extroverts and introverts are not types in the sense that everyone is either one or the other. It would be more accurate to look upon the terms as denoting the ends of a continuum, just as tall and short denote the ends of a continuum of height. Most people are intermediate between the extremes, tending one way or the other. Few are typical extroverts or introverts. Thus attempts can be made to measure degrees of extroversion and introversion, and to allocate a position in the continuum to a given person. This means that Galen's notion of types as clusters of traits is retained while rejecting his notion that people fall into only a few categories, and can be described satisfactorily by naming the particular category.

Other typologies, apart from extroversion-introversion, are used in modern psychology. It was noted over a hundred years ago that there was something in common also to the choleric and the

It might be thought that politicians are extroverted people. But this is not necessarily so. Do you agree with the psychologist's classification? (Introverts are shown in rectangular boxes, and extroverts in circles.) They are, from top to bottom: Gaius Cassius, who died in 42 B.C., one of the men who killed Julius Caesar; Sir Winston Churchill, 1874-1965, the British statesman, famous for his courageous and inspiring leadership in the second world war; Robespierre, 1758-1794, a dictator in the French Revolution who was in many ways an idealist, but was responsible for much of the Reign of Terror, and himself died on the guillotine; Cicero, 106-43 B.C., the brilliant Roman statesman, most famous for his gifts as an orator; Sir Stafford Cripps, 1889-1952, the British socialist politician.

251

melancholic types. They were both highly emotional, unstable, and neurotic. By contrast, the phlegmatic and sanguine types of person were seen as emotionally stable. This continuum, from stability to instability (or neurosis) cuts across the extrovert-introvert one, giving rise to a two-dimensional framework of personality description rather like that shown in Figure 1. This figure includes on the rim of the circle the various traits characterizing the particular combinations of extroversion-introversion and stability-instability which arise. People can have a position anywhere within this circle and combine any degree of extroversion-introversion with any degree of stability-instability. Most people will be found somewhere in the middle, being neither particularly extroverted nor particularly introverted, neither neurotic nor exceptionally stable. A person's position within this diagram is related in many important ways to his fate in life. Criminals come overwhelmingly from the choleric part of the diagram, hospitalized neurotics from the melancholic part. There are many other ways in which these two major dimensions of personality touch upon

social life, as well as our sexual behaviour and attitudes.

What determines a person's personality? What makes them behave in an extroverted or introverted manner? Many people would answer immediately that surely

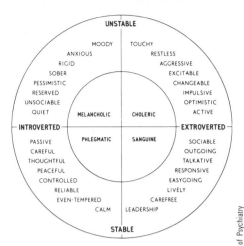

Institute of Psychiatry

Figure One

their manner of upbringing, their experiences in everyday life, their schooling, and their encounters with other people in general, determine their behaviour. This is, of course, true, but in fact surprisingly little is actually contributed to personality by these factors. Probably something like 75 per cent of all the factors which determine behaviour are inherited. Heredity determines very largely where in the circle of Figure 1 the newborn baby shall be placed, and while environment may push

him a little to one side or the other, it seldom exerts a major influence. The proof of this rather surprising proposition comes from extensive studies done on identical and fraternal twins.

Identical twins come from one ovum, fertilized by one sperm; the ovum then breaks up into two, and these two, sharing identical heredity, grow up into two separate individuals. In the case of fraternal twins, two ova are simultaneously released, and fertilized by two separate sperms; the two individuals that develop are no more alike than ordinary brothers and sisters. It is obvious that if a person's personality is largely determined by heredity then identical twins should be much more alike than fraternal twins. And this is what has been found. In one of the best-controlled and largest investigations ever conducted in this field it was even found that identical twins brought up in separation were more alike than identical twins brought up together. This may be due to the fact that identical twins often try to assert their individuality when brought up together and deliberately develop away from each other. However that may be, heredity is very important, indeed overwhelmingly important in determining personality. Extroverts and introverts are born and not made.

This fact clearly presents a problem. We cannot inherit conduct, but only physiological and neurological structures.

Mansell

It is possible that philosophers have a tendency to be introverts. The three shown here could be considered as such. **Left** *Baruch Spinoza, 1632-1677, the Dutch philosopher, lived a quiet life, working as a grinder of lenses, and spending much of his time studying and writing.* **Below** *Immanuel Kant, 1724-1804, the German philosopher, whose great work* The Critique of Pure Reason *examines the limits of human knowledge, spent all his life in Königsberg, teaching at the university.* **Right** *John Stuart Mill, 1806-1873, the English political philosopher and economist.*

Mary Evans

Radio Times Hulton

We cannot inherit sociability or emotional behaviour. There must be some physical structures in our nervous system which interact with other structures and with the environment to produce behaviour which we call extroverted or introverted.

Recent work has made it possible to identify these structures tentatively. Consider the stable-unstable continuum first, which is concerned with the arousal of emotions, their strength, and their persistence. In the stable person emotions are not aroused when not appropriate. They are not too strong to be coped with, and they do not persist when they have served their function. In the neurotic, emotional person the opposite is the case—emotions are too strong, are too easily aroused, and last too long. Now it is known that the expression of the emotions is mediated by a special branch of the nervous system, the *autonomic* system, which in turn is governed and co-ordinated by the *visceral brain* which is situated in the brain stem. It is inherited differences in the excitability of this visceral brain-autonomic system loop which govern a person's emotional reaction to environmental changes and determines his over- or under-reaction to such stimuli. Tranquillizers can act on this system to reduce its over-excitability and bring it back to a more reasonable level of functioning.

Extroversion-introversion is more closely linked with the central nervous system, particularly the cortex, that rind of grey matter immediately under the skull. The cortex is usually in a state of greater or lesser arousal and people differ in the degree of arousal which is present. It has been found that extroverts are typically in a state of low arousal, introverts in a state of high arousal. This may sound paradoxical. Should not the inhibited, introspective, passive introvert have the cortex with the low arousal? Such an objection misunderstands the function of the cortex; it acts to control, censor, and even abolish the activities of the lower centres, and it is these lower centre activities which emerge as the impulsive, uninhibited, outgoing behaviour of the extrovert. Alcohol illustrates this point well. This drug is a depressant and by reducing the level of arousal of the cortex it enhances extroverted behaviour. It is the internal activity of the introvert, his thinking, inhibiting, controlling functions, which are being heightened by cortical arousal. Typically the introvert is a man of thought, the extrovert a man of action. Sportsmen are usually extroverted, and philosophers, mathematicians, and scientists introverted. The sportsman might not run the risks he does run if he took time to think about them; the philosopher or scientist would get bored with his constant intellectual preoccupation, were it not for the high state of arousal of the cortex which nature has given him.

Cortical arousal is largely produced and regulated by a small agglomeration of cells in the brain stem, the reticular formation. Incoming nerve impulses send collateral nerves into this formation, while the main part of the neuron goes on up to the cortex; the message in the collateral neuron stimulates the reticular formation to send messages to the cortex in turn, instructing it to maintain a higher level of arousal (in order to be able to deal with the message received directly from the original neuron). The brain, in turn, can send back messages to the reticular formation, instructing it to keep on alerting the cortex, or to stop doing so. Thus there is a good deal of traffic between the cortex and the reticular formation and a very fine interplay to secure optimal levels of arousal. The differences in level between extroverts and introverts are thus the results of complex interactions, depending probably ultimately on the inherited lability of the reticular formation.

Direct evidence on these theories is available from electro-encephalographs (records of brain-waves) obtained from different personality types, and from other electro-physiological investigations. How do these mechanisms produce the observed differences in their social lives between introverts and extroverts?

The three writers shown here could be considered to be extroverts. **Right** James Boswell, 1740-1795, a Scottish lawyer, most famous for his biography of Dr. Samuel Johnson, had a great many friends among the literary personalities of his day. **Below** Samuel Pepys, 1633-1703, wrote a lively diary recording the details of everyday life of the seventeenth century. **Left** Alexandre Dumas, 1802-1870, the French novelist and playwright who lived an extremely active and adventurous life, and is famous for such exciting and romantic stories as The Three Musketeers.

253

A person's position in the 'personality-type circle' (Fig. 1), his position on the extroversion-introversion and the neuroticism-stability dimension, can have far-reaching consequences for his social conduct, his liability to become prey to neurotic disorders or criminal impulses, and his general sexual adjustment. How are such links established, and what are the causal factors which are responsible?

When unstable patients are tested by means of questionnaires, interviews, or in some other way, they can be seen to come predominantly from the 'melancholic' quadrant, having high scores on both introversion and neuroticism. Similarly, when criminals are tested they usually are found to have predominantly 'choleric' personalities, combining extroversion with neuroticism. This could, of course, be due to the circumstances in which these people find themselves. It could be that imprisonment or neurotic breakdown cause personality to change in these directions, rather than a personality having a predisposition to crime or neurosis. But it does not seem that this is likely.

There are several studies in which children of ten years of age were rated by their teachers for extroversion and neuroticism. The children were then followed over the years and a note was made of those who became habitual criminals or neurotics. When the original ratings were studied it was found that those who later turned to crime had been rated predominantly extroverted and emotionally unstable. Those who later succumbed to neurosis had been rated predominantly introverted and emotionally unstable. This and other studies provide evidence to show that personality is a powerful determinant of a person's future career and his expectations in life. The relationship is, of course, not perfect, but it is frighteningly close. There is much truth in the belief that criminals (or neurotics) are born and not made. It is far from the whole truth, of course, in that it neglects environmental influences which can alter the picture very powerfully, but it does give expression to facts which have been too long neglected.

How are these types of social behaviour linked with extroversion and introversion? One important link is the concept of conditioning as developed by Pavlov. Most people are familiar with the tale of Pavlov's dogs learning to salivate at the sound of a bell after he had paired the ringing of the bell with giving them food. Experiments with human subjects have shown that they, too, can be conditioned in just the same way as dogs by the simple pairing of a conditioned stimulus (the bell) and an unconditioned stimulus (the food). In the case of humans, it is usually emotions which are conditioned and, in particular, anxiety.

If a person is given a series of electric shocks always preceded by the sound of a bell, he will soon react with fear and anxiety to the sound of the bell. His emotional response can be measured by picking up electro-physiological signals such as the decrease in electrical resistance shown by his palm, due to the slight sweating induced by the fear response. That it is possible to condition anxiety and fear proved to be a very important discovery. It is linked with extroversion and introversion through another discovery made by Pavlov. He found that dogs differ profoundly in the speed with which they form conditioned reflexes and the strength of these reflexes. Dogs showing high cortical arousal conditioned well and dogs showing weak cortical arousal conditioned poorly. This suggests that introverts should condition well, extroverts poorly. Experiments have generally supported this deduction.

The relevance of this to social behaviour, particularly crime and neurosis, can be seen when considering the nature of neurotic disorders. Essentially, such neurotic symptoms as irrational fears and anxieties, phobias, and depressions, are conditioned emotional responses. They are caused by the chance presence of some otherwise neutral conditioned stimulus when a traumatic, fear-producing event happens. For example, a woman comes to a clinic with a cat phobia. She is so afraid of cats that she cannot leave her house for fear of seeing one. This has ruined her life and that of her family, for many years, and although she

INTROVERSION/EXTROVERSION   KEY

1. Do you sometimes feel happy, sometimes depressed, without any apparent reason?   YES NO
2. Do you prefer action to planning for action?   YES NO
3. Do you have frequent ups and downs in mood, either with or without apparent cause?   YES NO
4. Are you happiest when you get involved in some project that calls for rapid action?   YES NO
5. Are you inclined to be moody?   YES NO
6. Do you usually take the initiative in making new friends?   YES NO
7. Does your mind often wander when you are trying to concentrate?   YES NO
8. Are you inclined to be quick and sure in your actions?   YES NO
9. Are you frequently lost in thought even when supposed to be taking part in a conversation?   YES NO
10. Would you rate yourself as a lively individual?   YES NO
11. Are you sometimes bubbling over with energy and sometimes very sluggish?   YES NO
12. Would you be very unhappy if you were prevented from making numerous social contacts?   YES NO

By answering this questionnaire you can find out how you score on the introversion/extroversion and emotionality/stability scales. Mark your answer to each question, then turn to the chart at the end of the article for your rating.

realizes that the fear is unrealistic she can do nothing about it. How did it arise? When she was a little girl her father, in a mad temper, had drowned her favourite kitten in front of her eyes and beat her about the head with the corpse. The kitten was the conditioned stimulus which, through pairing with the unconditioned stimulus (the traumatic drowning and beating episode), now comes to evoke fear and anxiety. Had the girl been extroverted, she would not have formed such a quick and strong conditioned response. And had she been less emotional and unstable, her fear reaction would not have been so strong. Through the combination of her introversion and her instability the event produced a neurotic breakdown in the form of this phobia.

As far as criminality is concerned the position is rather different. Children are born savages and they have to be socialized through a lengthy and arduous process, jointly undertaken by parents and teachers, with the help, and sometimes hindrance, of the child's peer group. This process of socialization works through the mechanism of conditioning. Evil-doing (the conditioned stimulus) is followed by punishment (the unconditioned stimulus), leading to pain and anxiety. Through many thousand repetitions the child gradually acquires a conscience which is simply the generalized, conditioned anxiety and fear response to all temptations to socially unacceptable behaviour. It is this which keeps a person out of mischief and causes him to lead a socialized existence.

Extroverts, having low levels of arousal and so less easily conditioned, are handicapped in the acquisition of this conscience. They are less likely than introverts to acquire the socialized habits so essential in any society. This may be the reason why criminals are so often extroverted. They have not developed that guardian angel, the conscience, which alone can keep them out of trouble. And when extroversion is combined with a high degree of emotionality, as in the choleric personality, a very strong emotional drive is added to this mixture. The result is often a very unstable, potentially dangerous person, with strong antisocial tendencies. Extroverts lacking this strong emotional drive often

Shakespeare's Hamlet, prince of Denmark, is a typical introverted character—melancholic, brooding, and introspective. Here, holding a skull, he reflects on death.

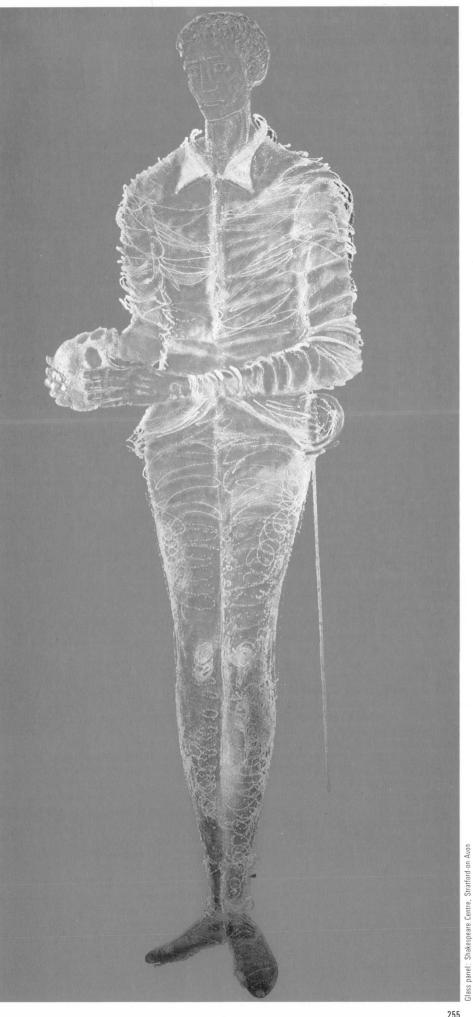

Glass panel: Shakespeare Centre, Stratford-on-Avon

indulge in activities which are frowned upon by society, even though they may not lead to prison. For example, they tend to be more sexually promiscuous and are involved in far more motor car accidents and traffic violations.

In their sexual relations one would expect extroverts to differ profoundly from introverts in being less inhibited, or in showing less social responsibility, or paying less attention to the niceties of social intercourse, of generally doing what they feel like, regardless of other people. Several studies were undertaken, both in England and in Germany, which bear out these expectations.

A study was carried out to compare the sexual activities of unmarried German students who were divided into extroverted and introverted groups by means of a questionnaire. At the age of 17, extroverted boys had had intercourse in 21 per cent of the cases, introverted boys only in five per cent, and for girls the figures were eight per cent and four per cent. By the age of 19, the percentage had gone up to 45 per cent and 15 per cent respectively for the boys, and 29 per cent and 12 per cent for the girls. This shows that extroverts have intercourse earlier than do introverts. They also have it more frequently. Of the boys and girls who had had intercourse at all, the mean frequency per month was over twice as great for extroverts as for introverts. Extroverts also tended to be much more promiscuous. Twenty-five per cent of the extroverted men, but only 7 per cent of the introverted ones, had had more than four sexual partners during the previous 12 months, while for women the figures were 17 per cent and four per cent respectively. Long premarital sex play, oral sex, and the use of many different positions for intercourse were all much more frequent among extroverts than among introverts.

Similar findings emerged from a study carried out in England. Extroverts were characterized by a liking for promiscuity and impersonal sex, by a lack of nervousness about sexual matters, by social facility with the opposite sex, a general liking for sexual activity, a contentment with their sexual life, and a lack of worry about it. Extroverts were found to be much more easily excited sexually than were introverts. Extroverts in general seemed to be sexually permissive while introverts by comparison seemed much more puritanical and inhibited in their behaviour and their attitudes.

These patterns seem to suggest that the extrovert has much the better of it, but this impression may be wrong. Youth is predominantly the time of the extrovert. Introverts tend to come into their own rather later. The philandering extrovert, sowing his premarital oats, is likely to become a figure of fun as a middle-aged Casanova, or suffer the stresses of the seven-year itch if he should marry. The reticent introvert is much more likely to settle into a happy marriage and remain content with his monogamous lot.

H. J. EYSENCK

Steve Hiett

In their sexual relations extroverts are less inhibited than introverts

SCORING KEY

INTROVERSION	EMOTIONALITY
0. Very introverted	Very stable
1. Introverted	Stable
2. Slightly introverted	Slightly more stable than average
3. Average	Average
4. Slightly extroverted	Slightly emotional
5. Extroverted	Emotional
6. Very extroverted	Very emotional

The odd-numbered questions refer to emotionality/stability. Your score on emotionality is the number of questions answered 'Yes'. Your score on extroversion is the number of even-numbered questions answered 'Yes'.